The
Jewels
of
Lalique

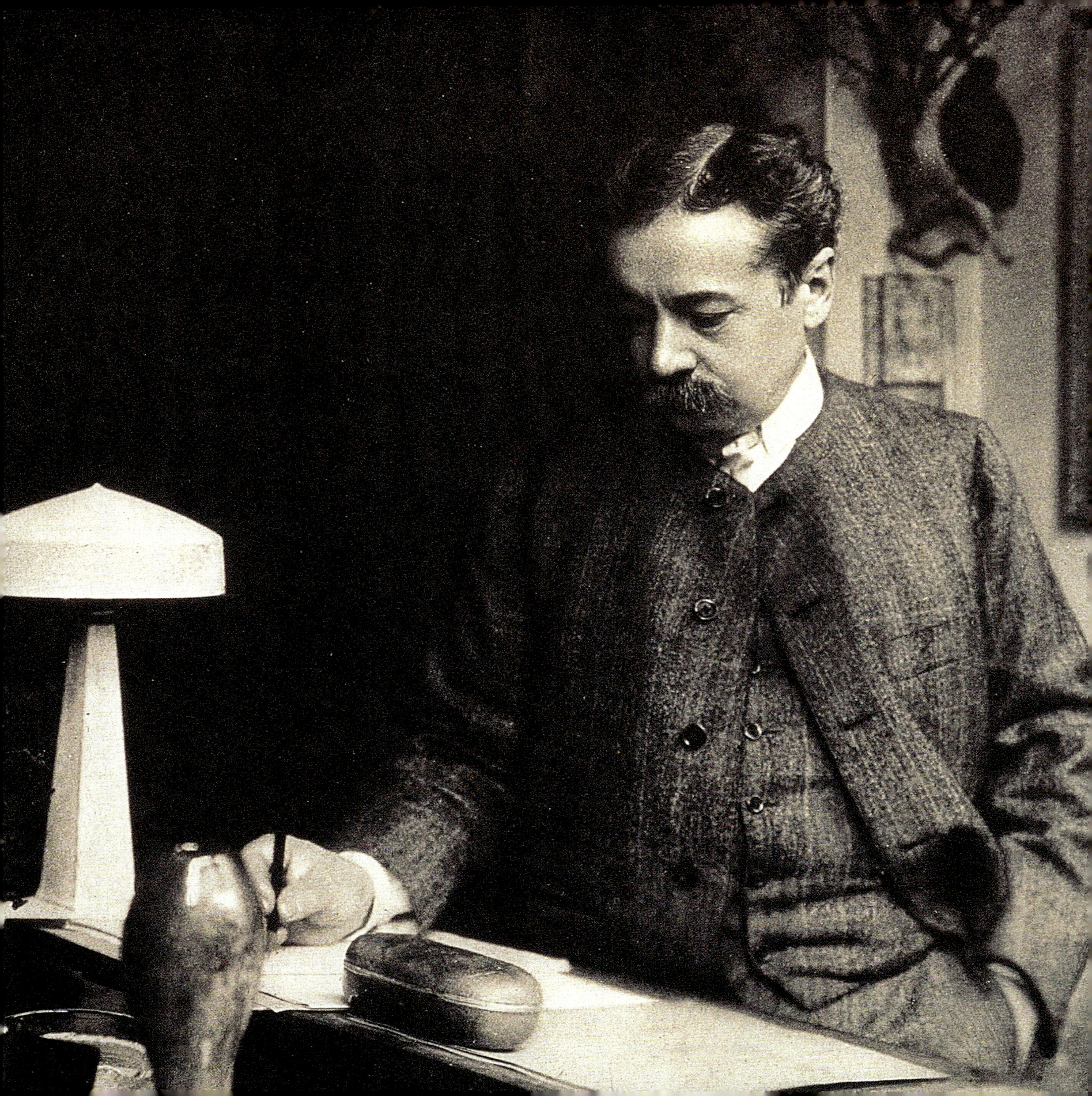

The *Jewels* of Lalique

Edited by
Yvonne Brunhammer

With contributions by
Sigrid Barten
Marie-Odile Briot
Florence Müller
Jean-Luc Olivié
Evelyne Possémé
Gabriel P. Weisberg
Joan T. Rosasco

Flammarion
Paris - New York

Editorial Direction: Suzanne Tise
Editorial Management: Philippa Hurd

Designed and typeset by Jocelyn Kargère
Copy-edited by Sheila Schwartz
Translations from the French (Brunhammer, Briot, Müller, Possémé, Olivié)
by David Radzinowicz Howell
Translation from the German (Barten)
by Jackie Smith

Flammarion
26 rue Racine, 75006 Paris

Website: www.flammarion.com

ISBN: 2-08013-632-1 (hardback)
ISBN: 2-08013-631-3 (paperback)
Numéros d'édition: FA363206 (hb); FA363107 (pb)
Dépôt légal: February 1998
Printed in France

Frontispiece: René Lalique in his studio.

Library of Congress Cataloging-in-Publication Data

Lalique, René, 1860–1945.
The jewels of Lalique / edited by Yvonne Brunhammer ; with contributions by Sigrid Barten ... [et al.].
p. cm.
Catalog of an exhibition held at the Cooper-Hewitt National Design Museum, Smithsonian Institution, New York, Feb. 3–Apr. 12, 1998 and the International Gallery; Smithsonian Institution, Washington, D.C., May 15–Aug. 16, 1998.
Contributions translated from French and German.
Includes bibliographical references.
ISBN 2-08013632-1 (hardbound). -- ISBN 2-08-013631-3 (softbound)
1. Lalique, René, 1860–1945--Exhibitions. 2. Jewelry--France--History--19th century--Exhibitions. 3. Jewelry--France--History--20th century--Exhibitions. I. Brunhammer, Yvonne. II. Barten, Sigrid. III. Cooper-Hewitt Museum. IV. Smithsonian Institution. V. Title.
NK7398.L36A4 1998
739.27'092--dc21 97-48532

Exhibition Schedule

February 3–April 12, 1998
Cooper-Hewitt, National Design Museum, Smithsonian Institution, New York, N.Y.

May 15–August 16, 1998
International Gallery, Smithsonian Institution, Washington, D.C.

September 13, 1998–January 10, 1999
Dallas Museum of Art, Dallas, Texas

Lenders to the Exhibition

The Art Institute of Chicago

Musée des Arts décoratifs, Paris

Calouste Gulbenkian Museum, Lisbon

The Cleveland Museum of Art

Corning Museum of Glass

Lalique Museum Collection, Paris

The Metropolitan Museum of Art, New York

National Museum of American History, Smithsonian Institution, Washington, D.C.

Virginia Museum of Fine Arts, Richmond

The Walters Art Gallery, Baltimore

Laurie and Joel H. Shapiro

Mr. and Mrs. Glenn S. Utt, Jr.

Mark Waller, Galerie Moderne, London

Mr. and Mrs. David Weinstein

Private collections

Contents

Acknowledgments

The present exhibition owes its existence to the vision and foresight of several key people. Gérard Tavenas, President of Lalique SA, and Yves Coléon, President of Lalique North America, together seized the opportunity that presented itself to sponsor *The Jewels of Lalique* in order to introduce to an American audience the early work of René Lalique, the founder of the company that they lead today. Odette Boulanger, Kim Friedman, and Catherine Vincent-Dolor were part of their dedicated, hardworking team.

This exhibition is not a replica of the one held in Paris; rather it focuses, as the show in Paris could not, on the Lalique jewels in museums and private collections in the United States. Private collections of Lalique are particularly rich, and many works that are featured have never been seen by the public before. The discovery of unknown or little-known works is one of the pleasures of this exhibition. Yet loans from abroad contribute to the breadth of *The Jewels of Lalique*. Unique circumstances involving renovations at both the Musée des Arts décoratifs in Paris and the Calouste Gulbenkian Museum in Lisbon, have made possible the presentation of a large number of important pieces from the two most inclusive and prestigious collections of Lalique's work in the world. Marie-Claude Beaud, Director of the Musée des Arts décoratifs, Evelyne Possémé, curator of the Art Nouveau and Art Deco Department, Jean-Luc Olivié, curator of the Glass Center and Contemporary Department, and Maria Teresa Gomes Ferreira, Director of the Calouste Gulbenkian Museum, have our deepest gratitude. Our thanks go also to Philippe de Montebello, Director of the Metropolitan Museum of Art in New York and Stewart Johnson and Jane Adlin of the Department of Twentieth-Century Art; Katherine C. Lee, Director of the Virginia Museum of Fine Arts, Richmond and Frederick R. Brandt, former curator of Twentieth-Century Art; William Johnston at the Walters Art Gallery, Baltimore; Henry H. Hawley at the Cleveland Museum of Art; David Whitehouse, Director of the Corning Museum of Glass, and Susanne K. Frantz, curator of the Twentieth-Century Department; Ian Wardropper at The Art Institute of Chicago; and Jean Benas at the National Museum of American History. We are also very grateful to Laurie and Joel Shapiro; David and Lynn Weinstein; Glenn and Marilou Utt, and to Mark Waller of Galerie Moderne in London, all of whom lent works by Lalique to the exhibition. A few lenders prefer to remain anonymous. All were very helpful, and it is their generous participation that makes this exhibition one of the finest ever mounted of the artist's work.

At the three venues, members of the museum staffs have contributed their time and effort to the effective installation and presentation of the exhibition. The unusual participation and cooperation of two sister branches of the Smithsonian Institution led to a fruitful collaboration. At the Cooper-Hewitt, National Design Museum, Smithsonian Institution in New York, the Director, Dianne H. Pilgrim, was ably seconded by Steven Langehough, Caroline Mortimer, Christine McKee, Jen Roos, Brent Rumage, Lindsay Stamm Shapiro, Deborah Sampson Shinn, Stephen H. Van Dyk, Susan Yelavich, and Egle Victoria Zygas.

At the Smithsonian Institution in Washington, Anne R. Gossett, Director, and Lori Dempsey, Assistant Director, led a team that included Rosa Aguayo, Rosemary Regan, and Tina Lynch Safreed.

Jay Gates, Director of the Dallas Museum of Art, and Deputy Director and Chief Curator Charles Venable were tenacious in their efforts to have the exhibition come to Dallas. It was accomplished with the help of Nancy Davis, Rick Floyd, Bob Guill, Suzy Sloan Jones, Antoine Leriche, Kathy Walsh-Piper, Debra Whittrup, and Gary Wooley, and with the support of The Chairman's Circle.

As organizers of the exhibition, Exhibitions International supervised and guided the myriad facets of this project. Many members of our staff in New York including Dorys Codina, Jan Spak, Dara Metz, and Cynthia Brown made valuable contributions over the past three years.

Our thanks also go to those who gave their help and advice in the preparation of the catalogue: Sigrid Barten, Geneviève Bonté, Ralph Esmerian, Raymond Guidot, Félix Marcilhac, Nicole Maritch-Haviland, Josiane Sartre, Claude Sorbac, and special thanks to Clémentine Vidal who assisted in the compilation of the Chronology.

The publisher, Flammarion, and particularly Suzanne Tise and Philippa Hurd in Paris and Jennifer Straus in New York, brought their taste and high standards to the production and distribution of this catalogue to which major scholars have contributed new research: Sigrid Barten, Marie-Odile Briot, Florence Müller, Jean-Luc Olivié, Evelyne Possémé, and Gabriel P. Weisberg. We are also grateful to Jocelyn Kargère, Sheila Schwartz, David Radzinowicz Howell, Jackie Smith, Bruno Bredoux, and Robyn Mahon for their contributions to the realization of this catalogue.

The publicity for the exhibition has been ably handled by Anne Edgar, Lindsey Gruber, and Luisa Kreisberg of The Kreisberg Group, New York. The complicated shipping arrangements were efficiently coordinated by David Epstein and Gloria Boudreau at Masterpiece International, Ltd. Jean-Pierre Royer of André Chenue SA in Paris, with the aid of Katherine Buckley in New York, dealt with shipping from France. Caroline E. Corvington of the Huntingdon T. Block Insurance Agency worked on the insurance for the exhibition.

Many other people gave us their help. David Behl and Laurent Sully-Jaulmes are responsible for many of the photographs taken expressly for this volume. Katy Homans designed the brochure, poster, and other graphic components for the exhibiton. Nancy McClelland, Barbara McLaughlin, and Sandra Joys at Christie's generously arranged for a symposium in New York. Frank Aucella, curator of the Woodrow Wilson House in Washington D.C. provided information about Mrs. Wilson's jewel. Jewelry historians Penny Proddow and Marion Fasel were unfailingly helpful. We want to thank Ingrid Grace at the Consulate of France in New York and Estelle Berruyer and Bernard Braem of the Cultural Services of the French Embassy in New York and Washington for their support. Virginia Budney, Dena Cook, Jeffrey Daly, Barbara Deisroth, Alistair Duncan, Edy Ferguson, Jane French, William K. Geiger, Gregory Kuharic, Mary Beth McCaffrey, Donald McClelland, David McFadden, Jessie Price, Faith Pleasanton, Dr. and Mrs. Joseph Sataloff, Usha Subramiam, and Lara Weber all deserve special thanks.

To all of the above we express our heartfelt gratitude.

Yvonne Brunhammer
Curator

Joan T. Rosasco
Exhibition Coordinator

Sponsor's Statement

Our fascination for René Lalique resonates on several levels: first, for the man himself who, having invented the modern Art Nouveau bijou*—making Lalique the undisputed master of the style—went on to become the greatest master glassmaker in the world of Art Deco.*

Second, for his talent: Lalique's interest in perfume led him to create highly expressive and symbolic perfume bottles, another passion broached the world of architecture and decorative arts with the creation of the fountains on the Champs-Élysées, the carriages of the Orient Express and the interiors of the luxury liner the Normandie*. And we should not forget those marvelous automobile emblems sought after today by all lovers of vintage vehicles.*

Third, this creative genius was able to combine the gifts of an exceptional inventor with a knowledge of technical developments, a combination which would ensure the continuing influence of his venture.

I am delighted and proud to see Lalique's talent recognised by the great museums of the world.

I am also very pleased to share this passion with many others, in particular Yvonne Brunhammer who initiated me into the secrets of René Lalique's creations, and who allowed me to share with them the emotion and beauty of his work.

Gérard Tavenas President, Lalique SA

Under the patronage of
His Excellency
François Bujon de l'Estang
Ambassador of France
Washington, D.C.
and
His Excellency Patrick Gautrat
Consul General of France
New York

Foreword

The work of René Lalique was appreciated in the United States during his lifetime. His jewels, displayed at the World's Fair in St. Louis in 1904, brought him the attention of fairgoers, and a large number of the pieces, purchased by Henry Walters, remained in the USA and are in the Walters Art Gallery in Baltimore today. In 1912, when François Coty opened a shop on Fifth Avenue in New York, he asked Lalique to create the decor for the elegant building. The large windows with a motif of entwined poppies are preserved in the store that has now become Henri Bendel. Lalique glassware has been sold in this country in major stores and in Lalique boutiques in several cities. The name Lalique is well-known, but the celebrity of the glass has tended to obscure the earlier jewels, and today many people are unaware of the fact that René Lalique, master glassmaker, began his career as a jeweler.

In 1991–1992, Yvonne Brunhammer capped her career as Director of the Musée des Arts décoratifs in Paris with a brilliant exhibition devoted to the jewelry of René Lalique. It was spectacularly successful, attracting the largest attendance in the museum's history and revealing to a new generation the wondrous jewels created a century before by one of the pioneers of modern design. Despite many requests, that exhibition could not be extended to travel to the United States, but now, four years later, propitious circumstances have made possible the organization of a new exhibition to present the jewels of Lalique in America. Again Yvonne Brunhammer has served as curator and as editor of the catalogue, making the selection of the works of art and bringing her erudition and enthusiasm to the creation of the present volume.

A unique feature of this exhibition was the harmonious collaboration of sister museums, both part of the Smithsonian Institution. The Cooper-Hewitt National Design Museum in New York and the International Gallery in Washington worked closely together and with us on shared elements of the installation and educational component for their two facilities.

David A. Hanks
Director, Exhibitions International

The Lalique Epoch

Yvonne Brunhammer

Brooch
Two Seahorses
c. 1902–1905
Chased gold, enamel
on gold and *plique-à-jour*
enamel, opals, pearls
4 x 2 1/2 inches
(10.2 x 6.3 cm)
(Cat. 100)

On the occasion of the 1933 Lalique retrospective at the Musée des Arts Décoratifs in Paris, Henri Clouzot subjected Art Nouveau to a close examination. His deep knowledge of arts and crafts—in which he had specialized first at the Bibliothèque Forney and then at the Musée Galliera, where from 1920 on he had organized major thematic exhibitions—led him to reject the commonly held assumption that Art Nouveau could be assimilated to the decorative arts alone. He saw it rather as the creation of sculptors, painters, and architects: "Only the cabinetmakers were missing!" Clouzot's target here was Émile Gallé's work as a cabinetmaker. "Though [Gallé] was clearly a master of the art of glass...in his furniture, he dispensed altogether too casually with practicality and logic....Above all, he carried...the nature school into a botanical pedantry, which has left us dahlia seats and poppy beds, dragonfly tables, and potato-flower sideboards."[1]

For Clouzot, successful works in the Art Nouveau style, from 1890 to 1900 were confined to the "precious arts," over which René Lalique's inventiveness loomed large. "A single artist, and one of the greatest—though today, at the summit of his career, he does not think highly enough of the works he produced in the last century—René Lalique had the gift of being able to transmit to the world the spine-tingling sensation of a new type of beauty. If only for his jewelry, one still ought to admire sympathetically this period of struggle and of fruitful faltering. Before Lalique, jewelry (*bijouterie*) was all gold, silver, pearls, diamonds, and precious stones. As early as 1896, he exhibited a bracelet in horn and ivory. Next came a pendant—*Winter Landscape*—in that engraved molded glass which was to oust rock crystal from his work.[2] He did not rest

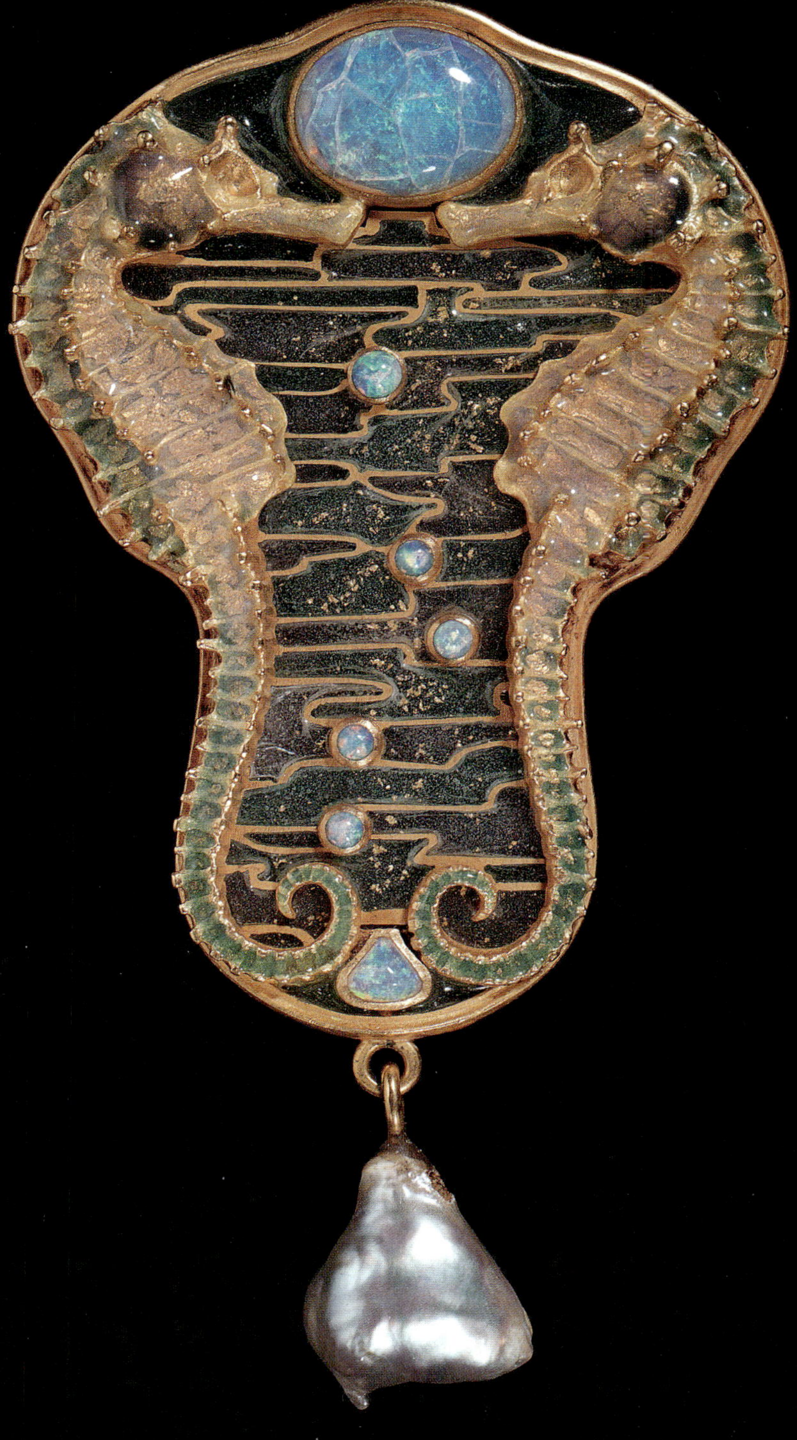

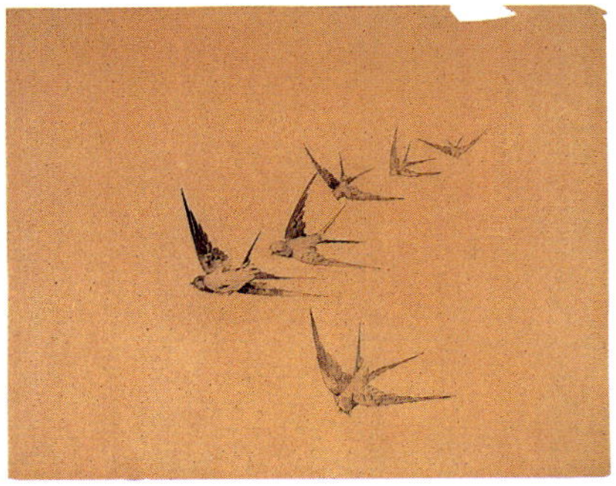

Design for a Corsage Ornament
A Flight of Swallows
1887
Ink on paper
6 1/4 x 9 inches
(16 x 26.4 cm)
(Cat. 16)

there; turning tradition on its head, he rehabilitated more modest gemstones that until then had been disdained: corundum, onyx, sard, jasper, coral, opals. He built up a complete range of parure for women: tiaras, combs, brooches, pectorals, pendants, rings, bracelets, in which the intrinsic worth of the materials involved was overshadowed by the sheer quality of his artistry and the efforts of his creative imagination. In his pantheistic jewel box, all nature has its part: flowers, fruits, insects, birds, fish, reptiles—but all created anew, the better to adapt them to jewelry-making."[3]

It was this quality of re-creation that it seemed Gallé's furniture lacked. Although Clouzot's judgment is severe, even unfair, it redounded to René Lalique's credit. Indeed, Clouzot was ready to rebaptize the whole Art Nouveau period as the "Lalique epoch." One might also speak of the "Lalique epic," since the artist's own story is that of a visionary, where the marvelous blends into reality and legend into history.

Lalique Before Lalique

Lalique's entry into his chosen trade was unobtrusive, as an assistant to one of the jewelers in the Palais Royal. His early creations, presented under the names of Boucheron and of Vever (cat. 3), were noted at the 1889 Exposition Universelle in Paris. He had started out as a designer of *bijoux*. (Although in common parlance there is often little distinction made between *bijou* or *bijouterie* and *joaillerie* and both can be translated as "jewelry," the words have different connotations, especially in Lalique's period, which are maintained throughout this catalogue. Traditional *joaillerie* depends for its effect on a single color produced by high-cut brightwork diamonds or other precious gems; *bijouterie* relies on artistic shaping, asymmetry, "humbler" materials, and different colors.) The few drawings Lalique exhibited in 1884 in a corner of the Salle des États in the Louvre during the Exposition Nationale des Arts Industriels, which accompanied the public showing of the Crown Jewels, were noticed by the jeweler Alphonse Fouquet (1828–1911), the greatest Parisian *bijoutier-joaillier* of the time. According to Henri Vever, Fouquet declared to the young man: "I was not aware of the existence of any contemporary jewelry designers, and at last, here is one!"[4]

Having set up business on his own by 1887, Lalique produced many designs and complete projects for pieces that were executed with *joaillerie* techniques. The materials and ornaments were also those of traditional brightwork, to which he added themes inspired by nature, the flowers and plants of his native Champagne—oxeye daisies, roses, either single or in bunches, branches of eglantine, ears of wheat, together with the insects which teem in the meadows—grasshoppers, spiders.

Vever writes that in 1887 Lalique

designed a "large *joaillerie* ensemble representing a whole flight of swallows, endeavoring to translate perspective in the diminishing size of the birds. He made a maquette...and presented it to Boucheron [who], finding it too fantastical, did not place an order." But Lalique had confidence in his project and executed it "entirely at his own risk." Won over by the finished product, Boucheron purchased it enthusiastically and sold "a large number," especially since the birds could be worn singly or as a group "in the hair or at the belt" (cats. 15, 16).[5] The flight of swallows derives from a childhood environment that Lalique never forsook. The dynamic diagonal composition proceeded from a close observation of a critical moment in the bird's flight, a characteristic also found in the pages of Hokusai's (1760–1849) *Manga*, that repertory of the plants, flowers, people, and animals of Japan, portrayed in their most typical attitudes. Did René Lalique know this book of prints that had been doing the rounds among Parisian artists since the beginning of the 1860s, shortly after Japan had been opened to the West? It is probable, though there is no proof.

There are two other certain influences on Lalique. Before entering professional life after the death of his father in 1876, Lalique had taken classes in drawing at the Collège Turgot. He was an apprentice under the goldsmith Louis Aucoc and signed up for evening classes at the École des Arts

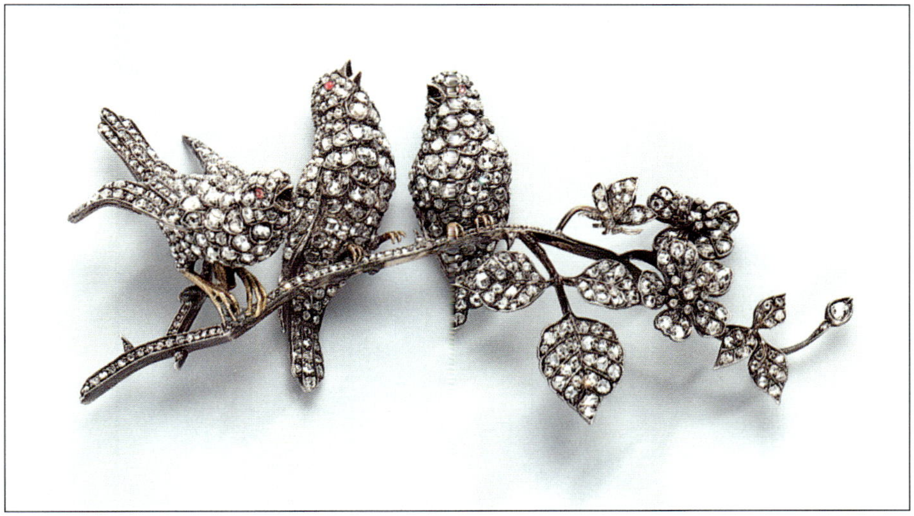

Corsage Ornament
Song Birds
1889 for the House
of Vever
Gold, silver,
diamonds, rubies
2 x 1/4 inches
(4.9 x 10.8 cm)
(Cat. 3)

Décoratifs before spending two years at Sydenham College to the south of London, where he produced drawings and studied ornamental composition. He immersed himself in the England of John Ruskin and William Morris, where the watchwords were arts and crafts, nature, and the period which represented—in the eyes of these writers—their supreme expression, the Middle Ages. The young man returned to Paris in 1880 and there found a second "mentor" of draftsmanship. It was the moment when the Musée de Cluny was organizing an exhibition of the drawings of Viollet-le-Duc, who had died in Lausanne the previous year. The architect had just published *Histoire d'un dessinateur: Comment on apprend à dessiner*, which amounted to a sort of last will and testament on the role of draftsmanship in artistic creation and in the observation of nature in all its forms, in particular the observation of a local, modest countryside—the French, Swiss, and Italian landscapes through which the architect frequently traveled.

In both London and Paris, the extensive practice of drawing was considered essential for the rejuvenation of those forms and ornaments which eclecticism had until then confined to rehashing the styles of the past. This attitude held sway at the first museum of industrial arts in South Kensington, opened in 1862, and among the founders of the Société du Progrès de l'Art Industriel then of the Union Centrale des Beaux-Arts Appliqués à l'Industrie, in 1864. René

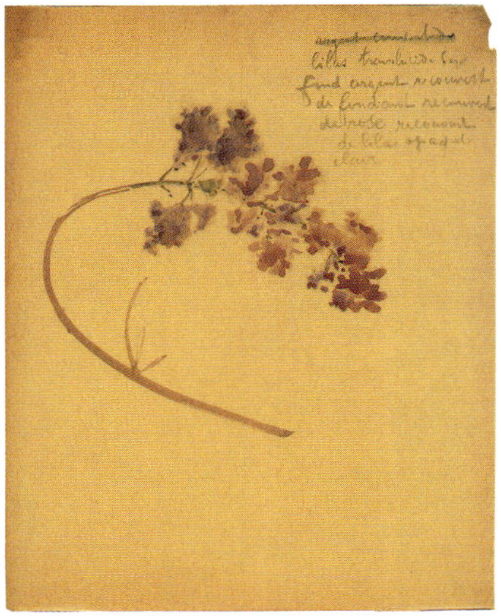

Fig. 1
Naturalist-style
Lilac Branch
Watercolor
M.-C. Lalique
coll. no. 8.1.003

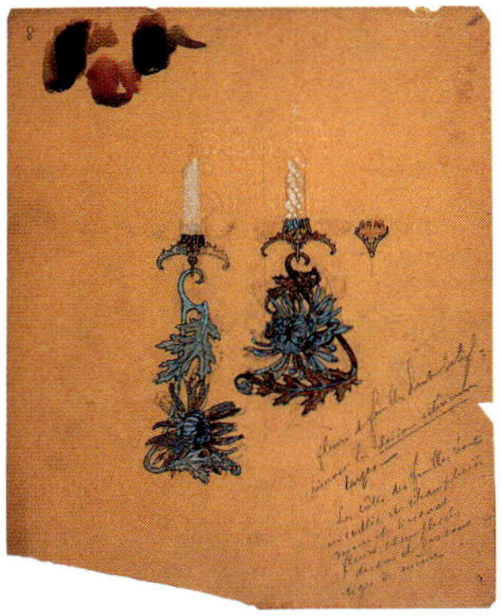

Design for Two Pendants
Chrysanthemums
c. 1898–1899
Pencil, pen, watercolor on paper
11 x 8 5/8 inches
(28 x 21.8 cm)
(Cat. 70)

Dog Collar Plaque
"Narcisse"
c. 1899–1900
Chased gold, opaque enamel on gold, glass
2 3/8 x 3 inches
(6 x 7.6 cm)
(Cat. 42)

While it is unclear whether the name traditionally given this plaque was supplied by Lalique, the solipsism embodied in Ovid's myth of the youth enamored of his own reflection was a central preoccupation of Symbolism. Yet this is another flower, with a name that refers to its chief characteristic: the golden color that gives it a solar radiance. Blue or green chrysanthemums are paradoxical and uncanny, belonging to a world of dreams whose mysterious nocturnal aura enshrouds these flower sprites.
A late-blooming flower, the chrysanthemum was a traditional symbol of autumn and the waning year. As such, they are worn in the hair of the allegorical figure of Autumn in a series of lithographs of the Four Seasons *by Alphonse Mucha (1896). Chrysanthemums, introduced from the Orient, enjoyed a great vogue in the later nineteenth century as part of the cult of Japan.* *JTR*

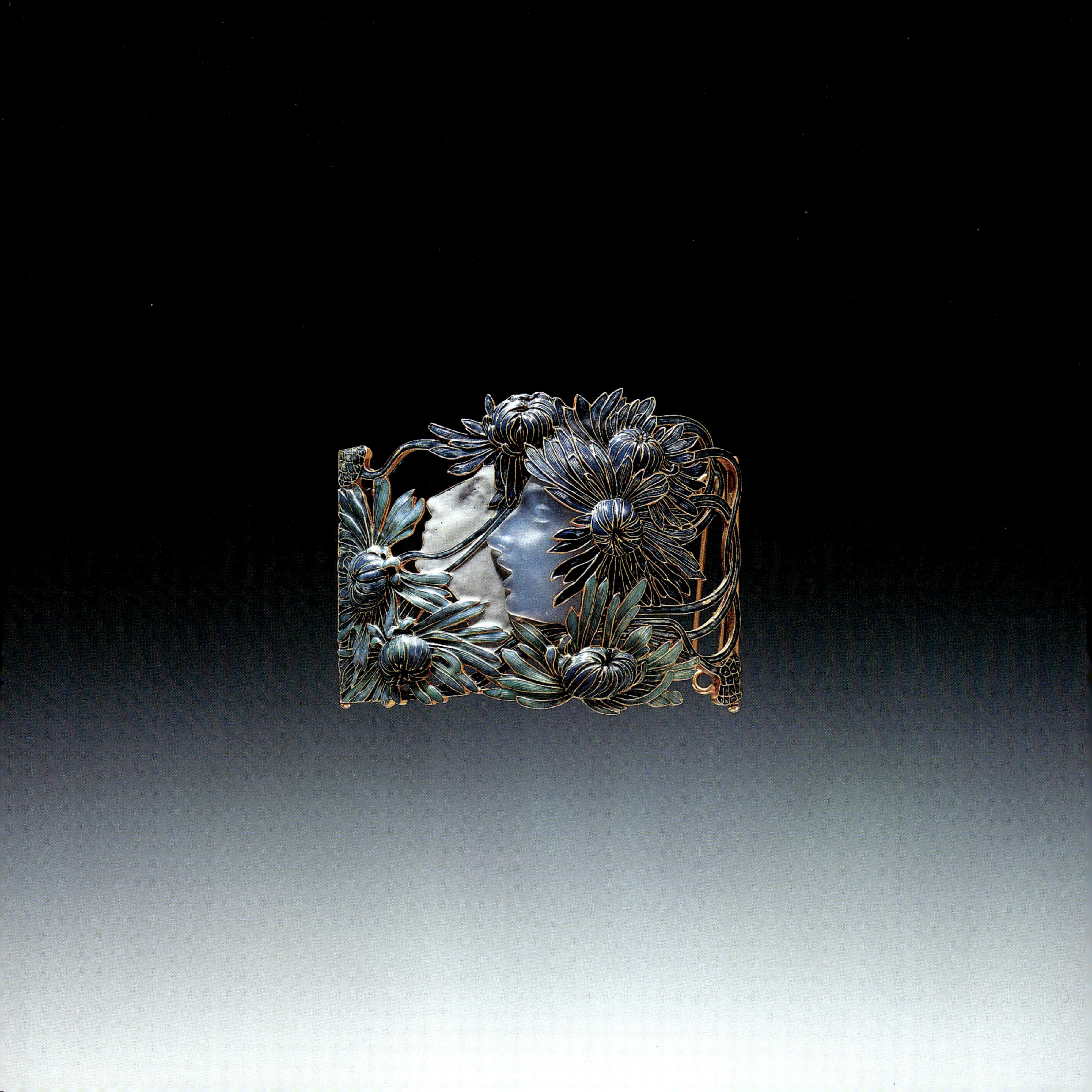

Lalique was a member of that generation of young artists who were to reap the benefits of a revolution in arts teaching that spread from Viollet-le-Duc's École de Dessin in Paris (later to become the École des Arts Décoratifs) to public and private education generally. He was able to further his taste for studying nature, while discovering how to apply it to ornamentation.

Lalique developed his repertory of forms and ornaments in gouache studies from life that he would vary and enhance unceasingly, a storehouse of images which Roger Marx saw as the artist's "Livre de Vérité."[6] In a lengthy chapter devoted to Lalique in a fundamental study of 1906–1908, *La Bijouterie française*, Vever described him in his studio on the rue Thérèse, where he had settled in 1890: "Seated at his work table, his brush or modeling tool in hand, always with those flowers that he had adored since his early childhood lying in abundance on the furniture, in every corner of the room, so as to have before his very eyes their delicacy of color, their elegant shapes which, with his exquisite taste, he knew how to analyze."[7] Around 1900, Lalique was portrayed in much the same way by the painter René Binet, in an attitude and in surroundings that evoke the portrait of Émile Gallé painted in 1892 by Victor Prouvé.[8]

Lalique's friends and contemporaries all showed their interest in that exceptional "picture library" that he pressed into service at every stage of his work, as he adapted motifs to the design of the *bijou*—or, at a later stage, of the glass piece—with the aid of numerous sketches and projects, which are a mine of information about his working methods.[9] No one, however, considered the importance of the photographs he took on his property in Clairefontaine, near Rambouillet, which had been acquired in 1898. These photographs, conserved by Lalique's granddaughter Nicole Maritch-Haviland, daughter of Suzanne Lalique, have cast new light on the artist's interest in nature and on his choice of themes; many are composed in such a way as to evoke one piece of jewelry or another, just as if he had the composition in mind as he took the picture.[10]

In Search of the "Modern *Bijou*"

At the end of 1885, René Lalique became head of the jewelry workshop of Jules Destapes, one of those who had been buying his designs on a regular basis. "I was perturbed, troubled," Lalique was to tell Vever, "at the idea of starting out on a new path, and I had many misgivings about tying myself down and wondered anxiously whether my new position as a head of a firm would curtail or enhance my liberty."[11] He need not have worried. Having inherited a well-organized studio complete with a competent work force under the supervision of Paul Briançon, who was to follow him as he moved from workshop to workshop until

1908, Lalique in fact gained just the sort freedom that enabled him to fulfill his true potential. At this time, he was providing Parisian master jewelers with both designs and pieces in which he would introduce his favored themes from nature. In 1894, for example, he composed a spatter necklace, with "ice blocks" of decreasing size set with diamonds, an astonishingly modern transposition in its abstract approach to the spray and droplets in a fountain of water.[12]

This nature lover was also a lover of the colors he found in the enamel used by Renaissance jewelers and in *objets d'art* from the Far East. Enamel was a vitreous substance that provided an infinitely varied range of tones derived from its metal oxides. Lalique's friend, the writer Pol Neveux (1865–1939), whose roots were also in Champagne, recalled the "wonderful days [they] spent long ago in the library at the École des Beaux-Arts, leaning over the old albums of Du Cerceau, Woeriot, Collaert and the Marot brothers."[13] In 1900, he saw Lalique as the heir to Benvenuto Cellini, as the one who had resurrected "the jewelry worn by the proud ladies of Cellini's memoirs or in the works of Brantôme," but "realized in keeping with our modern ideas."

Lalique exploited, in his effort to give form to the life of animals and plants, to their germination and birth, blossoming maturity, and final withering, every technical resource offered by enamel, with its exceptional chromatic range and natural rapport with gold, silver, diamonds, and colored stones. He employed translucent *cloisonné* enamels on gold for the stalks, leaves, and feathers but preferred openwork translucent enamel (*plique-à-jour*), the formula for which had been described by Cellini in the *Trattati dell'orficeria e della scultura* of 1568 and rediscovered in France during the second half of the nineteenth century by the craftsmen who, in the wake of the fashion for everything Japanese, strove to resurrect enameling techniques that had been lost since the end of the Renaissance. In 1872, Fernand Thesmar (1843–1912), close to the milieu of the *japonisants* and to the art critic Philippe Burty, who had published the seminal work on *cloisonné* in 1868,[14] had become greatly interested in the technique. It was Thesmar who rediscovered the difficult process of *plique-à-jour*. Lalique's earliest known work in this technique, dating from 1888, is a very small cup in which the enamel appears as if suspended within a fine gold mesh. This type of enamel allows light to pass through, and one can well imagine Lalique's enthusiasm when he used it to give life and movement to the petals of a large, pale-colored poppy which crowns a hatpin exhibited at the 1897 Salon or to make the jointed wings of an astonishing dragonfly woman (fig. 9) (part of his vitrine in the 1900 Exposition) look as though they are fluttering.[15]

Translucent enamel on gold opened up perspectives for Lalique that he would

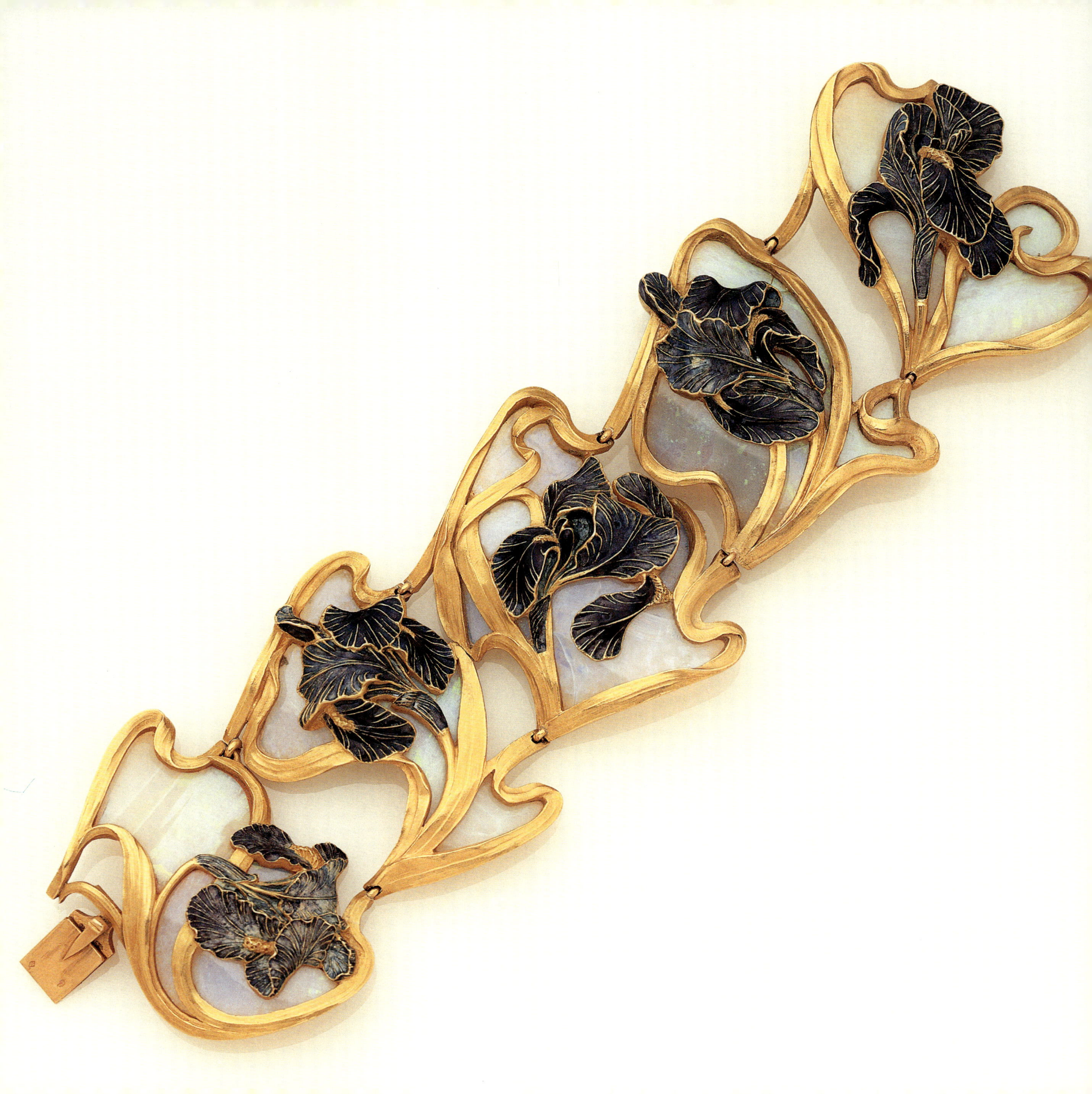

never cease to explore. On occasion, he would work the surface of the gold leaf, modify the consistency of the enamel by heating it short of complete fusion (cat. 54), model the enamel in overlapping layers, mix in gold flakes, and then, from 1891 on, even produce true mold-poured enamel reliefs.[16]

By the year 1890, the Lalique workshop employed around thirty artisans. It was at this time that Lalique decided to move to the larger and brighter premises on the third floor of 20, rue Thérèse, on a corner with the avenue de l'Opéra. He set up shop "like an artist," as Henri Vever puts it, designed models for tables and other pieces of furniture, and adorned the studio's walls and ceiling with a cavalcade of women, heralding perhaps the Valkyries on the music case exhibited in the 1894 Salon (cat. 170). This decoration was completed with the aid of two sculptors, Alphonse Ledru, father and son. It was also at this time that Lalique met Augustine-Alice Ledru, their daughter and sister, who was to be his companion and then his wife until her premature death in 1909 at the age of thirty-nine. She was the mother of two of Lalique's children, Suzanne, born in 1892, and Marc, born in 1900.

René Lalique had entered upon a phase of intensive research that would totally renew *fin-de-siècle bijouterie*. From 1892 on, he worked tirelessly, "making drawings, models, studies, and technical trials of all types without interruption, striving to achieve new results, to create something that has never been seen before."[17] When he recalled that decisive period of both his professional and emotional life for Henri Vever, he added that "it was a taxing time, one that exhausted [him] but which led to the Salons of 1895, 1896, and the rest."

Lalique now began to emerge from the anonymity in which those who commissioned his work had kept him. In 1893, he took part in a competition organized by the Union Centrale des Arts Décoratifs, the subject being a drinking vessel; he won a second prize (500 francs) and a commendation (cat. 169). He executed some stage jewelry, first for Sarah Bernhardt, whom he had met through his friend Georges Clairin in 1894,[18] and then for Julia Bertet, member of the Comédie Française. Lalique was now leaving forever the elitist world of *joaillerie* to enter the universe of true art to which he was to make an unexpected contribution: the *bijou*.

Lalique participated for the first time in his own right at the 1894 Salon de la Société des Artistes Français in the sculpture section, with the ivory music case illustrated with "The Valkyrie" (cat. 170). He sent an important piece to the 1895 Salon, which had for the first time opened its doors to the applied arts. The floral part of the undulating shape of a bracelet studded with iris quartz (cat. 53) lies tangent to recollections of the Renaissance, such as the large fastening made of two foliated scrolls set with amethysts and small diamonds, from which

Bracelet
Iris
c. 1897
Chased gold, enamel on gold, *plique-à-jour* enamel, opals
2 x 7 inches
(5 x 17.8 cm)
(Cat. 53)

Design for a Bracelet
Iris
c. 1897
Watercolor on paper
8 5/8 x 10 7/8 inches
(21.8 x 27.6 cm)
(Cat. 69)

The iris, along with the lily, was a medieval symbol of the Virgin and a favorite motif of the pre-Raphaelites. It was also much represented in Japanese art. Characteristically it grows beside water. Lalique exhibited two pieces of jewelry with an iris motif at the Salon of 1897, a belt buckle and this superb bracelet which was also included in his display at the Exposition Universelle in 1900. The opal is skillfully cut to fit into gold cells or cloisons, an ancient technique that had been perfected in Egypt. Lalique was surely acquainted with examples of Egyptian jewelry in the Mariette collection that had been acquired by Napoleon III for the Louvre. The design recalls a border ornament by Carlos Schwabe for his illustrated work, Evangile de L'Enfance de Notre Seigneur Jésus Christ, *published in Paris in 1891. There, too, iris blossoms are contained in a running frame of curvaceous leaves.* *JTR*

Design for a Brooch
Renaissance
c. 1893–1894
Pencil, ink, water-color,
gouache on paper
11 x 8 3/4 inches
(28 x 22.1 cm)
(Cat. 22)

Design for a Necklace
5 Scrolls
c. 1894–1896
Pencil, ink, watercolor on paper
11 x 8 5/8 inches
(27.9 x 21.7 cm)
(Cat. 19)

Necklace
3 Pomegranates
c. 1897
Chased gold, translucent enamel on gold, pearls, opals
7 5/8 x 7 5/8 x 3/8 inches
(19.4 x 19.4 x 0. 8 cm)
(Cat. 12)

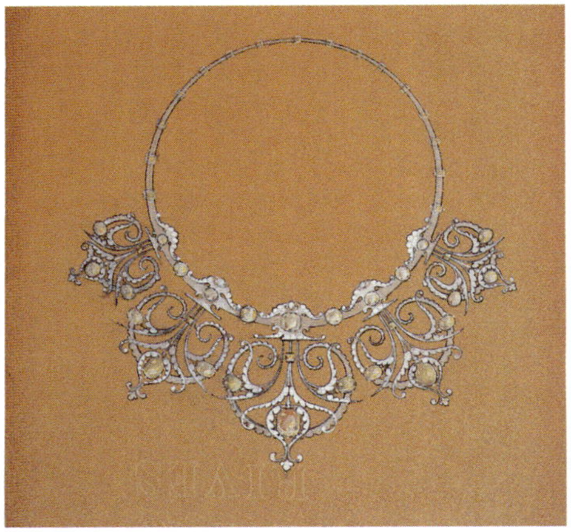

emerges, chased into the gold, a naked woman without arms (cat. 22). This marks the first appearance of a woman in Lalique's œuvre. She defies criticism, imposing her rather heavy, realistically fashioned body on the schematic floral design, a sort of proto-Maillol, provocatively modern yet remaining within the classical strictures of the *bijou*.

Lalique asserted himself in earnest two years later at the 1897 Salon at the Palais de l'Industrie with a showcase containing horn and ivory combs that were entirely novel in theme and execution. Both were inspired not only by Japanese art but also by a type of large comb used by Andalusian women. Parisian women used a wide, slightly concave comb to hold up two heavy gatherings of hair on either side of the head, sticking the curved tongs of another into the top of the chignon. The blondish, translucent horn and the ivory are carved and encrusted with gemstones and embellished with floral motifs in enamel inspired by Lalique's own botanical repertory as well as by the ornaments on those Japanese saber hilts he could have seen in the windows of Siegfried Bing's shop.[19]

What Lalique sent to the 1897 Salon impressed Émile Gallé, and in the columns of the Gazette des Beaux-Arts he placed the young artist in the context of the history of contemporary jewelry: "This year at the Palais de l'Industrie M. René Lalique was...the indisputable victor in the fine arts. He breathed new life into the art of *joaillerie*, and, I dare say, prepared the way for the final stages of the modern *bijou*."[20]

This, coming from an artist who had been striving for three decades to give expression in glass to emotions, to feelings of a purely plastic order is a priceless judgment indeed, one which amounted to the consecration of the "artist" in René Lalique.

Lalique's creations arrived at the right time to shore up Gallé's ideas in his fight to close the gap between the fine arts and the decorative arts—the so-called "major" and "minor" arts, respectively. Gallé employed the pages of the Gazette des Beaux-Arts to lambaste a French administration that could only recognize the *objet d'art* when "applied to industry" and made an irrevocable distinction between "applied and unapplied art." "Hence," Gallé continued, "Michelangelo's rights are not the same as Cellini's. Rodin has the right of life and death over the forgery of his work while, it must be said, Lalique would absolutely be denied this right for his delicate creations."[21]

Gallé shares with another writer on art from Nancy, his friend Roger Marx, the dogma, one might almost say the myth, of the Unity of Art as preached by the decorative artists of the time. At its foundation in 1864, the Union Centrale des Beaux-Arts Appliqués à l'Industrie had propounded this principle as doctrine. Lalique, wanting to create wearable jewelry for women as well as to extend his imagination, was a natural adherent of the doctrine.

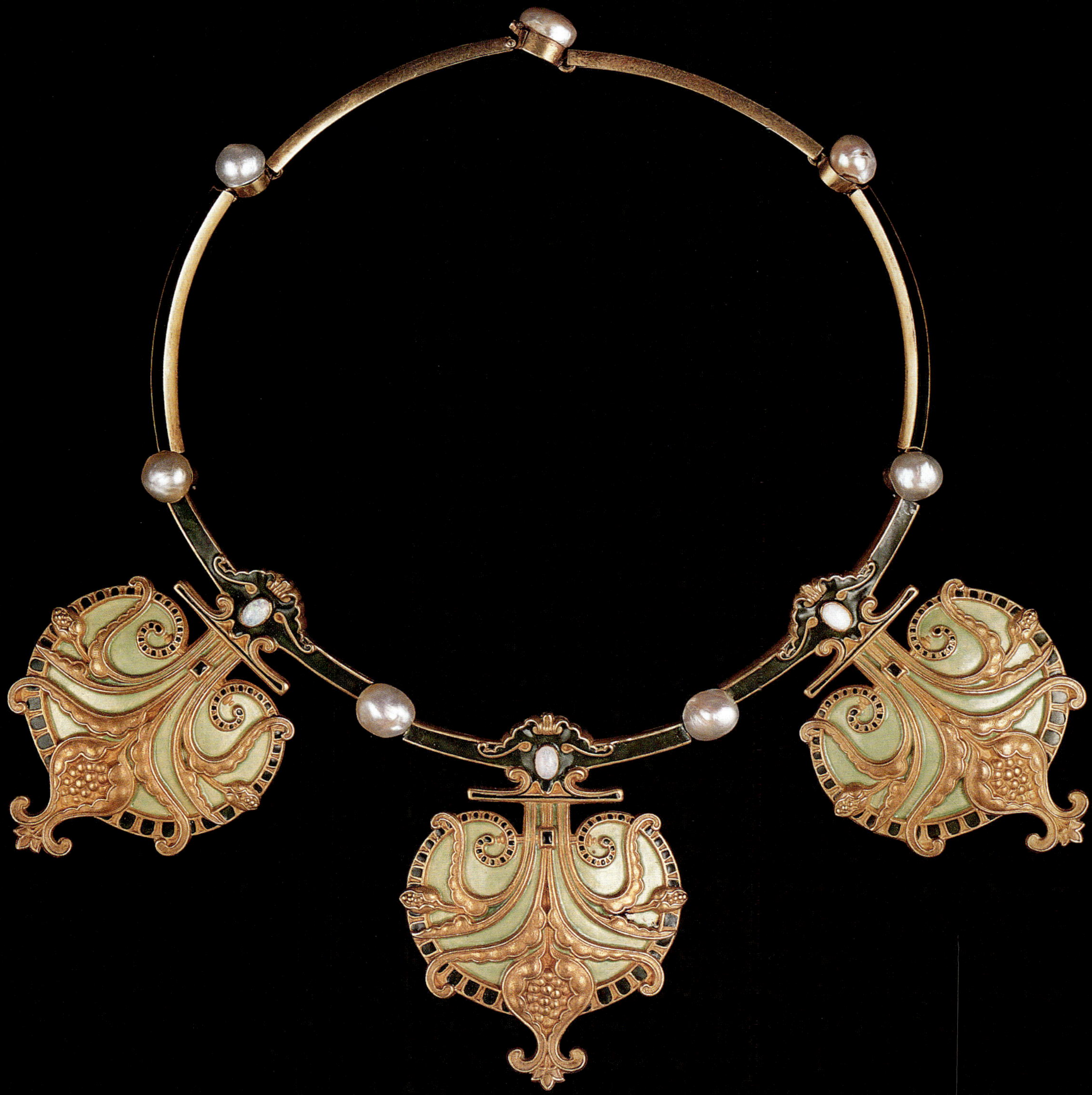

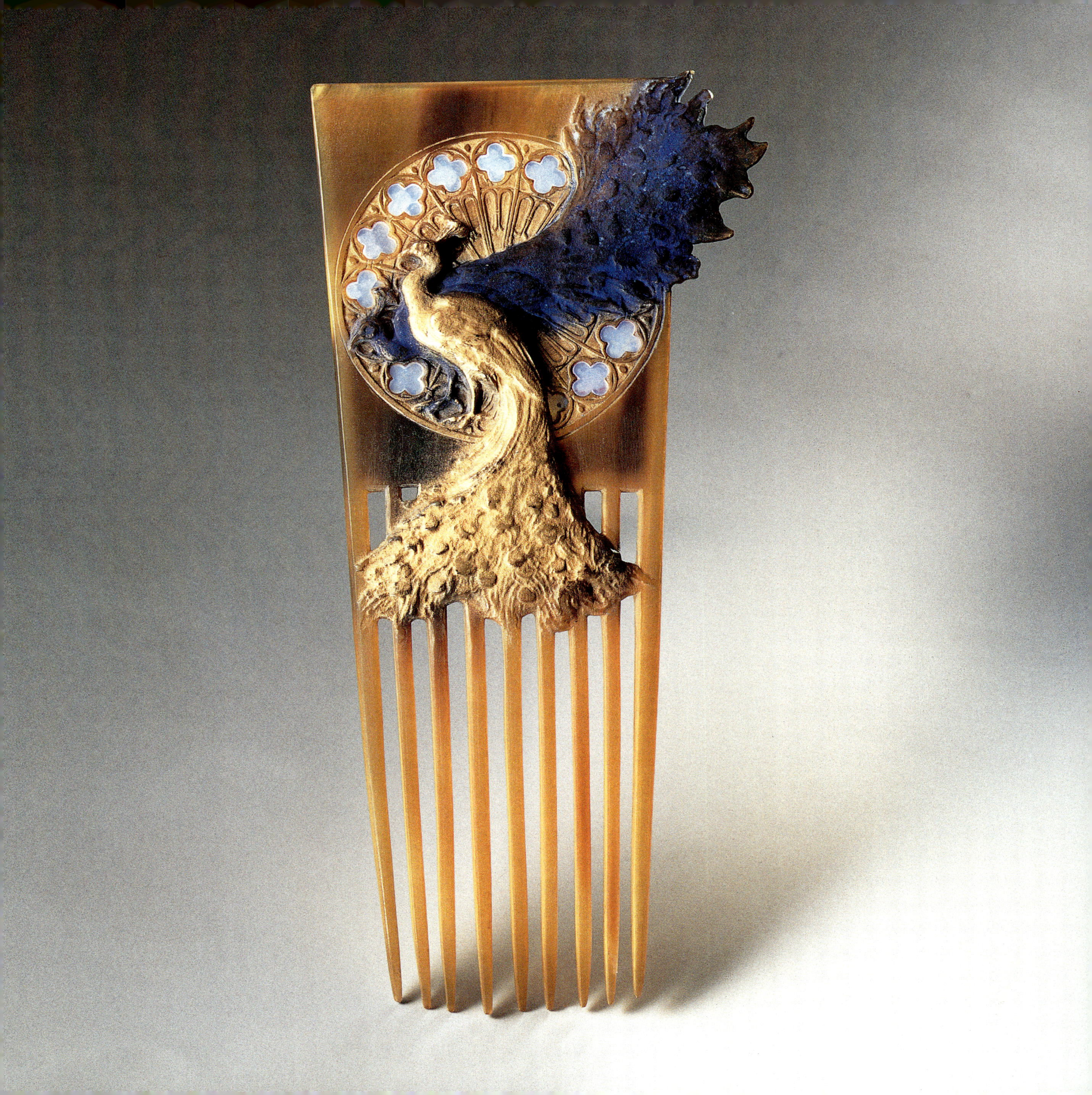

The "Modern *Bijou*" Realized

A foretaste of Lalique's vitrine at the 1900 Exposition Universelle could be found in his contributions to the 1898 Salon, when he was in the midst of a creative ferment. Though he still made use of outside ateliers (he entrusted metal-chasing to Georges-Pierre Deraisme, for example), he now had his own enameling workshop, directed by Eugène Feuillâtre (1870–1916). He also had a complete glassmaking concern where, according to Henri Vever, in 1890 he conducted his earliest experiments in the medium under the supervision of Jules Henrivaux, the director of the Saint-Gobain manufactory, and Léon Appert, a glassmaker who worked in Clichy.

Lalique's adventure as an artist in glass began in earnest within the intimate confines of rue Thérèse, where he presided, as Vever puts it, "like a true alchemist." At the outset, glass was treated as a replacement material, being easier to produce than relief enamel and less arduous to work than any stone—especially rock crystal. It was not long, however, before the material started to contribute not only a volume but a transparency, a reflection of its own that enhanced the qualities of other materials such as gold, enamel, and gemstones. Lalique also employed glass, however, in opalescent, enameled, and patinated forms.

But ultimately it was his exploration of volume, whether in bas-relief or in the round, that came to dominate his aesthetic conceptions. Lalique had trained as a sculptor as early as 1882, in a studio belonging to the city of Paris. He was thus able to execute his own large-scale models in wax or plaster. These were then made up in metal, ivory, or horn, by means of the reducing machine used by medal makers. According to Vever, Lalique also turned to the Ledrus, *père* and *fils*, for assistance.[22]

Through the articles that appeared in the specialized press it is possible to get a fair idea of the astonishingly wide range of jewelry Lalique exhibited in 1898, a veritable repertoire of all the types and themes found in his later work. The writer and poet Jean Lorrain was particularly intrigued by the combs. "Nine huge combs, of improbable dimensions which are difficult to imagine in a woman's coiffure."[23] Despite this reservation, he dwelt on three of them, among them the peacock comb—acquired by the Musée des Arts Décoratifs (cat. 26)—in which Lalique amalgamated two sources of inspiration, the Middle Ages and the East. The direct evocation of the Gothic cathedrals found in this opal rose window juxtaposed with the solar symbol of two peacocks is rare in Lalique's œuvre, the only other instance being an ogival arcade in a drawing for a comb (cat. 59). The opulent blue and gold enameled tails recall those which unfurled over the screens in the painted porcelain drawing room decoration James McNeill Whistler executed for the London

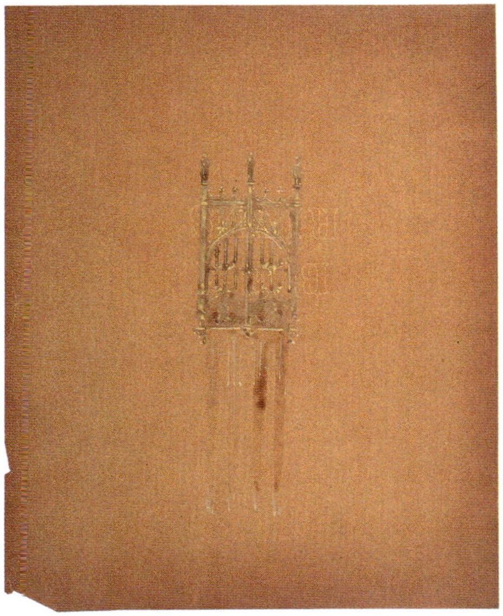

Comb
Two Peacocks in front of a Rose Window
c. 1897–1898
Brown horn patinated in blue and gold, disc of opals
7 1/4 x 3 3/8 inches
(18.4 x 8.6 cm)
(Cat. 26)

Design for a Comb
Gothic
c. 1897–1898
Watercolor on paper
10 3/4 x 8 3/8 inches
(27.2 x 21.3 cm)
(Cat. 59)

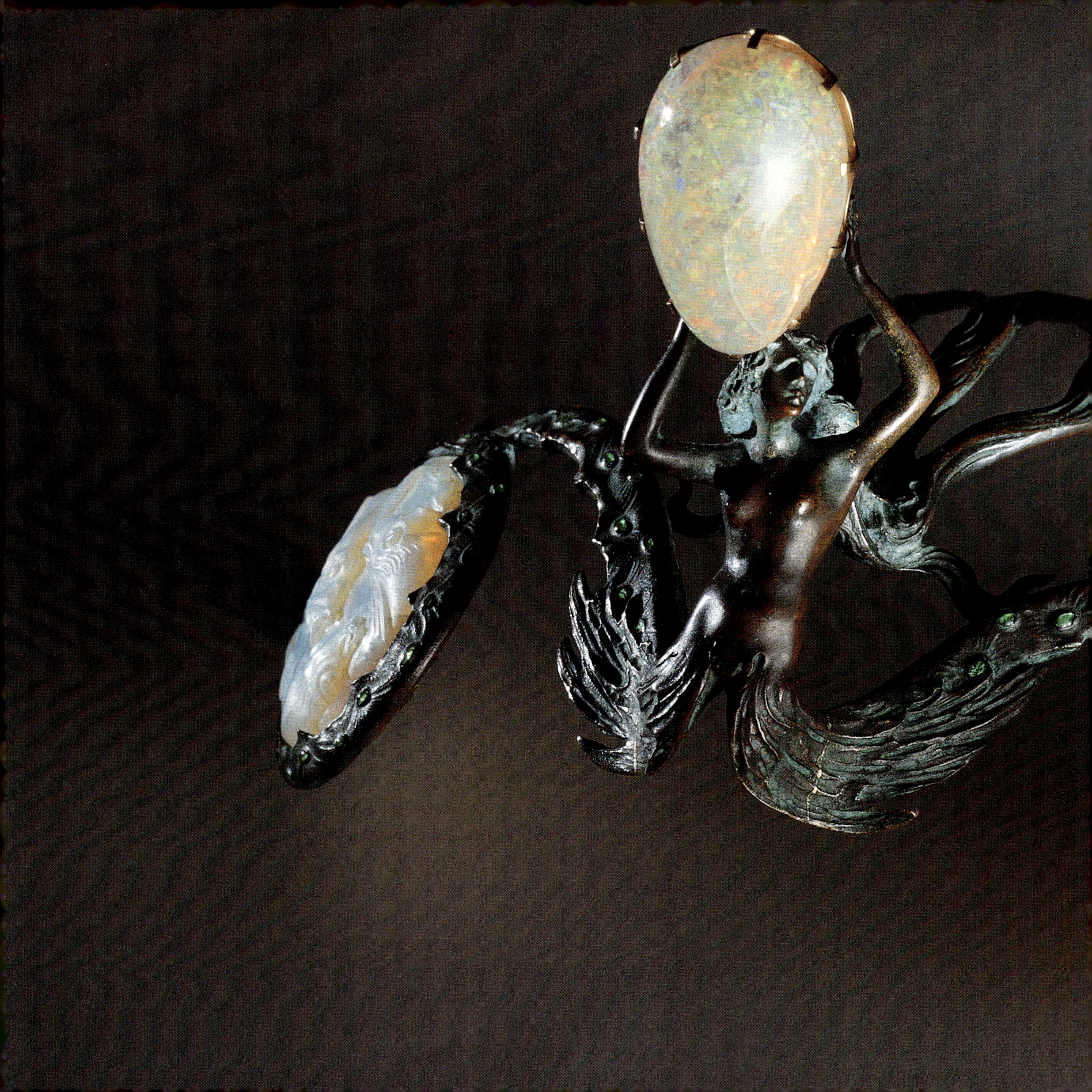

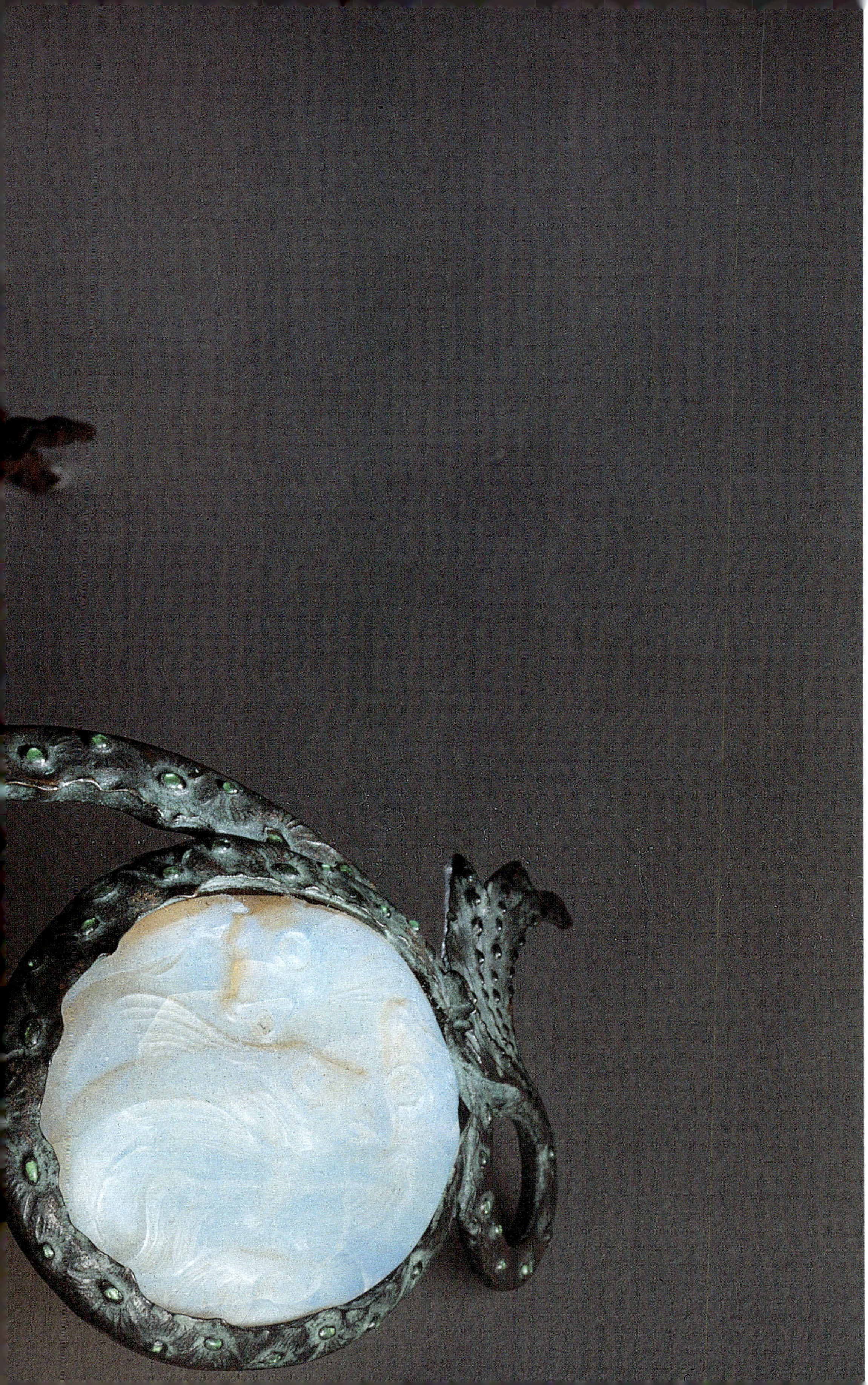

Tiara
Mermaid
c. 1897–1898
Bronze
with green and
brown patina,
enamel,
carved opals
4 x 5 1/5 x 5 1/4
inches
(9.7 x 14 x 13.3
cm)
(Cat. 37)

residence of his friend Frederick Leyland in 1876–87.[24] Peacocks, often found in pairs in Chinese painting, are a recurrent theme in Lalique's pantheon. He employs them as much for the decorative impact of their oceli-spotted plumage as for their ambiguous, culturally variable meaning. Lalique himself stressed the positive, cosmic symbolism of peacocks, following an interpretation frequently encountered in Symbolist painting, which associates the bird with Hera–Juno, wife and mother.

In his accounts of the 1898 Salon for *Art et Décoration*, Henri Vever had also lingered over the case containing these combs.[25] He denied them any practical use, even for "an ever so elegant woman....Not everybody can be Sarah Bernhardt or Cléo de Mérode." He noted the Japanese character of the umbel comb (cat. 48) and the fish comb that Jean Lorrain had seen as the "blue-green life of water solidified into the material of a comb."[26] He believed quite rightly that the mermaid tiara (cat. 37) was destined for a particular woman: Martine de Béhague, a lady very much of the upper crust who was at the time the wife of the comte de Béarn. It is in any case an uncommon piece, the sort Sarah Bernhardt would wear, placed on the forehead and sitting on the temples. A green and brown mermaid in patinated bronze stands upright beneath the weight of an opal she holds, arms extended above her flowing locks; two opals carved with fish are enclosed between the split fins of her tail. This piece is exceptional for a number of reasons: for the bronze material, which Lalique rarely used in his jewelry work (he normally imitated bronze with patinated or enameled gold), and for the carved opals treated like cameos. The theme too is original, combining as it does references to Japan and antiquity.

The mermaid tiara is also a tribute to opal, which was, despite its malevolent connotations, Lalique's favorite stone. It belonged to the Symbolist pantheon, where its pale-colored, ever-changing reflections and the drop of blood that it presents when viewed from a particular angle often figured in conjunction with the peacock's iridescent plumage. The poet Robert de Montesquiou also believed that the bird had its dangers. He entrusted the illustration of the cover of his collection of poems *Les Paons* ("The Peacocks") to Lalique, whose portrait can be discerned in a poem dedicated to the eighth gem, opal: "I know a jeweler of opals enamored/ Whom the purest diamond cannot tempt/ Only the pale flamed gem will he carve/ Whose iridescence has him for a lover kept."[27] The two men probably met around 1896 and, a year later, Montesquiou dedicated chapter VII of a collection of essays called *Roseaux pensants* ("Thinking Reeds") to Lalique and Gallé, "goldsmith and glassmaker." The text opens surprisingly with the poet amusing himself with the "jangling sound, rhyming with *relique*" of the name Lalique, who is predestined to become a "goldsmith, chaser in metal of shrines and reliquaries, of gleaming ciboria, radiant monstrances, of gem-encrusted sconces whose blazing tapers reflect the flaming tongues of their candlesticks in enamel and gems."[28] Despite Montesquiou's encomium, the production of objects for church use was exceptional in Lalique's work at that date.[29]

Montesquiou later changed tack and concerned himself with what was more personal to Lalique's art: flowers and plants, birds, milky, transparent opals, peacock feathers—all of which contribute to making Lalique "a master of iridescence and of shimmering, the prince of orients and reflections." "Peacock feathers with their opaline eyes" will become one of the jeweler's leitmotifs, the first example of which is the corsage ornament acquired by Calouste Gulbenkian at the 1900 Exposition.[30] Opal and moonstone were Natalie Clifford-Barney's (1876–1972) favorite gems. This fantastically wealthy young American woman had settled in Paris and had met Lalique in 1899 during her liaison with the famous *demimondaine* Liane de Pougy, who was to give her Lalique's silver ring chased with bats framing a moonstone heart (cat. 45).[31]

Other Lalique jewels were to follow, some of them presents from the poet Renée Vivien, who selected blue enamels set with opals and sapphires that matched Natalie's "virgin blue eyes" (cat. 92).

The Cult of Nature

"For M. Lalique, nature is a temple through whose living pillars...man passes as through a forest of symbols which it is his goal to select and to master. Suggestive power is one of his œuvre's central characteristics: by his desire to elicit meanings, to invite meditation, M. René Lalique is close to M. Émile Gallé...."[32] Although such a parallel is unavoidable today, it was probably less so at the time Roger Marx saw these two figures united in "such a fervent and intellectual cult of the flower." Despite their age difference, the careers of Lalique and Gallé are indeed comparable: both trained in the same technical and decorative tradition; both were receptive to all the fashions of their time—to the Renaissance, to the East and the Far East; and both blazed their own trail, creating, through the interpretation of nature, new, "modern" glass and jewelry pieces.

Émile Gallé and René Lalique shared an exact and serious attitude to flora that one might characterize as French, for it can be likened to the work of other Frenchmen. Pol Neveux, on perusing Lalique's *bijoux* and gouaches, was reminded of Bernard Palissy: "Both have observed nature with the same curiosity. They sensed the tiniest detail and have lingered long over the slightest events. They felt nothing trifling, nothing contemptible in the spectacle of things natural."[33] This is also the spirit not

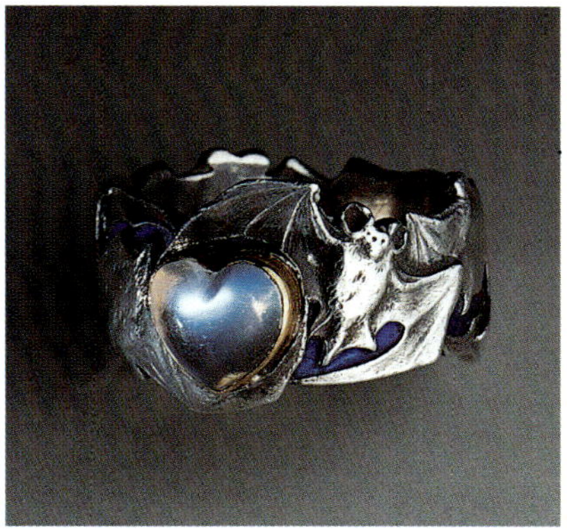

Ring
Bat
1899
Silver, translucent enamel, moonstone, gold
1/2; Diam: 3/4 inches
(1.2; Diam: 1.9 cm)
(Cat. 45)

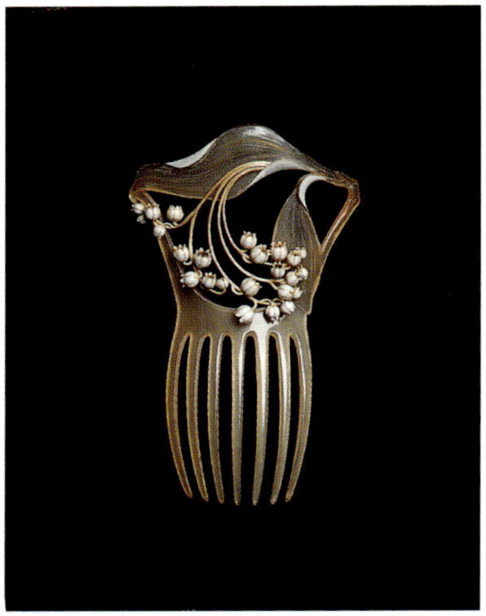

only of Viollet-le-Duc, but of that other Frenchman, La Fontaine.

The florilegium of plants in Lalique's jewelry derived from the fields and the woods, the gardens and bouquets he surrounded himself with: simple flowers, tender and rustic—violets, cowslip, dandelion; climbing plants such as morning glory and jasmine, and all those cultivated by the iconography of Art Nouveau—iris, wisteria, rose, poppy, honesty.

Lalique was concerned with every stage of the plant's life, from seed to withered stem, arranging the flora in bunches, bouquets or singly, depending on the piece he had in mind. His interpretation, though submitted to the laws of ornament, always takes as its starting point a real flower or plant, never one from some illustration in a botanical album. It seems that Lalique frequented the Paris botanical gardens, the Jardin des Plantes, as well as the natural history collection in its museum,[34] where he could have observed and drawn exotic and rare species, such as those cattleyas that he was to transmute into a sensual, sophisticated tiara (cat. 78). The timeless character of Lalique's jewelry was stressed by Pol Neveux: "Neither servile copying, nor pretentiously symbolic literary derivatives—such was his way." As Roger Marx put it: "The interpretations that M. Lalique gives of nature, far from falling prey to any formalistic stiffness, exude an emotive, wistful charm." These words evoke those jewels

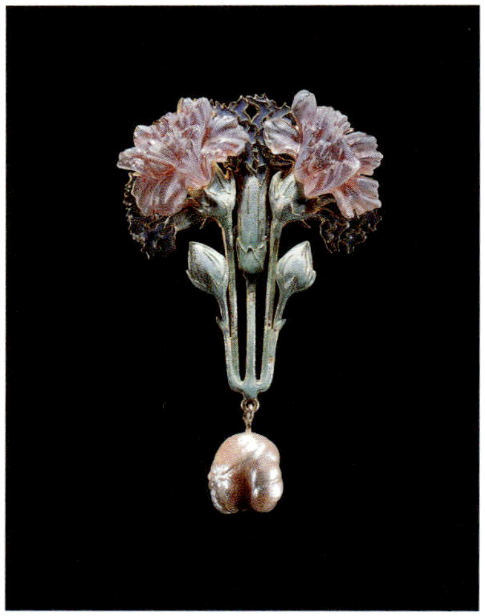

Comb
Lilies of the Valley
1900
Horn, gold, opaque enamel on gold
6 1/8 x 3 3/4 x 1 3/16 inches
(15.4 x 9.4 x 3 cm)
(Cat. 71)

Brooch-Pendant
Carnations
c. 1901–1902
Gold, opaque enamel on gold, *plique-à-jour* enamel, cast glass, pearl
3 1/8 x 1 7/8 x 7/16 inches
(7.6 x 5 x 1.11 cm)
(Cat. 123)

Handle of a Lorgnette?
Sweet Pea with Bust of a Woman
c. 1899–1900
Gold, enamel, cast glass
4 1/2 x 2 inches
(11.5 x 5 cm)
(Cat. 130)

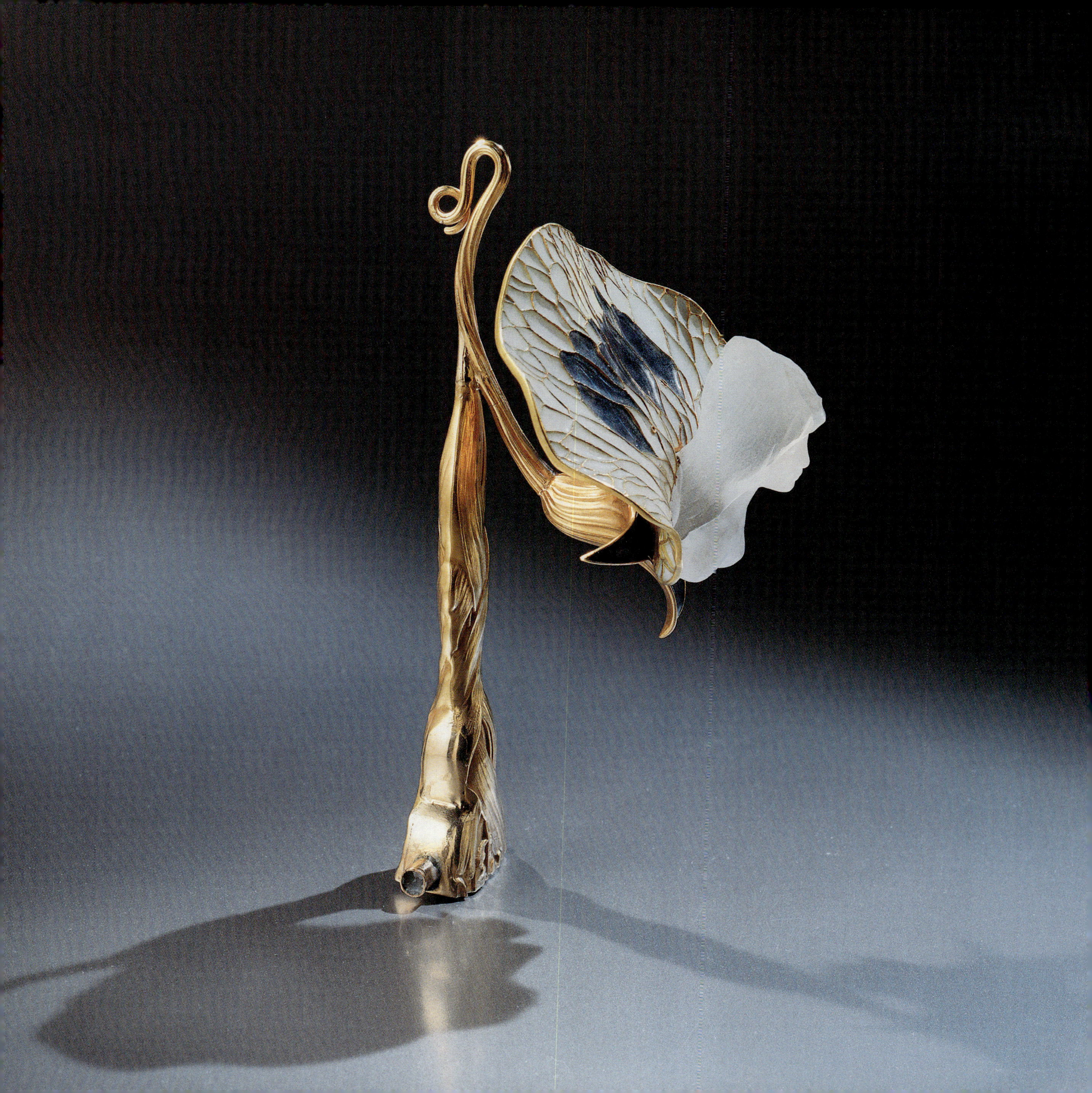

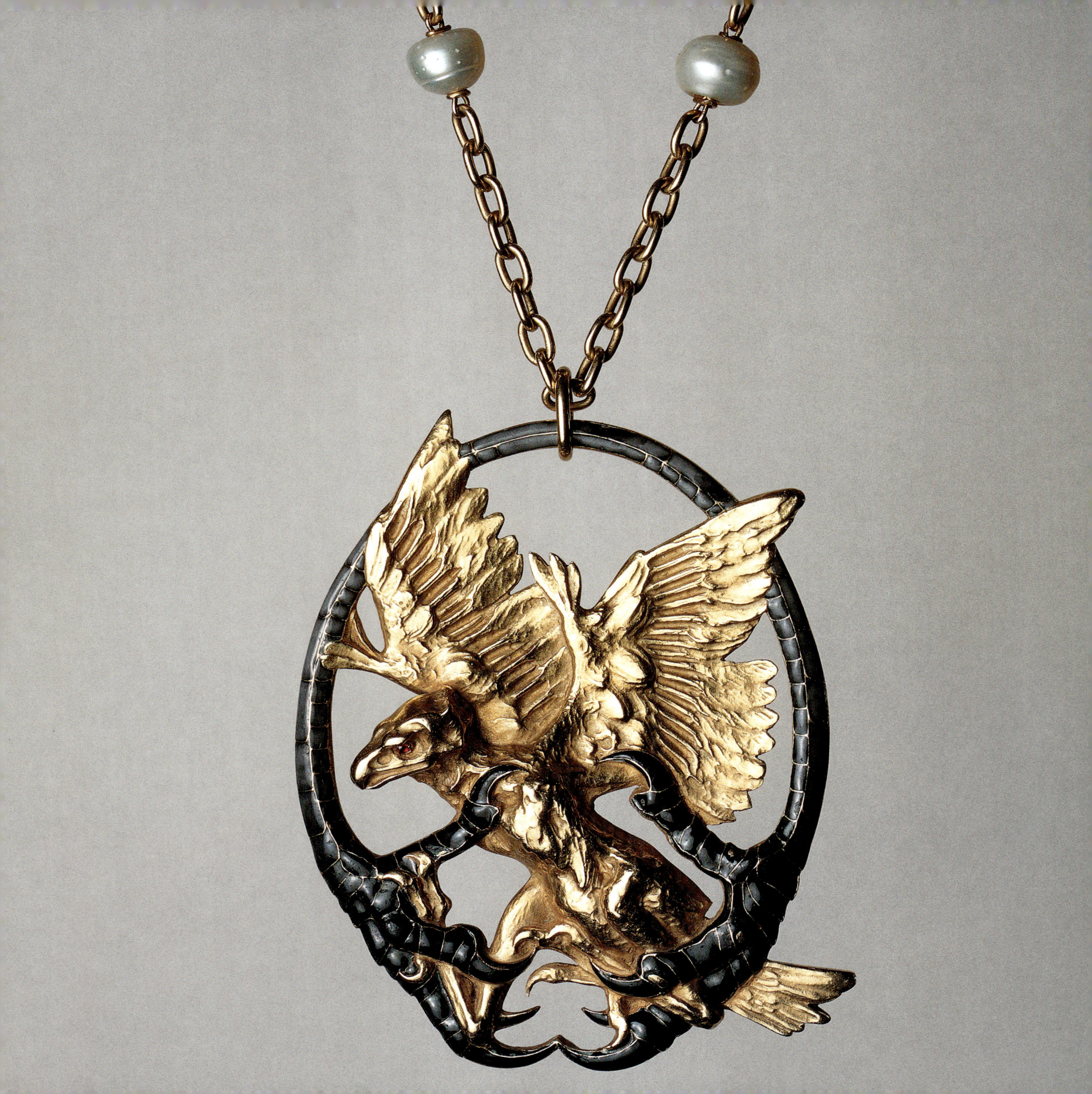

A great eagle with powerful upraised wings and outstretched talons is imprisoned within an oval frame that incorporates huge scaly talons executed in black enamel. This terrifying image of imprisonment, aggression and self-directed violence exemplifies the dark side of Lalique's imagery where talons, thorns, and the open jaws of serpents are interchangeably menacing. Lalique used a variant of this image for the cover of Edmond Rostand's play L'Aiglon *in which Sarah Bernhardt, playing one of her favorite principal boy roles, took the part of the "Eaglet," the ill-fated son of Napoleon who was imprisoned at Schönbrunn and died without matching the great deeds of the "Eagle," his father. Exhibited at the Paris Exposition of 1900, the pendant was apparently purchased by Sarah Bernhardt for Edmond Rostand, and it is known to have belonged to his wife, Rosemonde Gérard, who is represented wearing it in a portrait by Eugène Pascou painted in 1901 that is preserved at the Rostand family home.* *JTR*

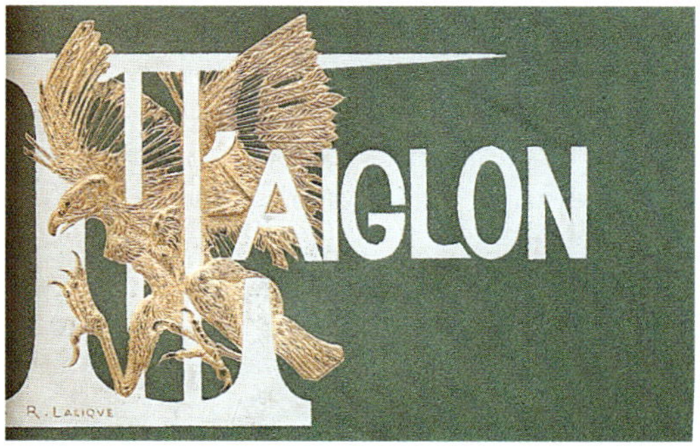

Pendant
Eagle
c. 1899–1900
Chased gold, enamel on gold, ruby, pearls
2 7/8 x 2 3/8; Chain 24 3/4 in.
(7.5 x 6; Chain: 63 cm)
(Cat. 97)

Frontispiece
"L'Aiglon"
by Edmond Rostand
1900
White ink on paper, gold
4 1/2 x 3 inches
(11.2 x 7.8 cm)
(Cat. 232)

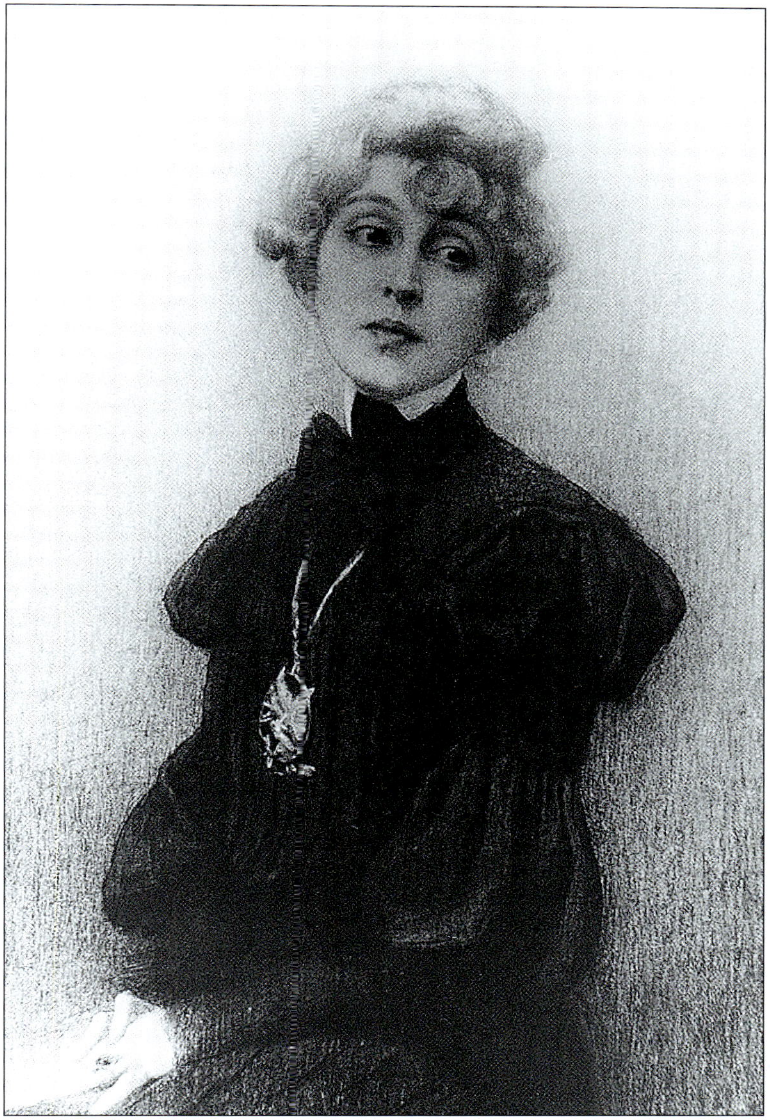

Fig. 2
Eugène Pascou
Portrait of Rosemonde Gérard
1901

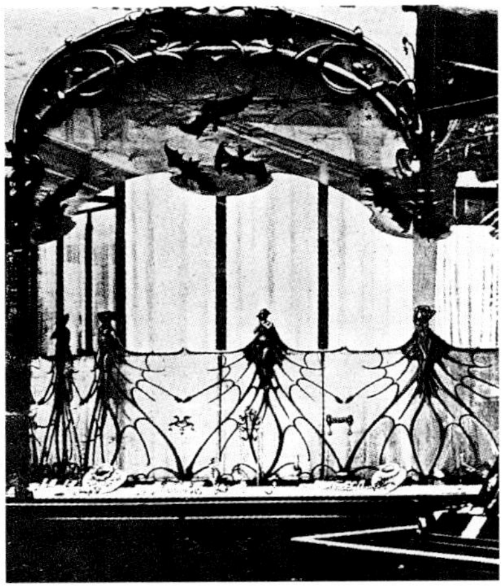

Above and pp. 32–33
Figs. 3 and 4
Lalique's Display Case at the 1900 Exposition Universelle in Paris

One of Two Sculptures
Butterfly Woman
c. 1899–1900
Bronze
Each: 39 x 40 x 13 3/4 inches
(99 x 101.5 x 35 cm)
(Cat. 172)

and drawings where the flowers and leaves are withered, shriveled (cat. 236), whereas for the most part Lalique portrayed plants in all their freshness, still dewy within the éclat of their enamel and glass.

Lalique also exploited the rhythm of the seasons and other natural phenomena. Rather than the leafy trees of high summer, he preferred the clear-cut lines of naked trunks and boughs, somber and dense, or branches of pine. In his work, he would capture the birds of both day and night, whether in flight or on the watch—swallows, bats, owls. He observed too the waters, flowing and still, and those animals that swim in the deep or live nearby—fish and seahorses, swans and dragonflies. He was well-acquainted with the teeming multitude of insects of the meadow that leap from stalk to stalk—butterflies and wasps, grasshoppers, bumblebees, and beetles, which, on occasion, can appear face to face as frightening-looking beasts, like the snakes, cockerels, and eagles which invaded his pieces for the 1900 Exposition.

There are metamorphoses, mutations, and transgressions from the vegetable kingdom to the animal and human realms. Lalique as a sculptor shows himself in the female and male faces, carved in pale chalcedony, gilded ivory, the green of the chrysoprase, rock crystal or glass (cat. 42); they have fine classical features, linked to mythology, to Egyptian or Greco-Roman antiquity. As a close associate of the Ledrus, he adopted a Rodin-like plasticity, with tangled, wrestling limbs of both sexes, often modeled in bronze before a definitive version in gold, ivory, and glass (cats. 173–176).

The Exposition Universelle, Paris, 1900

A print by Félix Vallotton showing a densely-packed crowd completely obscuring Lalique's exhibition case gives an inkling of the success the jeweler met with at the 1900 Exposition. It provided an opportunity for writers and art critics alike, as well as for the profession in general, to take stock of Lalique's contribution to the development of the modern *bijou* as it was extricating itself from the eclecticism and traditions of *joaillerie*. It was Lalique who paved the way for what has since been termed Art Nouveau; he was followed by the best of his fellow-artists, Georges Fouquet, the Vevers, Lucien Gaillard. They adopted from his work new techniques and materials, enamel and horn, for example, as well as a thematic repertory based on flowers and animals, on the symbolic imagery of woman, and a range of colors that monochrome *joaillerie* would never have employed. Grasset's designs for Vever or Mucha's for Fouquet utilize the whole gamut of natural materials—gold and silver, colored gemstones—along with metallic oxides to tint enamels of various types, matte or brilliant, opaque or transparent.

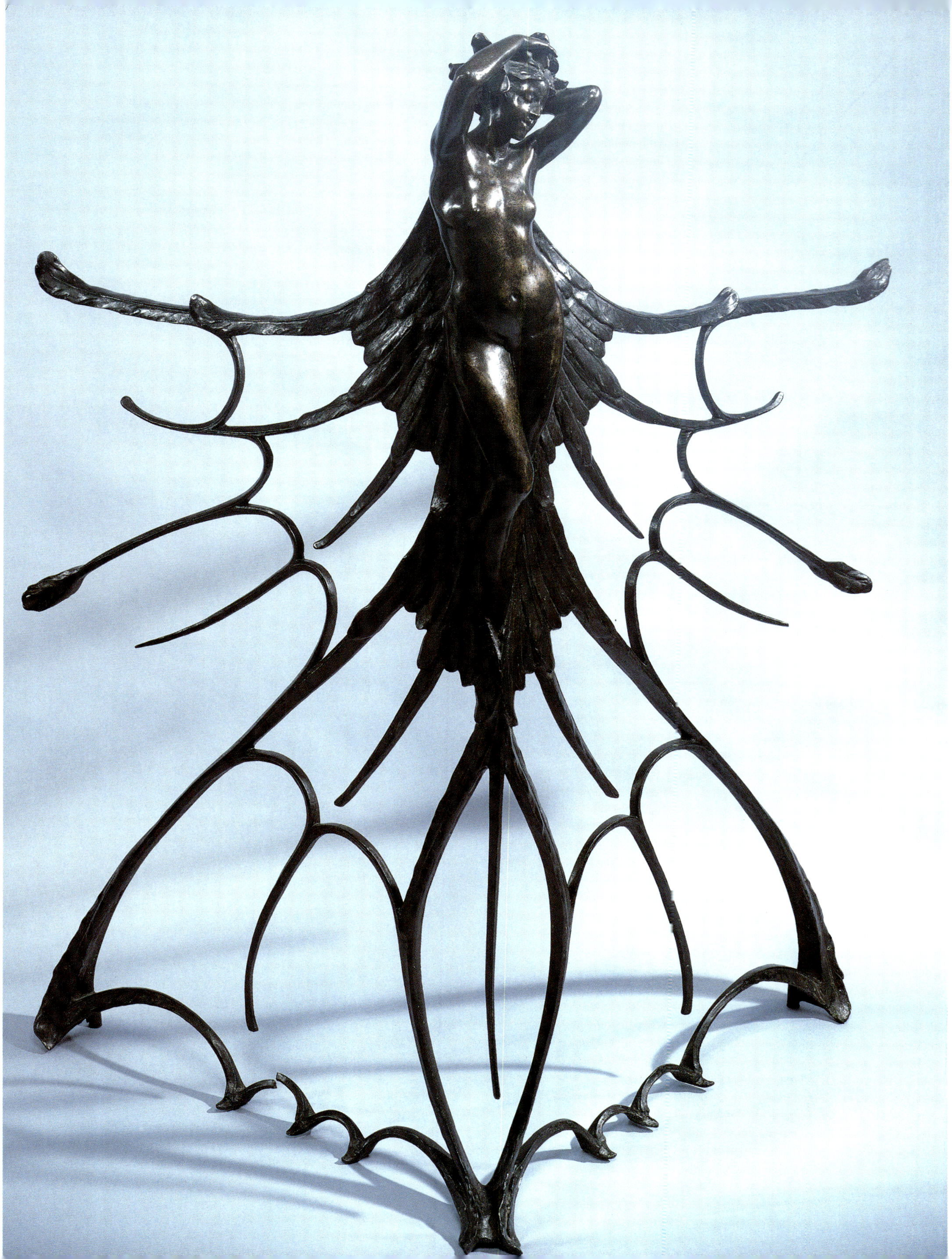

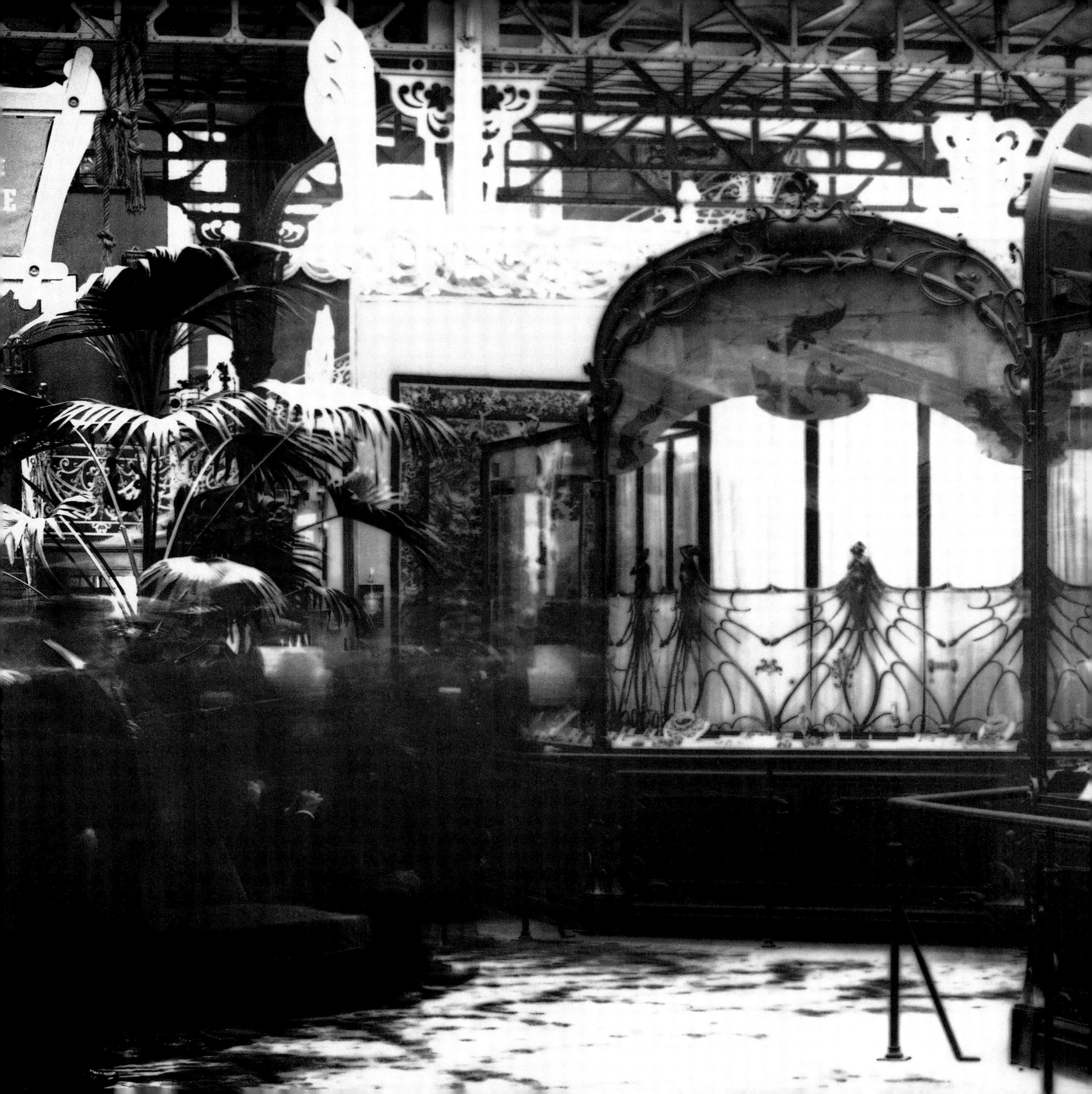

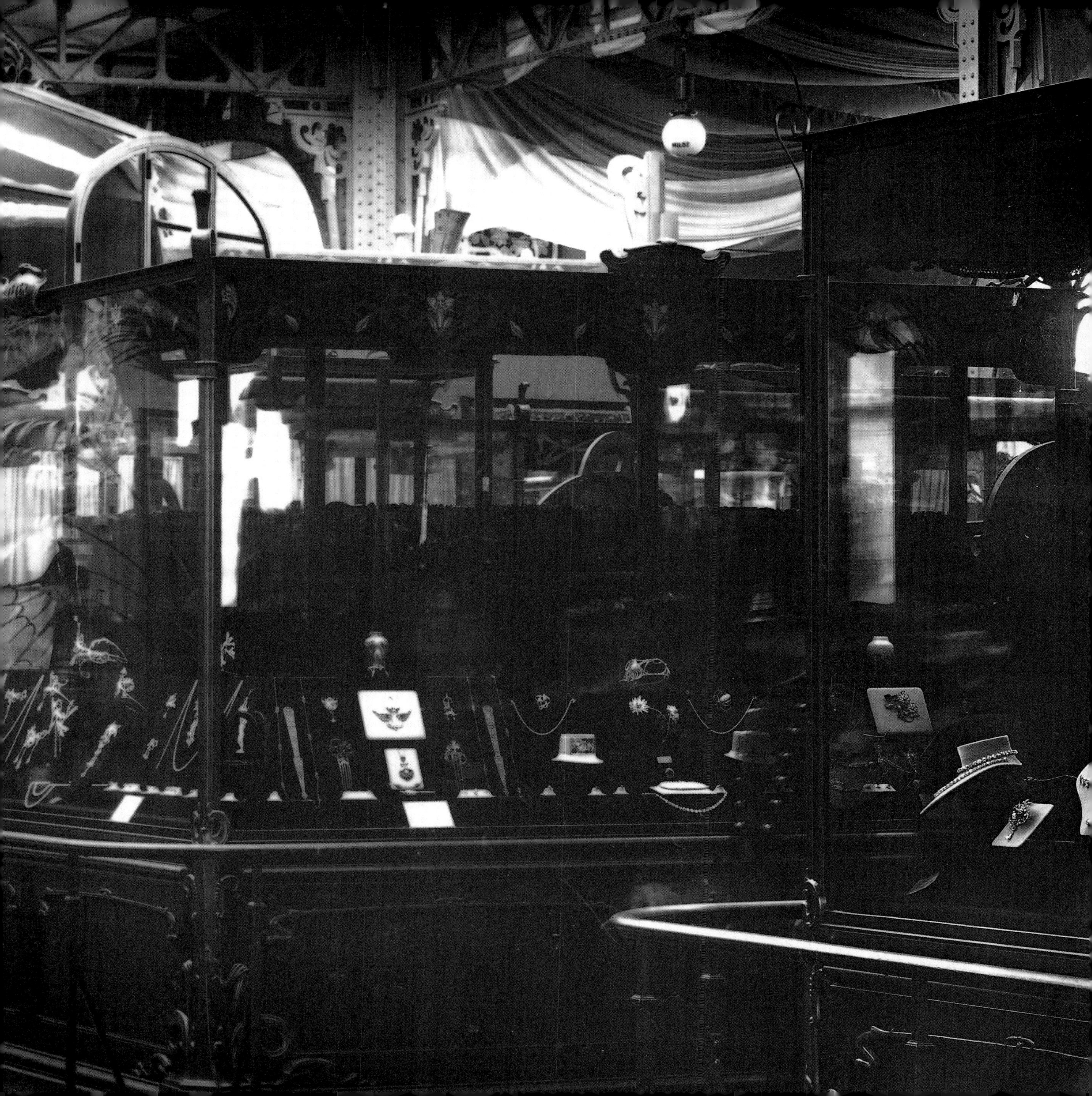

Lalique's jewelry pieces were, nonetheless, of quite a different order from those of his colleagues, which Émile Gallé had recognized as early as 1897 (p. 18 above). Pol Neveux, commenting on Lalique's presentation at the 1900 Exposition, failed to find any common ground between "René Lalique, the revolutionary, a precursor of a new art, and those intelligent manufacturers who exploit his discoveries and creations, and exhibit their green-eyed efforts on neighboring stands. Lalique refuses to call on more or less talented collaborators, he does not have to enlist the assistance of countless designers of questionable originality, and he can claim without fear of contradiction to be the legitimate father of every single *bijou* he sells; they are not the fruit of some dubious alliance, they were not spawned by the anonymity of some corporate appellation."[35] Although Neveux's judgment was hard on Lalique's contemporaries, the reception of Lalique's work was not without controversy. Henri Vever recalled a number of years later "the dense and fervent crowd [that] gathered round to see a body of work that was on everyone's lips. There were violent and often overblown altercations between devotees and detractors; however,...not many art critics proved hostile to the new style that Lalique had created, and many became wholehearted enthusiasts."[36]

The opinion of a fellow jeweler such as Vever on encountering Lalique's new work at the 1900 Exposition is all the more valuable since he can acknowledge Lalique's exceptional mastery, as well as his influence on contemporary "colleagues" and on the evolution of jewelry at the end of the nineteenth century. Vever stressed Lalique's role as a kind of agent provocateur for the public. "His other strong point was that...he did violence, if I may express myself this way, to a public which until then had been loath to take on novel ideas and forced it to accept that jewelry as *bijou* could, through the beauty of its workmanship, the originality of its artistic form and composition, acquire a value often far superior to that of the precious materials employed in *joaillerie*. Thanks to Lalique, the *bijou* has once again become an art object...."[37]

Lalique's contribution to the 1900 Exposition was worthy of the challenge that the international event laid down to all its exhibitors—to synthesize and propose a philosophy for the previous century as a whole. His showcase differed from the others in its architecture, decoration, and color scheme. Unlike his colleagues, who concentrated on contrasting tonal ranges, Lalique elected to use light, subtle, "natural/naturalist" harmonies. As Pol Neveux, one of those astounded by Lalique's genius, put it: "Beneath a flight of bats wheeling in a scabious-blue sky, women full of joy at living among such marvels twist their lovingly modeled torsos, unfurl their wings, whose nervures touch and intertwine in a loose round-dance before the fabulous treasures laid out at their feet. Picked out against a pale background, the jewels-rings and bracelets, chains and pendants, combs and corsage ornaments—lie next to each other, in varying colors, of differing lines, yet harmonious, together forming a diaphanous expanse, its tone blended like a spring meadow, or the clear, yet mysterious depths of some quiet hilltop rillet. This gathering of *objets d'art* also constitutes the least disputed—for it is indisputable—of all France's triumphs in this 1900 Universelle Exposition"[38] (see figs. 3 and 4).

Lalique's vitrine included a profusion of colored gems, nacreous pearls, pale ivory, blondish horn, bright golds and subtle enamels—in total more than a hundred pieces screened off by a lattice made from butterfly-women in bronze (cat. 172)—the product of ten years of unceasing labor, unstinting research, and technical trials. Some pieces were already known to those who had attended earlier Salons where Lalique had exhibited, but the public at the 1900 Exposition was of quite another sort, an international clientele from every walk of life. Lalique strove now to widen the range of his jewelry in both type and plan, proposing a "ladies' complete parure."[39] Yet at the same time he indulged in a number of individual, virtuoso pieces which naturally attracted the attention of public and critics alike. These *bijoux* were of exceptional dimensions, their highly structured architecture counterbalancing original, even strange themes. Lalique thus attained a rare degree of harmony between intention and realization, of appositeness of form, materials, and ornament. Can one still speak of ornament at this point? The question is certainly an open one for some pieces such as the tiaras, and for those decorative objects worn on the front of the corsage that are as wide as the pectorals of antiquity, the very ones in fact that European museums and a number of major collectors were so keen on acquiring.[40]

Not all the pieces found a purchaser, at least not before the Exposition had closed. This was the case for a necklace that was not mentioned in the press but which represented a fine example of Lalique's art and his technical and artistic approach at this date (cat. 36). It relies for its effect on the alternation and repetition of opal medallions and a hieratic composition, with black swans facing each other in pairs at the feet of bas-relief nude female figures on a ground of openwork translucent enamel elements in the shape of wings. A tiara in the form of a cockerel's head, rampant and aggressive-looking, holding in his open beak a yellow diamond which matches his feathers in translucent enamel, was acquired in 1904 by Calouste Gulbenkian.[41] Another piece, although well-received in the press, remained unsold, according to the artist's account book: a disquieting corsage ornament in the form of a writhing nest of snakes from whose open jaws poured forth

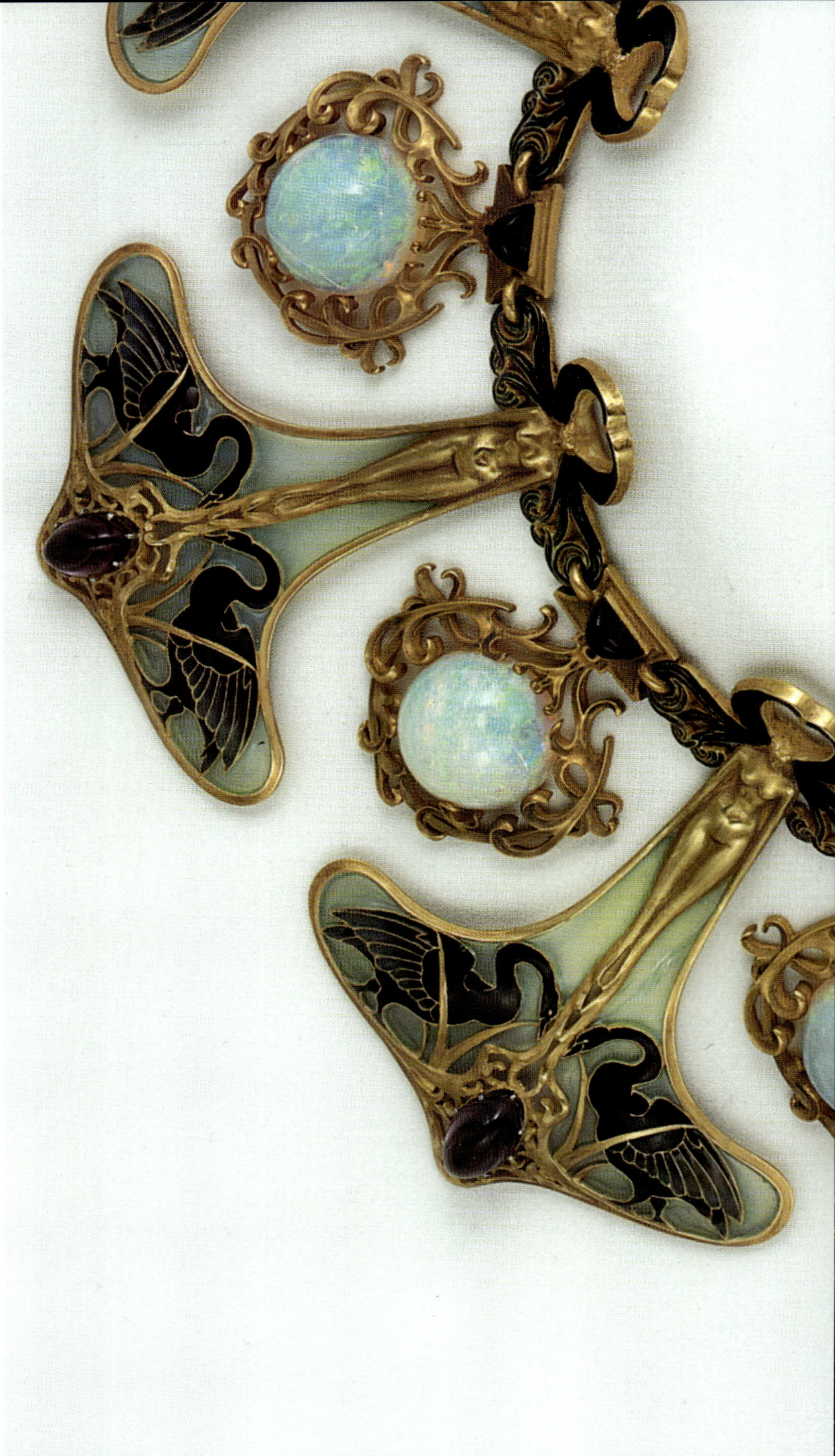

This spectacular necklace is composed of alternating radial components: nine gold and enamel spatulate pendants in the form of insect women and nine large circular opals in spiky settings. The disquieting image of a composite female, at once human, insectival, and avian, who effortlessly bridges several species anticipates the fluidity of natural categories characteristic of Surrealism. As is so often the case in Lalique's work, the trancelike quiet of the figure and the perfect symmetry of the design counteract the sense of strangeness, dispelling any anguish we might otherwise experience. This jewel, displayed at the Exposition Universelle in 1900, was then said to contain marquise-shaped diamonds, suggesting that the cabochon amethysts may be later replacements.

A symbol of whiteness, the swan also embodies notions of purity and solar radiance that the black swan inverses. Thus, in Tchaikovsky's ballet Swan Lake, *with choreography by Petipa and Ivanov, and performed in St. Petersburg in 1895, Odette, the white swan queen, is opposed by Odile, the malefic black swan. This image of confronted swans is curiously reminiscent of "Swan, Rush, and Iris," a design for a wallpaper dado produced by Walter Crane in 1877, where, in a composition derived from the age-old Tree-of-Life motif, a pair of standing white swans flanks a central cattail plant (later replaced by Lalique with a female figure). It is likely that Lalique encountered Crane's work during his years in London, but the English artist was also known and much appreciated in France.* *JTR*

Necklace
Insect Women and Black Swans
c. 1898–1899
Chased gold, enamel on gold, *plique-à-jour* enamel, opal, amethyst
Diameter: 9 1/2; Large pendants 2 3/4 x 2 1/4; Small pendants: 1 3/8 x 1 1/4 inches
(Diameter: 24.1; Large pendants: 7 x 5.7; Small pendants: 3.5 x 3.2cm)
(Cat. 36)

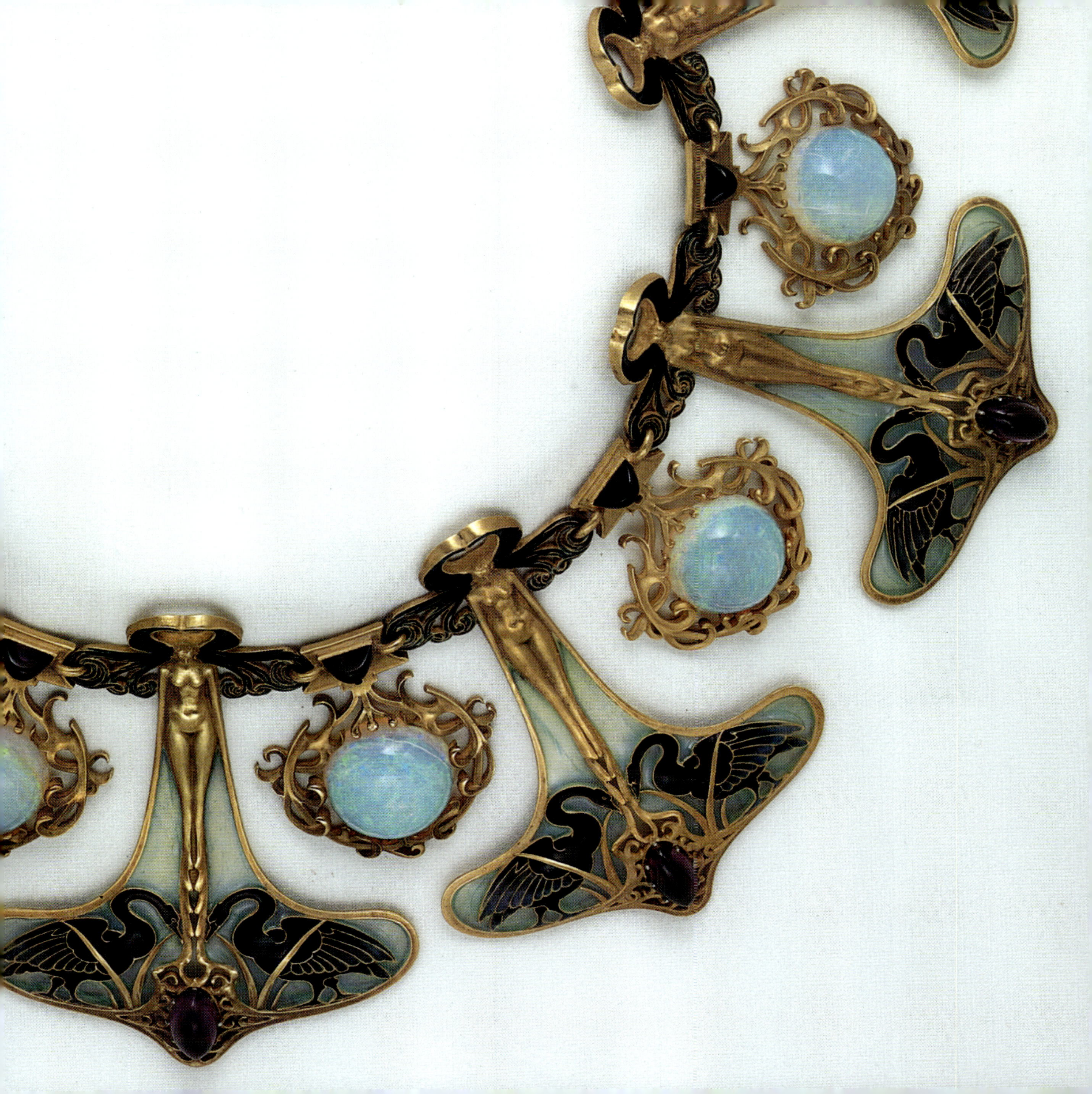

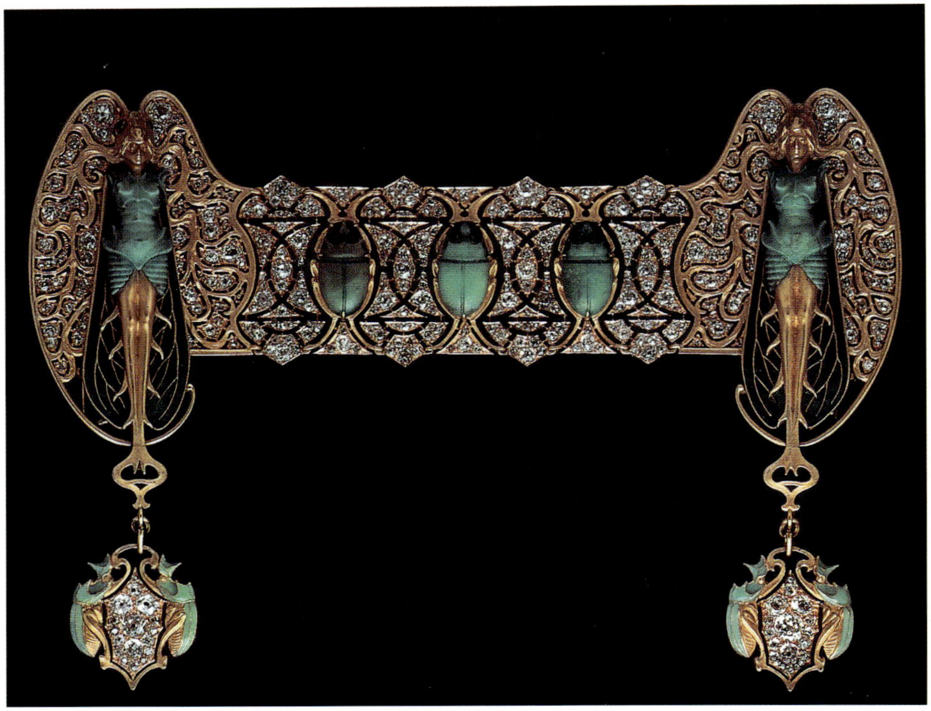

Fig. 5
Corsage
Ornament
Scarabs
c. 1897–1899
Gold, enamel,
brilliants

cascades of baroque pearls. The original can no longer be traced, but the model is known today from a replica made by Lalique (fig. 8), most probably for Gulbenkian, who purchased it in 1908.[42] The great collector waited until 1903 before acquiring one of the most bizarre pieces in the 1900 Exposition: a large dragonfly-woman, her chrysoprase torso emerging from a dragon's gaping maw. The translucent enamel of the jointed wings is suspended in a fine gold network; the wings spread wide before the beast's grasping talons.[43] A recurrent theme in Lalique's œuvre is the myth of the sphinx, recast in an Art Nouveau aesthetic: it reappears in another corsage ornament also shown at the 1900 Exposition, a piece probably from an earlier date, in which Lalique respected a symmetrical arrangement harking back to Egyptian models[44] (fig. 5).

The names of a number of several major European national collections appear in Lalique's account book, including decorative arts or applied arts museums (the adjective used depending on the country concerned). For these institutions, whether in Hamburg, Berlin, or Copenhagen, the 1900 Exposition Universelle provided an opportunity to enlarge their "modern" holdings. Copenhagen's Kunstindustrimuseum, for example, selected an astonishing pin whose head was made from a single large solar opal enveloped in enamel and gilt wasps (fig. 6).[45] The Musée des Arts Décoratifs in Paris, well-acquainted with Lalique's work, was more moderate in its taste, with a penchant rather for naturalist themes and technical perfection. It selected two fine pieces, the hazelnut necklace (cat. 54) and the pine-cone watch (cat. 55).

The list of those who purchased Lalique's work reads like a who's who: Russian, Viennese, and French aristocrats (among whom numbered Robert de Montesquiou's cousin, the comtesse Greffulhe); names in the worlds of politics and culture (Mme. Waldeck-Rousseau, Mme. Salles-Eiffel, Sarah Bernhardt, Julia Bartet);[46] and others whose names were among the donors to the Musée des Arts Décoratifs, such as the comtesse de Béarn (née Béhague) and the marquise Arconati-Visconti, both collectors of great renown. The comtesse de Béarn was an avid yet unerringly tasteful collector of everything from antiquities and first-rate Louis XV furniture right up to the Impressionists. Her name figures in Lalique's account book for the 1900 Exposition opposite the description of the mermaid tiara made of bronze and opals that had been shown for the first time at the 1898 Salon (cat. 37 and p. 24 above). She surely possessed other jewelry pieces by Lalique, among them a hair ornament with three lotus flowers, one design for which is now in the Musée Lalique in Paris (cat. 21).[47]

The marquise Arconati-Visconti (1846–1929) also bought a piece of jewelry from Lalique in 1900, a brooch comprising a woman's head topped by a dragon (cat. 38),

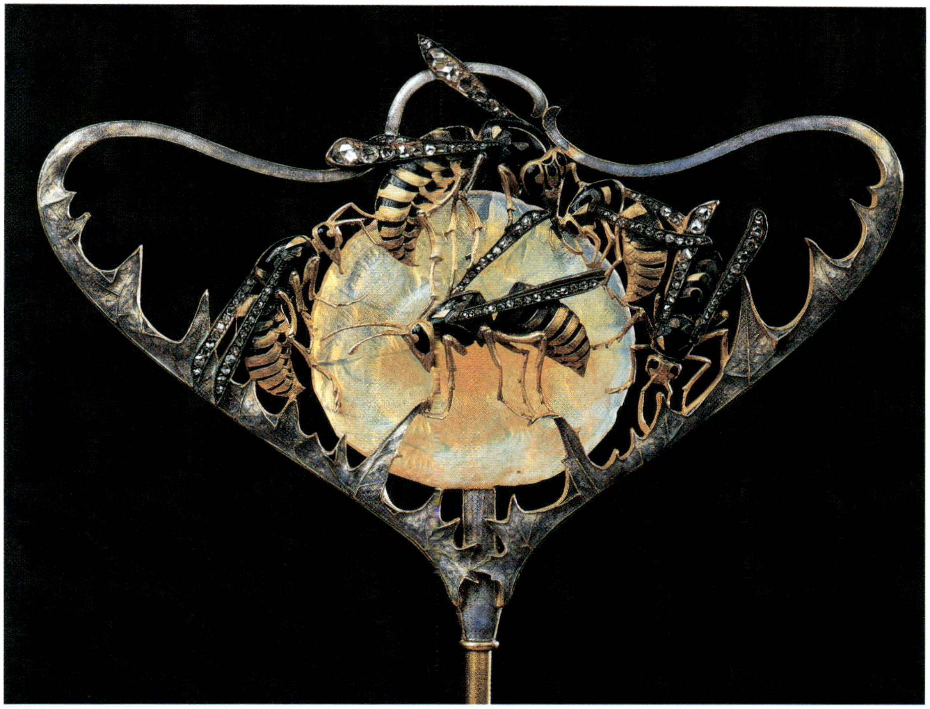

Fig. 6
Hatpin
Wasps
c. 1899–1900
Gold, enamel, opal, diamonds
8 1/4 x 4 inches
(21 x 10.2 cm)
Copenhagen, Det Danske Kunstindustrie-museum

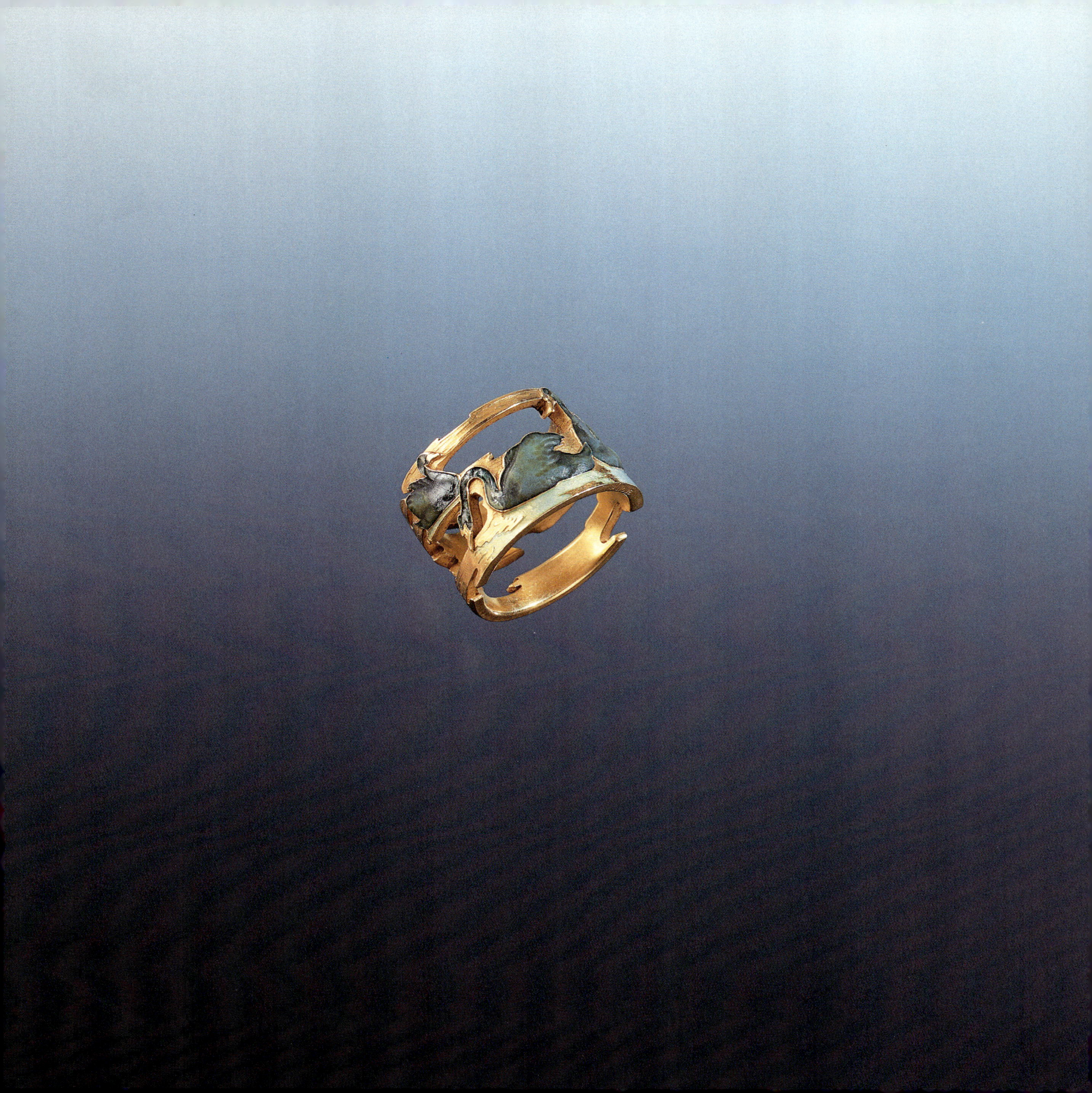

which she donated to the Musée des Arts Décoratifs in 1916, together with a group of pieces she had acquired or even commissioned from the rue Thérèse between 1895 and 1900 (cats. 4, 5, 8, 9, 14). Daughter of a journalist friend of Gambetta, she shared her father's republican ideas, surrounding herself with a political and literary coterie in which Jaurès, Briand, and Joseph Reinach rubbed shoulders with museum curators. She inherited from her husband large estates and collections in Italy and Belgium as well as a considerable fortune. Making her home in Paris, she established herself as a collector of works of incomparable quality, from pictures and furnishings of the French and Italian Renaissance to Lalique jewelry. Lalique's *bijoux*—especially those that, as Vever put it, "did violence" to the prevailing taste, were designed with a very select clientele, a financial-cum-cultural elite in mind, their high prices necessarily discouraging lesser mortals.

Lalique also wanted to produce simpler, less expensive pieces, which he did in glass, the medium that later provided him with an opportunity for mass production and became increasingly important in his work in the early twentieth century. Shortly after the 1900 Exposition, the vogue for Lalique was such that *Art et Décoration* ran a subscription offer for one of his pendants, which he had produced in one hundred copies. The form was typical of the dancing girls he had made in 1896–99, while the motif was that of a female head crowned by plane leaves. The piece was to be made in gold and enamel at the reasonable price of 150 francs, allowing women or collectors to realize the dream—hitherto impossible for many—of possessing "a Lalique," one that united all the principal characteristics of turn-of-the-century style.[48]

From Workshop to Factory

In 1900, René Lalique became the owner of a plot of land on the Cours-la-Reine, not far from the place de l'Alma, where he was to construct a large town house, combining on a single site private residence and professional premises, the latter with design offices, workshops, and exhibition spaces. Prior to this, he had received his clients in his workshops on the rue Thérèse, in a flat that soon became inadequate for his many activities, especially once he expanded into glassmaking. For reasons of safety, he decided not to build a smelter on the Cours-la-Reine. Instead, on an estate at Clairefontaine that he had acquired in 1898, he installed equipment that allowed him to produce large-scale pieces, such as the leaves for the doors of the carriage entrance and the interior doorway for the Paris town house. Completed in 1902 with the assistance of a certain Monsieur Feine, an architect who is otherwise little known, the building on the Cours-la-Reine puzzled devotees of new architecture by its dearth of originality.

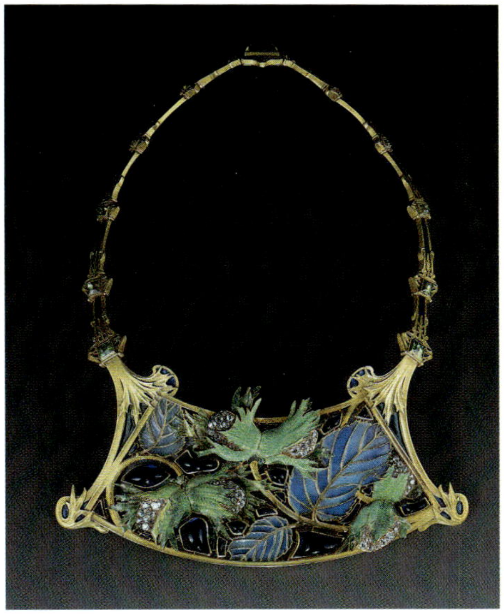

Ring
Swans
c. 1898–1899
Chased gold,
enamel on gold
Diam: 3/4 inches
(Diam: 2cm)
(Cat. 34)

Necklace
Hazelnuts
c. 1899–1900
Chased gold,
translucent
enamel on gold,
plique-à-jour
enamel,
diamonds,
peridots, glass
7 1/2 x 4 3/4;
plaque: 2 1/2 x
5 1/4 inches (19 x
12; plaque:
6.5 x 13.6 cm)
(Cat. 54)

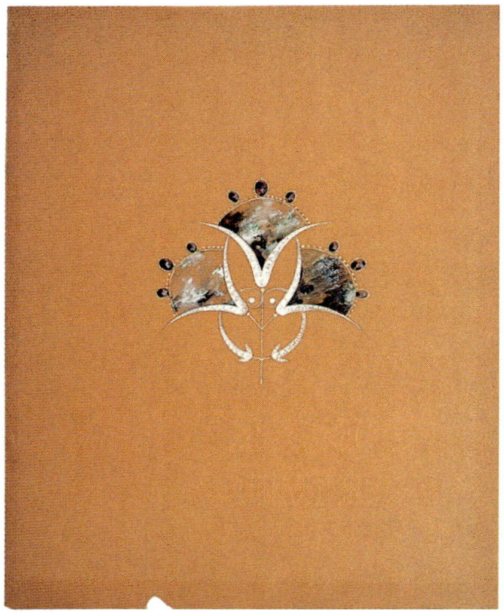

Design for a Tiara
Three Lotus Blossoms
c. 1893–1895
Pencil, ink on paper
10 3/4 x 8 1/2 inches (27.4 x 21.5 cm)
(Cat. 21)

"Was it want of boldness, or was [Lalique] simply incapable of creating something entirely new in an art other than that in which he was a past master, or again was it a fondness for a period, for a style whose works most appealed to his eye, to his mind?"[49]

Since Lalique was no architect, he merely conformed to the ideas prevalent among traditionalist practitioners of the art, who remained faithful to the styles of the past—in this case, to the Renaissance. A few details in the designs of the doorways and windows, however, show that the architect—or perhaps Lalique himself—knew that, since Hector Guimard, a facade of a building should express its interior layout. As for the decoration, spreading over the balconies and carved directly into the white stonework around the entrance door, it carries the Lalique hallmark, inspired by "all the different species of pines, from spruce to fir." The theme resurfaces on door leaves, made of molded glass mounted on steel, and the doorway to the hall, comprising four large pressed and patinated panels decorated with antique-style athletes.[50]

Lalique now possessed a real exhibition hall in which he could present the entire range of his work: jewelry, goldsmithery, items for the office, and the glass pieces that gradually became more and more dominant, until, by 1910, they had ousted every other form of artistic expression. Among the exhibition materials was a snake vitrine that Émile Molinier had admired at the 1901 Salon. "In truth, it is a strange concoction, four crawling serpents made of crystal, heads rearing, jaws agape, one in each corner."[51] Lalique's offerings that year, including the vitrine, had a new character, a whiteness that the critic Gustave Geffroy found fascinating. "It is a suddenly harmonious whiteness, one that spreads over the decoration of the showcase itself, flanked on all four corners by glass snakes which have the bright, grayish transparency of flowing ice. This delicious pale gray, alternating with an immaculate white, reappears too in most of the jewelry exhibited. It is a color of infinite buoyancy that blends with light and shade, gilded, but with a thoughtful meticulousness so as not to spoil the timbre of the prevailing whiteness, like snow turned golden under the sun or blue in the night, tinged with ivory, opal, silver...."[52]

The 1902 Salon saw the consecration of a type of object that, although not entirely novel in Lalique's œuvre, nonetheless provided a pretext for some extraordinary thematic and technical interpretations: the goblet—or chalice—an object he had already produced for the competition organized by the Union Centrale des Arts Décoratifs in 1893 (p. 17 above). For this new work, he employed a technique dating from 1898–1900, where the glass is blown into a metal armature (cats. 177, 178). He also used several materials, applying them in various ways—goldwork, ivory, cabochons, translucent enamels, and molded lost-wax process glass (cats. 179–181). To the familiar themes of pine and ears of wheat were now added the vine and wine, associated with the appearance of bacchanals and nude figures in his jewelry.

Ensembles of ladies' jewelry remained the core of Lalique's œuvre until 1911, when, at the Salon des Artistes Décorateurs, Lalique presented works exclusively in glass. The parures he designed continued to derive their effect from the inclusion of glass: a very white demi-cristal, which produced a kind of brightness, a liquidity that he associated with the theme of clear water and fish (cats. 131, 132, 134) as well as with a kind of innocence that also surfaces in his subject matter. Such innocence can be found in the two faces that join in a kiss, the one molded in relief on the obverse, the other incised on the reverse (cat. 138). The same tendency can be seen in the pigeons decorating a corsage ornament made around 1906–07 and presented to the wife of President Wilson in 1919 at the time of the Treaty of Versailles (cat. 139). Lalique designed several wide collars on which cockerels arranged in facing pairs or embroidered butterflies were embellished with glass and metal appliqué. For the Lyons silk manufacturers Atuyer, Bianchini-Férier et Cie., he produced, in 1907, models of four scarves brocaded in gold and brown plant motifs-wheat, oxeye daisies (cats. 190, 191)—and symbolic animals such as moths and peacocks.

The 1900 Exposition had thrust Lalique to the forefront of the international stage. Henceforth, he was to participate in every major foreign exhibition: Turin, 1902; St. Louis, 1904, which he attended, stopping over in New York; Liège in 1905, for which he decorated the French pavilion with embroideries on a floral theme.

In 1909, Lalique rented a glassworks near Paris at Combs-la-Ville, thereby providing himself with an industrial plant sufficient to fulfill an order for bottles from François Coty, the perfume manufacturer. Lalique now embarked on a new adventure, applying to glasswork the same working and research methods he had developed for jewelry. He utilized every known technique, both cold- and hot-working, depending on the final product desired. He invented new processes, took out patents,[53] and in so doing firmly established artistic glassmaking in the history of twentieth-century industrial arts.

According to Félix Marcilhac, in 1913 Lalique created between seven hundred and eight hundred models, two-thirds of which he continued to use after the war.[54] The majority were white in color, though they might on occasion be patinated or tinted. Following World War I, the factory, having become too small for an ever-growing output, was enlarged. The acquisition of a plot of land at Wingen-sur-Moder, in Alsace, enabled Lalique to construct yet another manufactory with new furnaces, which became operational in 1922. René Lalique

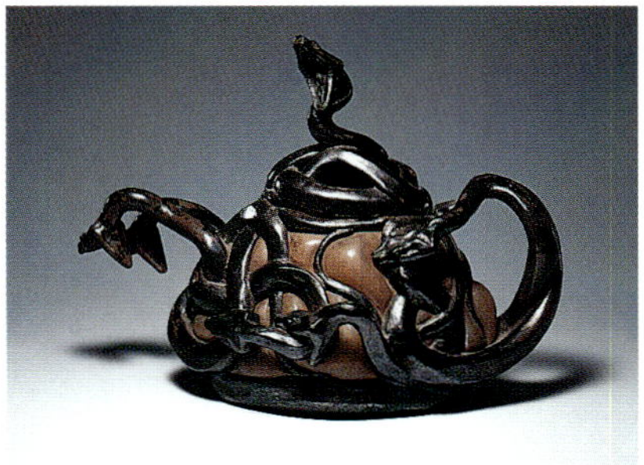

Sugar Bowl
Snakes
c. 1897–1900
Blown glass in silver setting
8 3/4 x 11 1/2 inches
(19 x 28 cm)
(Cat. 177)

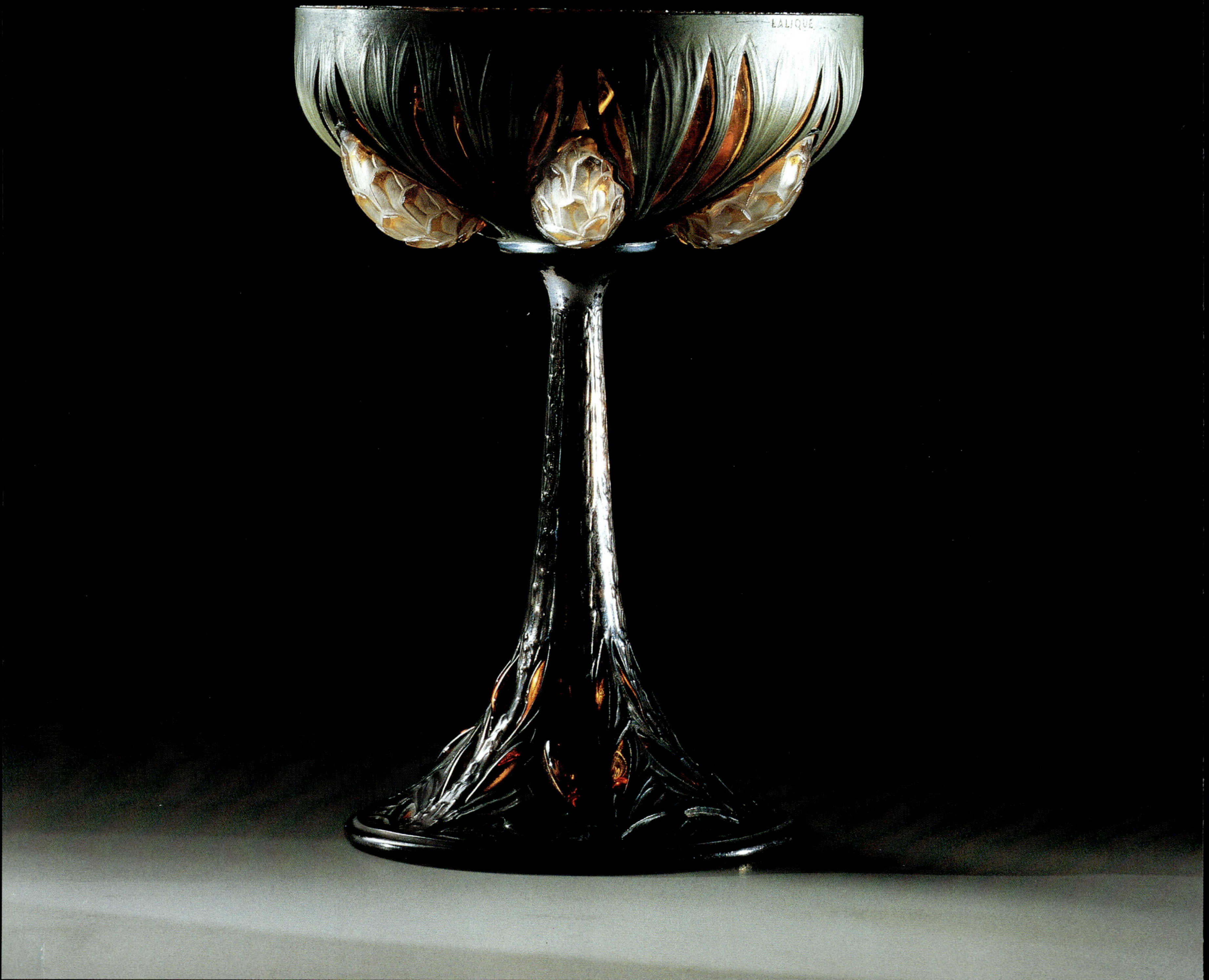
LALIQUE

was now able to buckle down to his most important task: mass producing designs so as to put them "within reach of as many people as possible."

Lalique and Gulbenkian: The Artist and the Collector

When, in 1933, the Musée des Arts Décoratifs in Paris presented the first retrospective of Lalique's œuvre, many a collector offered to lend their treasures. Among them were famous women from the worlds of politics or culture prepared to hand over the jewels they were in habit of wearing—Mmes. Waldeck-Rousseau, Bartet, and Salles-Eiffel[55]—and politicians such as Raymond Poincaré and Louis Barthou.[56] But the identity of the most important and most enigmatic amateur was concealed behind the initials S.C.G. The art critic Marcelle Oury, in a column of *Paris-Midi* devoted to the exhibition, gave an account of the pieces he had lent, exceptional both for their sheer number ("Monsieur S.C.G. lent enough to fill an entire room") and for their exemplary quality ("the great artist asserts that this room sums up all he has done to date.")[57]

For René Lalique himself, the jewelry, glasswork, and other objects that Calouste Sarkis Gulbenkian had been collecting since 1899 represented a synopsis of his art. It is in this guise that the Lalique collection is now presented in a newly refurbished treasure trove in the heart of the museum opened in Lisbon in 1969 to house the pictures and art works of the Gulbenkian collection. On view are some choice examples of French art. One can, for instance, travel to Lisbon to see the world's finest ensemble of furniture by French cabinetmaker Charles Cressent (1685–1768). There is also the eighteenth-century silverwork which was so popular in European courts (for example, that belonging to the Russian tsars, whose sale to some major European museums and wealthy collectors the Soviet regime negotiated around 1930). But most important for us are the works acquired by Gulbenkian from the most eminent contemporary artists living in Paris at the turn of century, among them Auguste Rodin and Lalique. Whereas the group of Rodin sculptures is interesting, Lalique's jewelry, glass, and *objets d'art* are exceptional: not only does the museum contain more than 160 examples, but their quality, variety, and originality are impressive.

Calouste Gulbenkian's selection offers a telling picture of the artist's multifaceted imagination and the collector's own tastes and personality. These two imposing men became true friends and had the same profound sensitivity for an exacting type of beauty forever renewed by their creative talents. In 1945, shortly after Lalique's death, Gulbenkian shared his feelings with the artist's daughter, Suzanne Lalique Haviland: "Your father was a very dear friend and the sadness of losing him is heightened by the infinite sorrow one

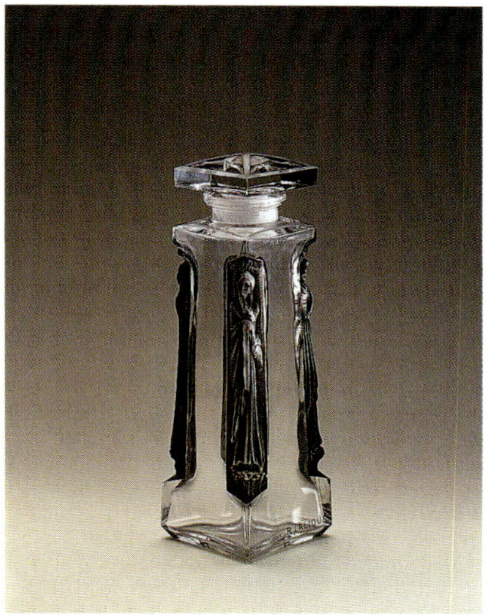

Chalice
Pine Cones
c. 1902
Clear blown glass, lined amber in an engraved silver structure
5; Diam. 3 3/4 inches (12.2; Diam. 9.5 cm)
(Cat. 180)

Perfume Bottle
Quatre Figurines
Model created in 1911
Mold-blown glass, neck and stopper in pressed glass, stained
5 1/2 x 1 1/2 inches
(13.3 x 4 cm)
(Cat. 216)

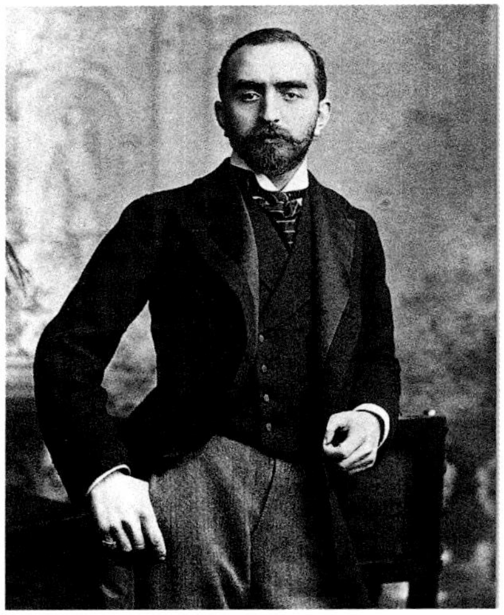

Fig. 7
Calouste
Gulbenkian

always feels at the loss of a great man." The collector also expressed his admiration for a "unique work [that] never ceased to grow during the fifty years that we were friends."[58]

By 1945, Art Nouveau had sunk into historical oblivion. Not even Émile Gallé, the glassmaking genius who had breathed new life into the art, transforming it into a medium befitting plastic expression, was spared. Lalique, however, managed to outlive the vicissitudes of taste; moving from jewelry to glassmaking, from Art Nouveau to Art Deco, he was neither spurned nor forgotten. The Lalique epic started out in solitary labor, as the artist designed, modeled, and performed technical trials of every kind in his unceasing quest for new territory. Calouste Gulbenkian, an oil tycoon, was made of the same stuff—relentless and unflinching in his creation of a world fit for the future. How like Lalique who, in the period prior to 1900, had developed the modern *bijou*, and in 1906 had designed perfume bottles that were the incarnation of the liquid they contained, before going on to build up a glassmaking concern that was to give material form to his dreams of transparency.

As a child and adolescent, Lalique had always enjoyed making drawings of his native Champagne countryside. He portrayed its slightest, its humblest details, spawning a repertory of grasses—common and rare—of insects, birds, flowers, and trees that he was later to combine into landscapes, arabesques, and soaring patterns of gold and enamel. Calouste Gulbenkian shared this love of nature. The collector wrote precise and sensitive descriptions of the Caucasus in his memoirs of a journey made there in 1890.[59] First bewitched by the gardens of Andalusia during a visit to Spanish museums in 1928, a few years later he acquired a property in Normandy, not far from Deauville. His retreat, named "L'Enclos," was a place where he could meditate and "enjoy some restful hours—few and far between in his busy life—gaze on the gnarled trees, breathe the fragrant shrubs and blooming flower beds, and delight in the many twittering birds with which his paradise teemed."[60] He directed his garden architect to treat the "open spaces, that is, the pastures, as meadows and not as lawns." Gulbenkian's wish was to preserve nature in its primeval liberty. Yet he remained aware that, "if we want to succeed in creating a dreamlike haven from which might issue a sensation of peace, we have to envisage the plantations, the reliefs and the views as a single harmonious ensemble that should inspire a sensation of order, that is, of nature both organized and disciplined."[61] René Lalique knew well this transition from design to jewel, from emotion to organization, from unbridled nature to the structured *bijou*. This and other similarities of character and taste cemented the friendship between the master of "black gold" and the "lover of opals."[62]

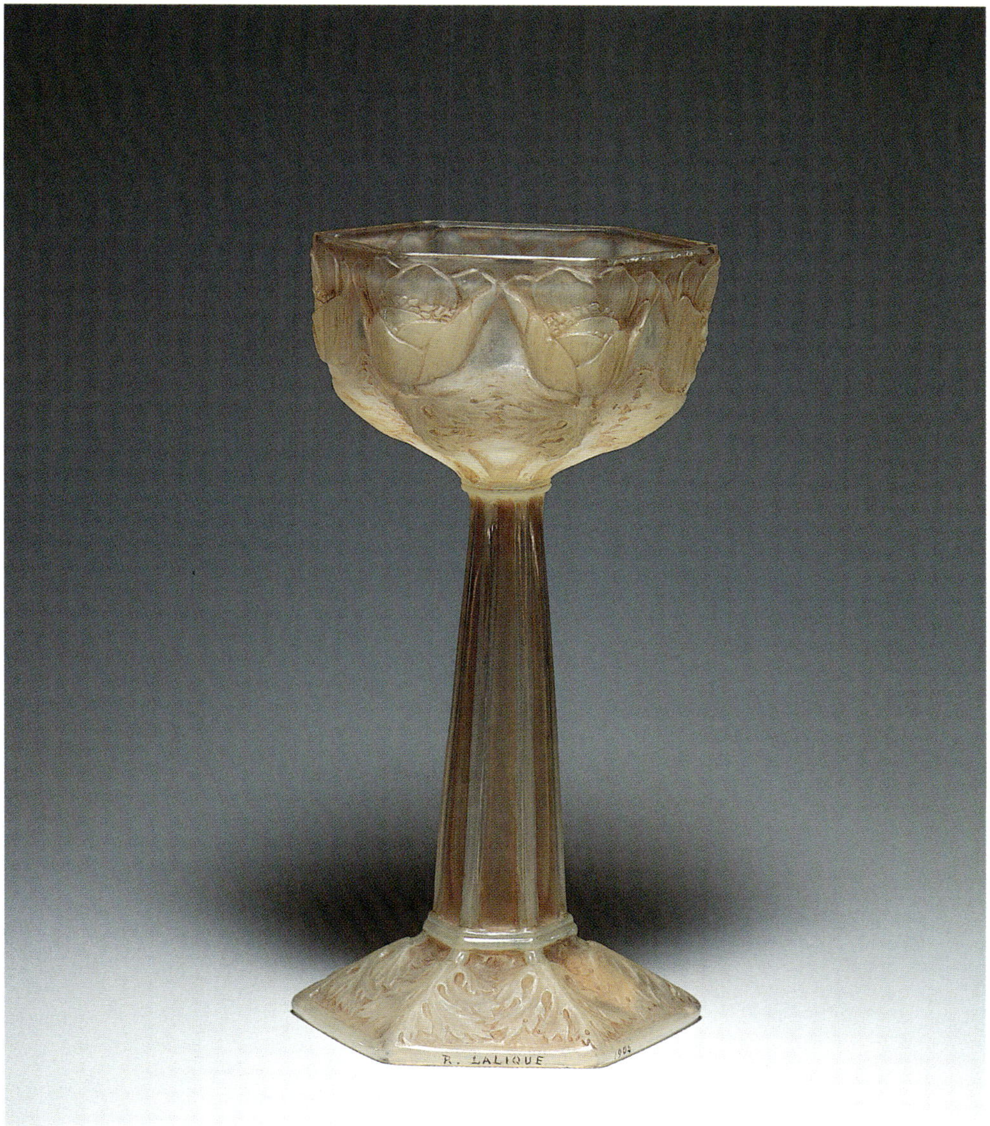

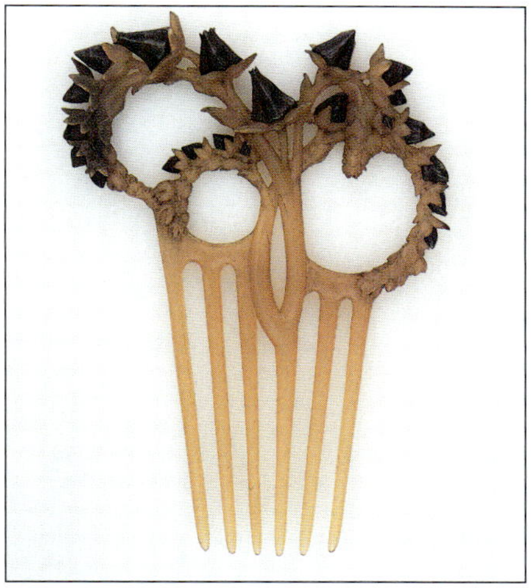

Chalice
Anemones
1904
Lost-wax cast glass
Height: 7 $^{1}/_{4}$;
Diam: 4 $^{1}/_{8}$ inches
(Height: 18.8;
Diam: 10.5 cm)
(Cat. 182)

Comb
Cactus
1902–1903
Horn, silver
6 $^{5}/_{8}$ x 4 $^{3}/_{8}$ inches
(16.5 x 11.6 cm)
(Cat. 73)

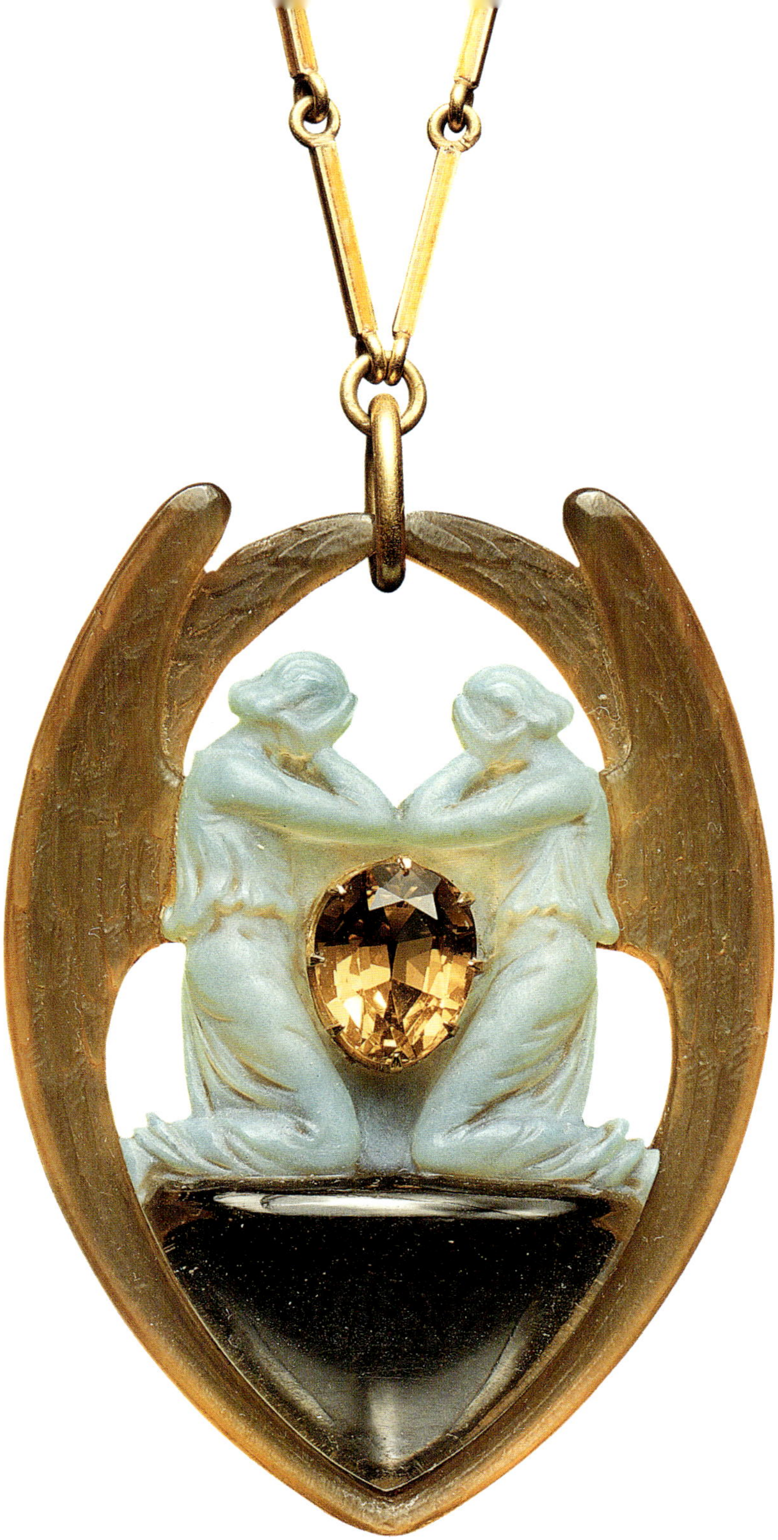

Pendant
Two Angels
c. 1902–1903
Gold, horn,
glass, topaz
2 1/4 x 1 1/2;
chain 21 1/4
inches (5.5 x 4;
chain 54 cm)
(Cat. 110)

Pendant
Entwining
c. 1900–1902
Gold, diamonds,
enamel, glass
2 3/4 x 2 3/8;
chain 21 1/4
inches (7 x 6;
chain 54 cm)
(Cat. 107)

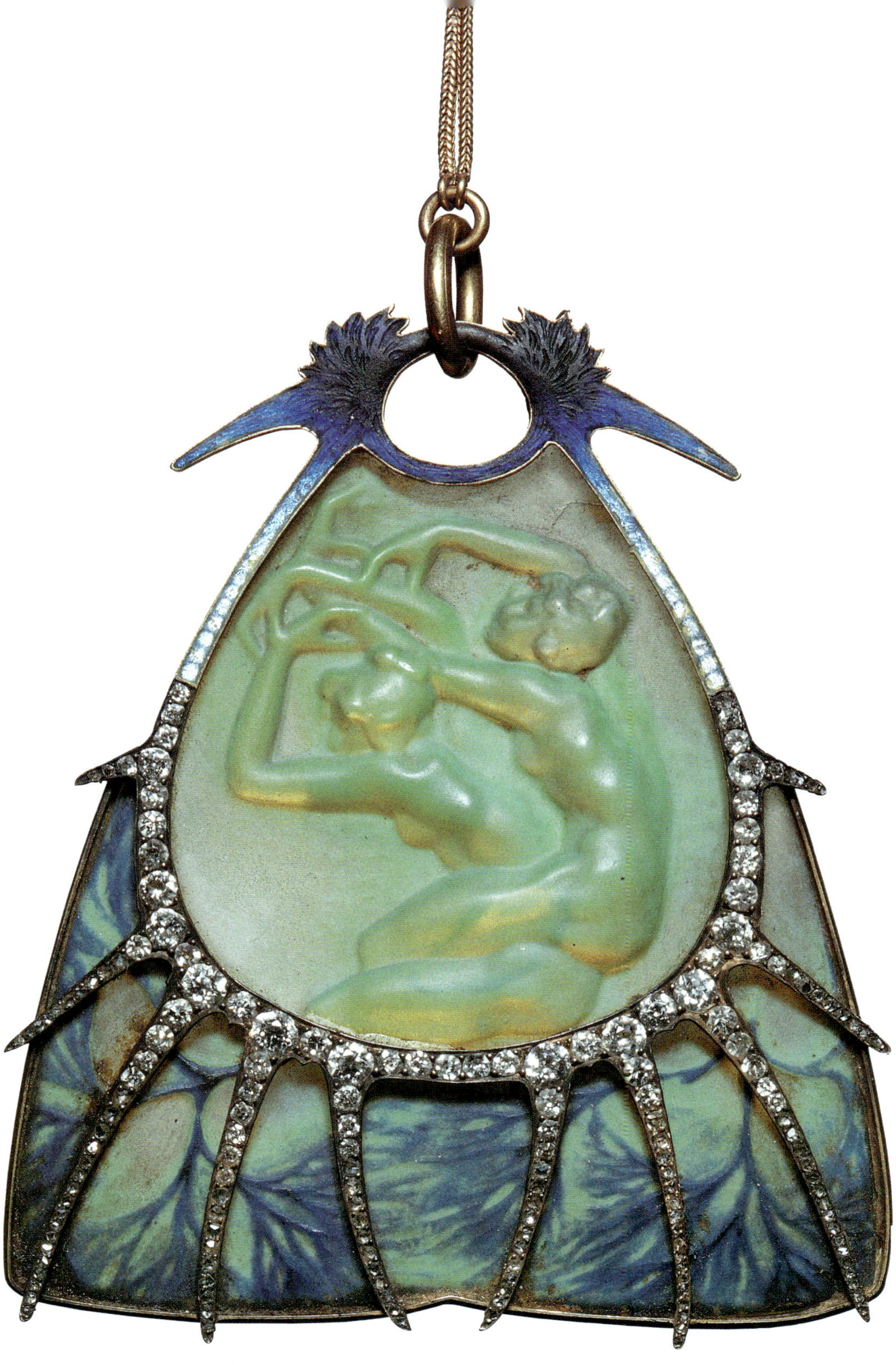

The Physics and the Metaphysics of Jewelry: "Something That Has Never Been Seen Before"

Marie-Odile Briot

In 1900, Lalique, already highly regarded by his peers, triumphed at the Exposition Universelle. The only precedent that comes to mind is that of Benvenuto Cellini.[1] Lalique had revolutionized the work of the goldsmith, creating mounts as sumptuous as the stones themselves and had even invented materials (enamels, *verre moulé*) which could replace or complement them. He spent two years (1887–89) developing this "different jewelry." But that, as he confided to Henri Vever, had been the easy part.[2] In 1892, how-ever, the invention of the concept—the Sym-bolists would have termed it a "synthesis"—which integrated a patchwork of materials and insights into the idea of the jewel itself had cost him "a truly extraordinary amount of effort." "I worked ceaselessly, making drawings, models, studies, and technical trials of all types without a moment's rest, striving to achieve new results, to create something that has never been seen before."

Lalique's innovativeness won him a place among the precursors of that modern art which forged, as Cocteau put it, "a tradition of novelty." "Prior to René Lalique, what was jewelry?" asked Gustave Kahn, creator of free verse and a friend of the critic Félix Fénéon. "Obviously ornament, but also a crude kind of luxury. The masterpieces of his predecessors, all founded on the brilliance of diamonds, seemed like portable cathedrals of light....The old jewel was based upon the idea of wealth; the new is built upon an artistic idea."[3] In the nineteenth century, society life in the rising bourgeoisie took up where the aristocratic court had left off. Industrial magnates dispensed with the red heels of court dress and adopted the comfortable sobriety of English fashion, transferring the conspicuous signs of their power to their wives. It was the great century of woman in all her finery, of fashion and of jewelry.

Brooch
Woman's Face Surrounded by Pine Boughs
c. 1898–1900
Silver, enamel, engraved stone
2 1/4 x 1 5/8 inches
(5.7 x 4.1 cm)
(Cat. 10)

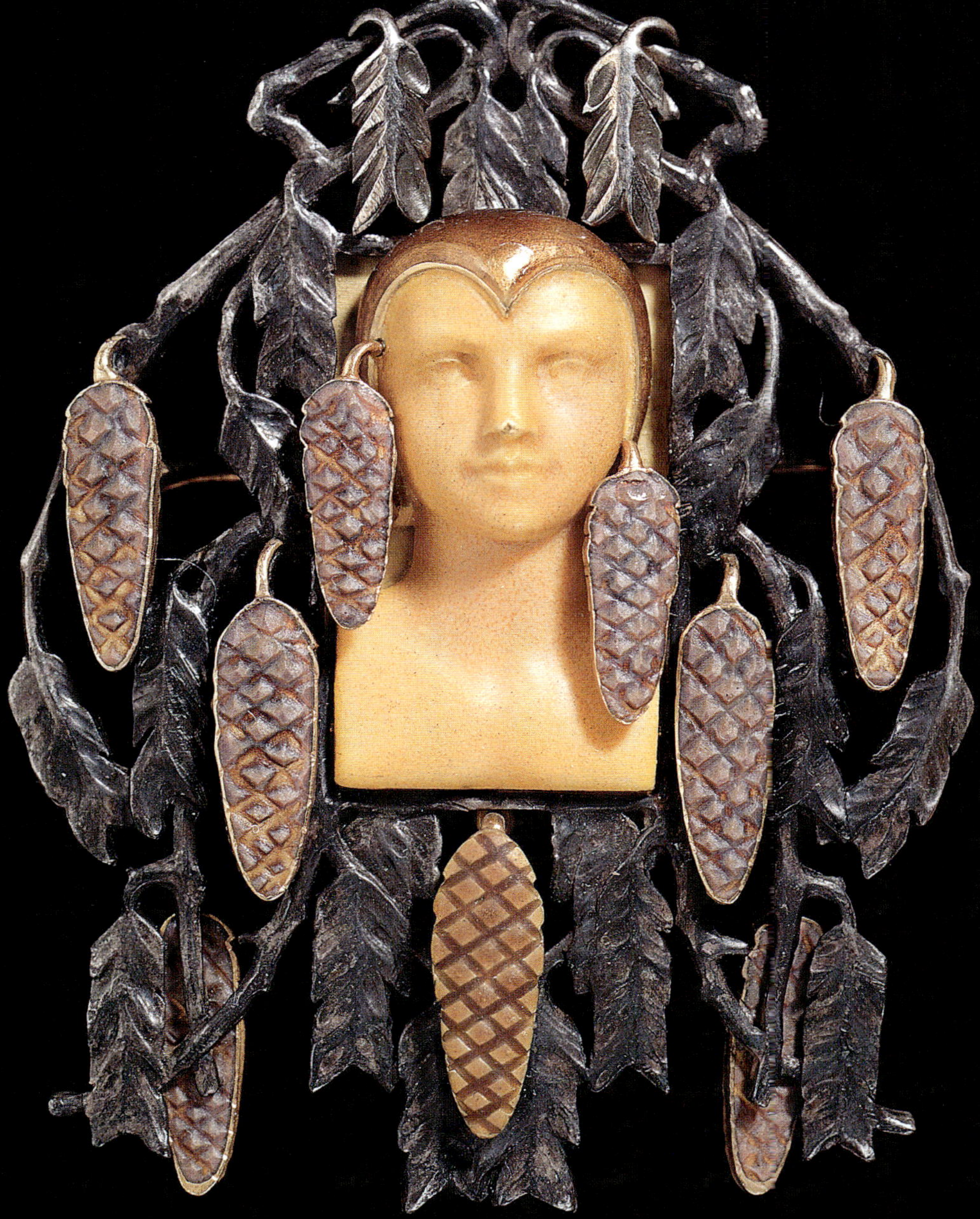

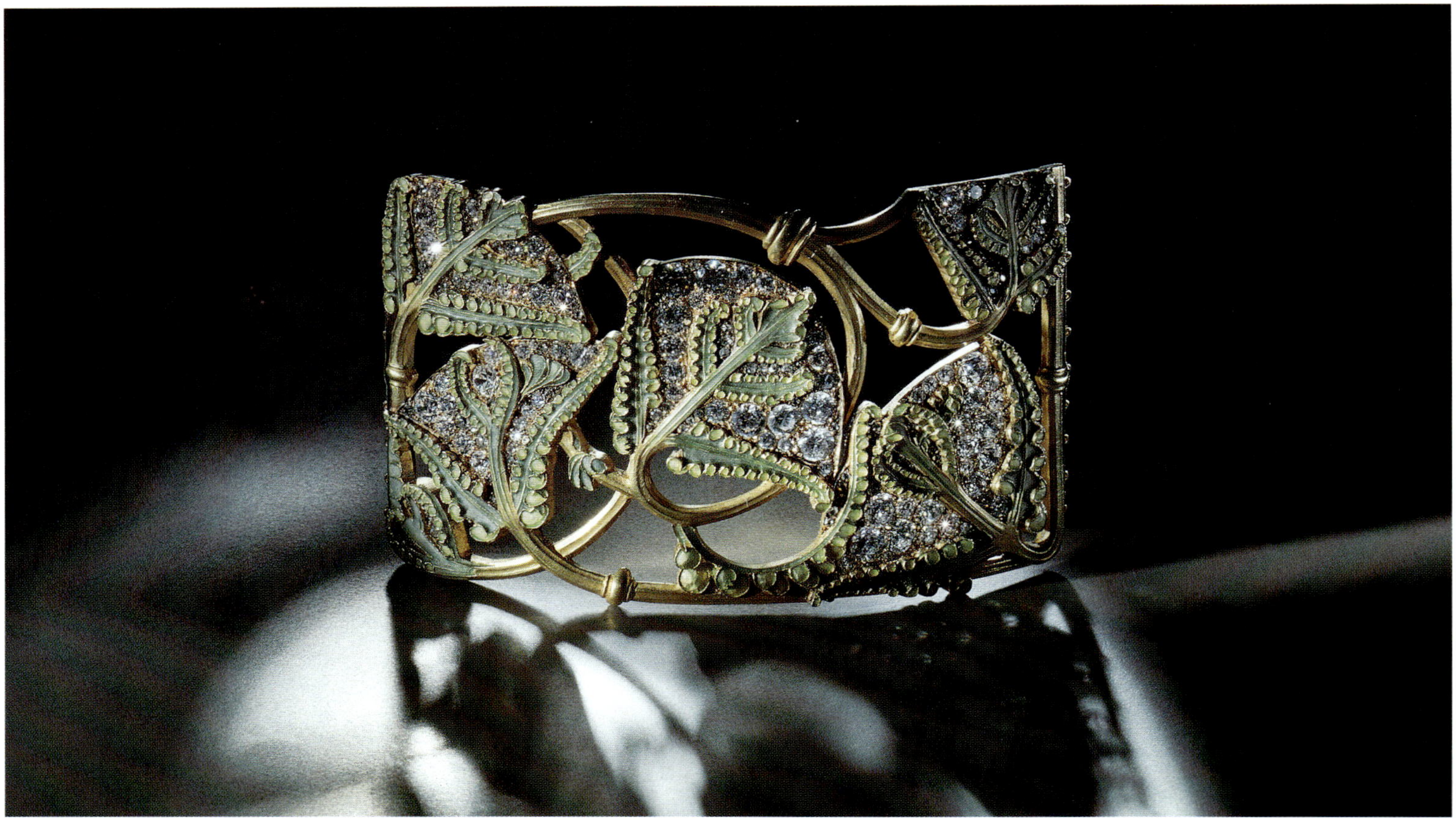

Dog Collar Plaque
Ferns
c. 1900–1902
Chased gold, translucent enamel on gold, diamonds (now replaced with zircons)
2 x 3 1/4 inches
(5.2 x 8.2 cm)
(Cat. 58)

Being an object of ornament, a jewel is highly symbolic. The origin of the French word *bijou* is obscure and two etymologies have been proposed. One finds the root of the word among the Celts.[4] The other derives *bijou* from *jouir* (to enjoy, to "come"). In vulgar parlance and slang, the word *bijou(x)* can designate both male or female genitals; this is the sense used by Diderot in his novel *Les Bijoux indiscrets*.[5] Jewels represent the imaginary Orient in paintings, from Delacroix to Moreau, and above all in literature. Jewels are a recurrent metaphor for poetry which, before the advent of free verse, was crafted like the bonsai Robert de Montesquiou gave Whistler.[6] The title of his 1852 book *Émaux et camées*, wrote Théophile Gautier, "expresses a desire to treat in a small form minor subjects, either in gold or copper plate with the lively colors of enamel, or else with the fine gem-engraving wheel on agate, carnelian, or onyx."[7] After Michelet had rehabilitated the witch,[8] Symbolism transformed the bourgeoise drenched in diamonds into a *femme fatale*, the most widespread variant being Salome, who had danced so lasciviously to celebrate the decapitation of St. John the Baptist.[9]

Though the debate was to continue unresolved well into the twentieth century, Art Nouveau represents the partial acceptance of the applied arts into the class of fine arts. The process began in England under the banner of the Romantic notion of the Unity of Art. Romanticism, dissolving the distinctions between the genres, found in medieval architecture the golden age of artistic synthesis. This quest for a synthesis encapsulated the crisis of a civilization which no longer identified with Greco-Roman classicism or with the images and forms it had produced. Art, whether "major" or "minor," needed to be "reinvented." This is the crux of our modernity: the cult of the new, the myth of the artist as creator.

In the middle of the nineteenth century, Japanese art, which eschewed easel painting, succeeded architecture as the model for the Unity of Art. The idea by then had become that of the *Gesamtkunstwerk*, the "total artwork," which served as a generalized aesthetic for life, or at least as the backdrop against which it might be played out. Throughout Europe, this concept was defended by movements that united all the plastic arts—except in France, possibly due to the diversity of the Parisian artistic scene. The Nabis (active between 1888 and 1896) certainly made unity their principle and attempted it in a number of productions under the aegis of patron and gallery owner Siegfried Bing, but there was no real studio work created in this vein. They were in truth painters who created murals, the primacy of the "decorative" for Sérusier and Gauguin being simply one more argument in favor of "pure painting."

In fact, the elevation of the "minor arts" in France was the result of a collective

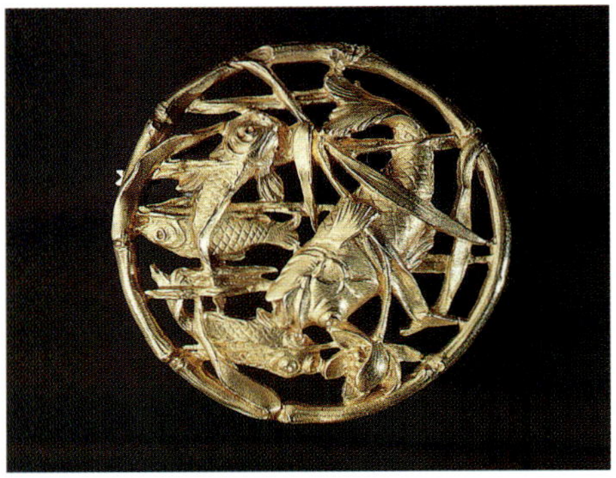

Brooch
Fish and Bamboo
1888
Cast and chased gold
Diam: 1 1/4 inches
(Diam: 3.1 cm)
(Cat. 1)

Comb
Umbel
c. 1897–1898
Blond horn, silver, enamel
5 3/4 x 3 1/4 inches
(14.8 x 8 cm)
(Cat. 48)

effort. By 1864, decorative art associations had formed their own museum, the Musée des Arts Décoratifs, and established in it a specific education curriculum.[10] Viollet-le-Duc created the chair for decorative composition and his work remained a benchmark. The study of nature was treated as an antidote to academicism. Nature provided a living dictionary of decorative motifs, together with an architectonic model of form. "Decoration functions for a building," wrote Viollet-le-Duc, "not as dress, but as muscles and skin function for man."[11] As an architect, he reintroduced in humanist language the Baroque notion of *natura naturans*,[12] which was fundamental to both Art Nouveau and Expressionism. Horta, Guimard, and Gaudí all read Viollet-le-Duc's books, and Rodin, Mucha, and Lalique were heirs to his teaching.

Japonisme dovetailed with this concept of naturalism; but Japanese art expresses a vision of nature which excludes all idea of human superiority over other living things.[13] Cultivating formal abstraction without projecting the deformation resulting from "human passions," Japanese art represents—compared to the Baroque—the softer side of *natura naturans*, and this was the path Lalique was to follow. He included in his art that science which makes decoration the very structure of the object. Free from all preconceptions, he borrowed from Japanese motifs "extravagances" that others denounced as "decadent"—serpents, bats, cockerels. He rooted them in his own personal animism or pantheism and in a "troubadour" poetics of an enchanted world bequeathed by Romanticism and reconstituted by Symbolism as a mythology.

The Jewel as Total Artwork

The "minor" arts made their entry into the Paris Salon in 1895. Lalique, however, had already entered the previous year as a "stowaway" jeweler in the sculpture section. Who introduced him to sculpture, one of the Ledrus (later his father- and brother-in-law), collaborators and Rodin's assistants? Though he had been supplying the great and the good with jewelry from 1880 and had had his own studio since 1886, the 1894 Salon marked the first time—in an act tantamount to a manifesto—that he actually signed a piece. Lalique exhibited an ivory music case decorated in bas-relief with "The Valkyrie" (cat. 170), which he had modeled and then reduced on a lathe like a medalmaker. This work was neither a sculpture nor a piece of jewelry; rather it constituted the *ars poetica* of the jewel. The aesthetic reference point was Wagner, who had made opera into the model of the *Gesamtkunstwerk*: "myth is the ideal subject matter for the poet," he had written.[14] The artwork is a re-creation of the world, a cosmogony. In the context of jewelry, the method is reduction. Creation in jewelry will thus be a miniature *opera mundi*.

The vogue for Wagner pervades the *fin de siècle*,[15] running parallel to the Baudelaire cult which recognized the poet as the master of *correspondances*, "seeing that things have always found their expression through a system of reciprocal analogy ever since the day when God uttered the world like a complex and indivisible statement."[16] In another equally famous text, Baudelaire had defined "that quality which you must allow me to call modernity, [that is] to extract from fashion whatever element it may contain of poetry within history, to distill the eternal from the transitory."[17]

Jewels are epitome of the eternal, the poetry of ephemeral fashion. As heirlooms, jewels were bequeathed from sovereign to sovereign just as they are still passed down from mother to daughter. No one ever hesitated to remove gems from one setting and remount them elsewhere to accommodate prevailing taste—but not, of course, a Lalique. For Lalique elevated the jewel to the quintessence of the eternal so that it might survive in its definitive form. The form itself might fall out of fashion; indeed it has. But even relegated to "the archaeological goldfish bowl in a museum," as Eugène Grasset put it,[18] it still signifies, in the absolute, the idea of the jewel. In the same way, Mallarmé in his verse strove to enshrine forever not so much a particular form as the very idea of poetry.

Lalique's faultless art was the result of a radical rethinking of the object. Lalique

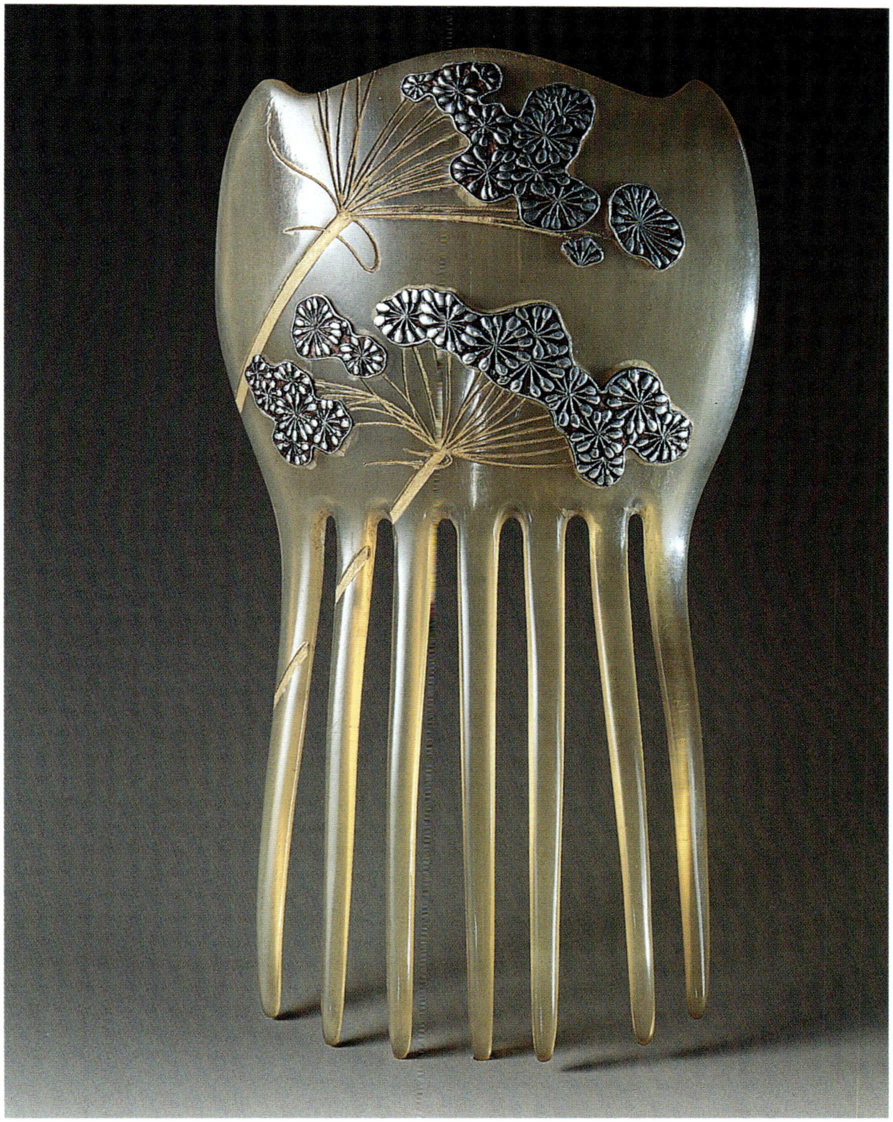

The
Jewels
of
Lalique

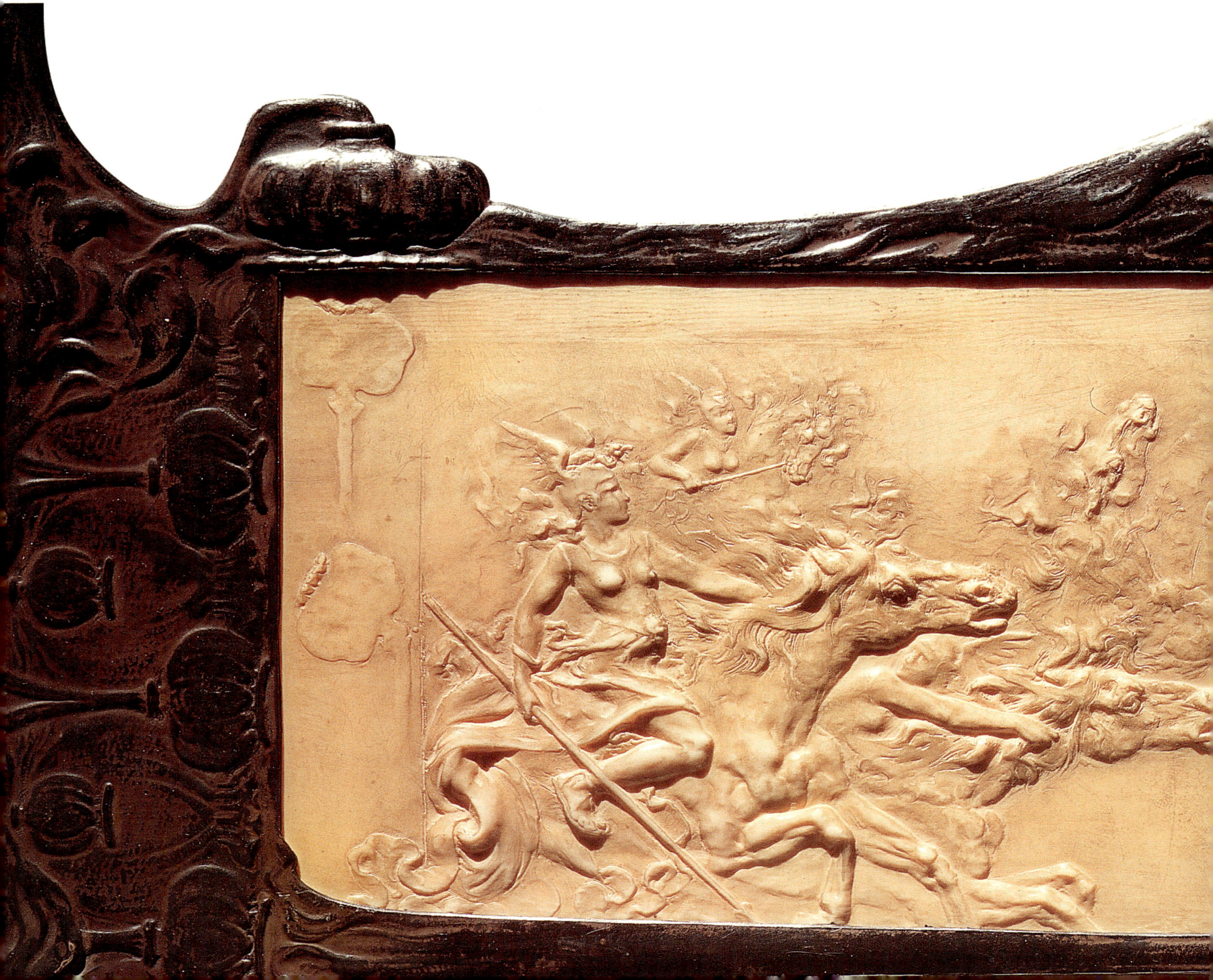

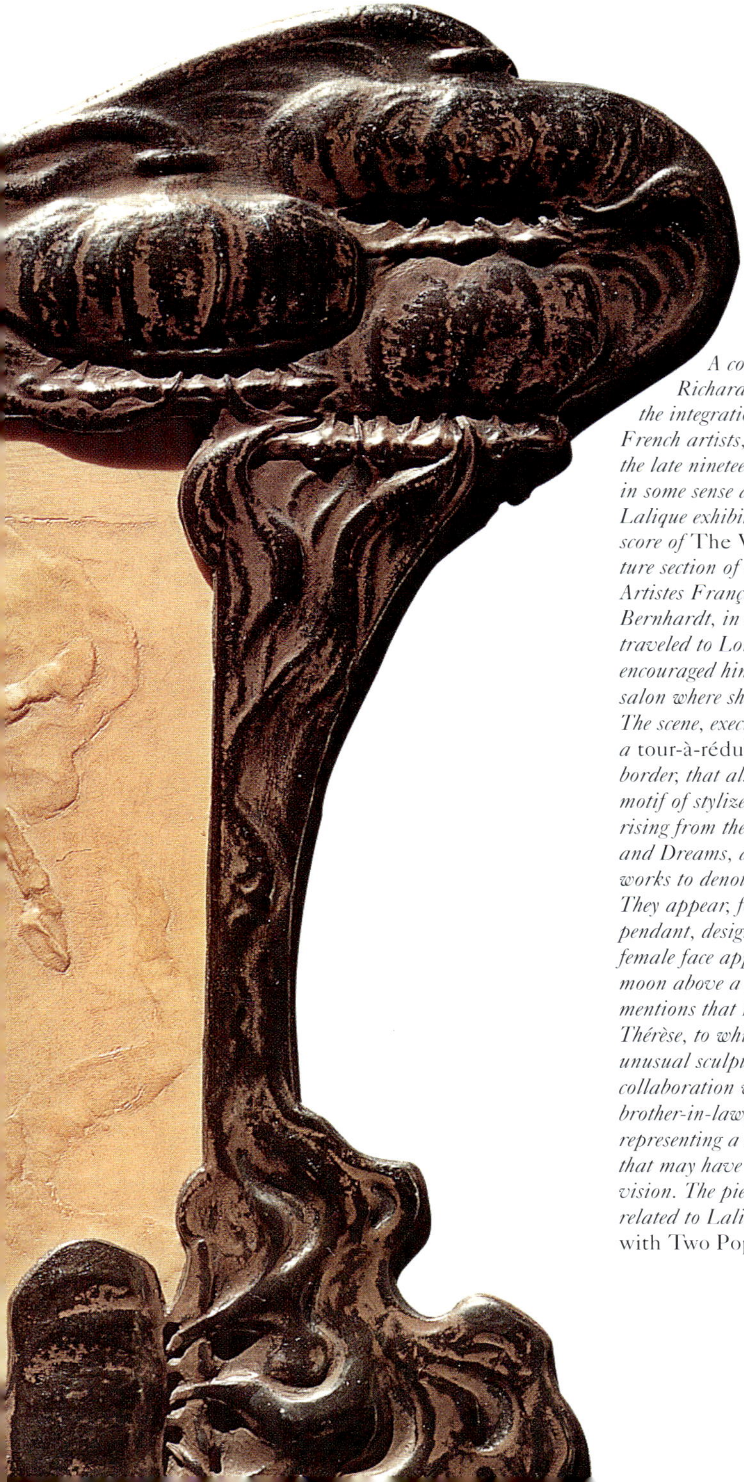

A common fervor for the music of Richard Wagner and for his vision of the integration of all the arts united many French artists, musicians, and intellectuals in the late nineteenth century. Art nouveau was in some sense an extension of this vision. Lalique exhibited this rich binding for the score of The Valkyrie *in 1894 in the sculpture section of the Salon de la Société des Artistes Françaises. It may have been Sarah Bernhardt, in whose entourage Lalique had traveled to London that same year, who encouraged him to submit his work to the salon where she herself exhibited sculpture. The scene, executed from a larger model using a* tour-à-réduire, *is contained within a silver border, that also bisects it horizontally. The motif of stylized poppy seedpods with fumes rising from them, a classical emblem of Sleep and Dreams, appears in many Symbolist works to denote the realm of the imagination. They appear, for example, on an ornate pendant, designed by Mucha, in which a female face appears within an opal crescent moon above a stylized night sky. Vever mentions that Lalique's shop in the rue Thérèse, to which he moved in 1890, had an unusual sculpted decoration made in collaboration with his father-in-law and brother-in-law, Auguste Ledru* père *and* fils, *representing a cavalcade of women, imagery that may have been related to this Wagnerian vision. The piece is undated, but is clearly related to Lalique's pendant,* Woman's Head with Two Poppies, *of c. 1898–1899. JTR*

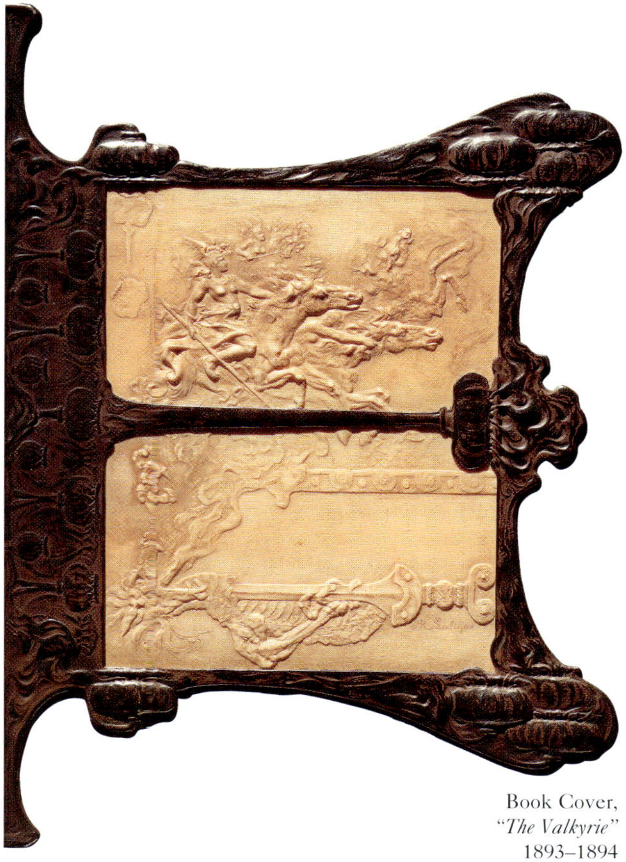

Book Cover,
"The Valkyrie"
1893–1894
Leather, silver, ivory
19 3/4 x 15 3/4 inches
(50 x 40 cm)
(Cat. 170)

possessed all the skill of the jeweler and knew the history of the art. Though his work redeployed the time-honored techniques of goldworking which gem-cutting had ousted in the seventeenth century, he had begun as a jeweler; in his dreams, gemstones had a life of their own. These rock-hard kernels of light which "ripen" in the bowels of the earth are regarded as the very essence of a natural perfection that no art can equal; they were even traditionally thought to have occult powers. Lalique, although never swayed by such magical considerations, nevertheless wanted to reclaim the tradition by creating "absolute" jewelry through the use of the color and material of gemstones. As in the age of the barbarians, each *bijou* he made would be a talisman. But it would have to be a modern talisman, or a purely intellectual one, like Sérusier's *Talisman* for the Académie Julian.[19]

A Symbolist Cosmogony of Light

The notion of analogy that gripped the nineteenth century reverted once again to symbols in its quest for a new mythology.[20] Numerous legends associate gemstones with the snake. The serpent is an archaic underworld god, chased out of the Christian Paradise. Just like a gemstone, its plastic perfection makes it a striking sign of the sacred in nature. The snake is the living abstraction of the line which Art Nouveau would see as the underlying "biomorphic" structure of form. Lalique drew his earliest snakes for Sarah Bernhardt. One might conjecture that he had found, through the Divine Sarah (La Berma of *À la recherche du temps perdu*[21]), the poetic vision of his own jewelry, for which the serpent is the prophylactic touchstone; and woman—regularly damned with him—is the tutelary goddess, the "living pillar."[22] In the beginning were woman, the stone, and the serpent. Lalique may have made his jewels for Calouste Gulbenkian, but he could not have made them without reflecting on Woman. His cosmogony is organized FOR Woman—it is her ornament—and THROUGH Woman, the mother-image.[23] A *femme nature*, hence a *femme fatale*. The female muse who had consoled Musset's unease, his *mal de siècle*, is by now thoroughly outmoded. Mallarmé lives his poem as if in childbirth. As a creator, he is a woman—and creation is the supreme notion of the late nineteenth century, full to term with the century to come.

The serpent, then, takes pride of place in Lalique's heraldry of the feminine. But for which female serpent does he wait? There is more than one and they are always twofold: Eve-Mary, Gorgon/Medusa-Minerva, Cleopatra-Isis. To whom should the Lalique beauty prize go in this Judgment of Paris? Certainly not to any Christian image. Unlike Baudelaire, Lalique puts no credence in sin. The Gorgon, even more than Minerva, has appeared on all too many classical ornaments, and Lalique's notion of beauty is

Fig. 8
Corsage Ornament
Snakes
1898–1899
Gold, enamel
8 1/8 x 5 2/3 inches
(20.8 x 14.3 cm)
Lisbon, Museu Calouste Gulbenkian

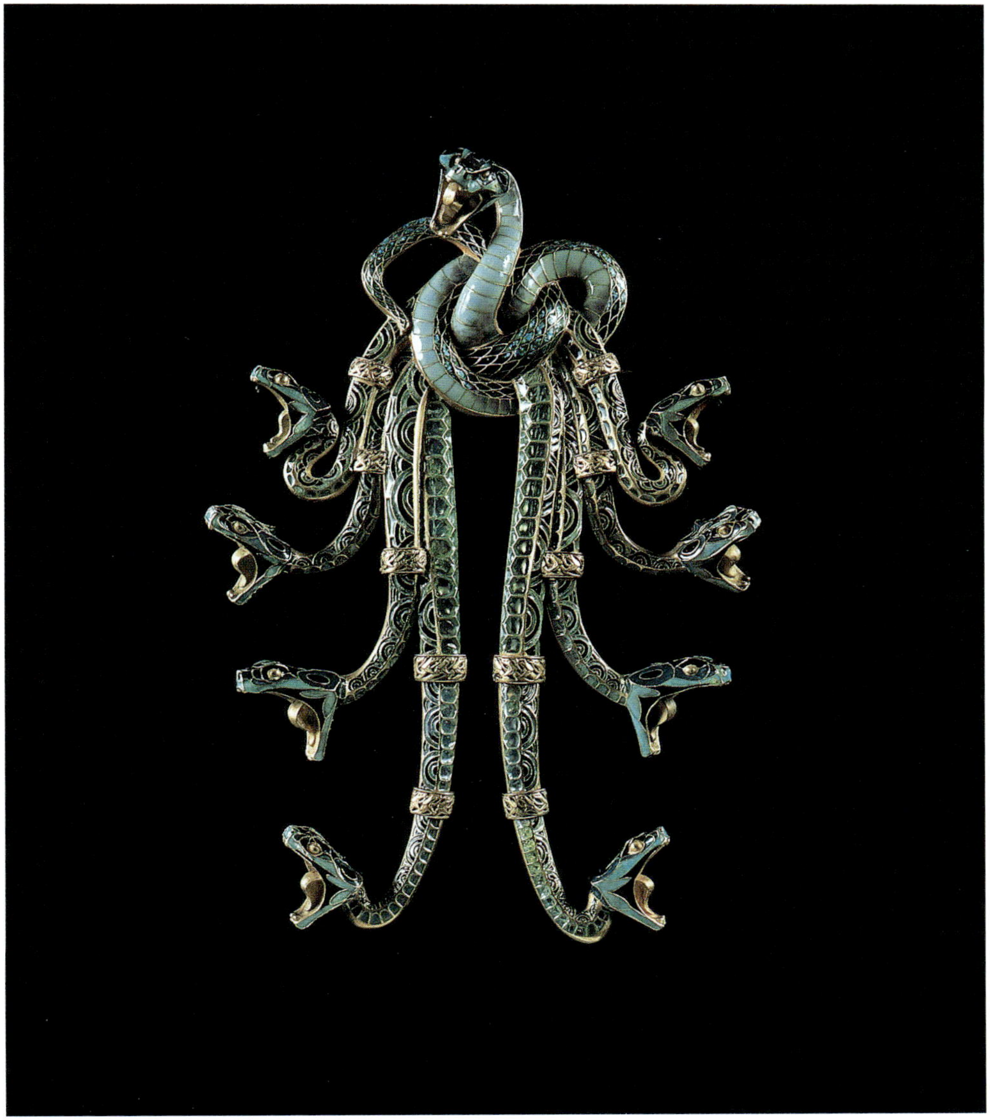

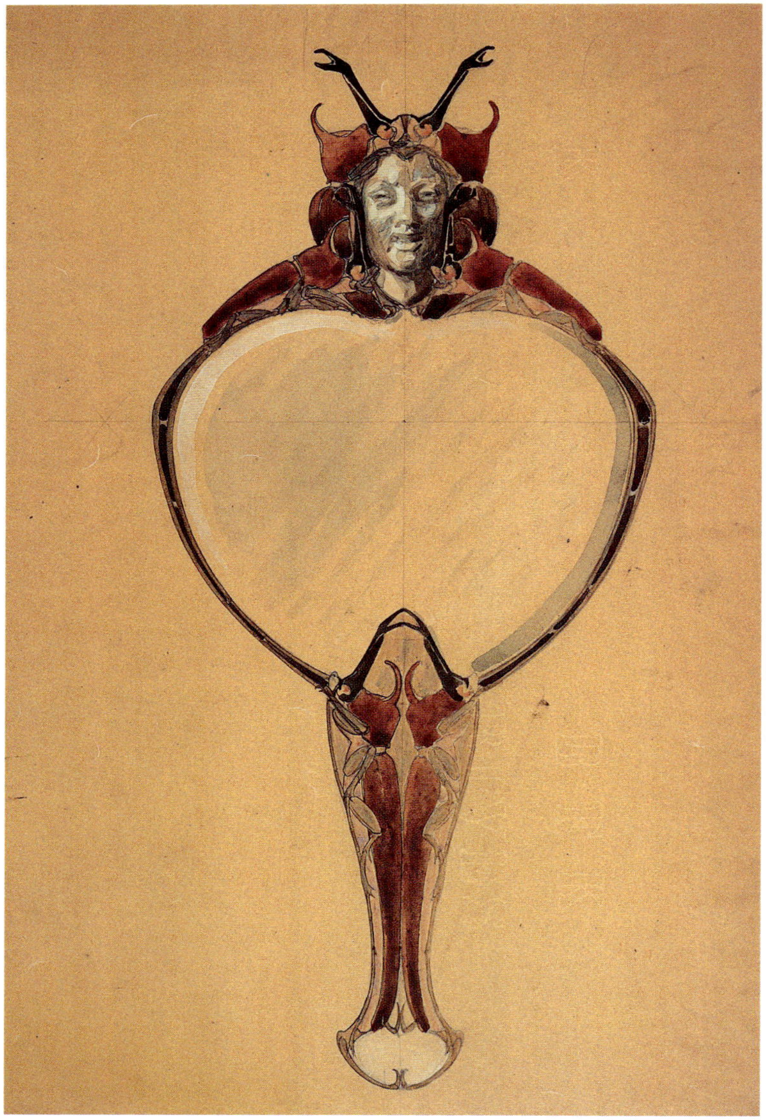

Design for a Hand Mirror
Stag Beetles and Face
c. 1898–1900
Pencil, ink, watercolor, gouache on paper
15 x 9 7/8 inches
(37.8 x 24.9 cm)
(Cat. 235)

Hand Mirror
Stag Beetles and Face
c. 1898–1900
Enameled bronze, glass, ivory, mirrored glass
13 3/4 x 7 1/16 x 1 7/8 inches
(34.8 x 18 x 4.5 cm)
(Cat. 188)

Throughout his career as a jeweler, Lalique designed luxurious toilet accessories. The bronze back of this menacingly exotic mirror is inset with two oval plaques of light-colored pâte de verre representing horned beetles. The strangely crested top section contains a small oval plaque with a beetle having a single extended horn. On the face of the looking glass, the mirror plate is surmounted by a human contenance set between enameled beetles and dressed satanically with their horns. The drawing for this uncanny object emphasizes the laughing male figure, a kind of Puck or sprite, who is clearly related to Lalique's jester figures with their leafy fool's caps. The inhuman forms of beetles with protruding horns frame the glass in which the reflection of the woman who holds the mirror will appear. The mirror thus reproduces imagery familiar from so many other jewels by maliciously reflecting the face of the woman in the circumference of the glass where it will be crowned with the horns of a terrible insect—Beauty among the Beasts. *JTR*

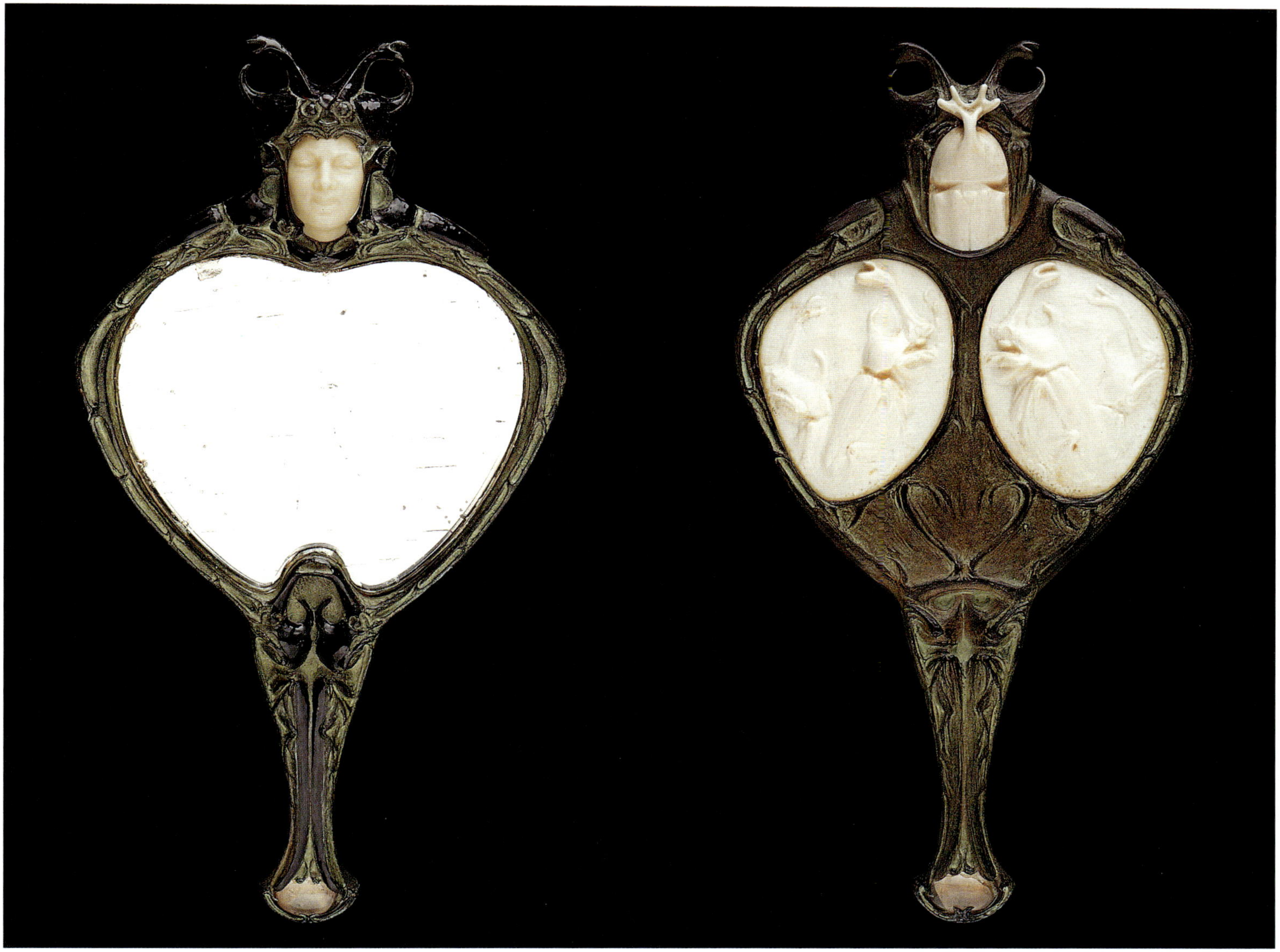

anyway not associated with horror. This leaves the Egyptians. Cleopatra is an Isis who took her own life. Yet, if death has a role in the strange work of the jeweler, it does not play it with such a tragic voice. In Lalique, death takes its own time, having the beauty of a withered leaf. Isis it is then, dressed in a knot of snakes charmed by the "general harmony,"[24] of her allure, in the fragrant movement of her dress, in the jangling of her jewelry.

In fact, of all these rather grandiose serpents, Lalique—who adores the countryside—prefers the wyvern, the dragonlike, two-legged winged creature who lives hard by springs and fountains because she possesses the stone. No longer quite a serpent in Lalique's metamorphosis, the dragon-dragonfly—a female torso, animal claws, wings, and snake's body—is an avatar of the female sphinx (fig. 9), to which Gustave Moreau was still giving a classical interpretation. The enigmatic "princesse lointaine" (the "faraway princess" penned by Maeterlinck and embodied by Sarah Bernhardt), is withdrawn into herself in a stillness of ecstasy and stone ("I am beautiful, o mortals, like a dream in stone"[25]); eyes unseeing, as in a pastel by Odilon Redon, she emerges from the water of the stone, in an airy metamorphosis, freeing her light-borne soul in the birth of a butterfly. It is the very metaphor for the *bijou*.

Classical jewelry (*joaillerie*), in which Lalique was trained, was an art of light, the only art in which transparency is named—and named twice in French: "l'eau," water, and "l'âme," the soul of the stone. Cutting gemstones is a highly abstract art, consisting in extracting from the water of the rock its luminous soul. It requires calculating angles so that they refract and diffract light to the best advantage, diffusing it across the colored spectrum of the diamond's white light or the characteristic frequency of the other waters. When—following the precepts of Viollet-le-Duc and Hokusai—Lalique the jeweler studies the motif both on and in nature, he has in mind a theory of light which is as exhaustive as that of the Impressionists and the Neo-Impressionists. He might even have read the color theories of Michel Chevreul. Lalique's art is entirely taken up by light, and his genius lies in knowing it.

Like the Impressionists, Lalique loved the countryside and the open air; like them, he was engaged in a search for a new principle of beauty—but within the miniature art of the *bijou*. The Impressionists have a wide-angle view of things; Lalique focuses on detail. Botanizing at the level of insects, he too has a sense for cosmic light, but also knows that it can be found in the bowels of the earth. He is a *cul-terreux* [a country bumpkin: literally, a "backside in the soil"] of the light. He has the same animist feelings that the Impressionists had, and is little touched by decadence. However, he individualizes animism, digging out the very

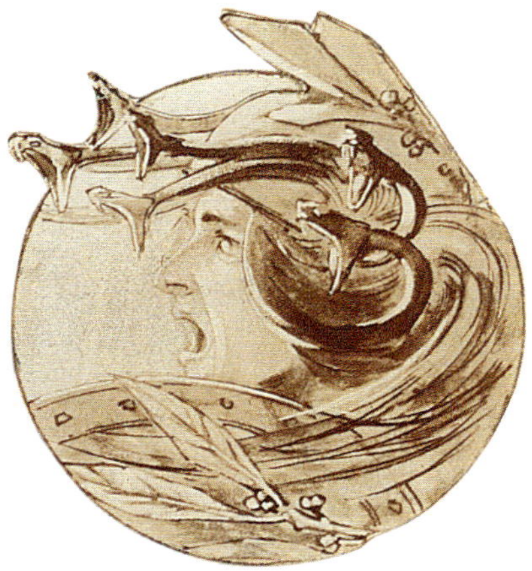

soul of the motif. His line delves into the details of nature's architecture (for example, thorns), into the anatomy of forms (fossils). Neither copying nor stylizing, his work is an interpretation—just as a musician interprets a score, infusing the music with life, without betraying the composer's intentions, or like an analyst teasing out a symptom. At once lyrical and intellectual, Lalique is also exact and imaginative. His wildflowers buzz in the summer heat, picked out one by one as in a medieval tapestry—among wasp-women, wasp-waisted in their hourglass corsets.

The peacock—that paragon of natural beauty—displaying or folding up his tail as the sun revolves round the earth, before vanishing (so both our deceived senses and the myths of old inform us), is the living embodiment of the solar drama. It inspired both *fin-de-siècle* poets and artists. Whistler was among the first to display this peacock splendor, in gold leaf on the four walls of The Peacock Room,[26] where the title—*Harmony in Blue and Gold*—evokes the twofold drama of light (between shade and brightness, night and day). The same title would have been appropriate for a Lalique comb, where one blue and one golden peacock are inscribed within a stained-glass rose window in opals (cat. 26). In 1901, Lalique executed the cover illustration of Robert de Montesquiou's *Les Paons* ("The Peacocks"). In 1888, Montesquiou (his seal and emblem was a bat) had given Whistler

Design for a Box
Allegory of War
c. 1898–1900
Collage on paper
10 5/8 x 9 1/2 inches
(27 x 24.4 cm)
(Cat. 234)

A pair of serpents, their delicate scales executed in fine translucent enamel, their tails enlaced to suspend a large pearl, frames this lozenge-shaped brooch. In the center, a glass "cameo" represents a slender nude figure with her arms extended widely to support voluminous cascades of gauzy drapery. She is cast in translucent blue-green glass set against a luminous golden ground. Lalique often uses shades of blue and green for his most dream-like figures, implying that they belong to a nocturnal realm. The use of gold foil behind glass to give it radiance is an ancient technique that Lalique would also use in some of his early glass vessels.

The name "Salammbô" alludes to the Carthaginian heroine of Flaubert's novel of 1862, a favorite text of the Symbolist generation that inspired an opera by Ernest Reyer first performed at the Théâtre de la Monnaie in Brussels in 1890. The serpent was the family totem of Hamilcar Barca, Salammbô's father, while the Zaimph, or great veil of the goddess Tanit, appears as an important element of the story. The female figure enveloped in drapery recalls images of Loïe Fuller whose performances in 1900 had attracted so many artists. However, while Fuller's movements were centrifugal and spiraling, this pas de danse *is stately, and the drapery falls in vertical folds. The figure thus seems closer to neoclassical models.* *JTR*

Pendant-Brooch
"Salammbô" or Salome
c. 1904–1905
Gold, glass, *plique-à-jour* enamel
3 1/8 x 2 1/2 inches
(8 x 6.3 cm)
(Cat. 140)

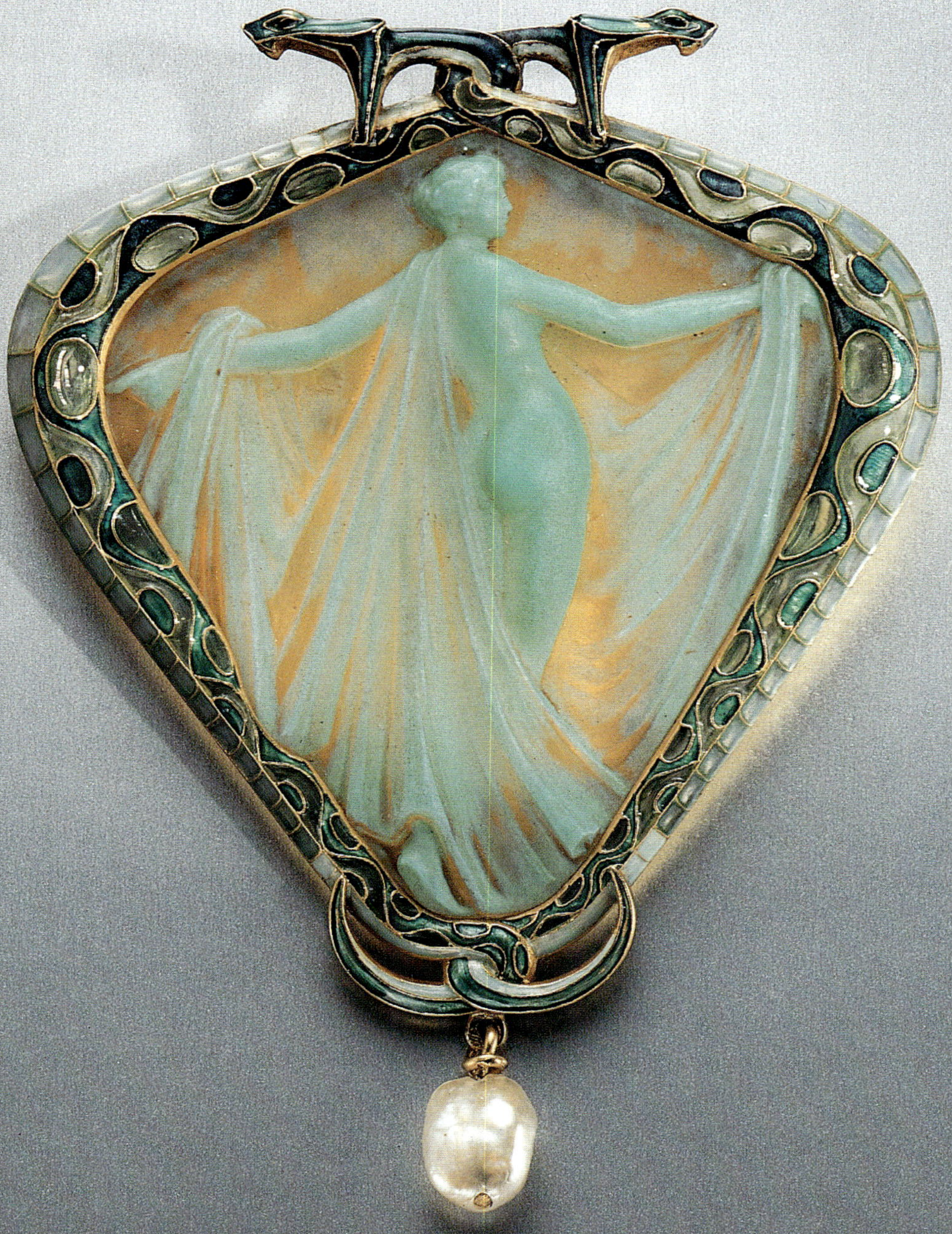

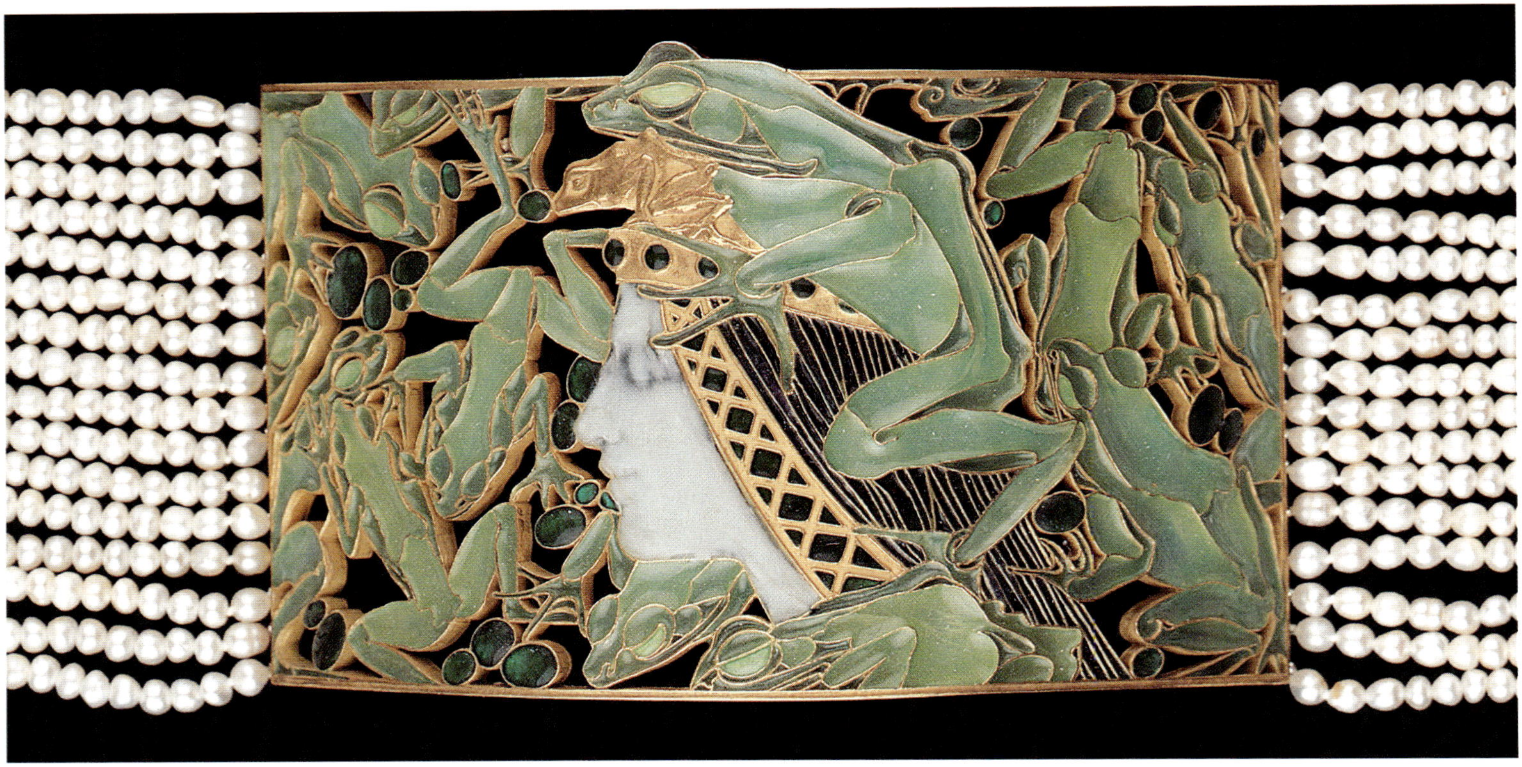

Female heads appear frequently in the work of Lalique amid many kinds of flowers, plants, insects, reptiles, and birds. This is one of the few of these enigmatic images which we know to have had a specific literary source. In an article recounting a visit to Lalique's studio in 1899, Jean Lorrain quoted the jeweler as having told him that the plaque had been inspired by Lorrain's own ballet La Princesse au Sabbat *with music by Louis Ganne that had been performed at the Folies-Bergère in January 1898. In his review of Lalique's display at the Exposition of 1900, Pol Neveux suggested that the bizarre motif was inspired by Lorrain's story with the same title, first published in 1895, and included in the 1902 collection* Princesses d'Ivoire et d'Ivresse . *In the ballet, Illys, a beautiful Egyptian princess, seeks the aid of sorceresses to preserve her beauty. Maliciously, they subject her to the horrors of the witches Sabbath where she is assailed by creatures of all kinds, including storks, toads, and a giant grasshopper. Lorrain's story tells of Ilsée, a princess enamored of her own beauty, who chooses to decorate her halls and gardens with innumerable grotesque statues of frogs. The plaque adopts the curious image of the lady and the frogs. Indeed, it may play on a less common French name for a frog, "reinette," a diminutive of "reine" or "queen," the word used by Neveux in his appreciative description rather than the more familiar "grenouille." "Narkiss," another tale included in* Princesses d'Ivoire et d'Ivresse, *bears the dedication "Conte pour mon ami Lalique." Indeed, the jeweler himself appears, with the pseudonym Barruchini, in Lorrain's decadent novel,* Monsieur Phocas, *published in 1902.* *JTR*

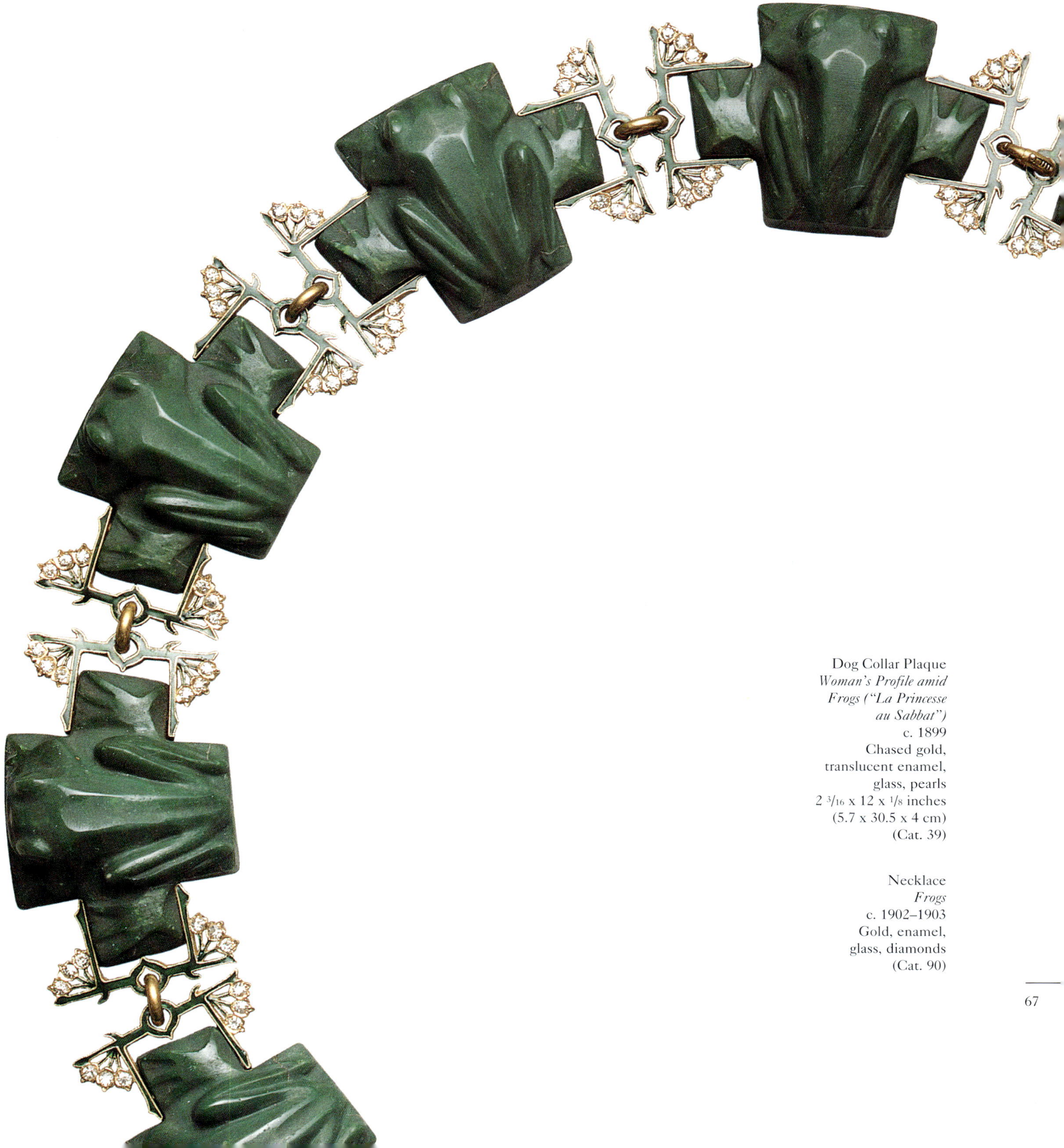

Dog Collar Plaque
Woman's Profile amid Frogs ("La Princesse au Sabbat")
c. 1899
Chased gold, translucent enamel, glass, pearls
2 3/16 x 12 x 1/8 inches
(5.7 x 30.5 x 4 cm)
(Cat. 39)

Necklace
Frogs
c. 1902–1903
Gold, enamel, glass, diamonds
(Cat. 90)

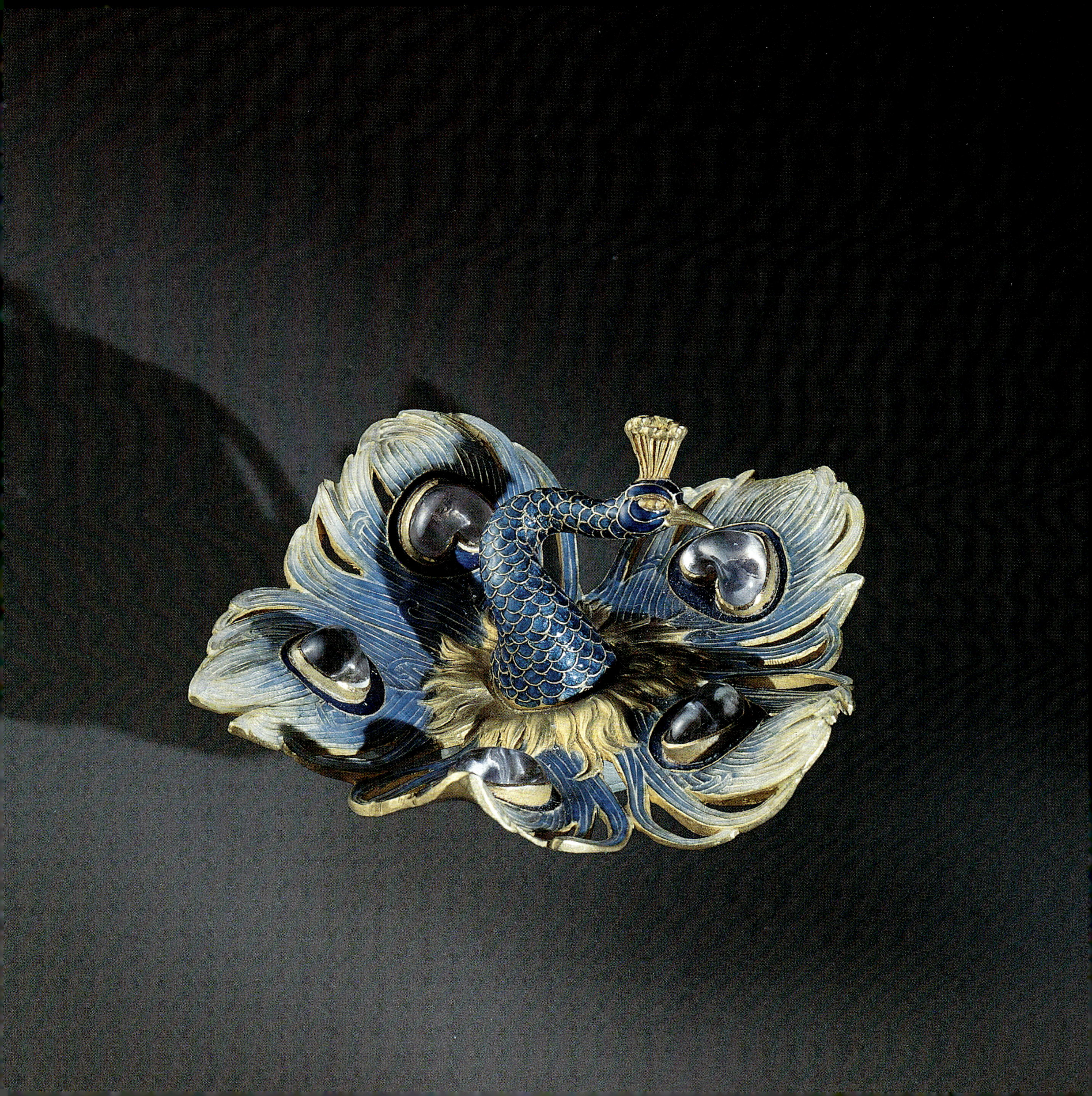

(whose monogram was a butterfly) a gold and glass butterfly attributed to Lalique—the jeweler was not yet signing his pieces—as a wedding present.[27]

It is light that rules Lalique's cosmogony. Unlike painters and writers, Lalique cannot lose himself in the space of the canvas or in words as he conjures up this utterly abstract "mystery." He has to encapsulate it in a motif. As with the stone and the serpent, the bat belongs to that empire of darkness which swallows up the sun every night so that it can be born anew on the morrow. The metamorphosis of the dragon-dragonfly, the bat is the incarnation of the twofold night, subterranean yet heavenly. On this solar drama is superimposed the alchemical dark work of jewelry, which harbors the secret of how to draw light from palpable night.

Lalique's vitrine at the 1900 Exposition Universelle was the outward manifestation of just such a vision. It comprised a jewelry "creation" halfway between a flight of bats and women-butterflies—whose flight remains affixed to the ground (cat. 172). In a watch, the bat-butterfly couple is turned into a representation of time itself, like the ultimate icon that art gave us (cat. 46). Henceforth, no one will ever venture to create another all-encompassing image of time. The face is dotted with black and white butterflies. On the back of the watch case is a flight of bats in a constellation of opals—night as the mirror image of time. The fob-ring is formed by one tiny uroboros.

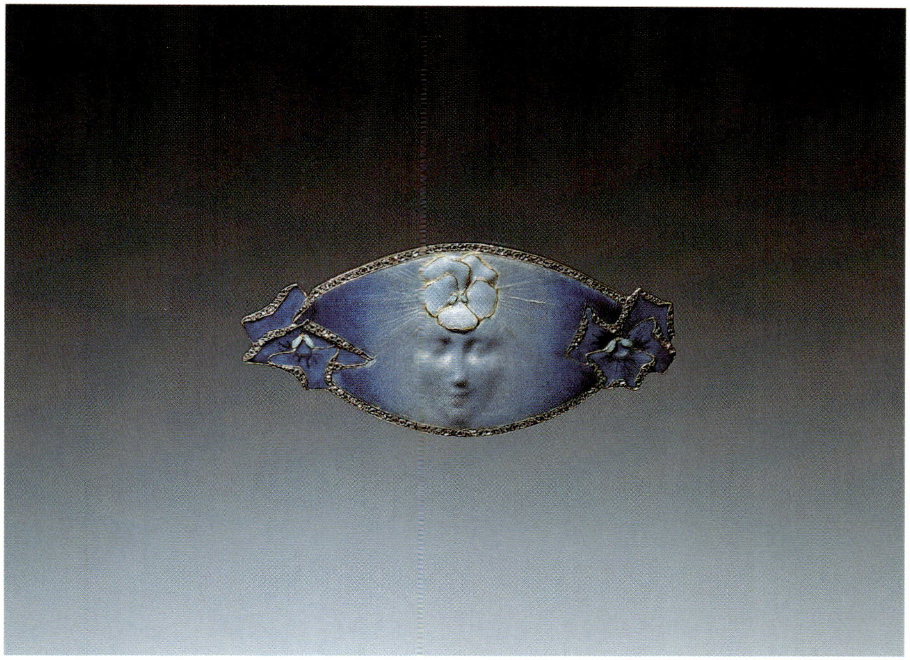

Brooch
Peacock
c. 1897–1898
Chased gold, translucent enamel on gold, moonstones
1; Diam: 2 1/4 inches (2.6; Diam: 6 cm)
(Cat. 27)

Brooch
Pansy / Thought
c. 1899–1901
Chased gold, engraved enamel on gold, diamonds
1 1/8 x 2 1/4 inches
(2.7 x 5.7 cm)
(Cat. 40)

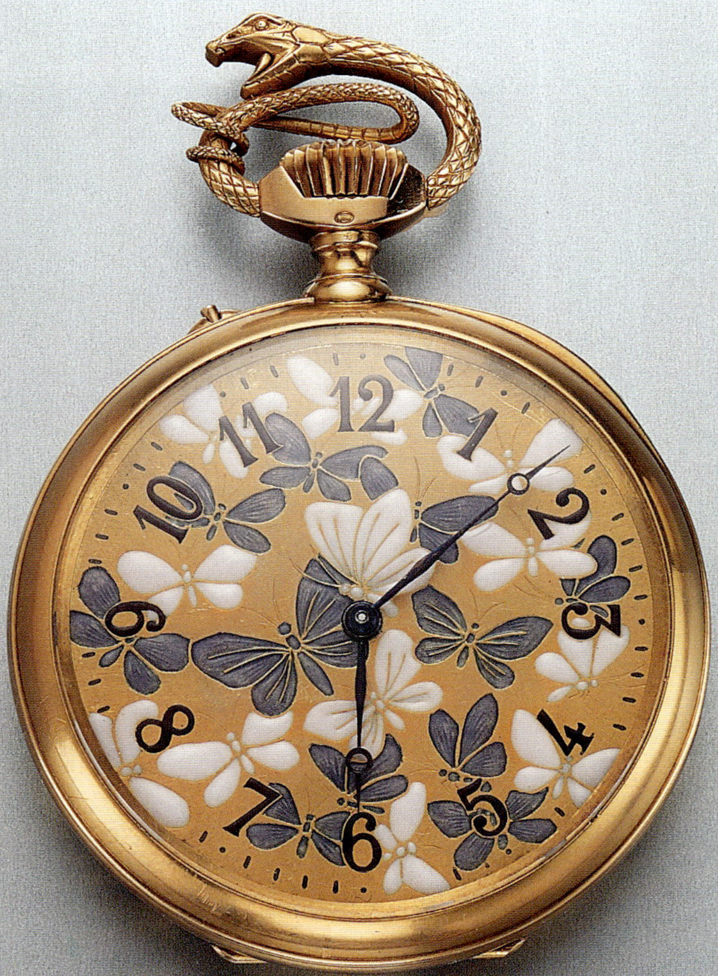

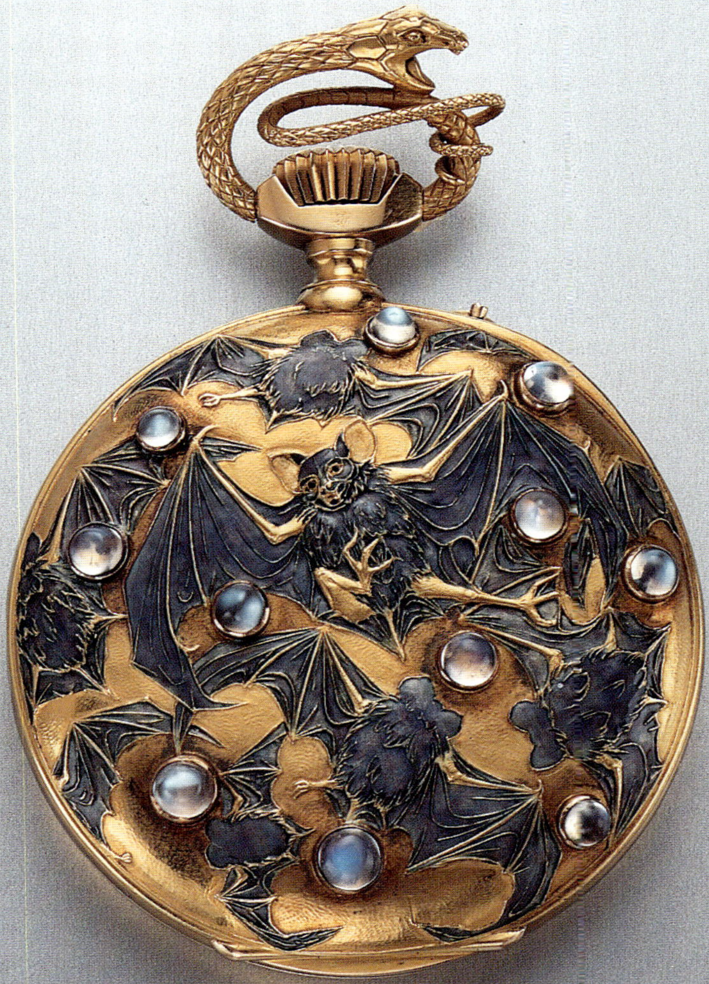

Previous double page
Watch
Butterflies and Bats
c. 1899–1900
Chased gold, enamel on gold, moonstones
Diam: 2 inches
(Diam: 5.1 cm)
(Cat. 46)

Brooch-Pendant
Butterfly-woman
c. 1894–1896
Gold, translucent enamel on gold, diamonds, rubies
2 3/8 x 2 5/8 inches
(6 x 6.5 cm)
(Cat. 6)

A "Necklace of Claws" for Nights Electric[28]

The mind-improving and aphrodisiac virtues of the bat, the winged mammal credited by some with being the first animal in all creation, are universally acknowledged. While in the West the bat embodies impurity, in the Far East it vouchsafes long life and happiness. According to some, the animal was born of a homosexual and incestuous union of the solar lord with his son.[29] The bat is apt to be Lilith, the vampire, or a female sphinx in the black light of creation, born, like Adam, of God and, like him, expelled from the Earthly Paradise.[30] Robert de Montesquiou, "sovereign of the transitory," as he called himself in a Baudelairean fashion in a 1892 work entitled *Les Chauves-souris* ("The Bats"), was the last nineteenth century dandy—as Huysmans' Des Esseintes in *À Rebours*[31]—as well as the first of the twentieth century—as Charlus in *À la recherche du temps perdu*.[32] But unlike Proust himself, Montesquiou openly vaunted his homosexuality: "Un honneur me viendra d'avoir aimé sans feinte,/Ce qui n'inspire encore à d'autres que la crainte." [33]

Sarah Bernhardt portrayed herself as a bat in her sculptures, had her room hung with a glossy black cloth embroidered with a bat motif,[34] and like Montesquiou—or he like her—had tamed one. Before launching Mucha's career, Bernhardt propelled Lalique into the art world by asking him to produce the jewelry for her role as Gismonda in 1894. But jewelry for the theater did not interest Lalique; it was the water of the diamond that was to play the starring role. Sarah would sport his pieces out and about in Paris and he remained a member of her clan, if not a member of what she called her "menagerie."[35] In 1896 he created the medal and the *bijou* which celebrated her consecration as a *trésor vivant*, and in 1899 decorated the yellow drawing room for the suite she had built in her last theater,[36] today the Théâtre de la Ville, formerly the Théâtre Sarah Bernhardt. One wonders when the eminence of this other "sovereign of the transitory"—that is, of dramatic art—will once more be acknowledged and the aura be restored to this first vamp in the long line of divas? Sarah's reading of Montesquiou's "La Couche de la morte" was the high point of the celebrations the aesthete organized at Versailles in 1894. Montesquiou sang her praises in a poem in *Les Chauves-souris*, describing her in the same guise as she immortalized herself in a photographic portrait in a coffin, and as "archaeologists" would one day find her intact, according to Montesquiou's poem: "She who dies so much was she loved."

When these archaeologists dig for the "secret of the invisible seam," "whatever remains of a butterfly's flight," then "a light-filled ash" will run through their fingers.[37]

It would not be long before electricity would "kill the moonlight," as Marinetti put

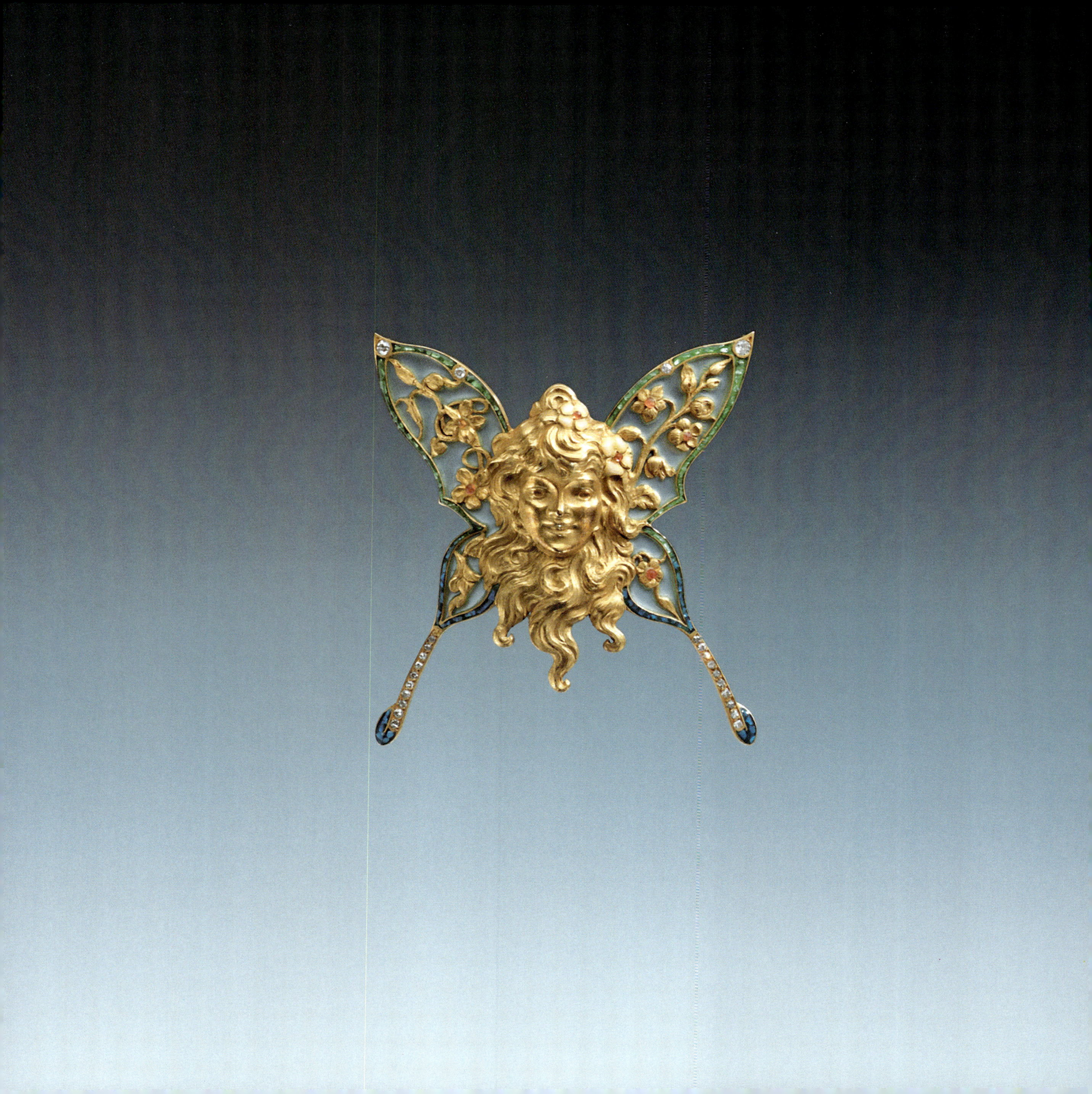

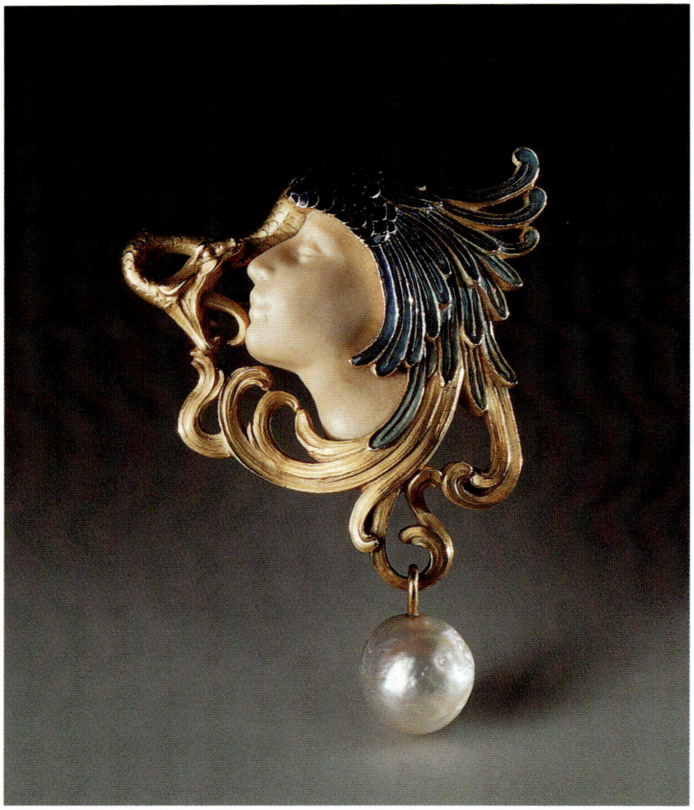

Brooch
Woman with Dragon Headdress
c. 1898–1899
Cast gold, enamel on gold, natural pearl, carved limestone
2 3/8 x 1 3/4 inches
(6.2 x 4.5 cm)
(Cat. 38)

Fig. 9
Corsage Ornament
Dragonfly Woman
1897–1898
Gold, enamel, chrysoprase, moonstones, diamonds
9 x 10 7/16 inches
23 x 26.6 cm
Lisbon, M.C.G.

it in the Futurist Manifesto of 1909. But before Balla decomposed the electric spectrum into a series in his *Compenetrazioni iridescenti* (1912–13) Loïe Fuller had projected beams of electric light onto a screen of veils, on which she represented nothing less than the soul of the dance. She drew out from darkness and movement the earliest dynamic abstract forms that the Lumière brothers were striving to fix on their cinematic negatives. The uses La Fuller made of electricity were soon to relegate the seven veils of Salome's dance to the prop box, though the stubborn Symbolist Jean Lorrain persisted in seeing in her a "human bat, dancing wrapped in a winding-sheet."[38] It is nevertheless preferable to assume that Lalique, who borrowed Lorrain's theme of the woman-frog, shared the point of view of another friend of La Fuller, Rodin. Lalique inevitably saw in her work the same architectonic principles that inhabited his designs and the same light moving within form which he was seeking in his polychrome transparency of gems, horn, enamels, and glass.

The *Bijou* in the Total Artwork: A Materialized Reverie of Light

Lalique had detractors as early as 1900. In a review of his London exhibition in 1905, an anonymous critic writing in *The Studio* took him to task: "Too much of his talent goes

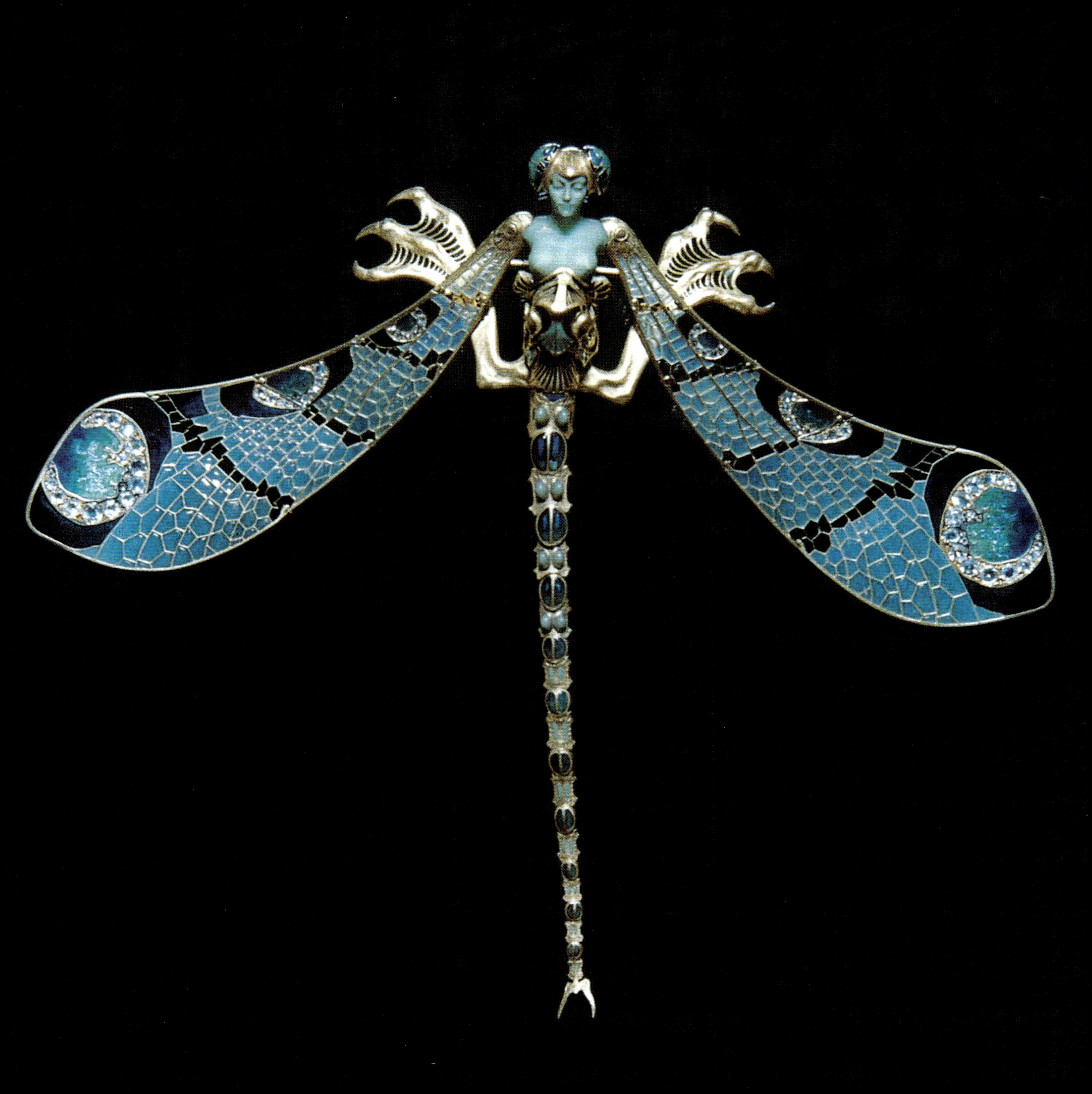

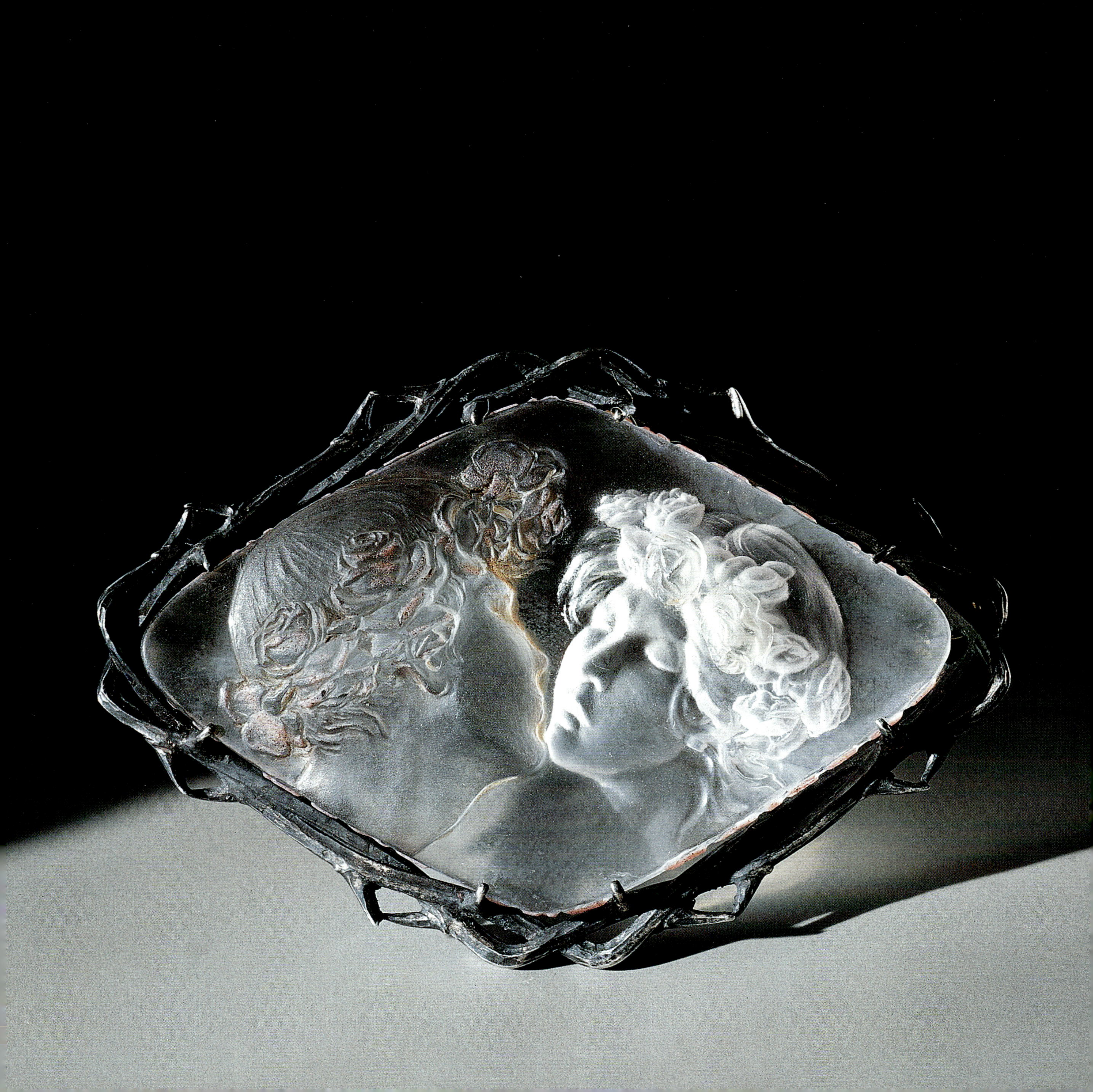

into the imitation of beautiful natural forms and flowers in unnatural-looking materials, which suggests sometimes an unpleasant decadence."[39] In France, it was his literary streak that was attacked.[40] It is true that Lalique had found in the Symbolist aesthetic a way out of the nineteenth century's crisis of the subject and of the naturalism which was its corollary. Romanticism had already been searching for a radically non-academic aesthetic, an unvarying and eternal subject in the *natura naturans*, as against the *natura naturata* of the classics. Both Impressionism and literary Realism, by rejecting all metaphysics, provided the opposite poles. Reacting against the materialism of the Realists, Symbolism provides naturalism with a conceptual framework through natural myths: woman, creation, light—all three of which Lalique was to "synthesize" in the mother-image of the gemstone-*bijou*. Symbolism, through recourse to folklore and a taste for the archaic, took the first steps in the direction of the idea of nature that twentieth-century primitivism—upon which Gauguin had already embarked—continued in the theme of lost nature. At the turn of the century, the aesthetic of the movement carried the idea of *natura naturans* to its paroxysm in Art Nouveau—before ending up as the "uprooted nature" that characterizes our time.[41]

The decadence of which the English critic accused Lalique can be read as artifice, as that "nature denatured" Baudelaire determined as one manifestation of the beautiful in the "transitory" of life.[42] Baudelaire, by conjoining in the "all" or "one" wherein "perfumes, colors and sounds answer one another,"[43] is the "guiding light" that links our "modernity" to that of Romanticism; and by naming it, he releases us from the grip of Romanticism. Reproaching Lalique with artificiality is like berating Van Gogh for his impasto, Seurat for his Pointillism, or Gauguin and Kandinsky for their blue horses.

While working with pure color, Lalique was encouraged to enlarge the palette of jewelry to include colored semiprecious stones and those artificial gems, enamel and glass, not only by the Nabis movement but also by the entire history of jewelry prior to the seventeenth century. The Nabis, through their simplified outlines, recaptured form, which had been dissolved by the Impressionist use of light. Lalique, however, never simplifies his draftsmanship—far from it. He makes of the complexity of a line encrusted into the void the essential architecture of his pieces. Or else he harnesses the science of the goldsmith to sketch in a filigree line through space or in openwork enamels some motif already dematerialized by light.

It was clear to Lalique that light does not destroy forms so much as it crisscrosses with them, depending on how dense a screen their substance presents. His genius resides in turning jewelry, the art of light, into a

Brooch
"The Kiss"
c. 1904–1906
Silver,
pressed glass
1 7/8 x 2 3/4
inches
(4.9 x 7 cm)
(Cat. 138)

passage through matter itself and in being able to use, even more than color, the grain, the opaque, the transparent, and the clear, the translucent nature of horn and enamel. Through this materialized conception of light, Lalique rescues jewelry as *bijou* from jewelry as *joaillerie* and from Gustave Kahn's "crude luxury." It is true that the masters of this latter type of jewelry were as much aware as Lalique that a gemstone is a cast of light. They nonetheless treated its water as a spotless surface which reflects and refracts light like a mirror.

Lalique conceives of transparency as the internal light of the jewelry piece, similar to those painters who try to uncover the interior light of painting. Lalique's *bijoux* do not glint; they radiate light. Light—in a woman's fleshy complexion or the animal nature of her falling hair—shoots through his pieces. It is the "invention" of glass that concludes this quest for an intimacy with the materiality of light.

Last of the goldsmiths and first of the "designers," the much admired leader of a school of artists plagarized the world over, Lalique stopped producing jewelry in 1910 to dedicate his art to that passion for glass which his earlier work had catalyzed. He returned, as an architect in glass, at the Exposition Internationale des Arts Décoratifs in 1925. He dedicated his pavilion to the memory of the pioneers, to the master glassmakers of the turn of the century—to Gallé, who had been among the first to recognize his work.[44]

Dog Collar Plaque
Two Fluteplayers
c. 1898–1900
Chased gold,
translucent enamel
on gold, opaque
enamel, diamonds
2 1/8 x 3 1/8 inches
(5.4 x 8 cm)
(Cat. 43)

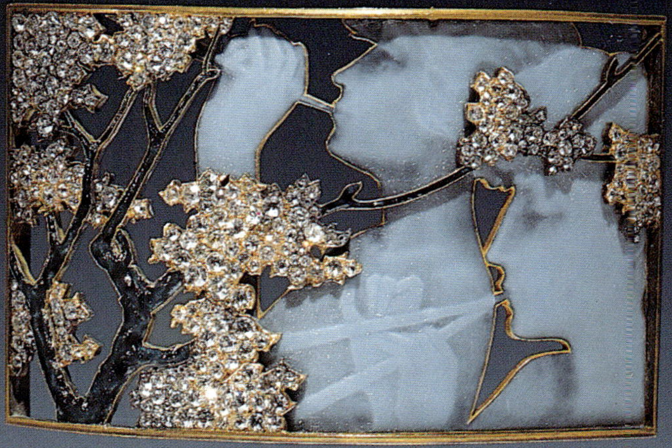

The Reception of René Lalique in America: 1901–1920

Gabriel P. Weisberg

Necklace
"Tigers"
c. 1903–1904
Gold, carved horn, tortoise-shell, enamel on gold, agate
Diam: 4 1/2 inches
(Diam: 14.4 cm)
(Cat. 98)

Following René Lalique's success at the Paris Exposition Universelle in 1900, growing numbers of Americans became interested in his work and came to appreciate his aesthetic.[1] Lalique was breaking away from the English and American style of jewelry, which emphasized sentiment and which had been linked with themes of grief, by focusing on brilliant jewels, shimmering color, and a more imaginative use of nature (insects, plants, flowers). His "new" aesthetic, emphasizing enamels, combined with varied colored stones, also created pieces that were more appropriate for display than for dress. Lalique's innovative style was described in the American periodical *The Craftsman* in 1902:

"The fresh and immediate ideas of Nature expressed in the flower-jewels of the French artist-craftsman speak volumes of hope for the continuance of the national art. In him history repeats itself. He has rejected the combinations of lines, the old meaningless symbols used by generation after generation of his predecessors, to draw inspiration from plant and animal life; just as the Gothic artists spurned the dead Byzantine decorative principles to create their own vigorous and vital ornament."[2]

Collectors and craftsmen alike considered Lalique a model of ingenuity, imagination, and craftsmanship. After examples of his jewelry entered public collections in France, including the Musée des Arts Décoratifs and the Musée du Luxembourg (the repository for the most modern achievements in the visual arts),[3] international periodicals directed greater attention to Lalique, and his work was featured in exhibitions in Europe and eventually the United States. Among designers Lalique was recognized as one who not only advocated an "art nouveau" (a term applied to only the most innovative in art), but also actively challenged others to surpass his achievements by setting a creative standard—an imaginative use of materials—on a very high plateau. By 1905 Lalique was

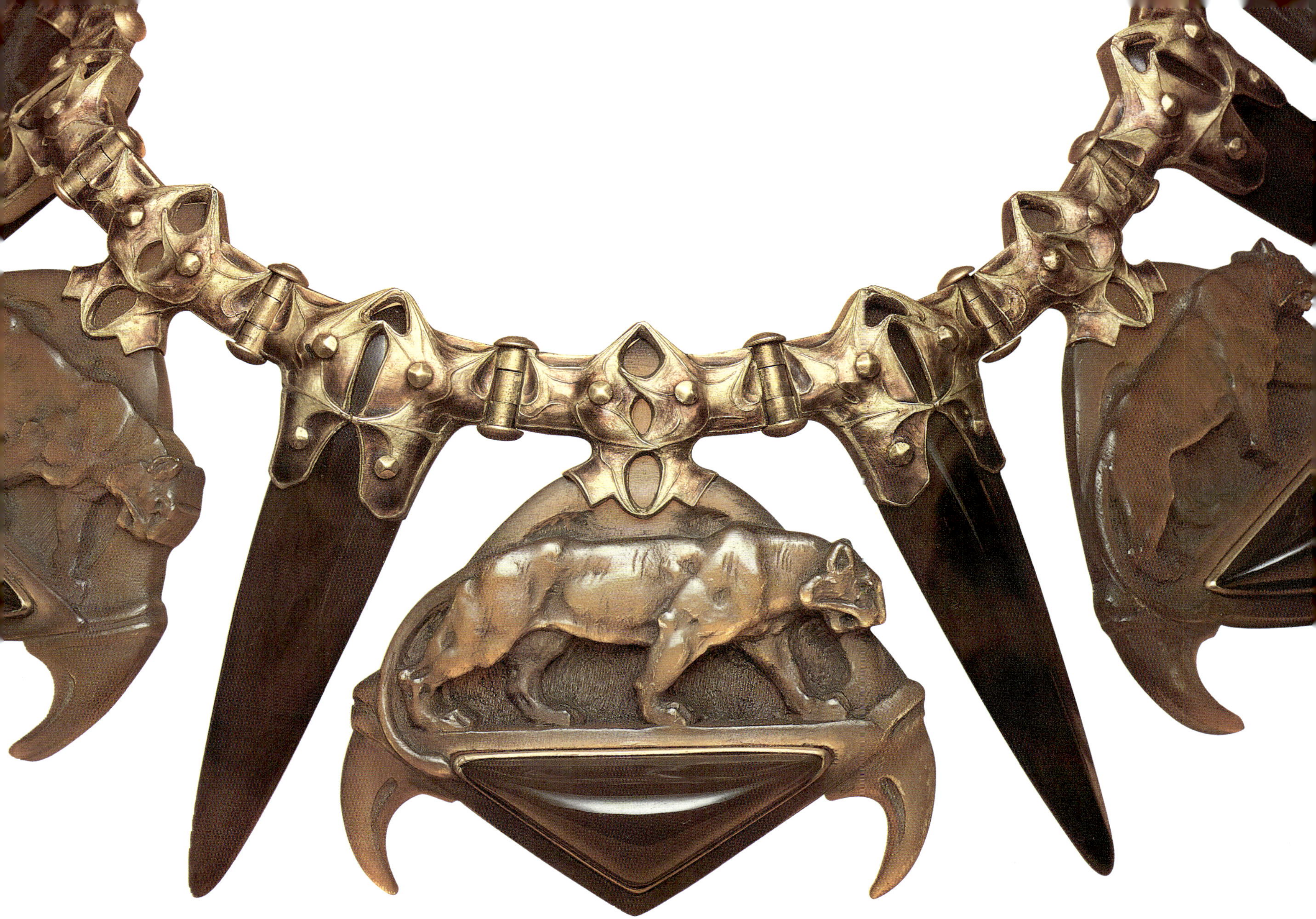

avidly discussed in America, both in the popular daily press and in creative periodicals published for the art field. This attention needs to be carefully assessed to form a clear picture of how Lalique attained his global position and to understand why he reached as broad a public in America as he did in France. Indeed, those who wrote about his creativity for American periodicals were well aware of his contribution to design, and they interpreted his achievements to make his ingenuity appear as a benchmark of the emerging appreciation for new, modern design in the United States.

Central to this movement in the opening decade of the twentieth century were the writings of Irene Sargent, a principal contributor to Gustav Stickley's *The Craftsman*, a magazine that promoted a lively discussion of the Arts and Crafts tradition in the United States.[4] As a professor of Romance languages and aesthetics at Syracuse University (Stickley had established his Craftsmen workshops in Syracuse), Sargent was well suited to translate a series of articles on French design that had first appeared in major French reviews and were subsequently published in *The Craftsman*.[5] Although several of the French publications supported Lalique's work in such contemporary perodicals as *Art et Décoration* and *L'Art Décoratif* (articles with lavish use of photographs of Lalique's pieces), Sargent added her own critical interpretation of his contribution to design. Her writings in 1902 and 1903 helped establish Lalique's favorable reception among American designers and collectors. She asserted that if the United States had a major pioneer designer in Louis Comfort Tiffany, then his creative drive was matched by Lalique's work in France.

Through Sargent's early efforts, Americans came to understand that Lalique's jewelry epitomized originality, utilized new materials, and successfully achieved an expressive freedom in jewelry that had rarely been seen before. Her widely read articles permeated the artistic community and gradually spread to collectors and other writers, who commented on Lalique in newspaper columns or reviews aimed at the general public. Sargent's early appraisal of Lalique set the tone and introduced the issues by which his work was judged. She wrote:

"Taken thus for all in all, M. Lalique is an artist of that type—the creative—which appears most rarely in the course of time. He has given a new direction to the art which he practices, and indicates to those that shall succeed him alluring possibilities of beauty. He has raised the objects which he creates from the rank of toy and talismans up to that of true works of art."[6]

While it is difficult to determine whether Sargent ever actually met Lalique, she did visit Paris in the late 1890s, perhaps in time for the Exposition Universelle of 1900. Certainly by 1901 she became one of the principal spokespersons for design issues in

The Craftsman, and quite likely she had used her time in Paris to discuss her ideas with European designers. Her articles, written with authority, conviction, and passion, reveal her deep and intimate awareness of issues in contemporary design. She clearly recognized that at public museums in France, especially the Luxembourg, the decorative arts were exhibited equally with painting, thus reiterating one of the basic concepts of the period—the unification among all the arts.[7] Sargent was clearly in the forefront of those who recognized that this concept would take American collectors and museums by surprise, since it was unheard-of for museums to present painting and decorative arts together in the United States.

In 1903 *The Craftsman* published a major article by Tristan Destève, "The Workshop and Residence of René Lalique," which had been translated by Sargent.[8] Illustrated with photographs of Lalique's home, (fig. 10) this piece provided specific information on where and how Lalique worked, yet it appeared at a time when Lalique was still not well known in America.[9] But it was also a moment when the methods of craftsmen and the operation of their ateliers or workshops was attracting critical attention in other locations. For this reason, Lalique was being used as a model, or at the very least others were aware of the way he worked with his designers. Sargent added to Lalique's "cult of appreciation" in 1903, when she based her interpretations on a review of the Paris Salon that had originally appeared in the popular magazine *Art et Décoration* (cf. pp. 41–42 above).

In the article, a French critic attacked pieces by Tiffany, claiming that the true center of the Salon revolved around the work of Lalique.[10] In her erudite summation of the original French review, Sargent furthered Lalique's cause in America by selecting the proper phrases and furnishing just the right inflection. She noted, for example, that Lalique was "still the wonderful artist that we have known," even if his works are not as "unexpected" as they had been—since artists, craftsmen, and collectors were seeing a larger range of works than before.[11] While Lalique's work was no longer a real discovery, he had nevertheless emerged as a designer worthy of imitation and emulation.[12] Sargent also capitalized on the implied rivalry between Tiffany and Lalique, although she was careful not to fuel any nationalistic fervor among craftsmen and critics.

Late in 1903 and into 1904, Sargent translated other articles that commented on the ways designers were exploring the insect world. In *The Craftsman*, Lalique was singled out as one practitioner who focused on grasshoppers and other humble "creatures of the animal and vegetable kingdoms"[13] (fig. 11 and cat. 96). Lalique's obsession with the insect world followed on earlier interests in birds, insects, and plants,

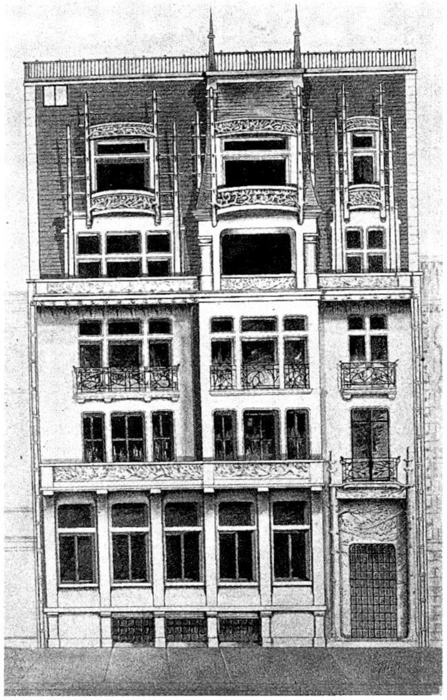

Fig. 10
Photograph of Lalique's home
Reproduced as frontispiece to the article "The Workshop and Residence of M. René Lalique," by Tristan Desteve, *The Craftsman*, 1903, vol. 4, pp. 1–8.

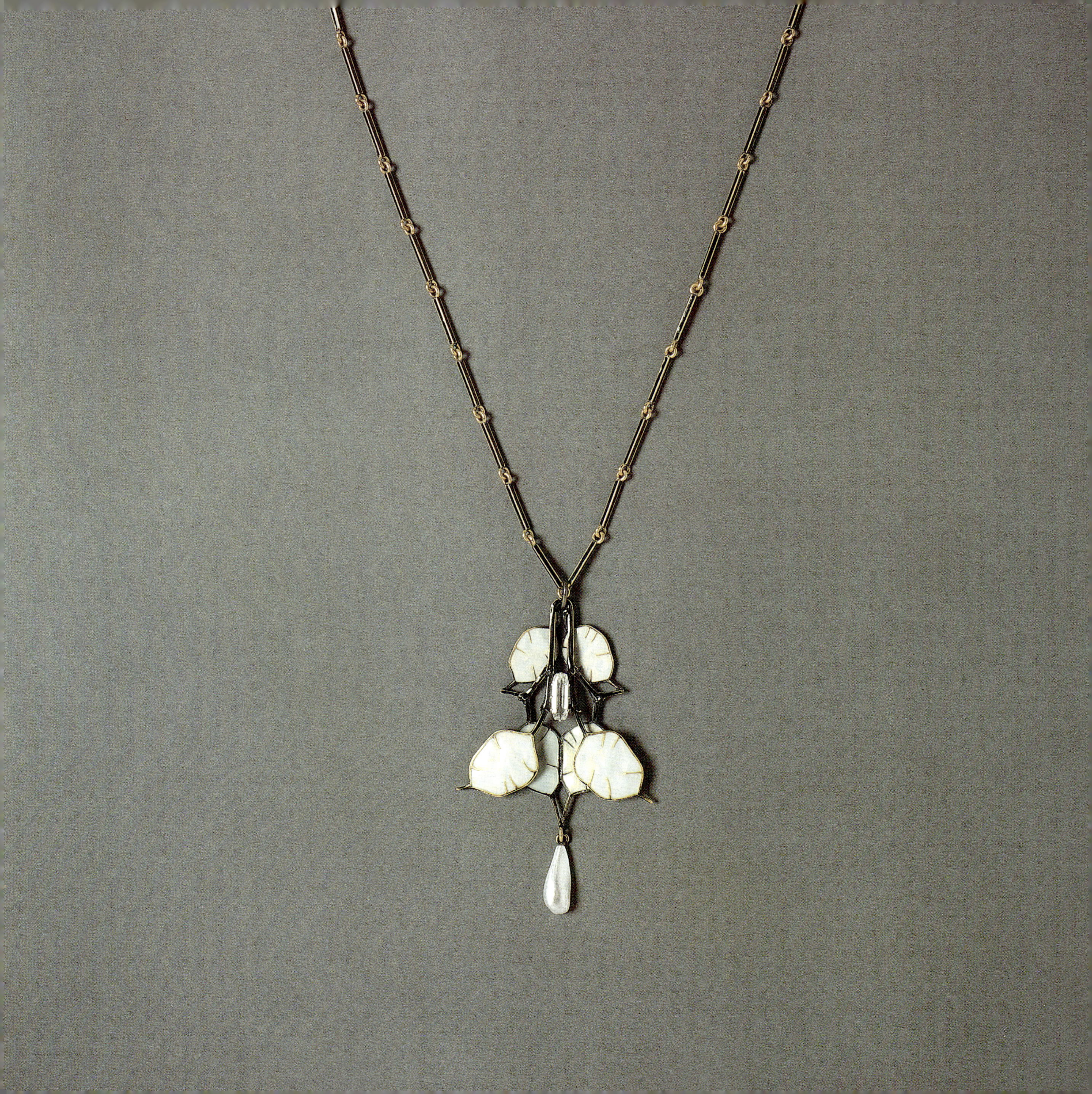

beginning with the *japonisme*-inspired ceramics of Félix Bracquemond (in the 1860s and 1870s, pieces that were reissued until well after 1900), the glass of Émile Gallé, the metalwork of Lucien Gaillard, and even in wallpaper produced for popular consumption. In 1904 *The Craftsman* called attention to critical investigations of Lalique and other jewelers on a global scale, and in particular the reception of Lalique's work in Germany. While the magazine did not elaborate on these discussions, it did signal the creative nature of designers and native critics who were eager to validate their creative responses.[14] Lalique's work in *The Craftsman* would have influenced the way design was being formulated and discussed in the United States.

The opportunity to demonstrate that American designers could indeed compete in the international design reform movement came when St. Louis hosted the Louisiana Purchase Exposition in 1904. Lalique's work was finally introduced to the United States—he had not appeared in previous American public exhibitions and this was the first opportunity to see his works in "real life." Primed for the Arts and Crafts renaissance by articles in *The Craftsman*, wealthy American collectors interested in the avant-garde were able to secure the best "jewels" at very high prices. Others among the general public were simply curious to see what the design reform movement had to offer.

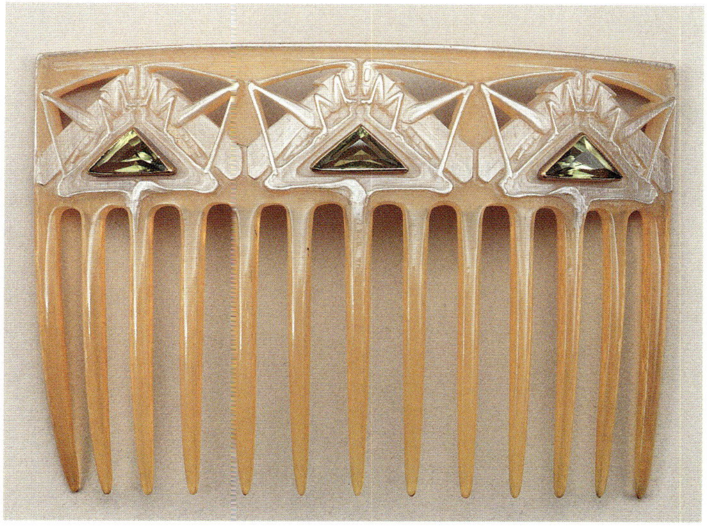

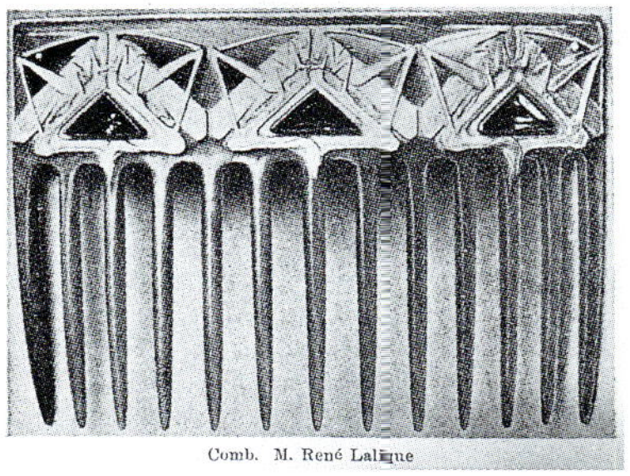

Pendant and Chain
Honesty Pod
c. 1902–1903
Gold, enamel, diamond, pearl (replacing diamond)
Pendant: 2 3/8 x 1 1/2; Chain: 21 1/2 inches
(Pendant: 6 x 3.8; Chain: 54.6 cm)
(Cat. 136)

Fig. 11
Comb
Reproduced in the article "The Insect in Decoration," by P. Verneuil, *The Craftsman*, 1903–4, vol. 5, p. 573.

Comb
Grasshoppers
1902–1904
Carved horn, tourmalines
2 1/2 x 3 1/2 inches
(6.4 x 8.9 cm)
(Cat. 96)

The Louisiana Purchase Exposition

As the largest international exposition held to that date, the Louisiana Purchase Exposition dwarfed earlier presentations in Chicago (1893), Paris (1900), and Buffalo (1901).[15] Although the exposition provided an opportunity to compare the fledgling Arts and Crafts movement in the United States with achievements in other countries, the popular press barely covered the decorative arts.[16] Significantly, outside of the Palace of Arts, where the American pieces were shown, a series of room interiors, complete in every detail, announced the Jugendstil, Art Nouveau, and Secessionist styles that were then evolving in Europe. Visitors could see the latest in interior room design and discover an alternative to the academic revivalism that often dominated the decorative arts.[17] By situating this display within the Palace of Varied Industries, near the exposition's entrance, the fair's organizers signaled an interest in crafts, new designs for room interiors, and promoting the innovative.

The installation of Lalique's imaginative "jewels" marked the first time that his pieces had been put on public display at a major American exposition. Some have argued that Lalique's works were not even shown in the Palace of Arts. Recent investigation, however, has determined that his jewels were housed in this pavilion as part of the section devoted to "original objects of art workmanship."[18] Collectors and the general public received notice of his rank in the decorative arts from a critic for *Scribner's Magazine*, who deemed him the best representative of Art Nouveau in France.[19] His work would have been compared with that of such stalwarts as Auguste Delaherche, Albert Dammouse, and Taxile Doat in French ceramics, and his creative accomplishments mentioned in league with those of Jules Habert-Dys, Edmond Lachenal, and Louis Majorelle.[20] Lalique, however, was clearly a "star" whose reputation preceded him.

Naturally, Lalique was readily compared with Tiffany, another major exhibitor in St. Louis. The perceived rivalry between these designers was exacerbated by the American press. In an article published in *The Craftsman* in 1904, the writer stressed that "Louis Tiffany resembles M. René Lalique, but he is much less radical, less original, and far more conventional than the distinguished French artist."[21] The author used Lalique as a model worthy of emulation, noting that Tiffany often found himself "a competitor of M. Lalique," although when it came to producing "jewels," the American was only a "brilliant amateur."[22] The article did acknowledge several of Tiffany's innovations and endorsed his presence at the exposition in St. Louis, yet Lalique's work demonstrated a level of quality and creativity that was seemingly unattainable for the American designer. Nevertheless, so many visitors crowded the exhibition to see major pieces by Lalique and Tiffany, including the latter's Favrile pottery and glass, that armed guards were hired to protect the displays, particularly those of Tiffany and his craftsmen.[23] Through such awareness from critics and the public alike, the applied arts came of age in the United States.

Among those who avidly appreciated Lalique's achievements were Alice Roosevelt, eldest daughter of President Theodore Roosevelt, and Helen Gould, a member of a wealthy socialite family in New York, whose mansion on Fifth Avenue was regarded as a showplace of elegant taste. Miss Roosevelt, repeatedly photographed at the exposition, (fig. 12) was keenly interested in current trends, and her fascination with Lalique suggests that politically and socially prominent families in the United States closely followed the latest trends in French decorative arts, for they wanted to obtain pieces by those craftsmen who were developing a reputation.[24] The *World's Fair Bulletin* (October 1904) noted the presence of these two young women examining Lalique's display: "A rare collection of artistic hand-wrought jewels,...executed by the celebrated Parisian artist, René Lalique, is an attractive feature of the French exhibit in the Art Palace. Since the opening of the Fair the cases containing these jewels have been visited by many persons including Miss Alice Roosevelt and Miss Helen Gould, both of whom expressed much admiration for the artistic workmanship."[25] The attention Lalique's pieces received from the popular press as well as from wealthy American socialites elevated his work to a far more visible public platform and clearly added another dimension to his favorable reception and growing reputation in the United States.

Americans from every state in the Union traveled to St. Louis to see the World's Fair, with a surprisingly large number coming from Maryland, and particularly Baltimore.[26] One among them was Henry Walters, whose wealthy father had been amassing an extensive collection of paintings and sculpture in Baltimore.[27] Evidently, sometime during the fair, young Walters attended the exhibition of Lalique pieces.[28] A collector in his own right, Walters wanted to move beyond the appreciation of work by Tiffany that had been stimulated by his purchases at the Paris Exposition Universelle in 1900, and he acquired several pieces that Lalique exhibited in St. Louis.[29] The purchase of these pieces revealed Walters' growing interest in jewelry and goldsmithing, as well as his awareness that Lalique's work bridged the gap between the fine arts and the applied arts, qualities that he admired in the Japanese decorative arts that he was amassing in his collection. As a result of his trip to St. Louis, Walters emerged as an early leading collector of Lalique in the United States. His positive response to the French craftsman who was influencing American

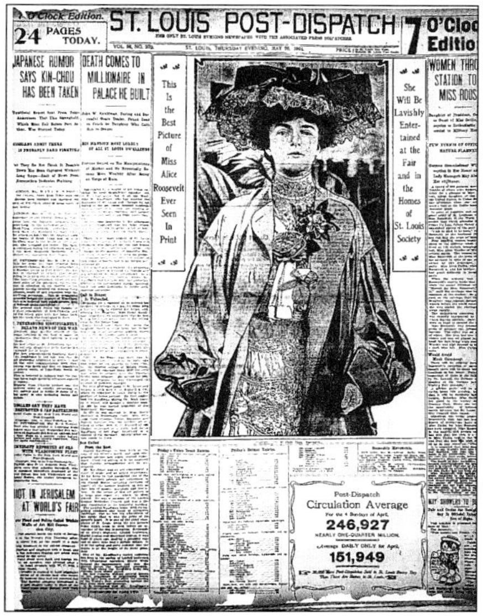
7 O'Clock Edition.
24 PAGES TODAY.
ST. LOUIS POST-DISPATCH
7 O'Cloc[k] Editio[n]

JAPANESE RUMOR SAYS KIN-CHOU HAS BEEN TAKEN

DEATH COMES TO MILLIONAIRE IN PALACE HE BUILT

This Is the Best Picture of Miss Alice Roosevelt Ever Seen In Print

She Will Be Lavishly Entertained at the Fair and in the Homes of St. Louis Society

WOMEN THRO[NG] STATION TO [SEE] MISS ROOS[EVELT]

NOT IN JERUSALEM AT WORLD'S FAIR

Post-Dispatch
Circulation Average
For the 4 Sundays of April,
246,927
NEARLY ONE-QUARTER MILLION.
Average DAILY ONLY for April,
151,949

Fig. 12
Photograph of Miss Alice Roosevelt
Reproduced in the *St. Louis Post Dispatch*, May 26, 1904, p. 1.

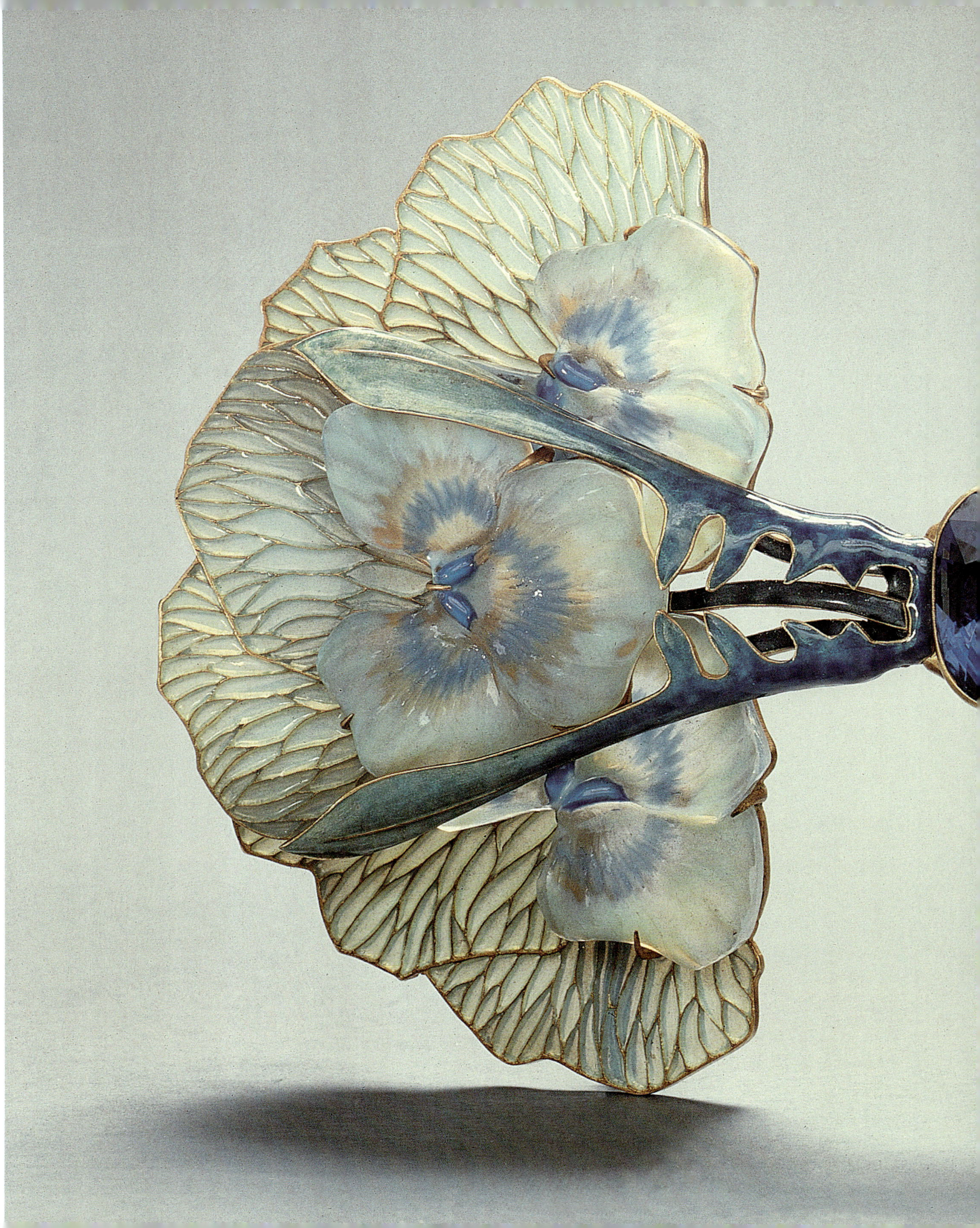

Corsage
Ornament
Pansies
1903–1904
Gold, enamel
on gold, *plique-à-jour* enamel,
cast glass,
sapphire
3 1/16 x 5 1/2
inches
(8.1 x 13.9 cm)
(Cat. 124)

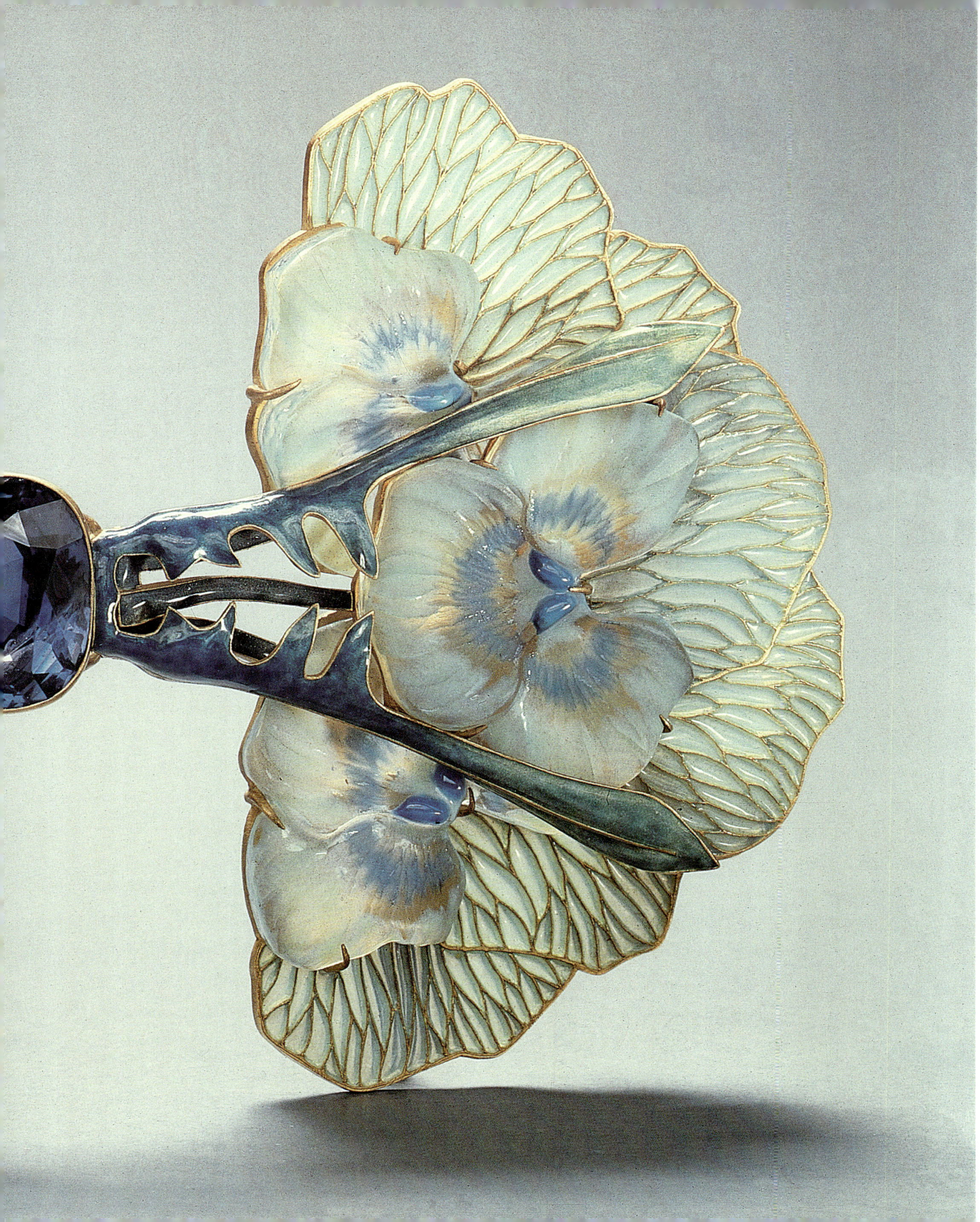

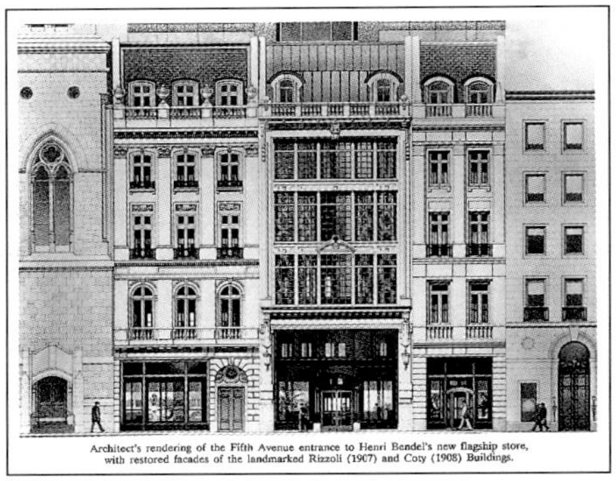

Fig. 13
The Coty Building in New York
1912

designers and creators played a crucial role in attracting Americans to Lalique. Walters' acquisitions, which did not receive attention in public or artistic journals of the time, disappeared into his private collection of jewelry, where they could be seen only on request. This was perhaps done to maintain secrecy about the high prices he paid, and it may well have been in keeping with his own reclusive personality. Only in later years was his collection identified as an outstanding example of the Art Nouveau aesthetic in America[30] (cats. 98, 126).

Among the nine pieces that Walters purchased in St. Louis were several, such as a pansy brooch, that demonstrated Lalique's ability to create natural forms by using a *plique-à-jour* enamel process. The variation of color in the "blossoms" is indicative of the Art Nouveau aesthetic (cat. 126) that stressed the creative utilization of nature. Other, less radical brooches showed a more symmetrical style that eventually dominated Lalique's work in glass, a material he increasingly employed after 1909.[31] Even so, Walters' large acquisition in 1904 confirms that he, like so many others in the United States, had been captivated by Lalique's design and craftsmanship. Lalique's status had been so magnified by the press that the Frenchman had assumed an almost cultlike significance in America.

Lalique visited the United States at the time of the St. Louis Exposition, arriving in New York City on April 24, 1904. While we know that he stayed in New York at the elegant Waldorf-Astoria Hotel, accompanied by his wife, Alice, it is now established that he traveled on to St. Louis before going to Buffalo (May 1, 1904) and returning to New York (May 19, 1904) prior to embarking on the *Savoie* for the return journey to France (May 26, 1904).[32] A notation in the original manifest of "alien passengers" aboard the *Savoie*, Lalique's ship for both Atlantic crossings, curiously gave the jeweler's destination as the Waldorf Astoria hotel in New York rather than St. Louis.[33] In Alice Lalique's letters to her daughter, Suzanne, in Paris she noted that they were "installing the vitrines" in St. Louis (May 3, 1904) and that by May 7 the "installation (of Lalique's jewels) while very difficult to do" was widely admired. "It was a great success."[34] Still, the fact that Lalique had other contacts in America beyond those associated with the St. Louis Fair, and that he noted in the official ship's registration that he had been to the United States at an earlier time (although the exact date was not recorded) raises the issue of whether Lalique had more extensive knowledge and contacts in America than has yet been fully discovered.

Further American Perceptions of Lalique

In June 1905, Lalique's work attracted considerable attention in the staid *New York Times*. In a section dedicated to "Society at

Home and Abroad," Lalique's pieces were discussed in a column that stressed the "personal and otherwise," another indication of how owning one of his pieces had become a status symbol.[35] His jewelry for the hair was deemed "attractive ornaments," and his technical mastery of enameling was appreciated. Indeed, as if well aware of discussions in the specialized art press, the writer pointed out the lavender or mauve tints in Lalique's combs, two tones that were thought appropriate for the era. By emphasizing the artist's penchant for "flowers as designs" and his use of butterflies or insects on brooches and pendants, the writer suggested that the best way to appreciate a Lalique object was through an interest in nature. More important, the author set Lalique apart from those jewelers who relied almost exclusively on the use of diamonds. He distinguished between what was vulgar—a dependency on diamonds—and refined—the incorporation of a variety of materials.[36] Commenting on Lalique's inventiveness, the author emphasized the use of stones and other materials, such as horn and mother-of-pearl, and the ability to enhance a piece's brilliance by varying the colors and sizes of stones. "Why the diamond should have ever attained its great prestige must ever remain a mystery to the artist. Diamonds are merely glitter and alone suggest nothing, but wealth....Lalique is a master of the art of enameling and leans toward amethysts, peridots, and topazes."[37] Lalique's work was deemed supremely artistic, one of the higher compliments of the day, and his new creative aesthetic was presented to the general public who read *The New York Times*. That the discussion of Lalique took place in the society pages suggests that a wide range of Americans, from the average reader to the upper elite who traveled abroad, had become aware of his international reputation. It also indicates that collectors were increasingly willing to acquire a piece by Lalique because he created in the Art Nouveau style, which was then becoming popular in America, and his jewels had assumed a degree of prestige that made them attractive to high society.

By 1912, interest in René Lalique as a master craftsman was furthered by the appearance of an insightful pamphlet prepared under the auspices of Haviland and Company, manufacturers of ceramics, in New York.[38] The author, J. Nilsen Laurvik, correctly assessed the contribution of Lalique's turn-of-the-century jewelry as having "commanded special attention." His recognition that the pieces introduced a "new style" of jewelry went far in giving Lalique credit for having fostered the appearance of Art Nouveau. The impact that the jewelry had on other craftsmen and potential owners was notable. Laurvik wrote that from this moment jewelry was "regarded as a spot of color in which the *tout ensemble* of a lady's apparel finds its fitting culmination: the final touch that accents and

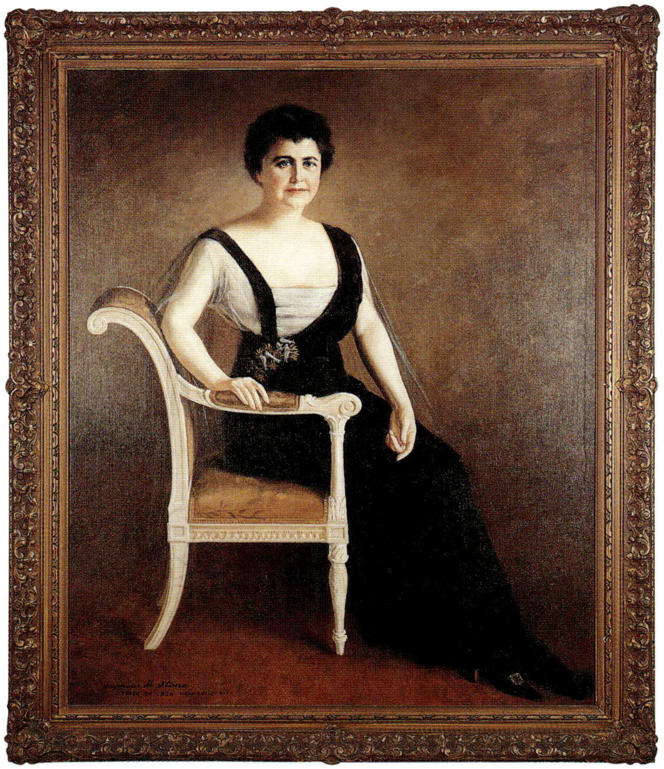

On December 13, 1918, President Woodrow Wilson, accompanied by his wife Edith Bolling Wilson, arrived in France for the negotiations that would forge the peace treaty at the end of World War I. On December 16, the Wilsons were received with great ceremony at the Hôtel de Ville. After the official speeches, President Wilson was presented with a specially struck gold medal and with a gold pen to use when he signed the peace agreement. Edith Wilson was then surprised to receive "a corsage brooch—the work of René Lalique—composed of olive branches set with diamonds and on which sit eight white enamel doves."

Annotations on the preparatory drawing for this piece (which also shows a pendant stone) indicate that the birds were originally conceived as pigeons. While nearly indistinguishable ornithologically, pigeons and doves are far removed iconographically. Apparently, more than ten years after the creation of the brooch, the birds were reinterpreted as doves, identifying the brooch's iconography as a symbol of peace.

When in 1920 the First Lady had her portrait painted by Seymour Stone, the Lalique brooch was very prominently featured at the waist of her stylish black and white gown. Originally intended for the White House, the portrait hangs today above the fireplace in the dining room of the Woodrow Wilson house in Washington. *JTR*

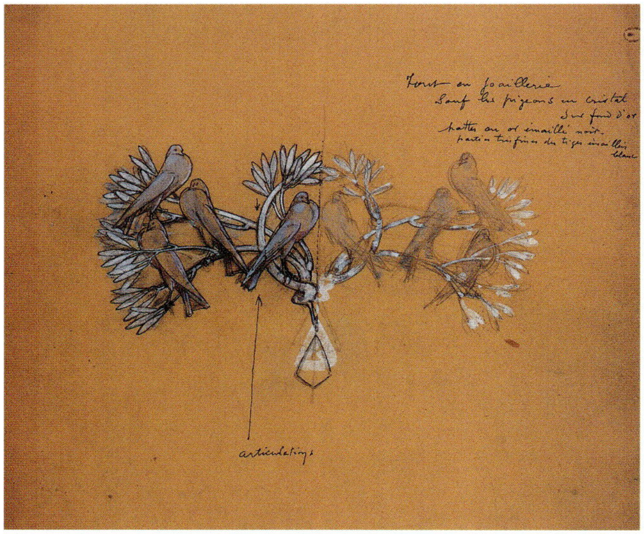

Fig. 14
Seymour Stone
Portrait of Edith Bolling Wilson
1920

Design for a Corsage Ornament
Pigeons on Olive Branches
c. 1905–1906
Pencil, ink, watercolor on paper
11 x 8 5/8 inches (27.8 x 22.1 cm)
(Cat. 164)

Brooch
Doves on Olive Branches
c. 1905–1906
Gold, enamel, cast glass, diamonds
6 x 2 1/2 inches (15.5 x 6.5 cm)
(Cat. 139)

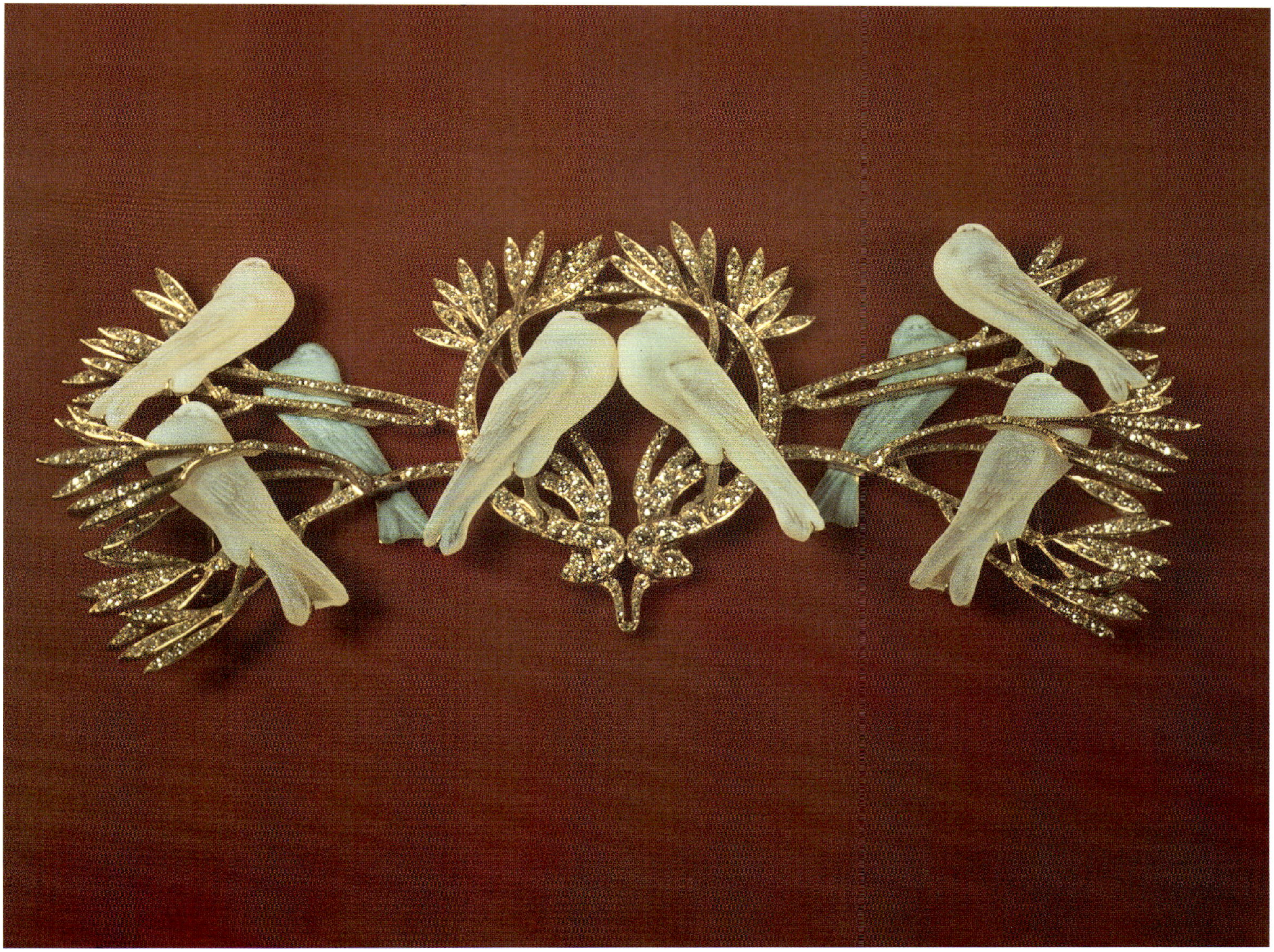

This remarkable, archaeologically based corsage pin, exhibited at the Exposition Universelle in 1900, is unique in Lalique's œuvre. The flat, oval-shaped openwork scene depicts a nude female figure, presumably a maenad, confronted by three satyrs. The figures are enhanced on the obverse with grayish enamel carved in low relief, an exacting technique that Lalique used at this time for a number of pieces. The scene is carefully chased in gold on the reverse. This medallion reproduces, with slight modifications, and in reverse, part of a figural group on a fifth-century B.C.E. Attic red-figure cylix, or drinking cup, by the Brygos Painter in the British Museum, which Lalique may have seen on one of his trips to London. JTR

Corsage Pin
Finial
or Hat Pin
Maenad and Satyrs
c. 1899–1900
Gold, translucent enamel on gold, opal
3 3/8 x 3 7/8 inches
(8.7 x 9.7 cm)
(Cat. 106)

Following double page
Brooch-Corsage Ornament
Fish
c. 1904–1905
Gold, *plique-à-jour* enamel, diamonds, glass
4 7/8 x 2 3/4 inches
(12.4 x 7 cm)
(Cat. 134)

reveals the general harmony of the whole."[39] Lalique was seen as an initiator of a fashion in which jewelry helped create an overall artistic or aesthetic impression. It was no longer regarded just as an expensive accessory.

Throughout the discussion, Laurvik also emphasized Lalique's qualities as a designer and craftsman who placed his reliance on "good work." The pamphlet carefully argued that Lalique had not degenerated into a figure willing only to pander to popular commercial taste. He was recognized as someone ever interested in pursuing the "fertility of invention," qualities that had first been visible in his jewelry. At the same time, while acknowledging that new technology had often led to the general "decay" of craftsmanship, Laurvik praised Lalique's ability to use the "machine without in the least affecting the artistic quality of his productions."[40] This ability was seen as one of Lalique's primary contributions to design and placed his "artistic jewelry" at the forefront of his creative excellence.

In response to this renewed recognition of Lalique's work, *The Craftsman* once again discussed another aspect of Lalique's significance in America. Not only did his objects meet the fashionable needs of the elite, but they made him one of the principle creators of a "new art" in France. "Lalique, of all the modern Frenchmen, has done [much] to freshen and rejuvenate the art spirit."[41] The critic stressed Lalique's interest in simplicity as an aesthetic hallmark of his creative approach. He saw Lalique as fearless in his "design, in his color, and yet never without purpose....He has never ornamented purely for the sake of decoration...."[42] This subtle evaluation of Lalique's place as a creator further cemented his esteemed position in the United States. When this article is paired with the detailed examination of Lalique's work by Laurvik, it becomes clear that the years just before World War I marked a moment of intense recognition in the United States for Lalique's overall creative contribution. With these publications keeping his work before the public and interpreting what he had achieved, there is little wonder that Lalique's name was not far from the lips of those who wanted to secure a meaningful gift for an important person.

When the people of Paris decided to honor President Woodrow Wilson in 1918 by presenting him with the Freedom of the City award, they gave Mrs. Wilson something that would be appropriate and widely understood: a Lalique brooch in gold studded with diamonds in the shape of "doves of peace" perched among the branches[43] (cat. 139). In this way, the people of Paris and the French government not only honored what had been achieved between the two countries, but they also acknowledged Lalique's status in America. This gift verified that Lalique's imagery and creative artistry had assumed a level of recognition and importance that crossed all barriers of nationality and class.

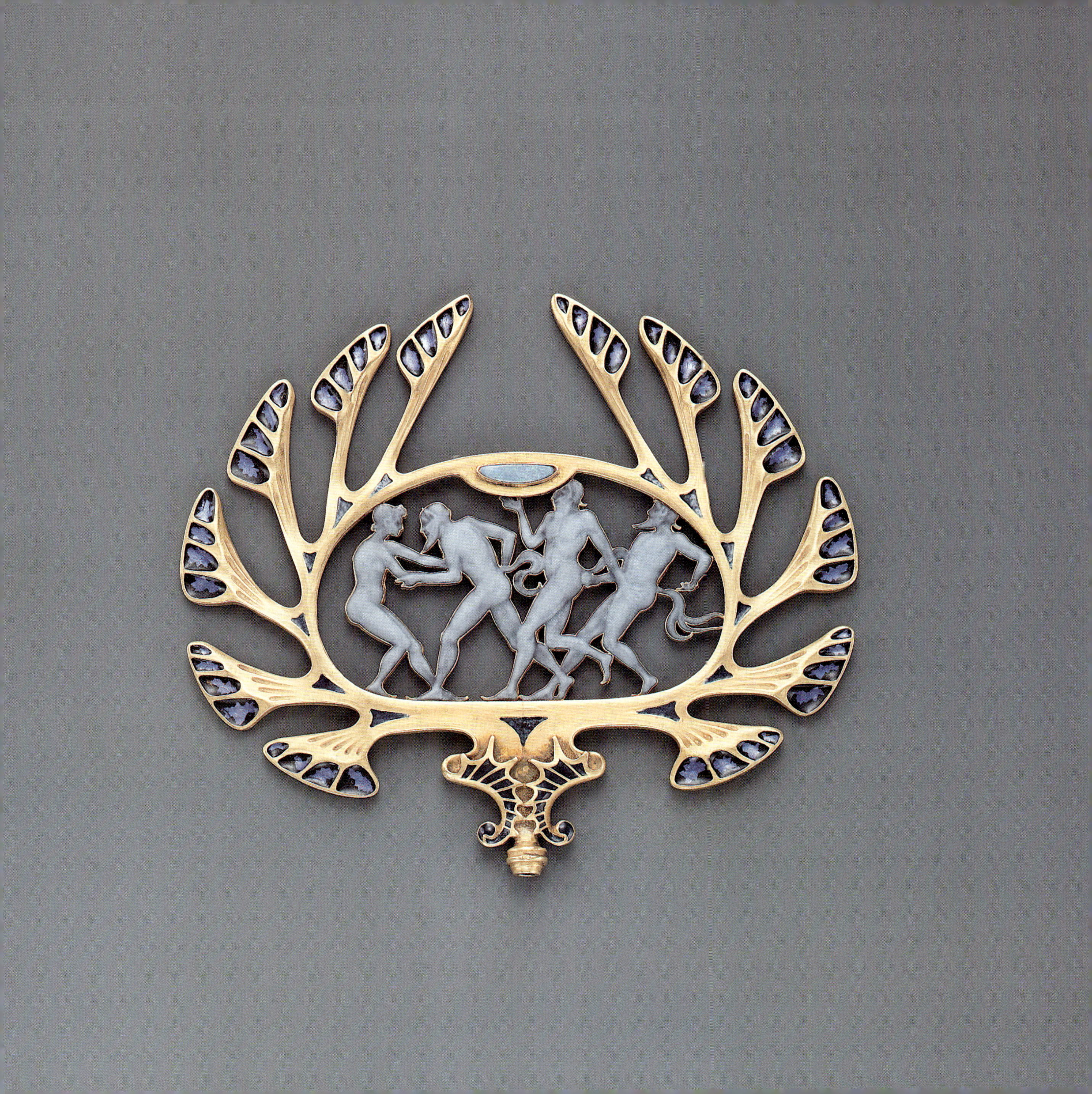

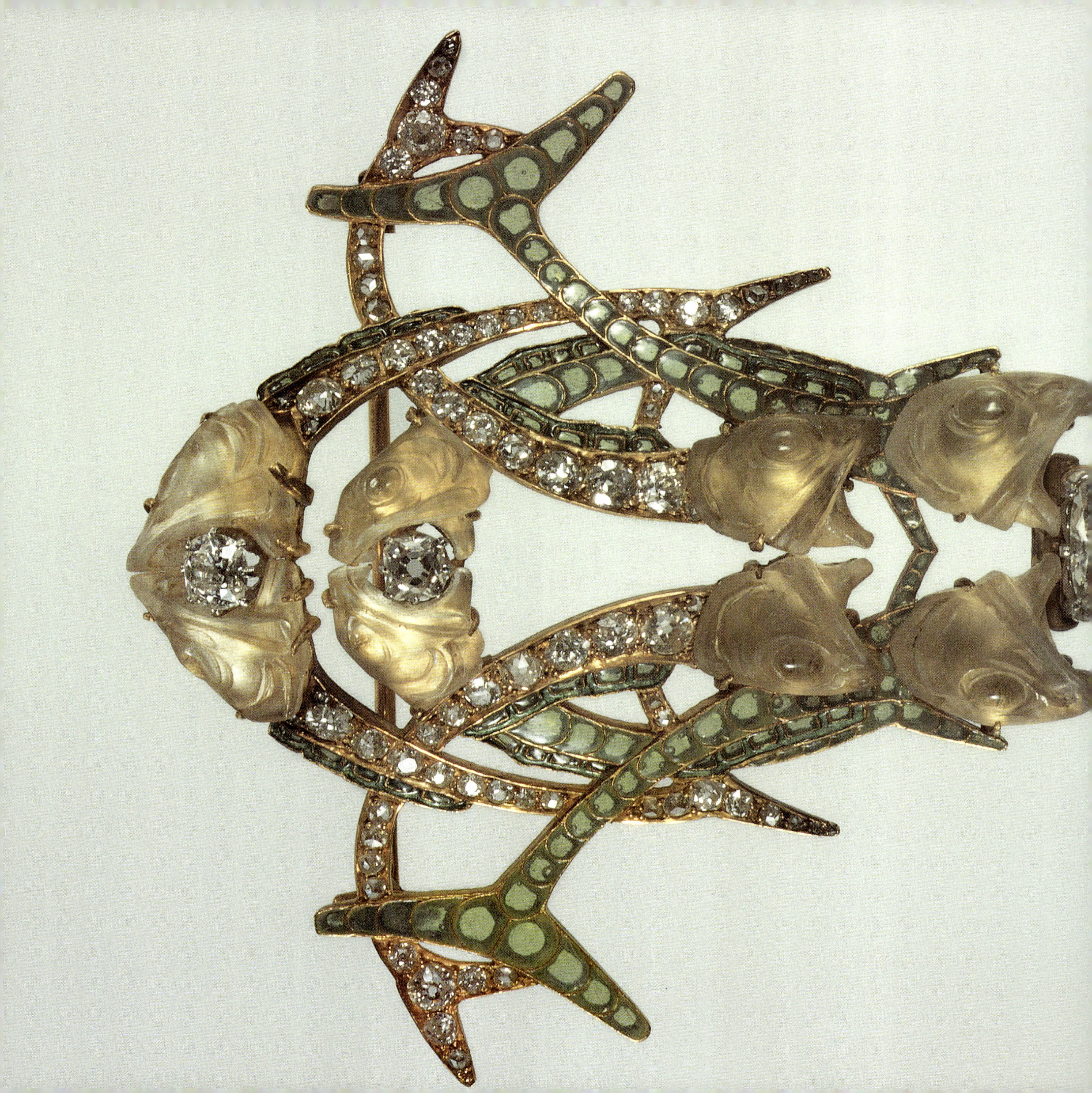

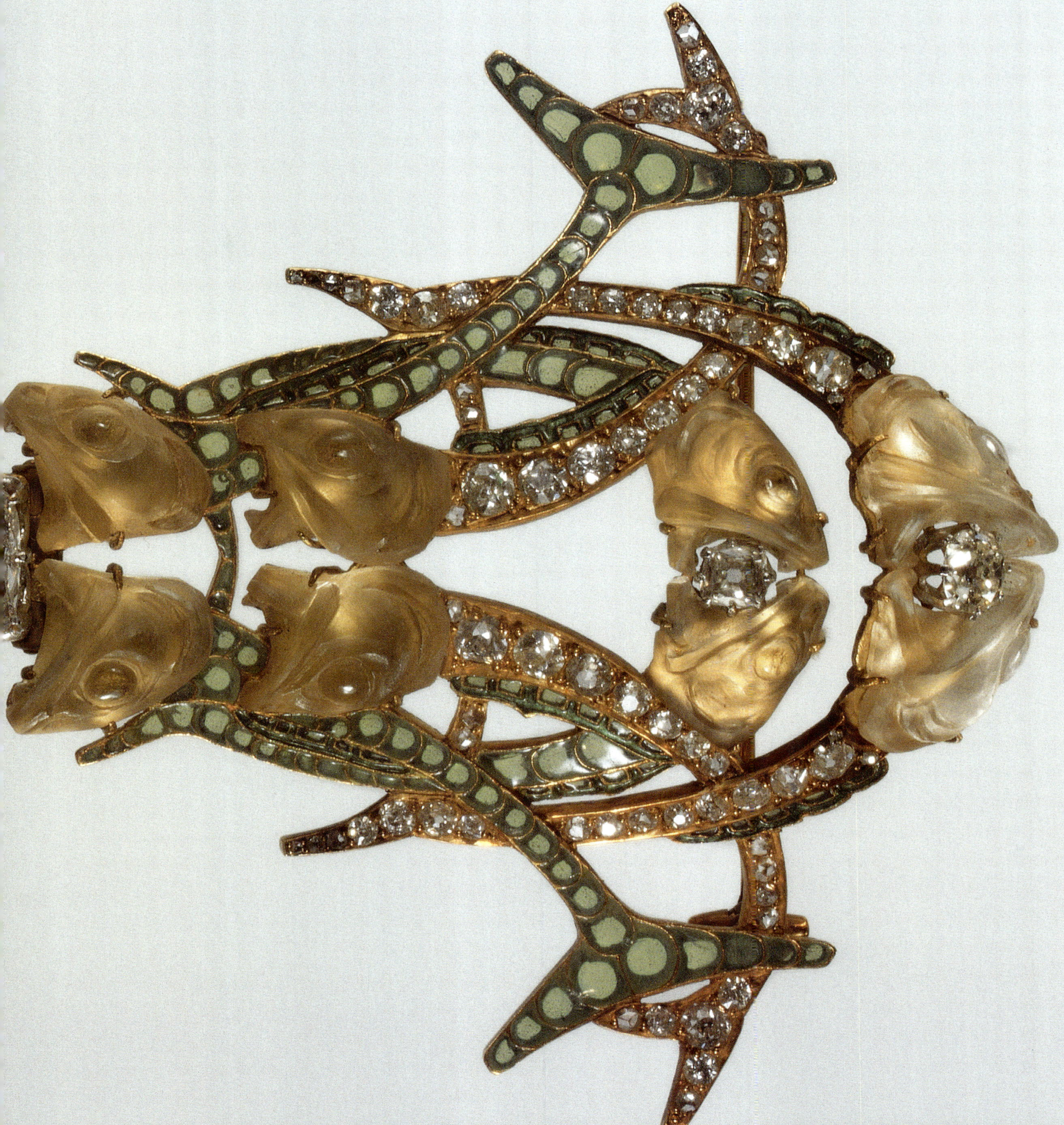

Lalique and Fashion

FLORENCE MÜLLER

As regenerator of the art of jewelry and the sworn enemy of the historicism and mannerism which held sway over the *fin de siècle*,[1] René Lalique stood out in contemporary eyes as an artist of the avant-garde. In those days, fashion was all too pleased to bow to convention and follow a measured, middle course. The toilettes for which Lalique made his pieces were styled to this environment of conformism. Paradoxically, though the artist was admired by all, seldom did his works meet with the approbation of women brave enough to wear them, since his jewelry conflicted with the *bon ton* which determined the attire of Belle Époque beauties. The links between Lalique and fashion lie outside the domain of style, and go beyond the design of the feminine toilettes of the period. For Lalique, the ample formal vocabulary of fashion seemed to offer merely a pretext for new creations.

The taste of the Belle Époque for jewelry parures was by no means unconnected with the interest that Lalique's work aroused. The period adored jewelry: "fashion dictates that one should wear as much jewelry as possible."[2] This penchant for jewelry, which at the time was attributed to American women, favored excesses of every kind: diamonds were worn in the day, men chose the finest stones and pearls for hat- or tiepins, for rings, buttons, watch chains, and chatelaines. For Christmas 1897, the voguish English jewelers offered curious pieces on a cycling theme: bracelets made of miniature bicycles together with chain bracelets and belts in the form of spoked wheels! Every day, new trinkets were created: jointed dolls, enormous hearts enclosing portraits, and fetishes such as the tortoise, the four-leaf clover, the little pink pig, or else, with a hint of modernity, St. Christophers intended to protect the

Tiara
Ivy Leaves
c. 1904–1905
Horn, gold, diamonds, tortoiseshell
3 1/2 x 7 3/8 x 6 inches
(8.9 x 18.7 x 15.2 cm)
(Cat. 77)

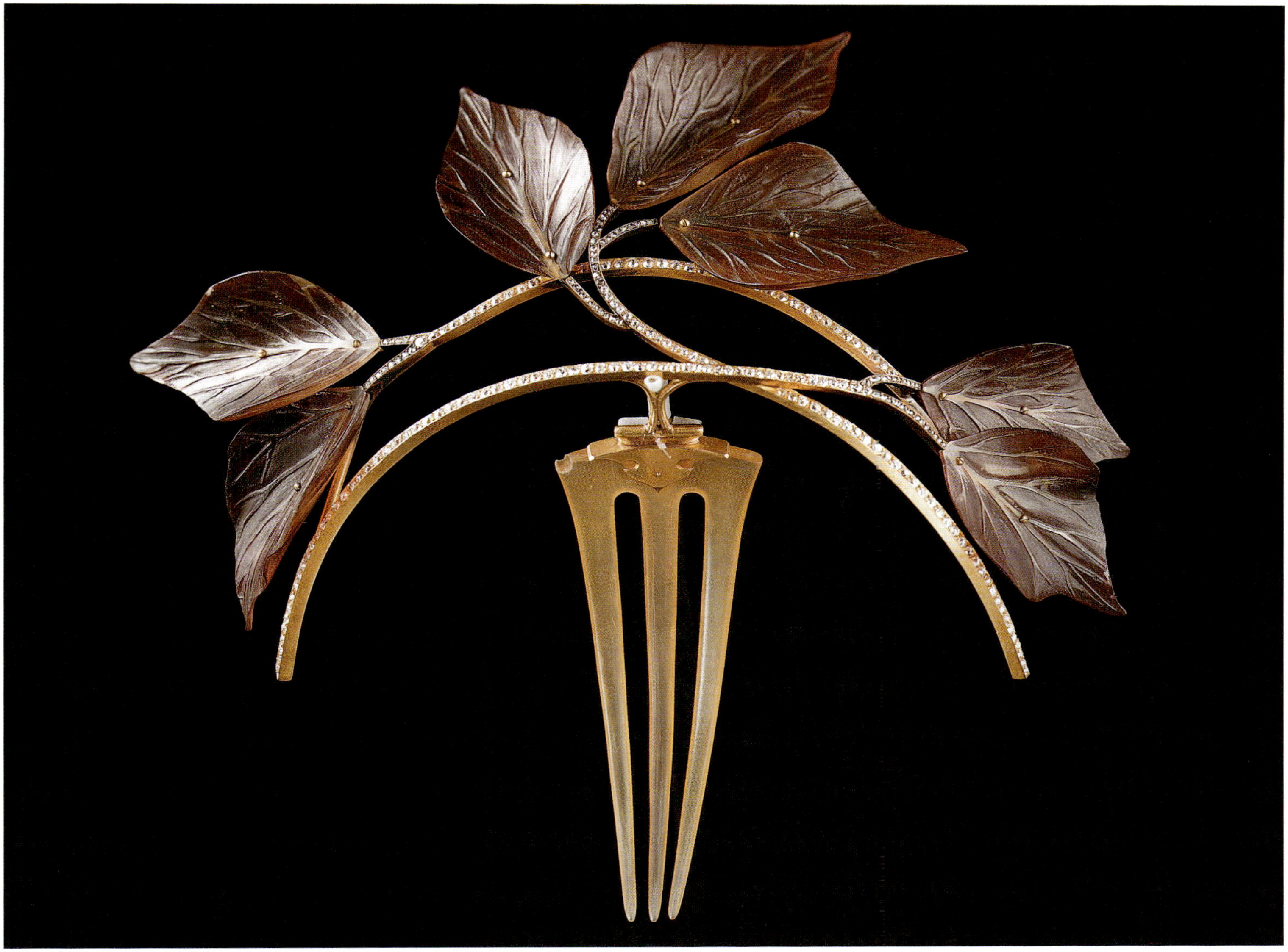

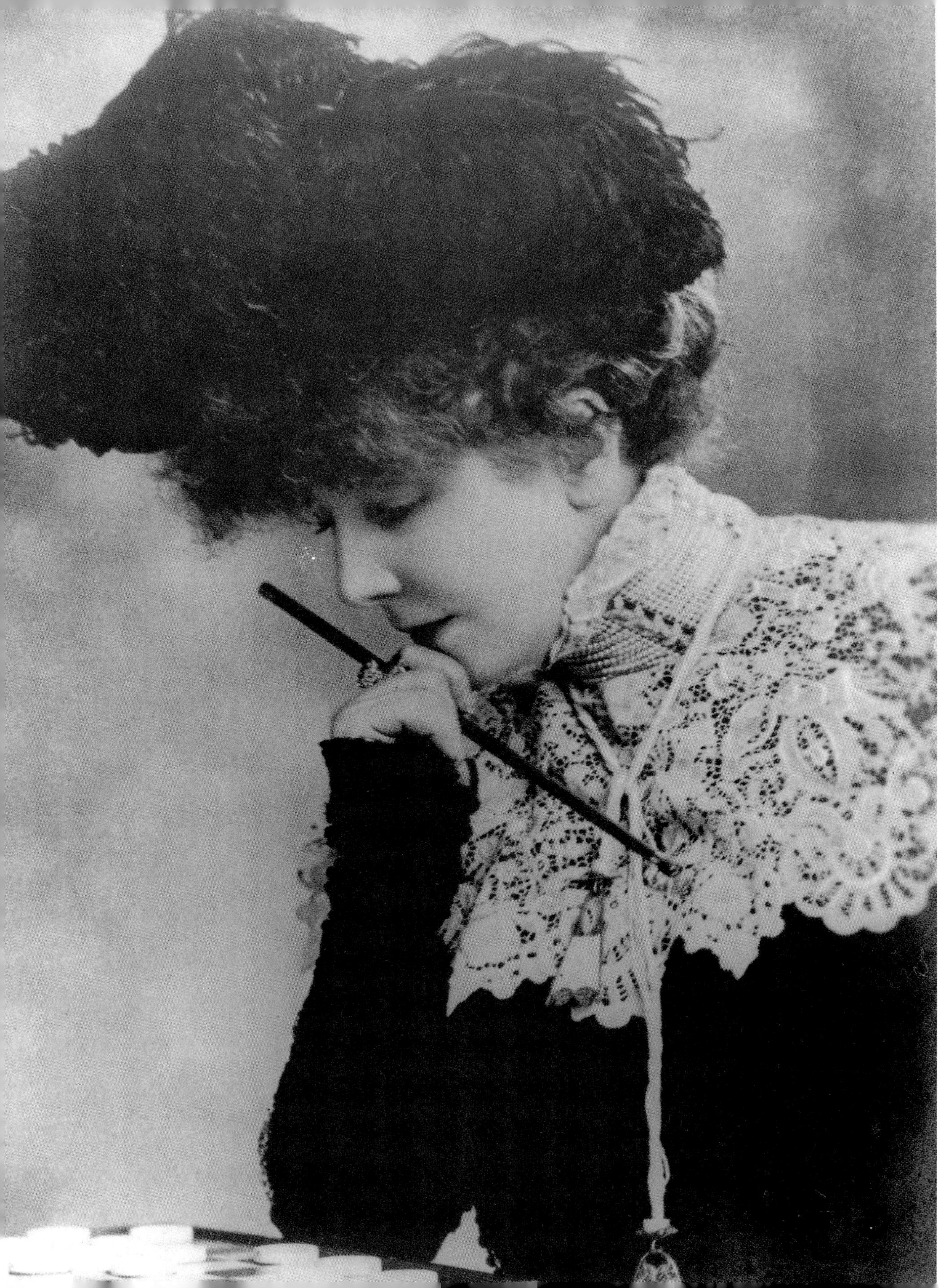

Left
Fig. 15
Sarah
Bernhardt
at a Game of
Checkers
Photograph
showing the
actress with a
bayadere chain
by Lalique, a
dog collar, and
a ring.

Right
Fig. 16
Sarah
Bernhardt
Dressed for the
City

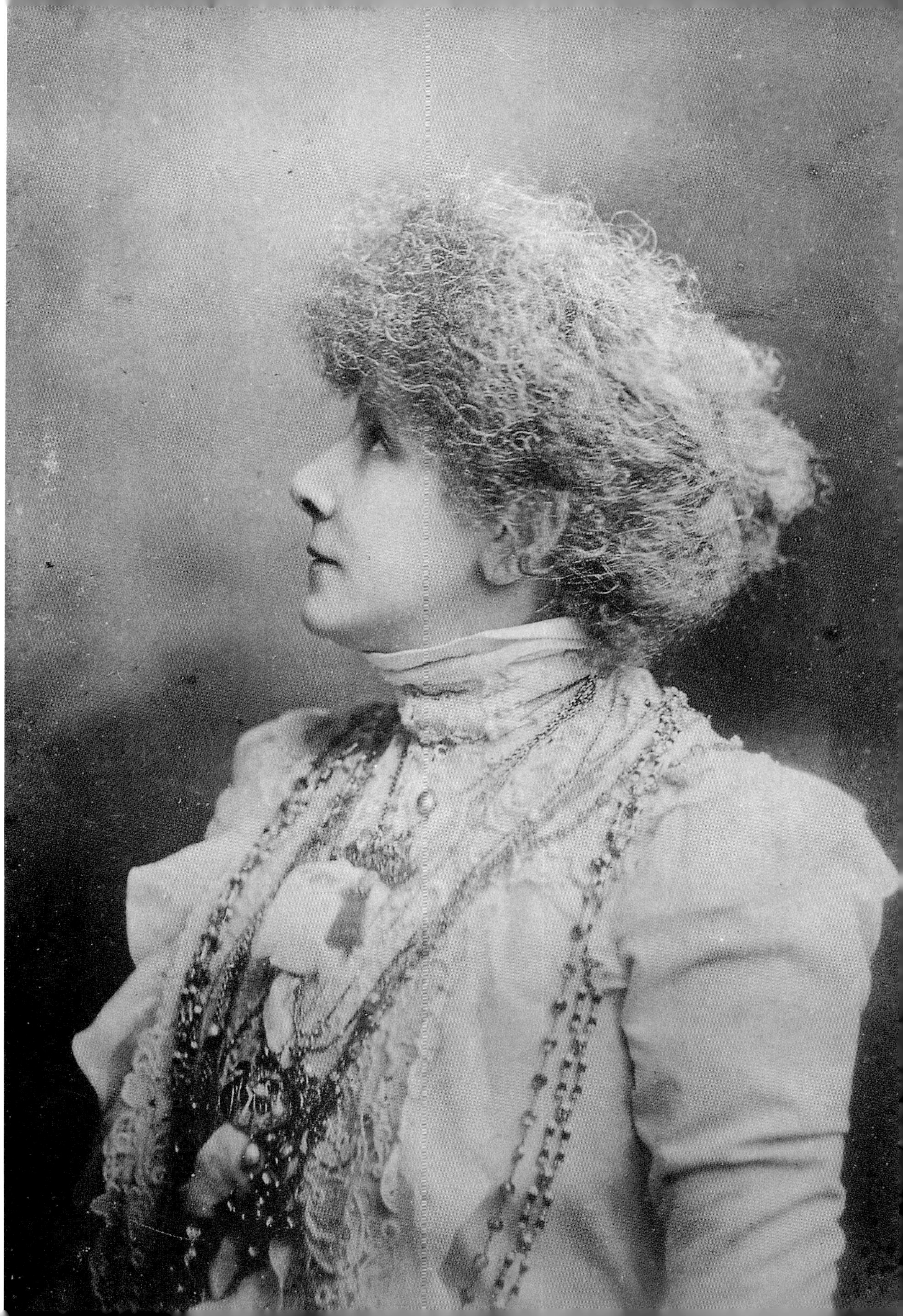

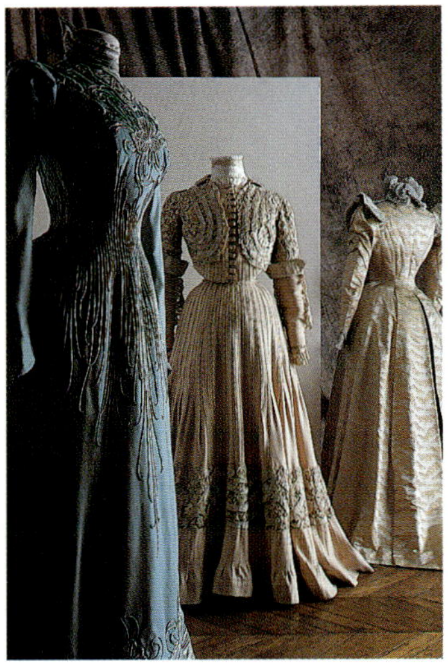

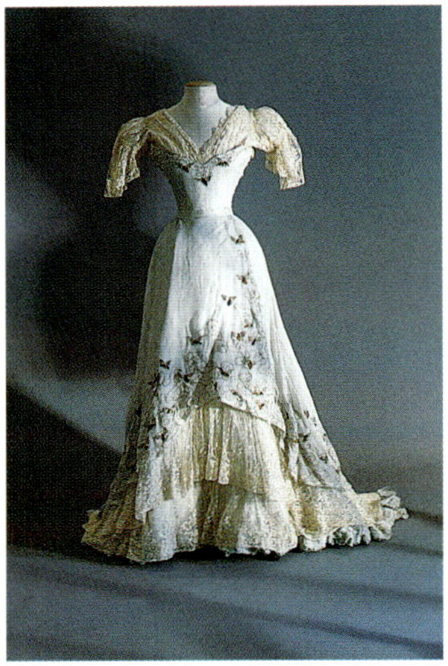

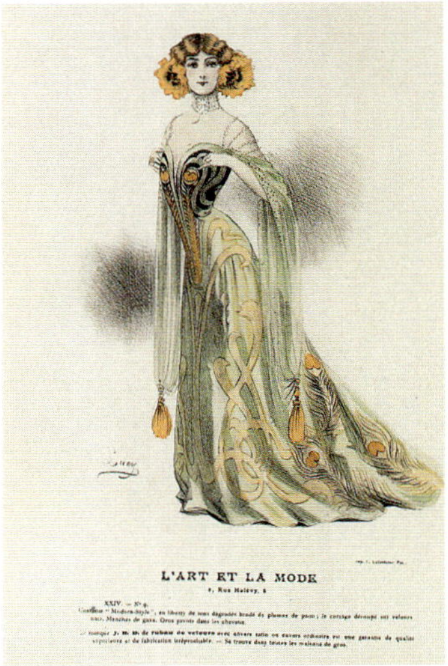

Left
Fig. 17
Dresses from the Collection E. Cogenheim of 1898
UAD Coll. inv. 32188AB
Musée des Arts de la Mode

Center
Fig. 18
Dress by Jacques Doucet Embroidered with Wasps
UFAC Coll. inv. 55-58-26

Right
Fig. 19
Drawing of Lucy wearing a "Modern Style" Costume
From *L'Art et la Mode*, February 28, 1903, no. 3, pp. 178–79.

automobile traveler on the road. The famous "slave" chains known as *esclavages* typify a desire to have woman set like a gem, chained even in the morning with pearls and diamonds—like those of Mme. de Yturbe, a lady of society—with a belt of seven rows of fine pearls and a chain of rings of diamonds slung over the shoulder. A woman of elegance would encase herself in these *esclavages* by rolling them around her waist and arms, hanging watches, powder compacts, or lorgnettes from them, and binding up her hair in enormous ropes of pearls. In the evening, not content with strangling herself with high dog-collars around the throat, she let several long rows of pearls hang down almost to the floor, positioning them like epaulettes above the sleeves. The pearls, ranged on both sides of the décolleté or over the shoulder, and held in place by some pretty jewel, emphasized the ample curve of the bosom. Such a woman was a prisoner, beset on all sides by jewelry, held fast in a tight dress and a suffocating corset. Yet these articles of personal adornment also enshrine the triumph of femininity, particularly that of those professional beauties and wily courtesans who would blithely spend fortunes at the jeweler's. Thus the celebrated *demimondaine* depicted by Jean Cocteau: "Fist on hips, decked out in pearls, girded in diamonds, Liane de Pougy advanced through the tables at Maxim's with all the indifference of a planet."[3]

As one fashion editor noted, the all-pervasive *bijou* "is such an integral part of our toilette that it turns up at our couturier's, our milliner's and our hairdresser's."[4] Everything that had been, until then, a simple accessory—belt clasps, chains, hair- or hatpins—was treated as *joaillerie*: "Right down to her hatpin, everything is lavish in a Parisienne's attire."[5] Women were quick to plant vast strings of real pearls on a hat to keep it perched atop the gossamer framework of some hairstyle, and hairdressers offered customers wavy combs studded with pearls and diamonds. In 1898, Lady Hertopp appeared at the Duchess of Devonshire's ball, dazzlingly costumed as the Empress Josephine in a dress covered with emeralds and diamonds.

Viewing such a splash of precious stones, one would naturally associate the splendor of the gems with the illustrious rank of their owners. The grandest of ladies often resorted to such subtle subterfuge as a way of affirming their status in a dignified manner. At Vienna in November 1896, for the wedding of the duc d'Orléans and the Archduchess Maria-Dorothea of Austria, the duchesse de Broglie, so as to appear in her best finery at the various events, had brought the family jewels with her. An episode recounted by her daughter, however, reveals the truth behind contemporary appearances: "When the hairdresser came to dress my mother's hair before the gala performance at the Imperial Theater, he looked piteously at her diamonds, which were tiny and set in an old-fashioned style. Then, with some aplomb, he drew from his valise a superb tiara of false emeralds and stuck it in the middle of her chignon, adding: 'worn by a princess like you, everyone will believe that it is a family heirloom. One must do one's best to impress these people.'"[6]

The practice of wearing fakes doubtless contributed to the gradual acceptance and widespread use of costume jewelry in elegant parures.[7] At the time, such jewelry was termed *bijou artistique*, and appeared prominently in the coverage of fashion magazines such as *L'Art et la Mode*. In the constant search for the novel and the unexpected, costume jewelry can always outdo work in authentic gemstones. This meant that people looked approvingly on the work of artists such as Falize or Lalique, "who bestow nobility on even the most humble of objects."[8] Women once again found semi-precious stones fashionable, such as the opal and amethyst promoted by Lalique in 1898 and 1903 respectively.

Lalique had relatively little influence on fashion, apart from a few fads generated by some of his jewelry. But his contemporaries held his work in high esteem, acknowledging it as art rather than craft. Such accolades,

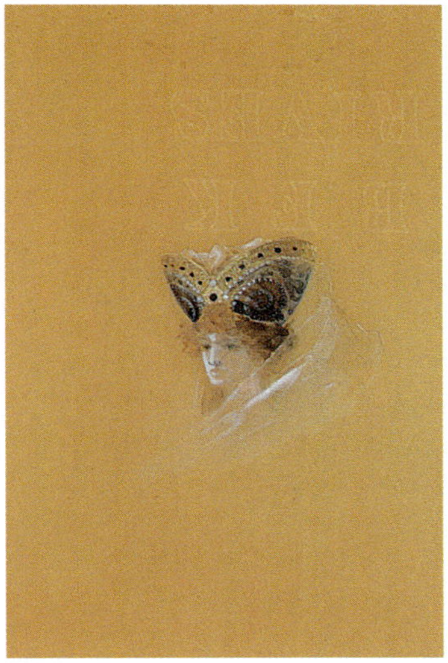

Drawing
Sarah Bernhardt in Theater Headdress
c. 1894
Pencil, watercolor, gouache on paper
10 1/2 x 8 3/8 inches
(26.6 x 21.3 cm)
(Cat. 24)

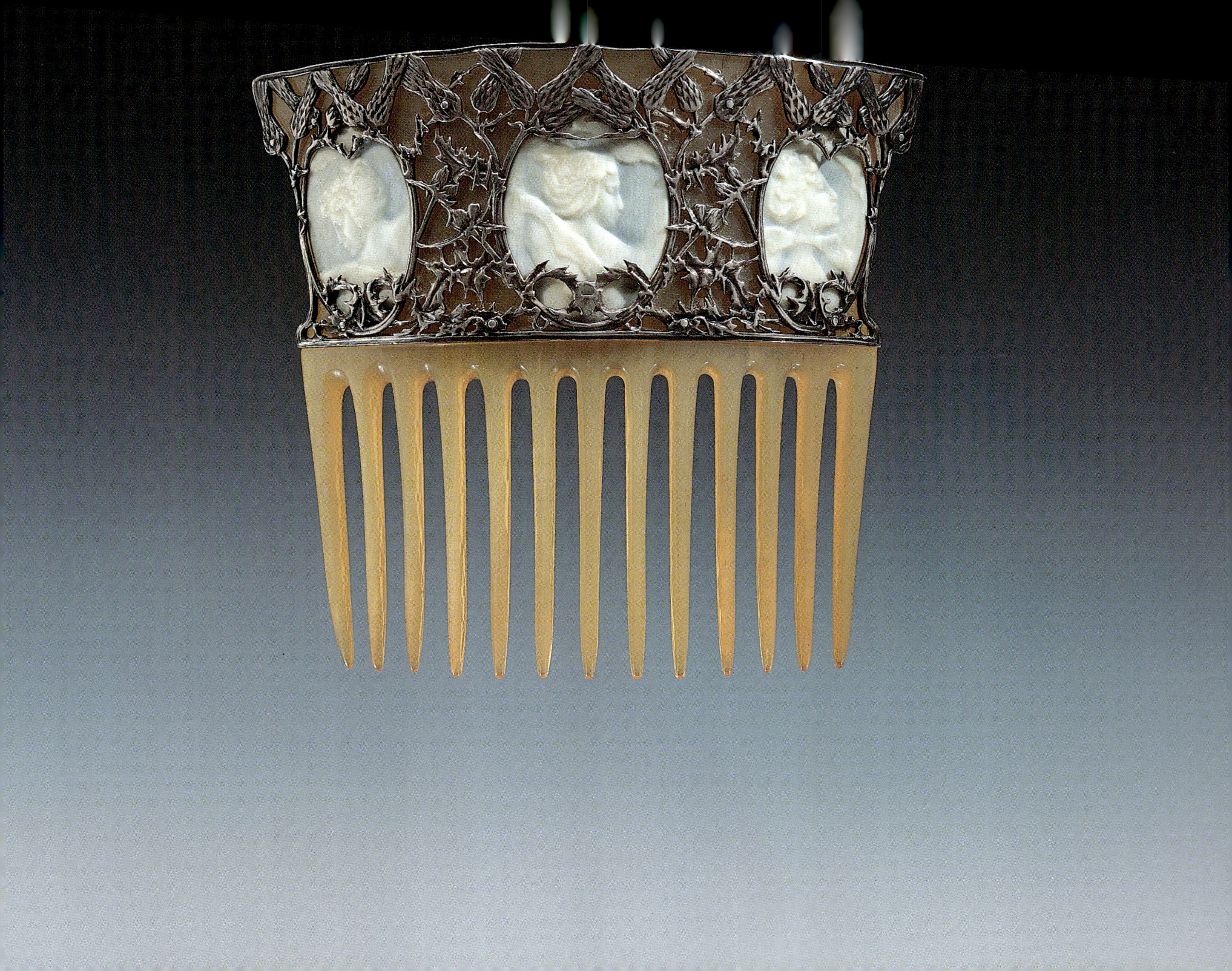

however, were of no use to the wearer. Critics were quick to lambast the overly original character of these pieces as "eccentric, unwearable, mere showpieces or museum objects....It is incontrovertible: Lalique's jewelry is seen but very rarely in society and is almost never met with in the street, at the theater or at grand receptions."[9] The few women audacious enough to sport Lalique's pieces belonged to artistic circles, those furthest removed from convention, and they were able to appreciate the beauty of an object despite the inexpensive nature of the materials from which it was made. Actresses and courtesans practiced the arts of seduction and mystery. Like Sarah Bernhardt, (figs. 15, 16) Emma Calvé, Natalie Clifford-Barney, Liane de Pougy, or even Madame Meurlot-Chollet the sculptor, they were glad of objects which told a story or elicited feelings, which struck a chord with their entourage or provoked astonishment. Even if the richness of the motifs in Lalique's work is difficult to transmit from a distance, such women remained partial to "the solemn profundity of his symbolism."

Only a few high-society ladies, such as the comtesse de Béarn and the marquise Arconati-Visconti, dared to ornament their toilette with jewelry by Lalique. In general, however, such women opted for ornament whose magnificence would best proclaim their family's illustrious ancestry or the extent of its wealth. If Lalique's jewelry often adorned the baskets of gifts presented

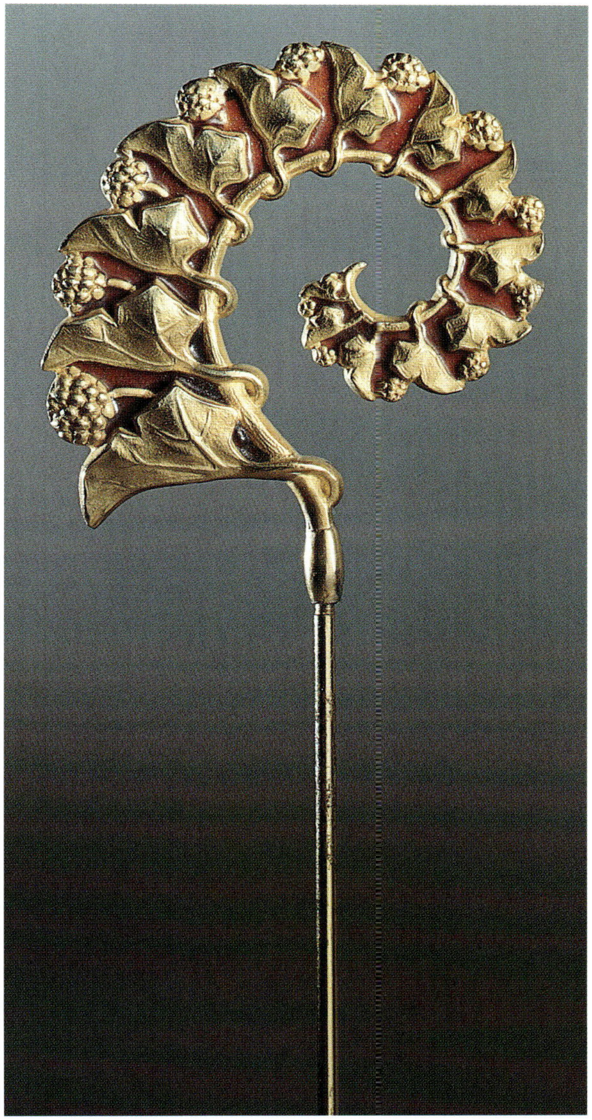

Comb
Medallions and Thistles
c. 1901–1903
Horn, enamel, ivory, silver
4 x 4 1/4 inches
(10 x 10.7 cm)
(Cat. 115)

Hatpin
Ivy and Clover
c. 1900
Chased gold, translucent enamel on gold
7 3/4 x 1 1/4; motif 1 1/4 inches
(19.8 x 3.4; motif 3.3 cm)
(Cat. 74)

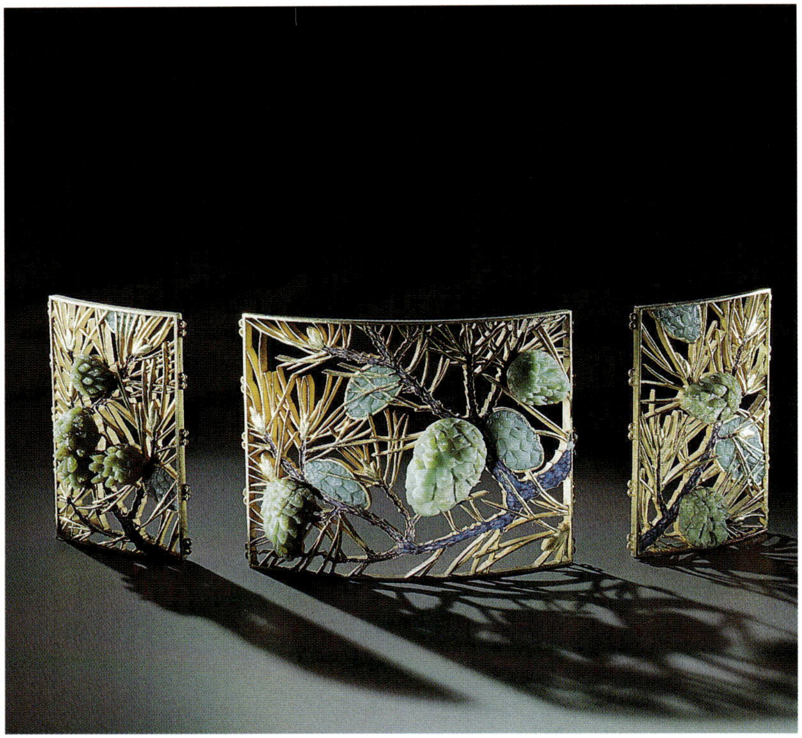

Dog Collar Plaque
Pine Cones
c. 1900
Chased gold,
translucent enamel
on gold,
chrysoprases
Central plaque: 2 x 2 1/2; side plaques: 2 x 1 1/4 inches
(central plaque: 5 x 6.2; side plaques: 5 x 3.4 cm)
(Cat. 56)

at the grander weddings, such as those presented by the prince and princesse de Polignac or M. and Mme. de Bonnières to princesse Hélène de Brancovan at her marriage in 1898, for the most part they were not seen to leave the jewel caskets in which—like museum pieces—they were conserved. In the realm of contemporary haute couture, fashion designers were reluctant to give their creations too personal a stamp, a dress being judged good or bad on the quality of the fabric and its decoration. The taste for grandiose adornments which characterized Jean-Philippe Worth might easily be distinguished from the predilection of someone like Jacques Doucet for the delicate style of the later eighteenth century, but for the most part it is not easy to tell the work of one fashion house from another, so subtle are the stylistic variations. It is only with the second generation of couturiers in the years 1910–20 that each "label" was able to build its own individual identity and style. Around 1900, the heads of the most popular and already venerable fashion houses (haute couture had by then been in existence for forty years) were unwilling to approach the artistic avant-garde or to refer to it in their creations. Jacques Doucet—who was by then forty-seven—only turned to amassing and commissioning modern art in 1912, after the sale of his eighteenth-century collection.

On the rare occasions when a Lalique piece was actually worn, the portrait photographer's eye would highlight the extreme ambiguousness of the jewelry, always full of signs, seemingly intended to be read like a book, and "delight the gaze in the pleasantly snug atmosphere of an inner circle."[10] Willfully ignoring the delicacy of the subjects themselves, these jewels, just like any other parure of the period, were drowned in the sort of overwrought confections that were then considered to be the height of chic in a toilette. Lalique's chokers were worn over a high neckline already decked out with fine lace, while pendants would be immersed in the flounces of a chemisette.

Proust—who was wont to describe how clothing exemplifies the soul—took great delight in this decorative profusion, reflecting on one of the characters in *À L'Ombre des jeunes filles en fleurs* that the "complexity of these 'accessories' without any practical use, with no apparent raison d'être, added a disinterested, thoughtful, secretive note, which harmonized with that melancholic air which Mme Swann always wore."

Paul Poiret was to experience much the same feeling when working as a youthful fashion apprentice for Jacques Doucet on the rue de la Paix. His talent had already been acknowledged and he had been entrusted with creating a coat for the actress Réjane in the fourth act of *Zaza*, which she was getting ready to play at the Théâtre du Vaudeville. The description Poiret has left in his memoirs, written in the vocabulary of the jeweler, shows how an attempt was

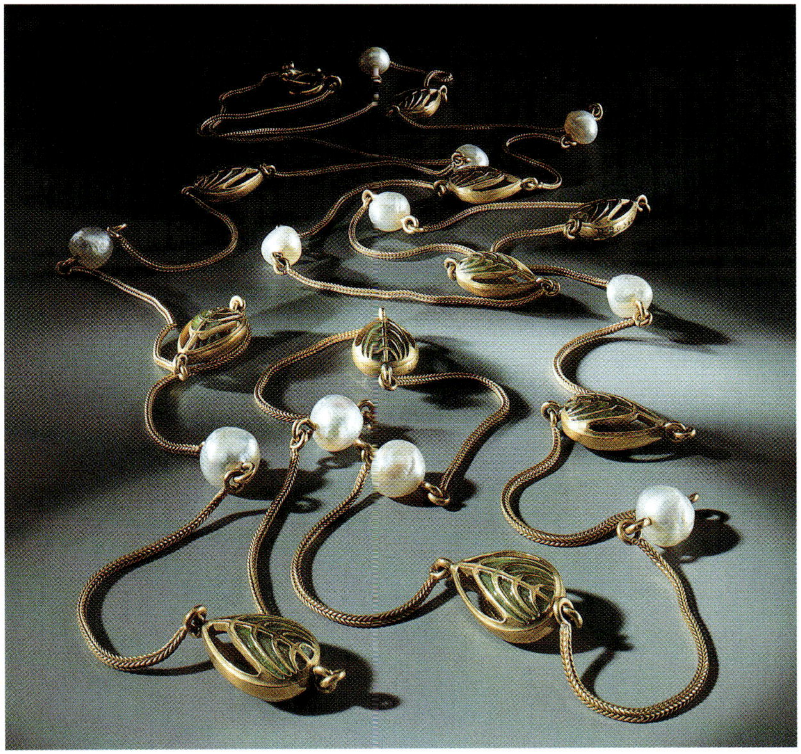

Locket Chain
Leaves
c. 1898–1900
Electrum,
baroque pearls,
plique-à-jour
enamel
6 inches
(14.9 cm)
(Cat. 76)

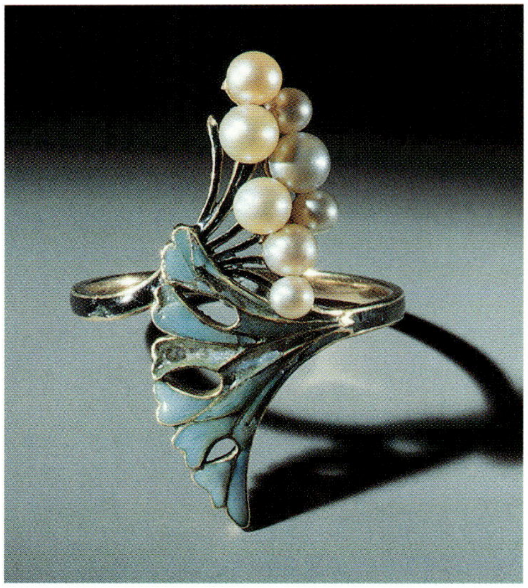

Ring
Flowers
c. 1900
Gold, opaque enamel on gold, *plique-à-jour* enamel, pearls
2 1/4; Diam: 3/4 inches (3; Diam: 2.1 cm)
(Cat. 81)

Buckle
Two Cocks
c. 1898–1900
Enamel, metal
3 3/4 x 5 1/2 inches
(9.5 x 13.8 cm)
(Cat. 93)

made to introduce expression and feeling into this costume, which was "in black tulle veiling a black taffeta painted by Billotey [a then celebrated fan painter] with vast mauve and white irises; an enormous ribbon in mauve satin and another in violet, running through the tulle and hugging the shoulders, fastened the coat in front with a complicated knot."[11] Poiret adds that the sensational effect produced by the actress's appearance on stage made him famous. "All the sadness of a romantic denouement, all the harshness of a fourth act was in that most expressive coat and, when it appeared, the public could already sense how the play would end." Whether it was a dress or jewel, the excess, the opulence, or the complexity of the piece generated the same charm.

The multiple meanings that crowd Lalique jewelry sometimes approximate the complicated arrangements of contemporary attire. In the pendant *Old Man with a Woman Curled Up in His Beard* or in the mermaids and fish belt fastener (Lisbon, Museu Calouste Gulbenkian, inv. 1157 and 1172; hereafter MCG), it is impossible to tell what constitutes the main subject, the frame or the motif. Framing, secondary on most other occasions, is here all of a piece with the subject. The fashion of 1900 has left us with striking images of its line and of the extreme stylization of the sheathed body. Woman, reassembled from a succession of curves and hollows, appears in the guise of a flexible vine, as a natural element, something taken out of the vegetable kingdom and then idealized by a dress designer. This sinuous, unfurled line became the main attribute of femininity of the period, and turned every woman who was to sacrifice her natural comfort on the altar of artful fashion into a poison-scented sorceress. Society portraitists of the day such as Boldini stress just that line, pausing only to take snapshots of the garments as they whirl in eddies around the body. Lalique, too, was to harness this very same movement in his 1901 pendant *Two Women Dancing* (MCG, inv. 1140). Asked to design a handbag for Sarah Bernhardt (cat. 186), that queen of *femmes fatales*, did not Lalique choose the theme of the snake, in the form of a two-pronged reptile twisting around itself so as to represent the dual nature of femininity? Animal subjects inspired fashion and accessory designers alike. For one cocotte—the protégée of M. Gaston Meunier—Jacques Doucet devised a blue chiffon dress covered in an embroidered swarm of hovering wasps over arabesques, symbol of the wantonness of the easy-come-easy-go young female. Lalique's brooch *Blackthorn and Wasps* of 1904 (cat. 128) is doubtless not invested with the same meaning but shares a related iconography. One drawstring bag is decorated with a peacock fanning its tail (Paris, Union Française des Arts du Costume, inv. 71.54.15; hereafter UFAC), and there is a parasol fixed with an owl's-head handle (UFAC, inv. 67.1.65).

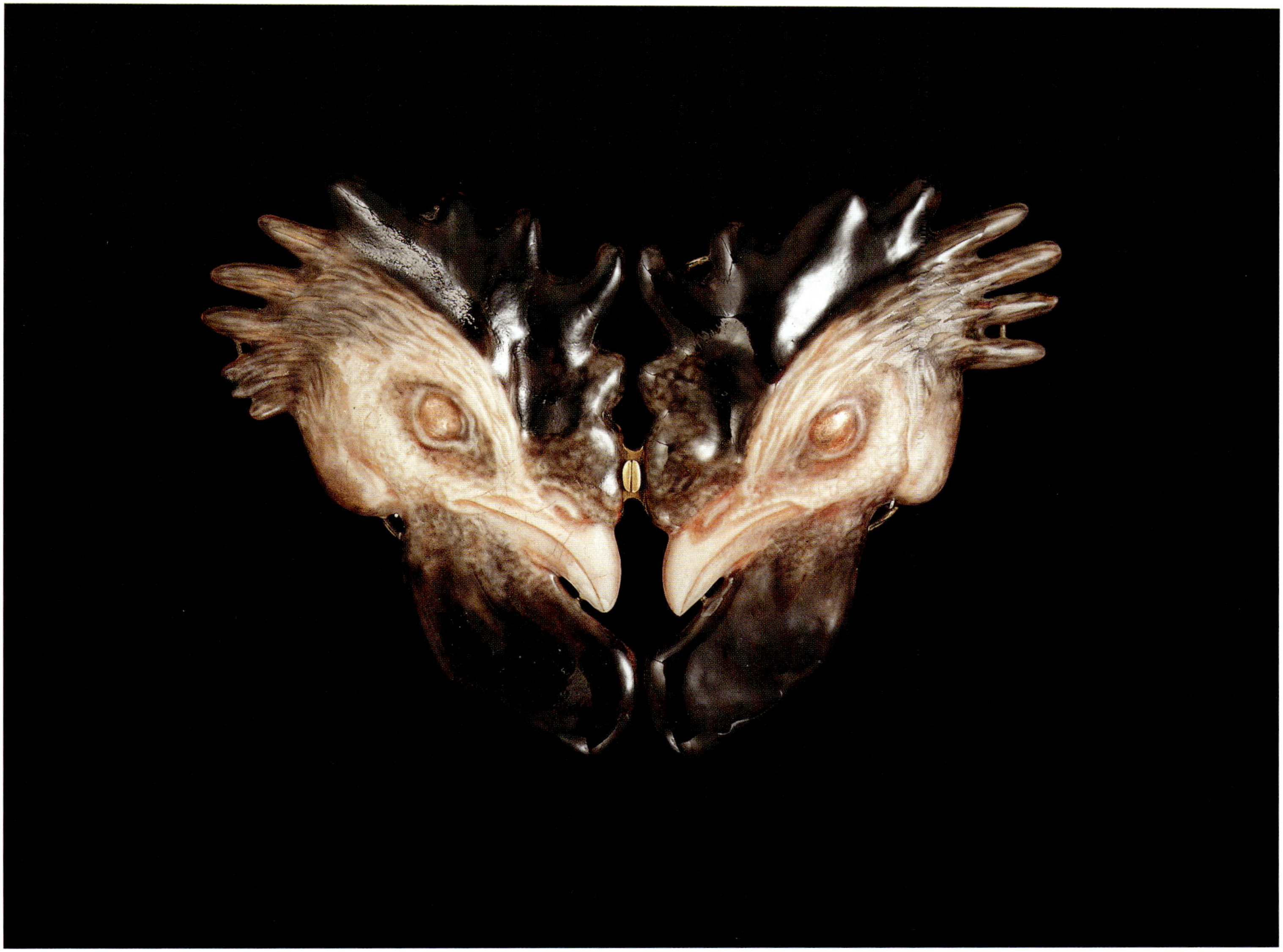

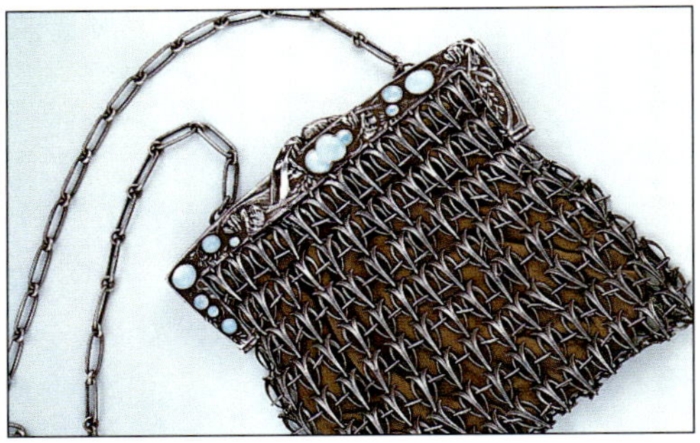

Handbag
Wasps
c. 1901–1903
Silver,
moonstones (?)
7 1/8 x 7 1/4
inches
(18 x 18.5 cm)
(Cat. 187)

Lorgnette
Lizard
c. 1899–1901
Gold, enamel
on gold, *plique-à-jour* enamel,
optical glass
6 3/8 x 1 5/8
inches
(16.2 x 4 cm)
(Cat. 89)

Handbag, *Two Snakes*
c. 1901–1903
Silver, silk,
leather
9 1/8 x 7 inches
(23.1 x 17.9 cm)
(Cat. 186)

More often, however, fashion delved into the wealth of themes offered by the plant world and simply picked out certain motifs whose delicacy evoked the evanescence of Lalique's flowers, such as a dress by Doucet decorated with wisteria blooms (UFAC, inv. 55.58.4). Orientalist themes, which were latent in Lalique's work, also furnished the artificers of fashion with a trove of decorative motifs, as in the ivory Buddha head clasp for an evening clutch bag (UFAC, inv. 86.02.22) or in a grimacing Japanese netsuke head hung from a parasol wrist-loop (UFAC, inv. 86.05.2).

If Lalique's work forms part and parcel of the Art Nouveau movement that reigned supreme in the decorative arts at this time, fashion was to follow it only with regard to the celebrated slinky silhouette. Elements from Art Nouveau *per se* were rarely employed as adornments in dress, though exceptions did exist, such as an 1898 model in celadon blue woolen cloth embroidered with entwined white caterpillars (Paris, Union Centrale des Arts Décoratifs, inv. 32188 AB). This type of stylistic exercise seems to have been the province of painters and draftsmen, such as Georges De Feure, a virtuoso of the arabesque and the *entrelac.* A number of light mantles and coats, such as a Redfern design in midnight blue wool are decorated with soutaches or jade embroidery in the form of curves and scrolls, but these appear somewhat watered-down in spirit.

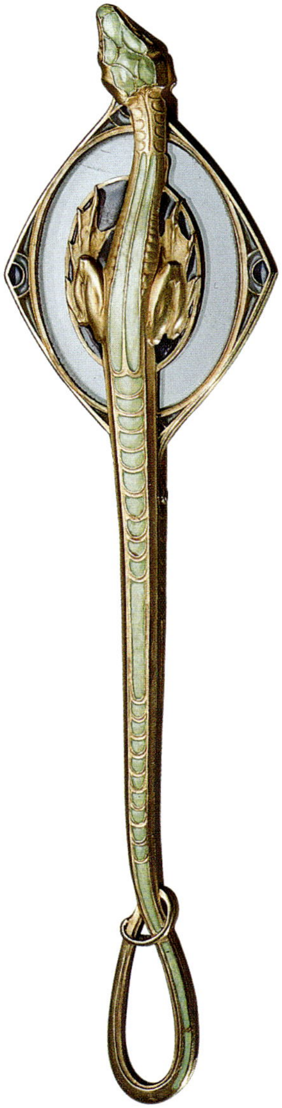

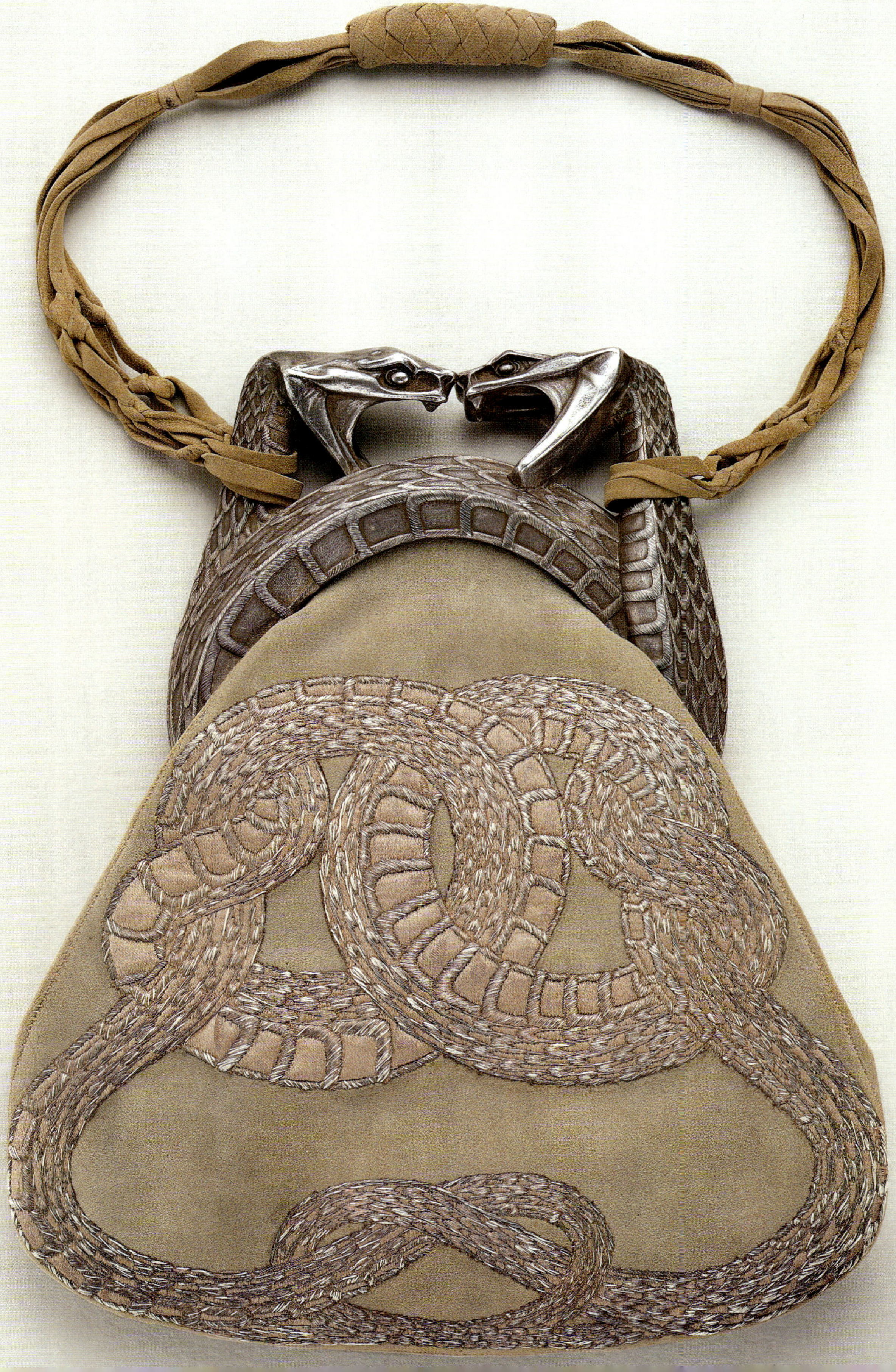

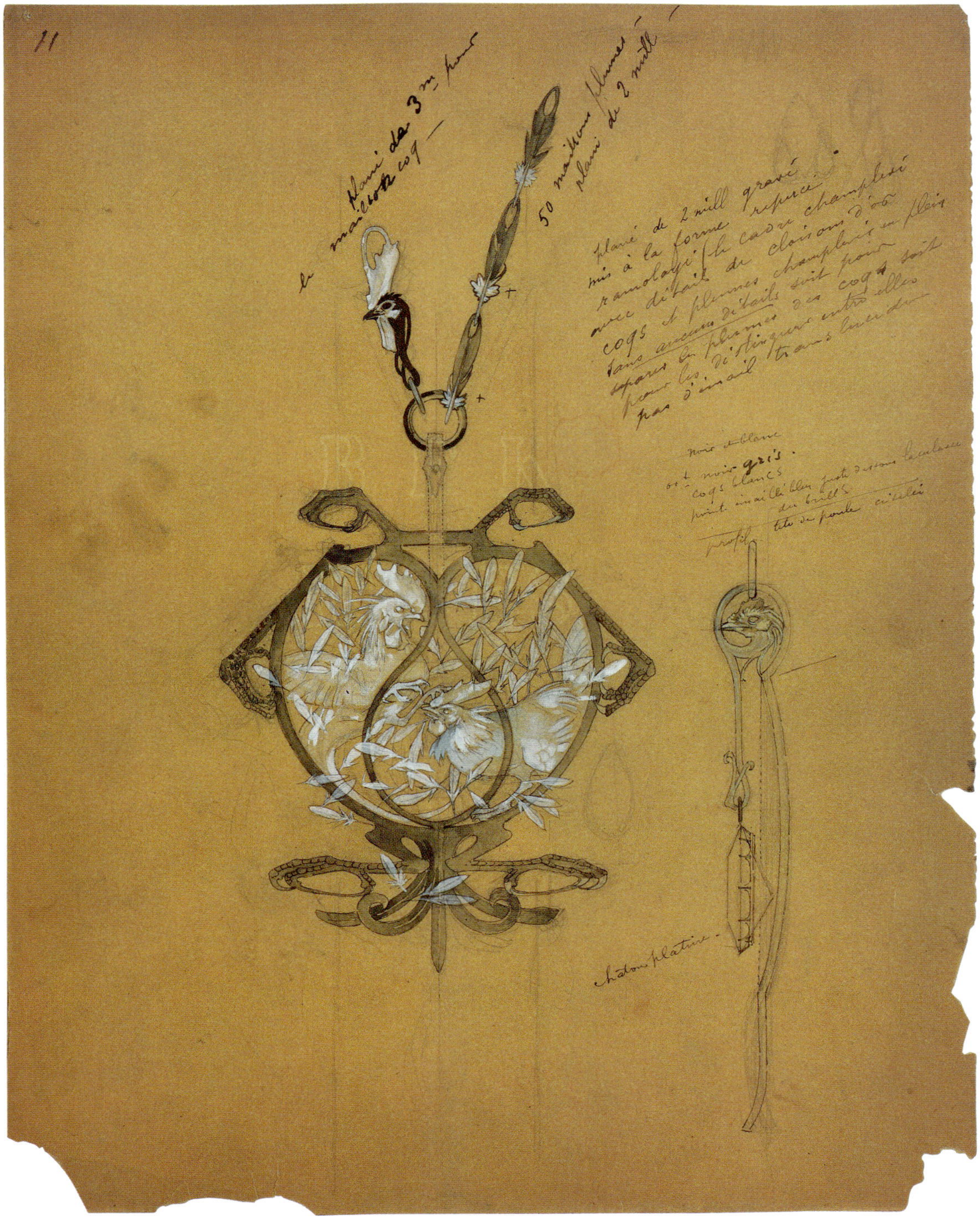

Design for a Pendant
Two Fighting Cocks
c. 1899–1900
Pencil, ink, watercolor, gouache on paper
11 x 8 3/4 inches
(28.2 x 21.9 cm)
(Cat. 156)

Corsage Ornament
Blackthorn and Wasps
1904
Gold, enamel, pressed glass
1 3/4 x 4 1/2 inches
(4.7 x 11.2 cm)
(Cat. 128)

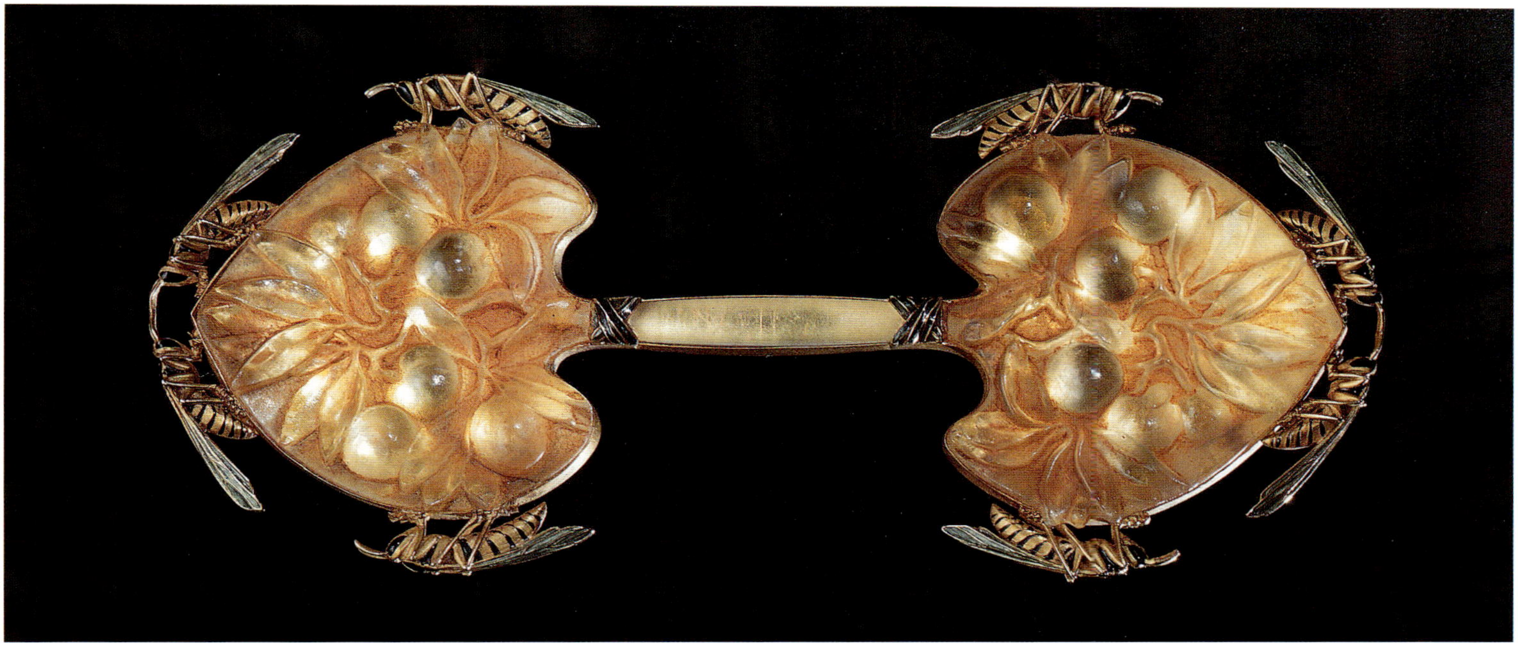

Some shared sources of inspiration and a few strong underlying lines are not sufficient to establish a connection between Lalique and the world of fashion. Going beyond the "feminine" attitude which suffused Belle Époque art and which was responsible for an unconscious complicity between Art Nouveau and fashion, Lalique knowingly placed his talent in the service of woman generally, all the while respecting and observing the precise ways in which jewelry and accessories were used. (According to Léonce Bénédite, it was Sarah Bernhardt who might have inspired Lalique to forge his path to Art Nouveau *bijouterie.*)[12] Tiaras, combs, chokers, corsage ornaments, pendant earrings, brooches, hatpins, chatelaines, lorgnettes, looking-glasses, fasteners, barrettes, pendants, armlets, ensembles for the hand, fans, handbags—the list of the objects for which Lalique composed designs is indeed a long one. But the items in the list confirm that Lalique limited himself to designing ornaments for the feminine toilette, the sort that could be used to spotlight some part of the total effect, such as the

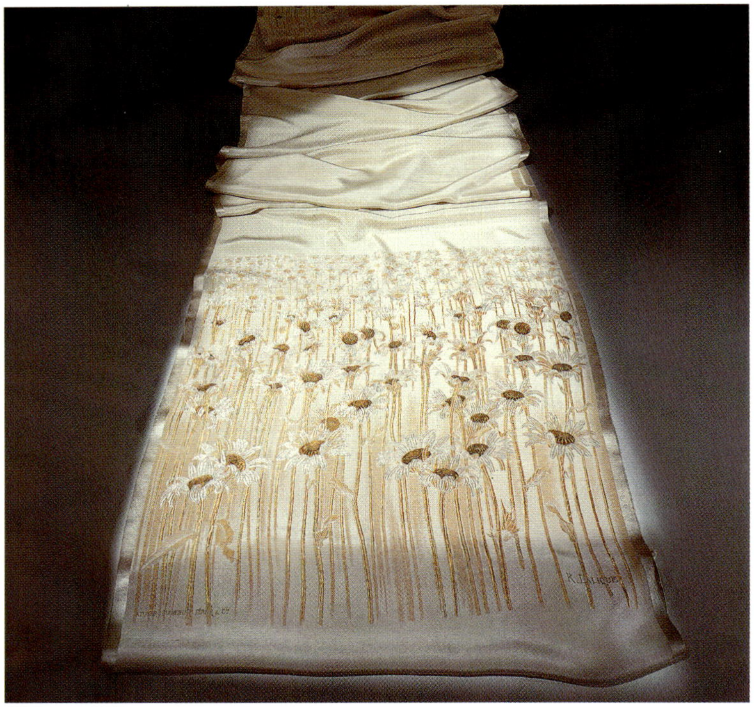

Stole
Field of Daisies
1907
Silk, metal, figured crêpe, gold and brown brocade
124 x 22 7/8 inches
(315 x 58 cm)
(Cat. 191)

Bracelet
Wheat Stalks
c. 1901–1903
Gold, *plique-à-jour* enamel, diamonds
1 1/2 x 7 inches
(3.7 x 18 cm)
(Cat. 86)

neck, décolleté, shoulders, or waist. And so he continued at the 1904 Salon, where he presented three collars embroidered with facing cockerels, peacocks, and a scene from a tournament. In 1906 he attempted once more to revive the art of embroidery and fabric design, creating a coat collar and four scarves for Bianchini-Férier, graced with butterflies, moths, and peacocks.

Women customers of the day, going beyond the dictates of fashion, sensed the great originality and personality of the artist and were receptive to the strength and magnetism of an œuvre with which they did not want to or could not compete. The very subjects of Lalique's jewelry designs are at odds with the basic approach of contemporary fashion.[13] The dresses of 1900 covered the whole body up to the neck, placing the face in a case, as it were, and enframing it in a lace collar, while bright pearls and diamonds were chosen to emphasize paleness of complexion. The symbols and allegories in Lalique's miniature sculptures could not fail to introduce a more somber note: withered flowers, the ghost of Ophelia, uncanny sacred woods, bats, snakes, monstrous eagles, a procession of frozen nuns—such subjects were hardly designed to accord with the purely decorative style of the period's fashions.

All too devoted to the thrall of appearances and of convention, Belle Époque fashion was unable to come to terms with the enigmatic, disturbing character of the works of Lalique.

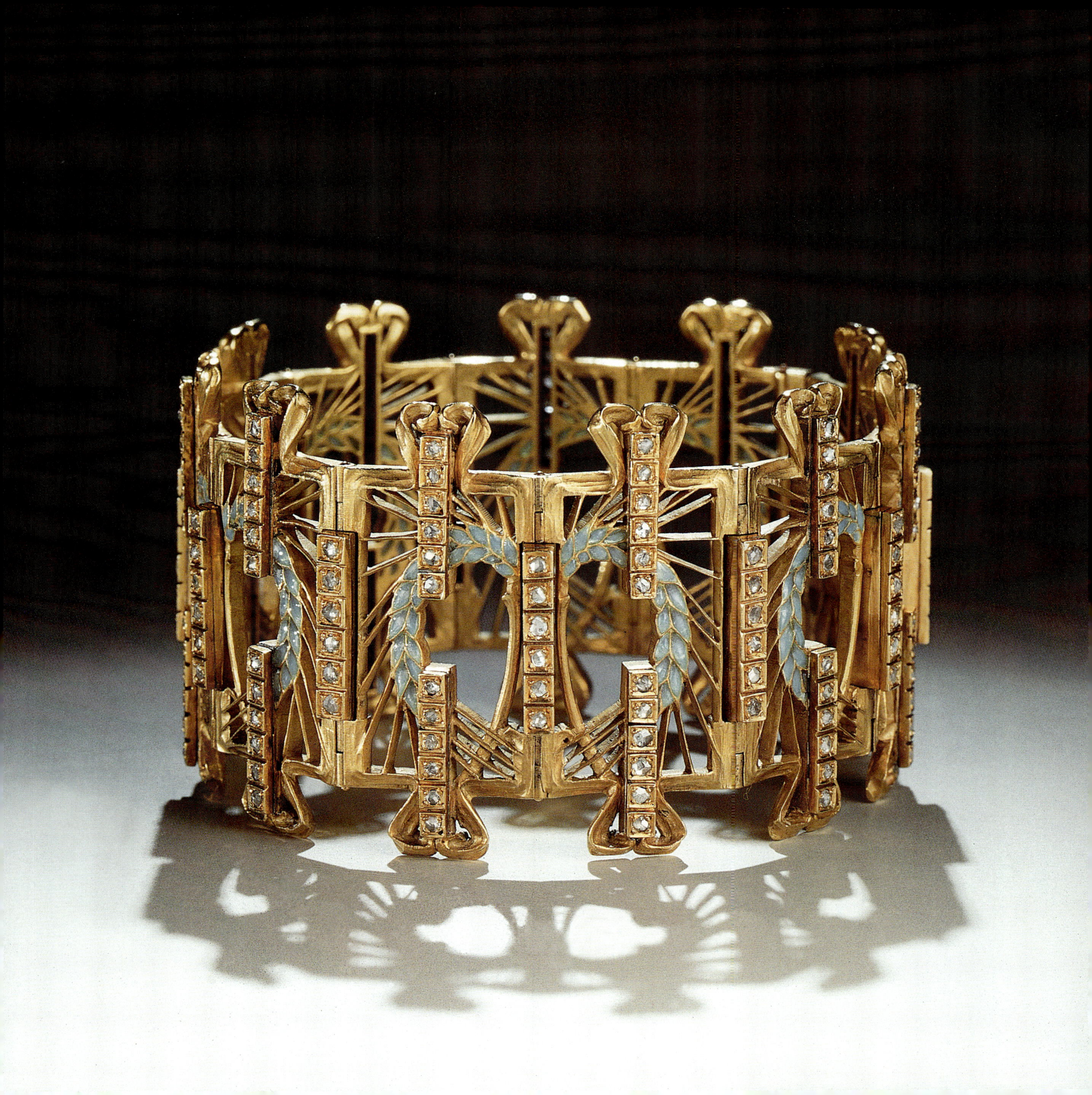

Design for a
Pendant-Brooch
c. 1890–1892
Pencil, ink,
watercolor on
paper
10 7/8 x 8 1/4
inches
(27.8 x 22.1 cm)
(Cat. 20)

Necklace
Chrysanthemums
c. 1897–1899
Gold,
translucent and
opaque enamel
on gold, pearls
2 3/8 x 15 inches
(6 x 38.2 cm)
(Cat. 13)

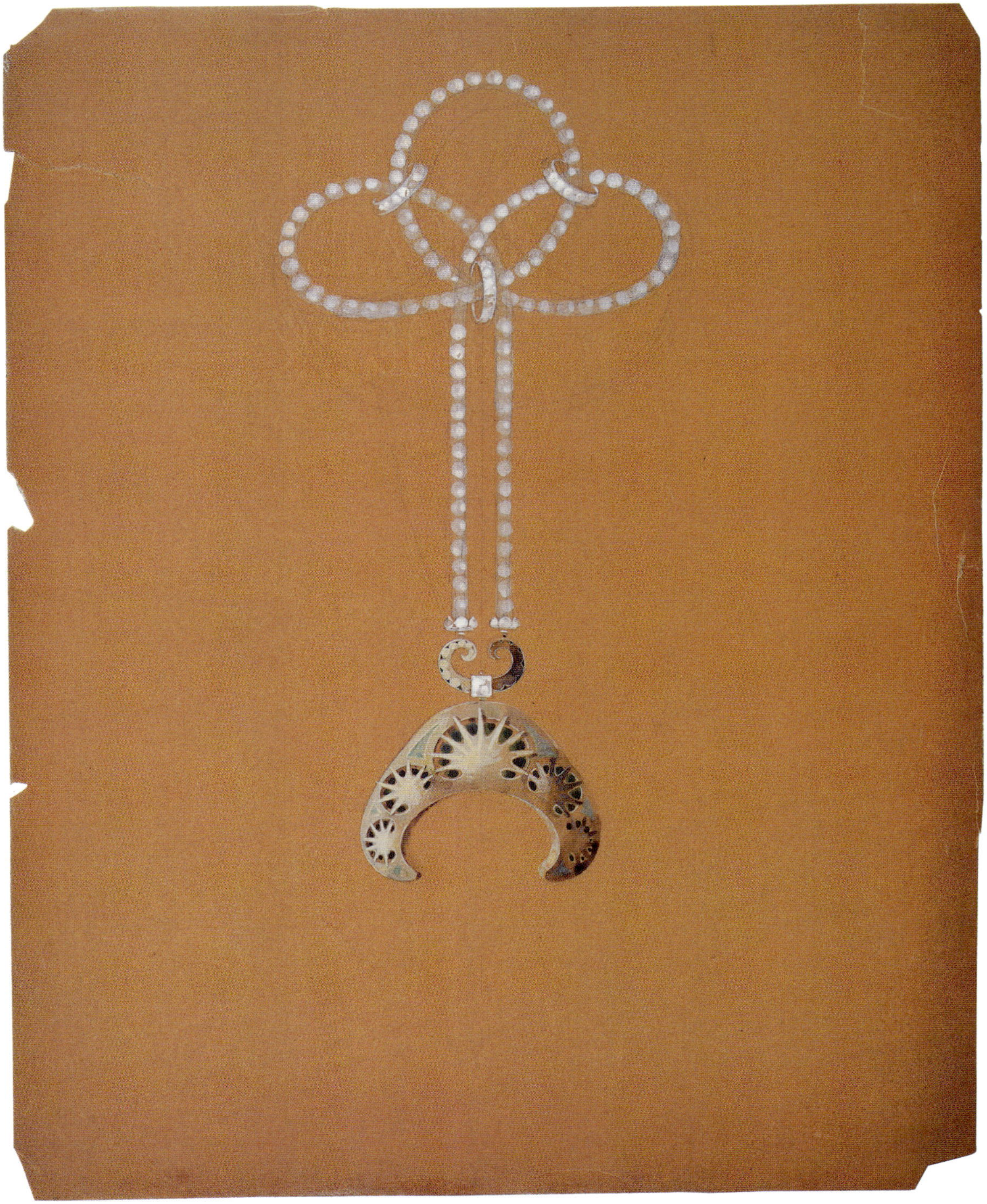

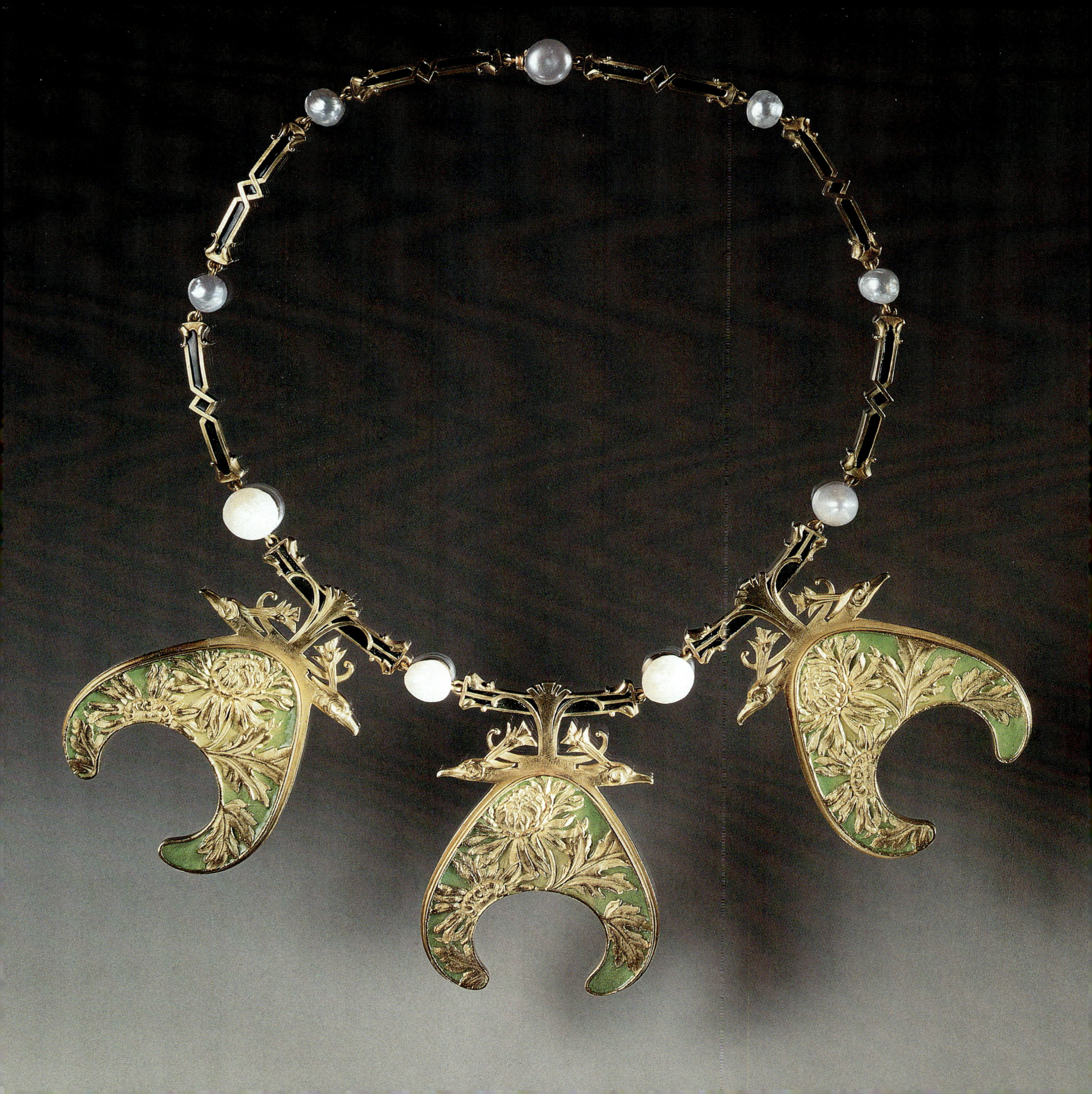

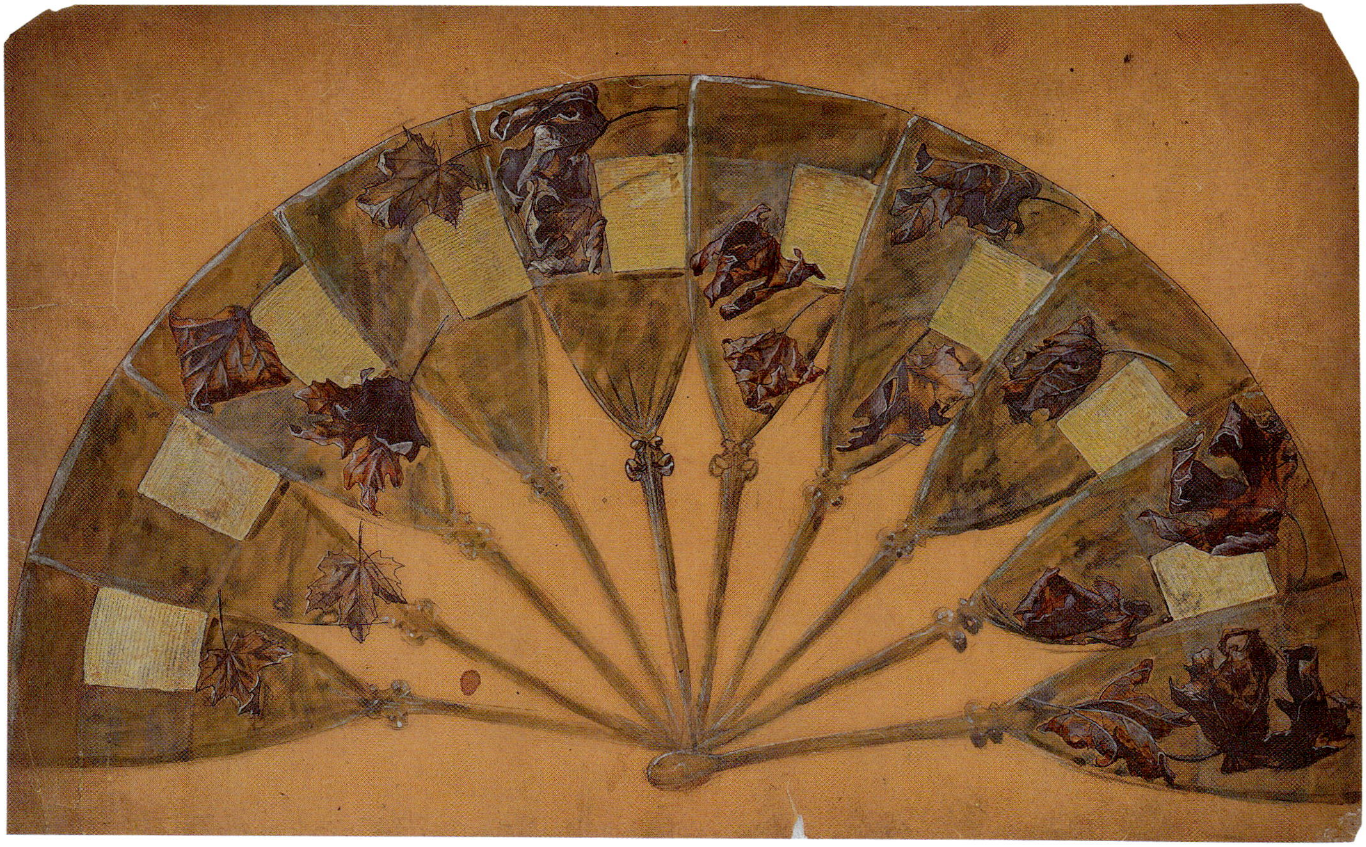

Design for a Fan
Falling Leaves
c. 1899–1900
Pencil, ink, watercolor on paper
10 5/8 x 21 inches
(27.5 x 53.6 cm)
(Cat. 236)

Design for a Corsage Ornament
Pine Boughs and Cones
1905–1906
Pencil, ink, watercolor on paper
11 x 8 5/8 inches
(28 x 21.8 cm)
(Cat. 152)

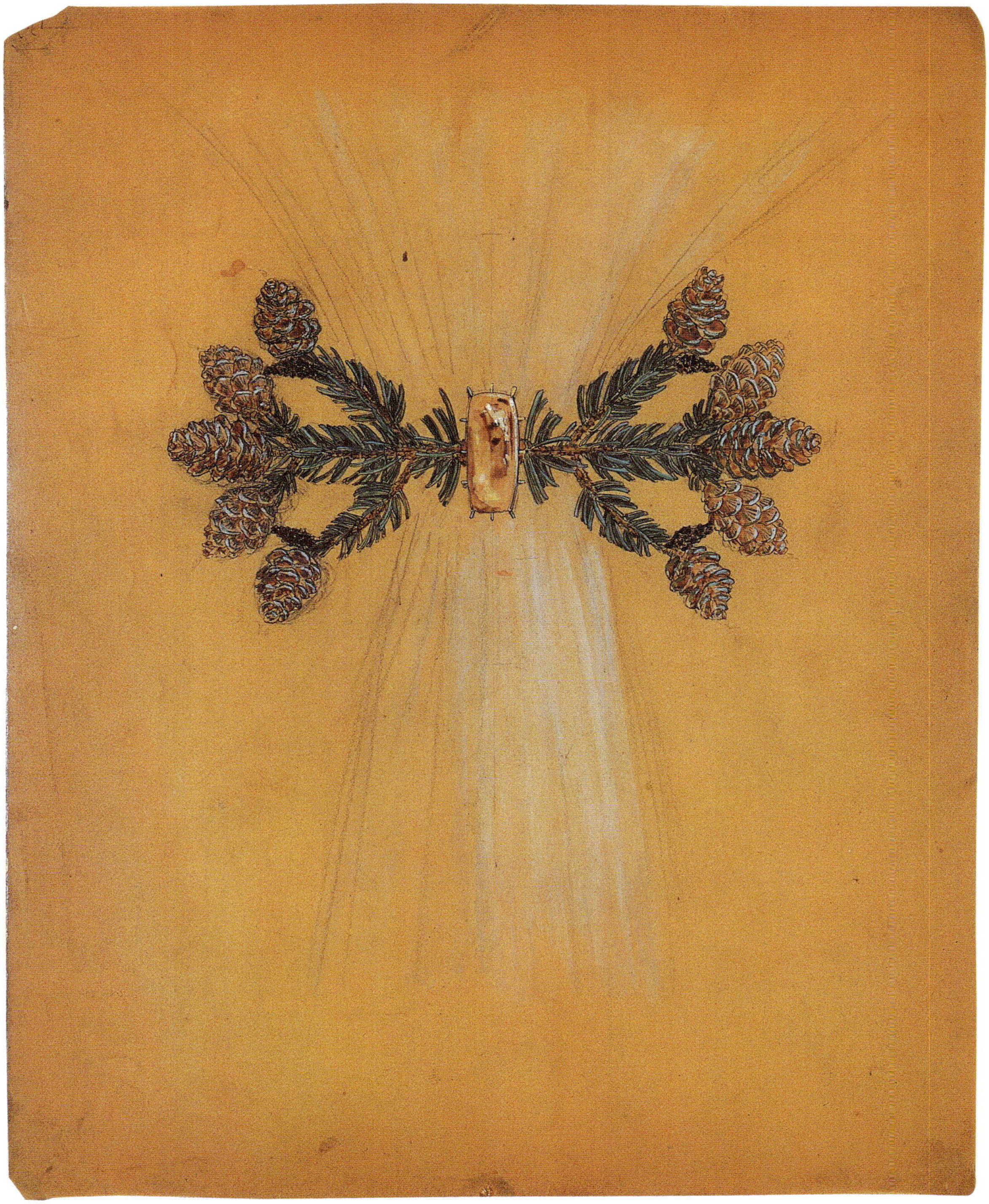

Materials and Techniques in the Jewelry of René Lalique

Sigrid Barten

By brilliantly mastering the technical aspects of his profession as a goldsmith and by working freely with an extended range of materials, René Lalique succeeded in creating jewelry with unique characteristics. The artist also used great skill and insight in incorporating elements from the disciplines of painting and sculpture: subtly matched enamels, colored stones, iridescent pearls and dull-gleaming gold were formed into three-dimensional representations of objects and figures. Later, in his second career as a glassmaker, Lalique put his innovative ideas into practice by developing new techniques.[1] It was his own inventions and technical equipment that gave him the freedom he needed to attain his artistic objectives.

Each item of Lalique jewelry is immaculately crafted. This is evident not only on the front of his work but invariably on the back as well. For example, spherical shapes were perfectly finished even on the back; the reverse of a gold-plated mount of a bas-relief might have an additional design that would never be seen when the piece was worn. The creations of the great goldsmiths of the Renaissance had served as a formal model for René Lalique early in his career, and as far as craftsmanship was concerned, they remained a source of inspiration until the beginning of the twentieth century.[2]

The only known comments by Lalique himself on the techniques used in creating his jewelry are the notes which accompanied his working drawings. These instructions to his colleagues at the studio contained details of the thickness of the gold foil and of how it was to be worked, details of the precious and semiprecious stones and how to cut them, and of the type of pearls to be used. Here and there we find the name of a client, a date, or even the name of an outside

Brooch
Pine Sprig
c. 1900–1902
Gold, enamel, cast glass
2 3/4 x 2 inches
(7 x 5 cm)
(Cat. 121)

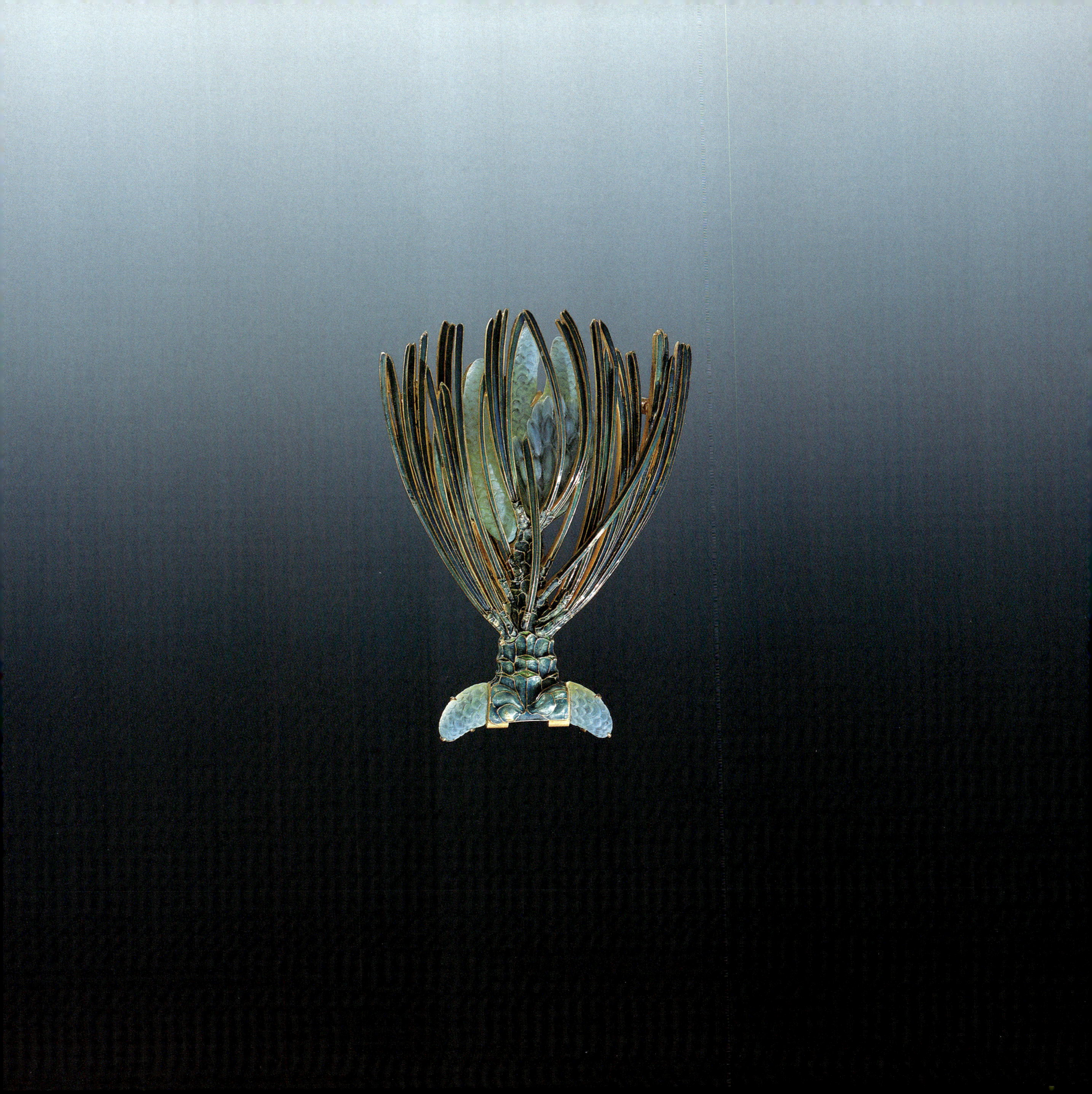

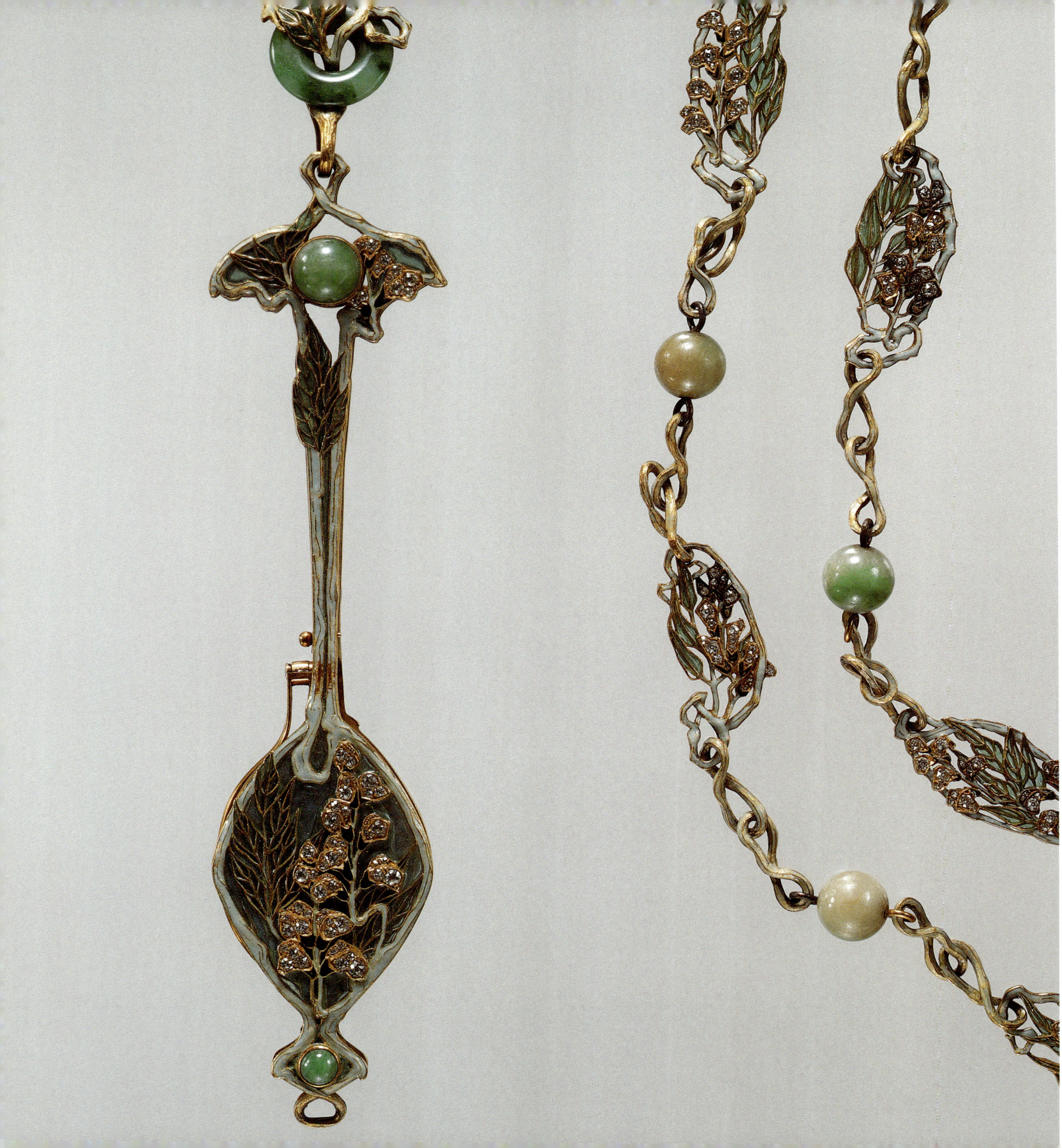

craftsman. The frequently quoted history of French nineteenth-century jewelry by Henri Vever is useful as a secondary source.[3]

The materials selected and the unconventional ways of combining them reflected the fact that Lalique was concerned not simply with their value, but rather with the effect they would produce and their power of expression in relation to one another. For the first time in the history of jewelry, we find glass relief next to polished diamonds. René Lalique used horn, mother-of-pearl and ivory, precious stones and pearls subtly combined with the dull shine of the gold. A range of enamels in numerous intermediate shades provided him with a wide variety of colors.

Each item of jewelry produced in Lalique's studio was based on a full-scale working drawing. The thick bundle of thousands of drawings was rightly described by Roger Marx in 1899 as the artist's "Livre de Vérité."[4] The artistic origins of all the jewelry pieces by Lalique are recorded in it. The master delegated the subsequent transformation into three-dimensional form to craftsmen who specialized in individual techniques, though he monitored their work at every stage.[5]

He employed up to thirty people at his studio at 20, rue Thérèse from 1890 to 1902 and later at 40, Cours-la-Reine. Until 1905, his home and workshop were never far apart.

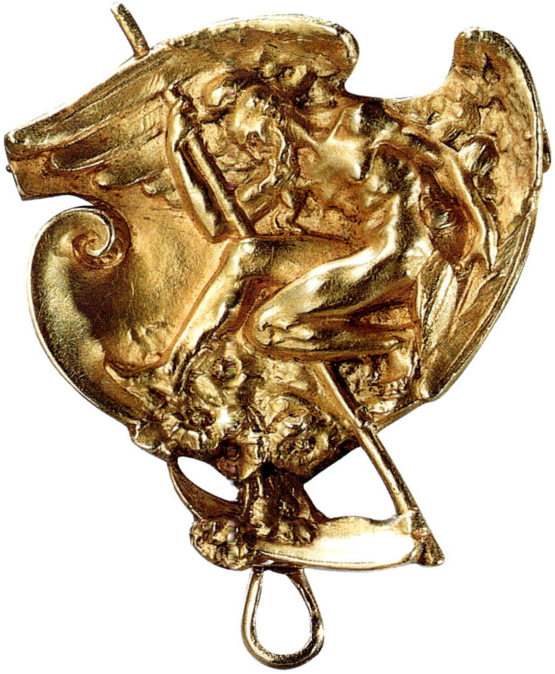

Lorgnette
and Chain
Wisteria
c. 1899–1900
Gold, opaque white
enamel on gold,
diamonds, jade,
glass
6 1/2 x 40 inches
(16.5 x 101.6 cm)
(Cat. 88)

Chatelaine-Brooch
Figure of Time
c. 1888–1890
Chased and
embossed gold
1 1/2 x 1 1/4 inches
(4 x 3.2 cm)
(Cat. 2)

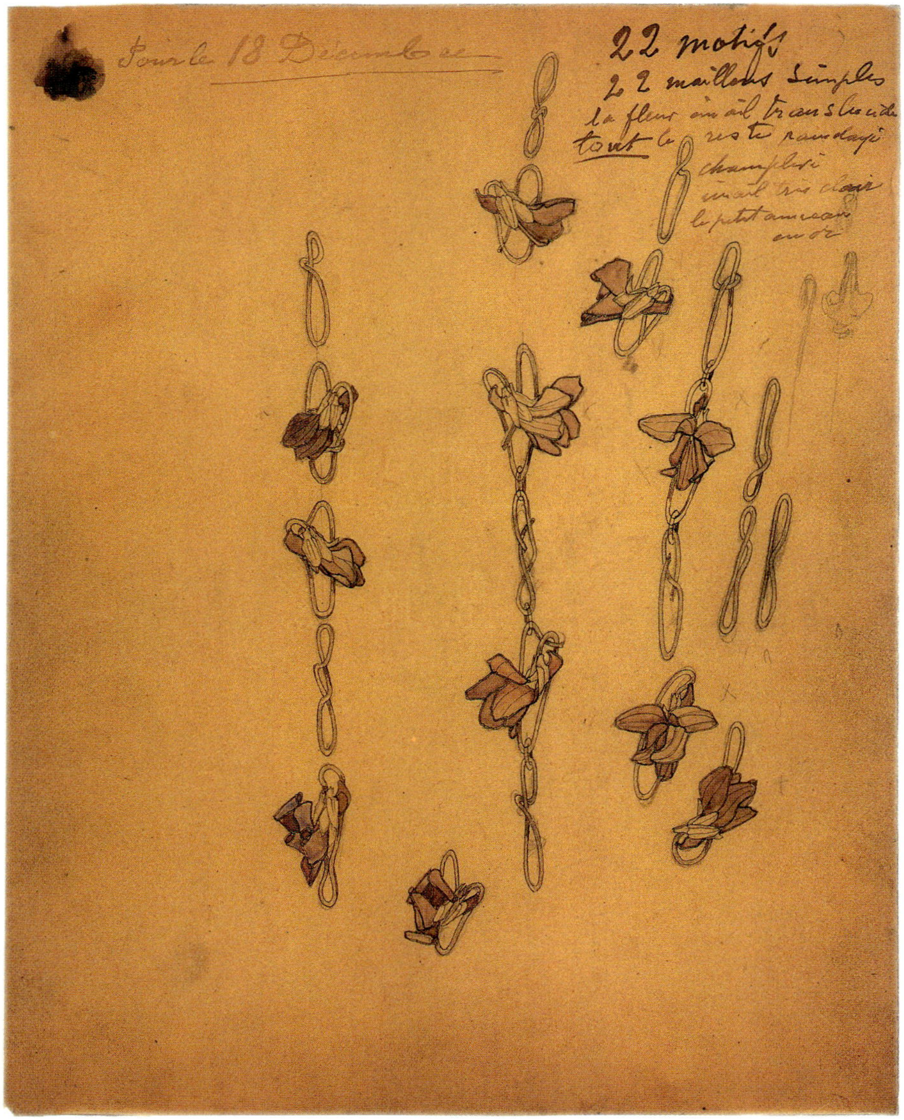

Gold as the Primary Material for Jewelry

Lalique preferred to work with gold, usually yellow gold with a high millesimal fineness (750/000) and occasionally green gold, which gets its coloring from the cadmium present in alloy form. Solid-gold items were cast using the lost-wax process.

However, pendants, brooches, necklaces, and bracelets were usually crafted in fretworking. In this case, the goldsmith would start with a plate of gold rolled to a thickness of 1.5 to 2.5 mm (the minimum and maximum thicknesses are 0.5 and 4.0 mm), which was cut out, following the outlines of the drawing, and fretted out on the inside to produce the internal detail. The outer edge was given the necessary strength by reinforcing it with beading. The edge would sometimes also be designed as a plant stem or branch and at the same time served as a border for the enamels.

The shaping of the gold plate began with the "ramolayer" method, which involved engraving it with a graver and engraving needle; then it was chased to produce fine reliefs and to carve out depressions, if enamels were to be used.

If the gold relief was going to cover a fairly large area, the best way of working it to the desired shape was to emboss it, using a die.

Creating Color and Light Through Enamels

Between 1895 and 1908, hardly a piece of jewelry left Lalique's workshop which did not use enamel to give it color. Enamels were as important for the decorative effect as casting and engraving were for the sculptural form. Enamel consists of finely ground glass flux to which a little water is added to make it easier to apply with a brush, just as in the *pâte-de-verre*, or glass paste, method. Enamel gets its colors from metal oxides. The enamel only turns to liquid and adheres to the surface of the gold when it is heated in the oven. Gold is particularly suitable for enameling since it hardly expands, even at very high temperatures, and, furthermore, has a very high melting point. This largely eliminates the risk of the glass flux cracking when the metal contracts again as it gradually cools down.

In the case of *champlevé* enameling, Lalique's preferred technique, cells were engraved into a plate, leaving only dividing ridges. These latter served either as the figure or as the ground of the motif. The deeper the hollow, the darker and more intense the color of the enamel. Lalique worked principally with translucent enamels, so that the light was reflected by the gold behind. This also ensured that the internal pattern of the engraved base remained visible. If the gold plate was thin, the reverse side had to be coated with a counter-enamel to equalize the tension (Lalique is known to have used light blue, dark green, and purple counter-enamels). Opaque enamels could be applied in several layers and in varying colors and could later be cut to produce the effect of a veined gemstone (e.g. the watch, *Pine Cones*, cat. 55).

Items of jewelry were endowed with greater radiance and delicacy by *plique-à-jour* enameling. This technique, described in 1568 by Benvenuto Cellini, had been forgotten and was rediscovered by French enamelers in the mid-nineteenth century. The effect is similar to that of a stained-glass window in miniature. For this technique, Lalique started with an openwork gold plate. The parts which were to contain the windows had a copper plate attached to their backs, and the enamels were melted in the oven as in the *cloisonné* and *champlevé* techniques. After cooling, the copper was etched away, using nitric acid to expose the glass so that it would be visible from both sides. The *plique-à-jour* method is one of the most elaborate techniques used in Lalique's jewelry (e.g. the lorgnette and chain, *Wisteria*, cat. 88).

Sparkling Jewels and Opaque Gems

Since relief and color provided by gold and enamels dominated representational Art Nouveau jewelry, precious, polished gemstones were used as a special feature.

Design for a Chain
Violets
c. 1899–1901
Pencil, ink, watercolor on paper
11 x 8 1/2 inches
(27.8 x 21.7 cm)
(Cat. 149)

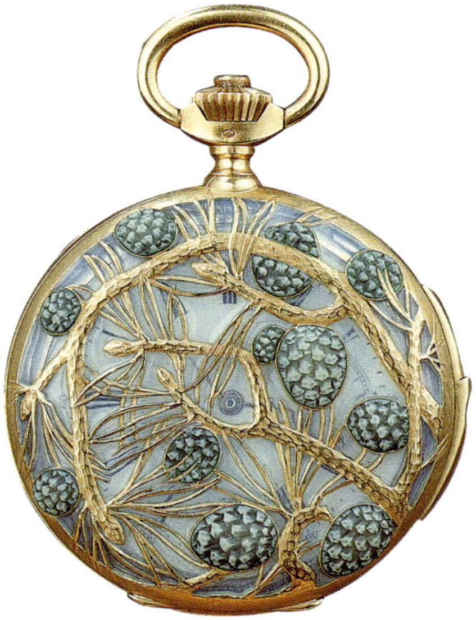

Watch
Pine Cones
c. 1898–1900
Gold, *plique-à-jour* enamel, opaque enamel on glass
2 3/4; Depth: 5/8; Diam: 2 inches
(7; Depth: 1.5; Diam: 5 cm)
(Cat. 55)

Brooch
Female Head with Dragonflies
c. 1904–1905
Gold, mold glass, *plique-à-jour* enamel
2 x 6 5/8 inches
(5 x 16.8 cm)
(Cat. 129)

Following double page
Pendant
Woman's Face and Wisteria
c. 1898–1900
Chased gold, opaque enamel on gold
4 x 1 1/4 inches
(10 x 3.2 cm)
(Cat. 44)

Lalique was not concerned with the intrinsic value of the stones, although he always picked exquisite examples, but with their color, refractive qualities, and size. It is characteristic of his jewelry that the colors of the enamels and precious stones are always matched to each other.[6] Of the different varieties of cut stone, Lalique showed a preference for blue and green stones, such as the dark blue sapphire and the water-colored aquamarine, the dark green emerald and the yellowish green peridot. The brown and yellowish shades of topaz, yellow diamond, and citrine harmonized beautifully with the warm tone of the gold.

Dazzling white diamonds are of particular significance since they were incorporated both individually and in clusters. Lalique liked to use arrangements of small diamonds to represent flower stems, the turned-back undersides of petals or—in dense clusters—stamens. About 1905, the diamond took on an even more prominent role when it was used in panels of clear, cut glass to produce a transparent and white color effect.

Among the translucent stones suitable for working into cabochons, Lalique showed a preference for the opal between 1898 and 1903. Its opalescent appearance, which changes with the light to reveal a wide spectrum of colors, appealed to his sense of color. Before Lalique, goldsmiths had avoided the opal because, according to superstition, the stone with its indeterminable color possessed evil powers. Lalique used the opal not only for peacock feathers and the center of flowers, but also for small panels, employing it instead of *plique-à-jour* enameling, for example, to represent water.[7]

Between 1898 and 1900, before Lalique started concentrating on glass as a component of jewelry, he often created female faces—resembling a cameo—from opaque gems, surrounded by gold and enamels. The matte, velvety surface of a whitish-colored chalcedony carved into relief (e.g. cat. 41 and MAD, inv. 9146) and even the cool green of a chrysoprase (MCG, inv. 1133) evoke soft skin better than any other material. However, from 1900 onward, Lalique began to make greater use of a similarly opaque, whitish material: ivory.

Ivory and Horn

Elephant tusks had been highly prized since late antiquity for their durability and relative ease of carving. Lalique used it in various ways for representational work, either in the form of flat relief panels, or as free-standing, three-dimensional sculpture.[8] He tried it out for the first time in 1894 in the music case with "The Valkyrie" (cat. 170). Over the following years, he extended his use of ivory to a wide repertoire of objects, including reliefs for pendants and brooches, hair combs, tiaras, sculpted paperweights, bottle stoppers, letter openers, a handbag handle, and the back of a pocket watch. Lalique even managed to invest the creamy

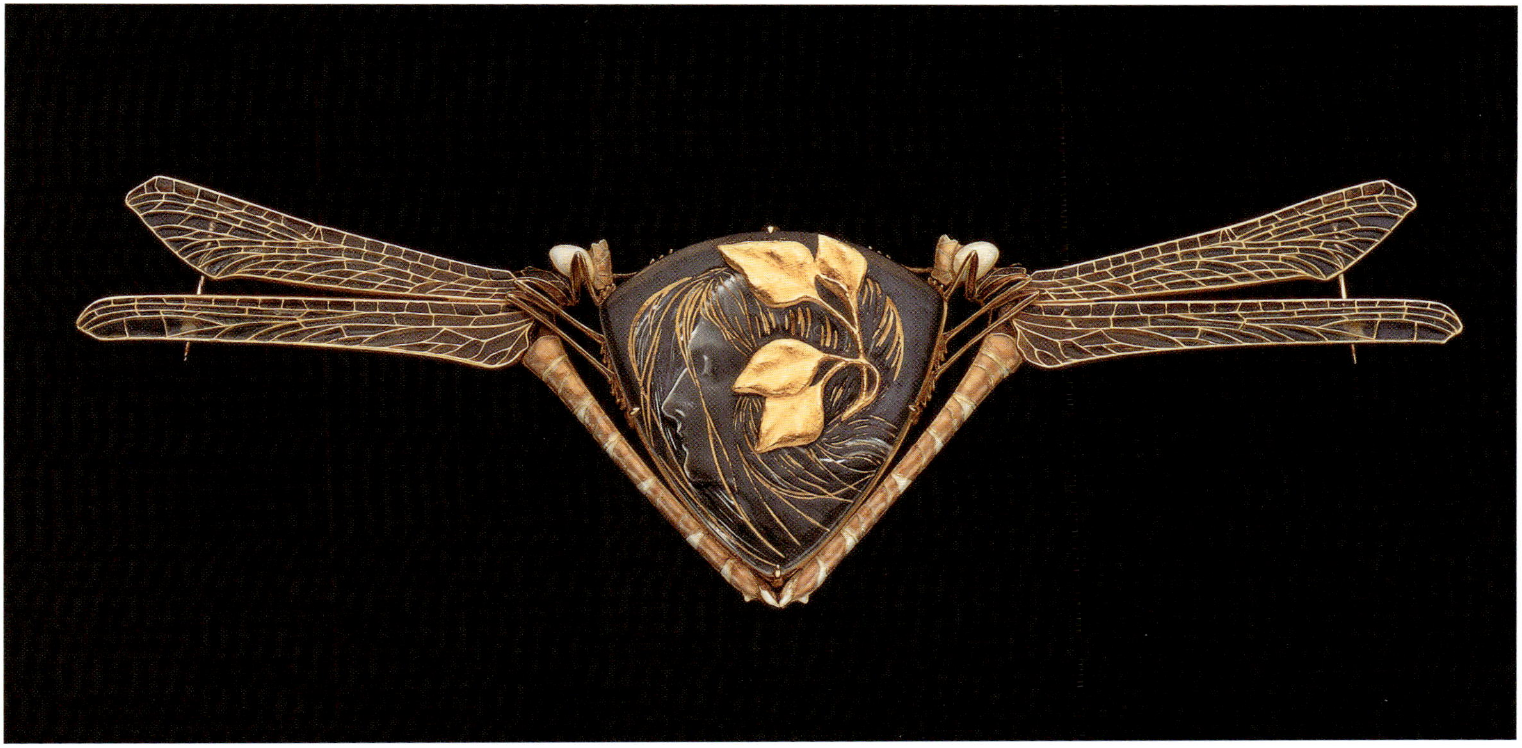

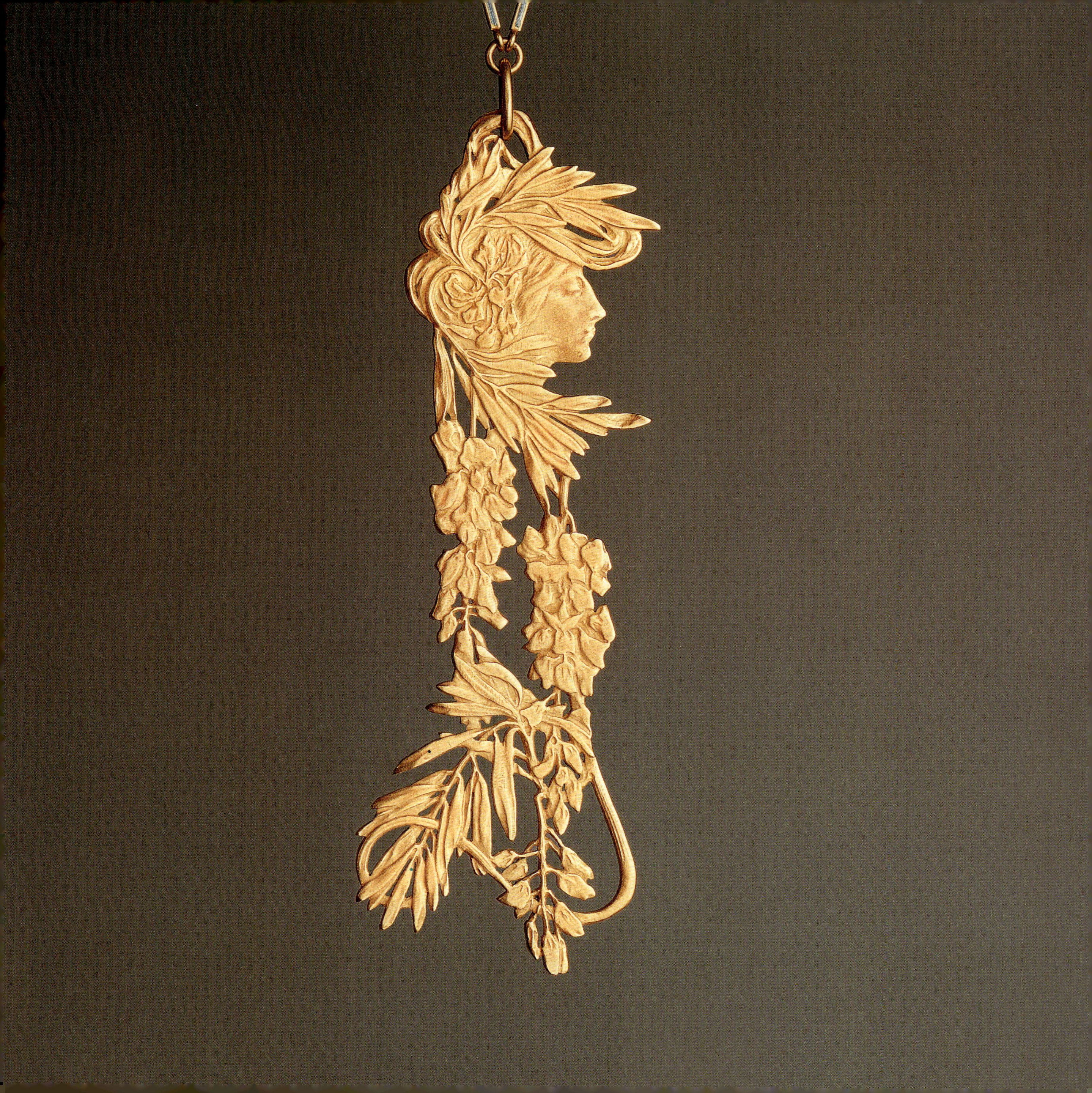

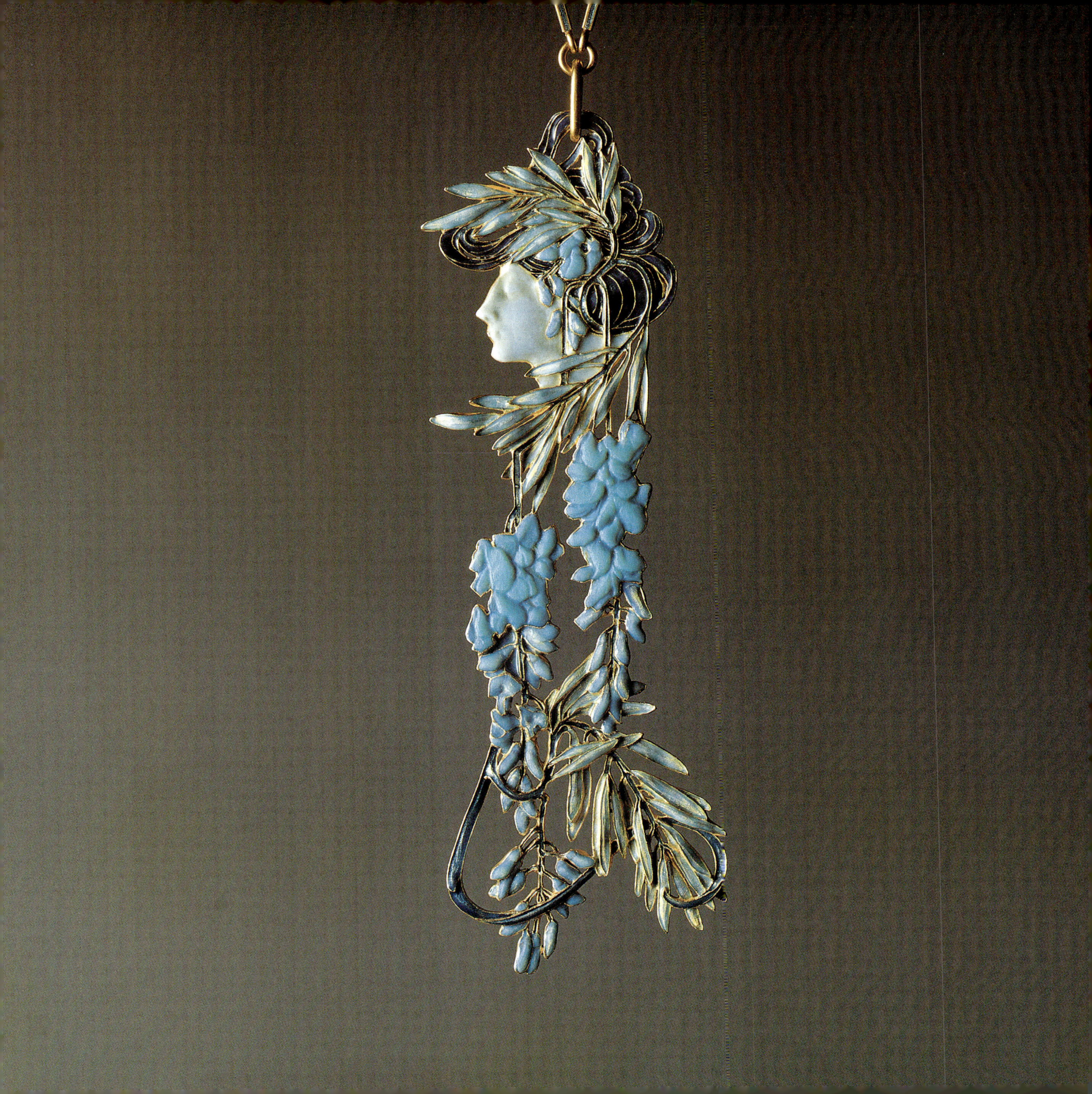

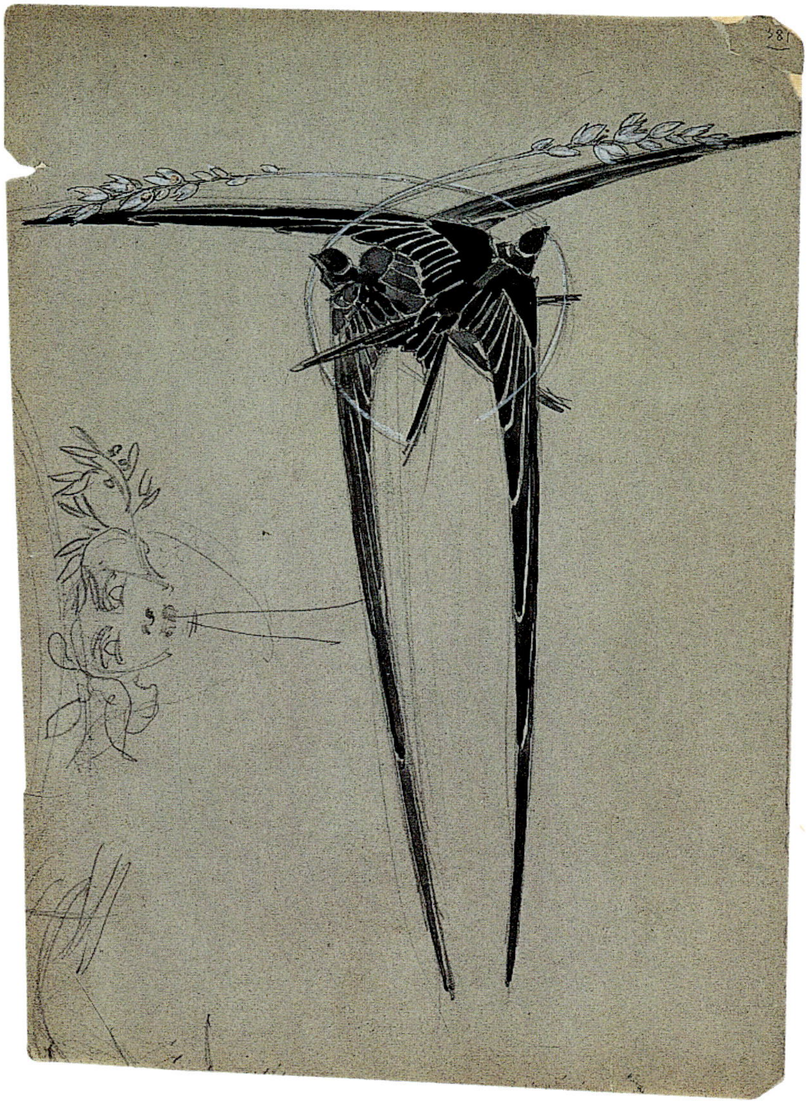

Comb
Two Swallows with a Stalk of Oats
c. 1906–1908
Gold, carved horn, diamonds
6 1/2 x 8 1/2 inches
(16.7 x 21.8 cm)
(Cat. 99)

Design for a Hairpin
Two Swallows with Wheat
1906–1908
Pencil, ink, watercolor on paper
8 3/4 x 6 1/2 inches
(22.2 x 15.6 cm)
(Cat. 158)

ivory with soft color by carving the background of the relief panels to such a degree that it became translucent. When a gold plate inlaid with colored enamel was placed behind the ivory, it glowed through in a subtle tone. The artist also made exquisite use of ivory in the three-dimensional representation of orchid blooms on a tiara (cat. 78 and Baltimore, Walters Art Gallery, inv. 57.936).

It was even more unusual to come across horn in a goldsmith's workshop. In 1896, Lalique became the first craftsman to produce jewelry from horn. He appreciated it for its transparency as well as its pliability and malleability. However, he preferred the finer buffalo horn from India and South America to European cow horn. It goes without saying that horn was the best material for hair combs. Lalique embellished the heads of the combs with gold elements, combined with enamel or even precious stones, which he fixed in place with hidden screws and rivets. He realistically carved the teeth of the comb to look like stems andthe tops to look like leaves. Then he added flowers made from precious materials. He worked so skillfully with these combinations of materials that they appeared completely natural. Lalique was also fond of using light horn for the supporting structures of tiaras, or when he wanted to represent prunus branches on a brooch. He used this material until 1908, in other words, almost until the end of his career as a jeweler.

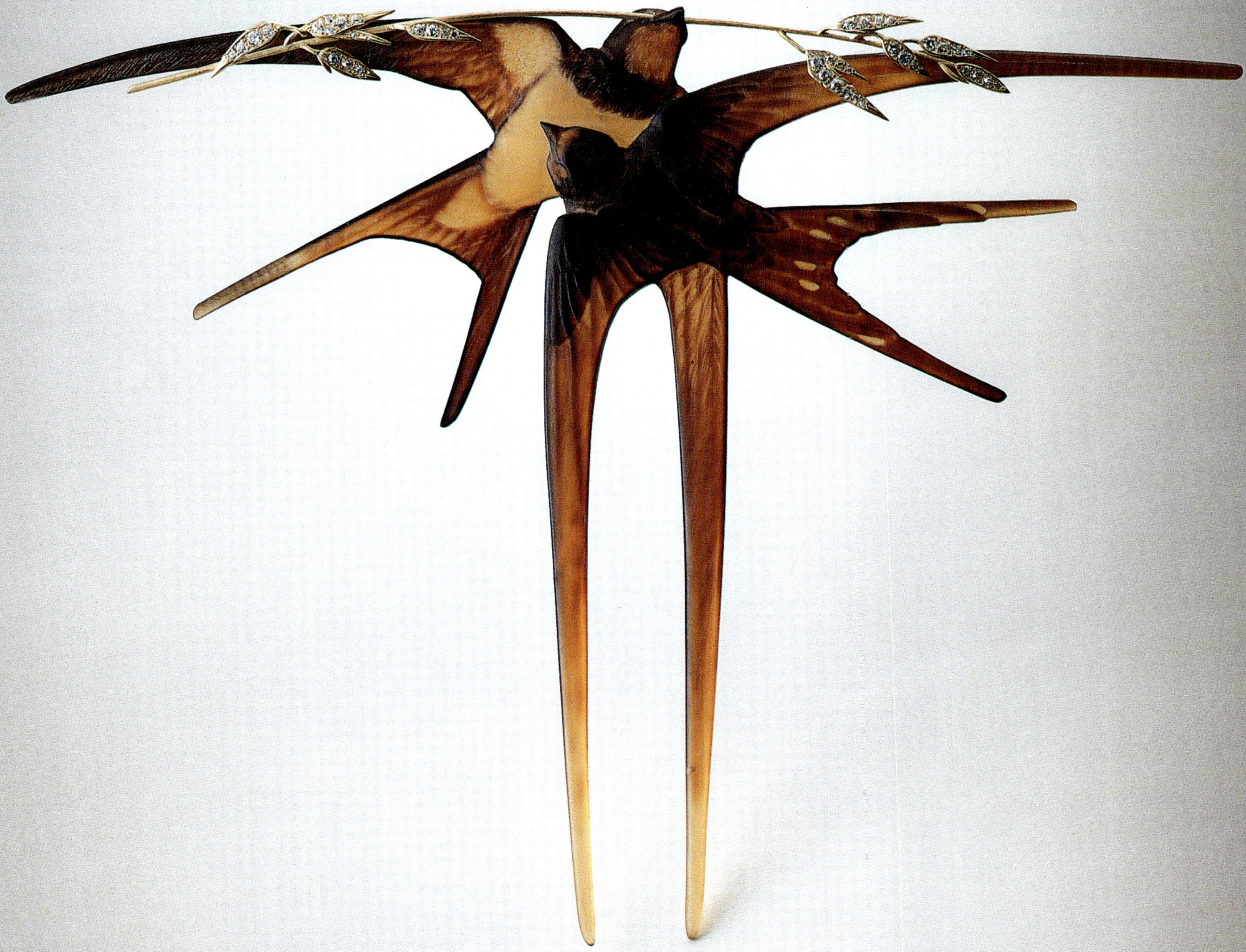

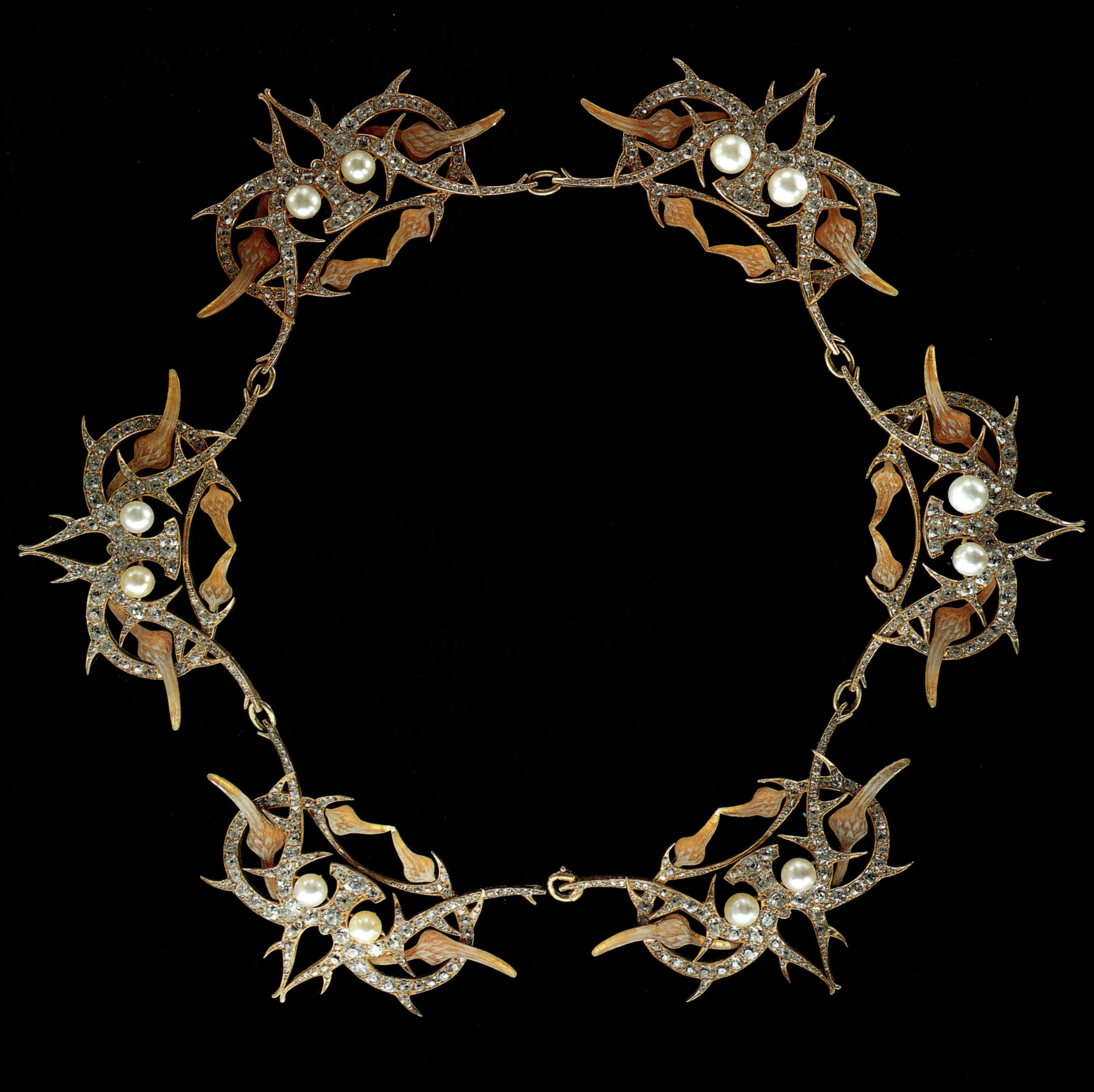

Tour à réduire

As well as being an exceptionally talented artist, Lalique was also technically gifted. When producing reliefs in precious metals, ivory or horn, he made use of the *tour à réduire*, or reducing lathe. Miniature-format representational sculptures and reliefs, and even scenes portraying several figures designed to be incorporated into jewelry, could rarely be produced in his studio by an engraver or ivory carver without first creating a large three-dimensional model. Lalique had frequently employed the technique of embossing gold or silver plates, which required accurate dies. From 1892 on, he employed an instrument that had only previously been used by medallists: the *tour à réduire*. This reducing machine, as it is also known, made it possible to create a scaled-down version from a relief in plaster, metal, or wax. The device operated on the same principle as a pantograph, but in three dimensions. A blunt tracing needle followed the contours of the relief, while at the other end of the shaft—the movement having been transmitted by gears and levers—a steel cutting tip recreated the same relief on a smaller scale. This technique enabled the artist to produce a larger-scale model, for example, in plaster, and then a reduction appropriate to a smaller piece of jewelry. The reduced version could be used as a die mold or, in the case of gold or ivory relief, could be incorporated directly.[9]

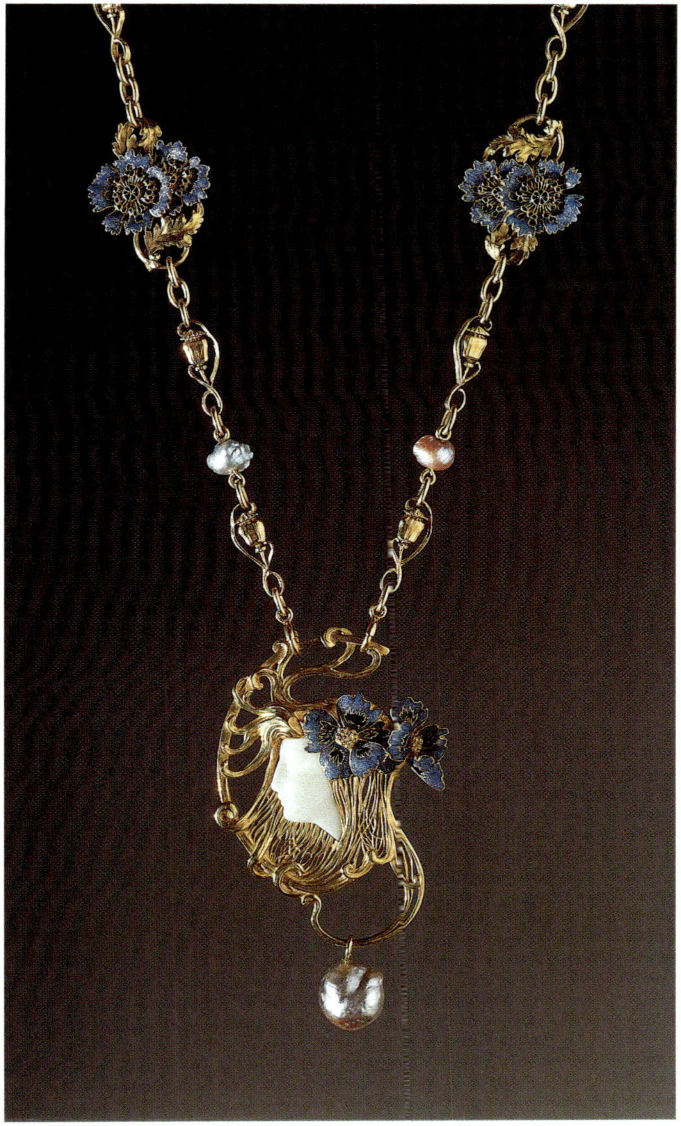

Fig. 20
Necklace
Thistles
c. 1904–1905
Gold, diamonds, glass, enamel, pearls
Each segment: 2 3/4 x 1 1/2 inches (7 x 4 cm)
Private Collection

Pendant and Chain
Woman's Head with Poppies
c. 1898–1899
Cast and chased gold, carved white chalcedony, translucent and opaque enamel on gold, pearl
4 x 2 1/4; chain: 28 1/4 inches
(10.2 x 5.7; chain: 71.6 cm)
(Cat. 41)

The exotic flora of the New World inspired botanists and artists from the time of the discovery, and throughout the following centuries plants were collected for the gardens and greenhouses of Europe. Some American painters of the Hudson River School extended their interest in the unspoiled natural paradise of North America into the southern continent. Martin Johnson Heade traveled to Brazil in 1863 and returned to South America in 1867. His particular interests were the hummingbirds and exotic orchids found in the lush tropical forests. A typical example is his painting Study of an Orchid *of 1872 in the collection of the New York Historical Society. At the Paris Exposition of 1889 the American firm of Charles Lewis Tiffany presented a group of twenty-five spectacular orchid brooches. Naturalistically colored with painted enamel in brilliant tropical colors: yellow, pink, and, in particular, magenta and mauve, and highlighted with diamonds, these astonishing jewels were based on a series of botanical studies made for the firm on expeditions to Brazil, Mexico, the Philippines and other exotic locales. They were extravagantly admired and imitated by Parisian jewelers.*

Lalique made no attempt to emulate this virtuosity, although in the 1890s he produced memorable belt buckles incorporating the flower. On one, a ladyslipper orchid, executed in gold, hangs above its own reflection in pale green translucent enamel water like a floral Narcissus. On another, a similar gold orchid, cruelly ensnared by black enamel thorns, sheds drops of ruby blood.

The great series of orchid tiaras belongs to the years 1903–1904 when, having turned away from the more bizarre designs that were now so pervasively and vulgarly imitated by others, Lalique produced a series of jewels incorporating quite naturalistic representations of leaves and flowers, many of them executed in carved horn or ivory. Among the most beautiful was a series of tiaras each in the form of a single ladyslipper or cattleya orchid. Here, the flower is sensitively carved in ivory while the narrow leaves are made of translucent enamel with a central vein of diamonds. Abstention from color in the representation of the showiest of flowers makes this tiara in the form of a cattleya orchid a tour de force *of sublety and sophistication.* *JTR*

Tiara
Cattleya Orchid
c. 1903–1904
Carved ivory, horn, gold, enamel on gold, diamonds
4 5/8 x 8 1/8 x 6 1/4 inches
(11.8 x 20.5 x 16 cm)
(Cat. 78)

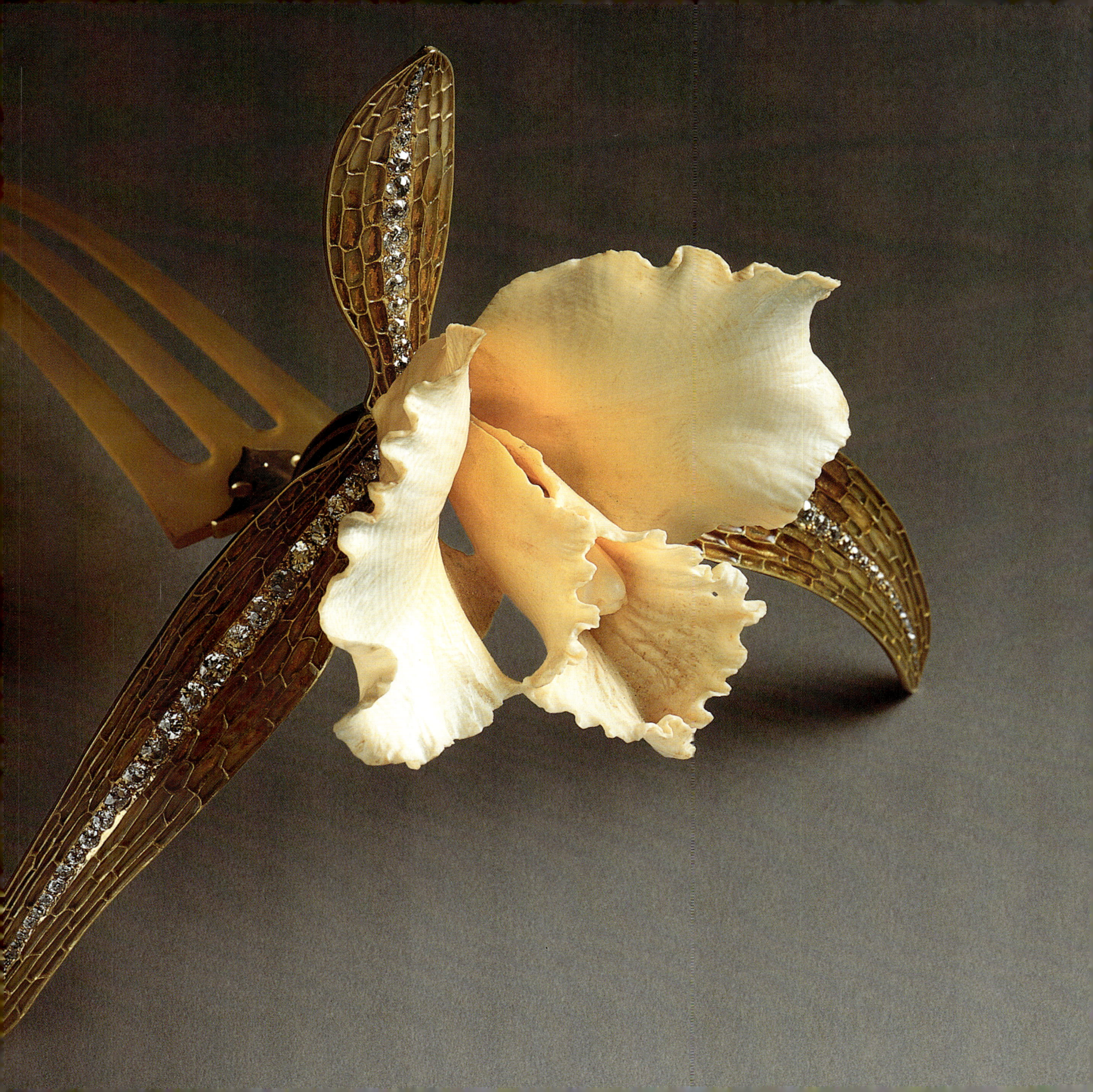

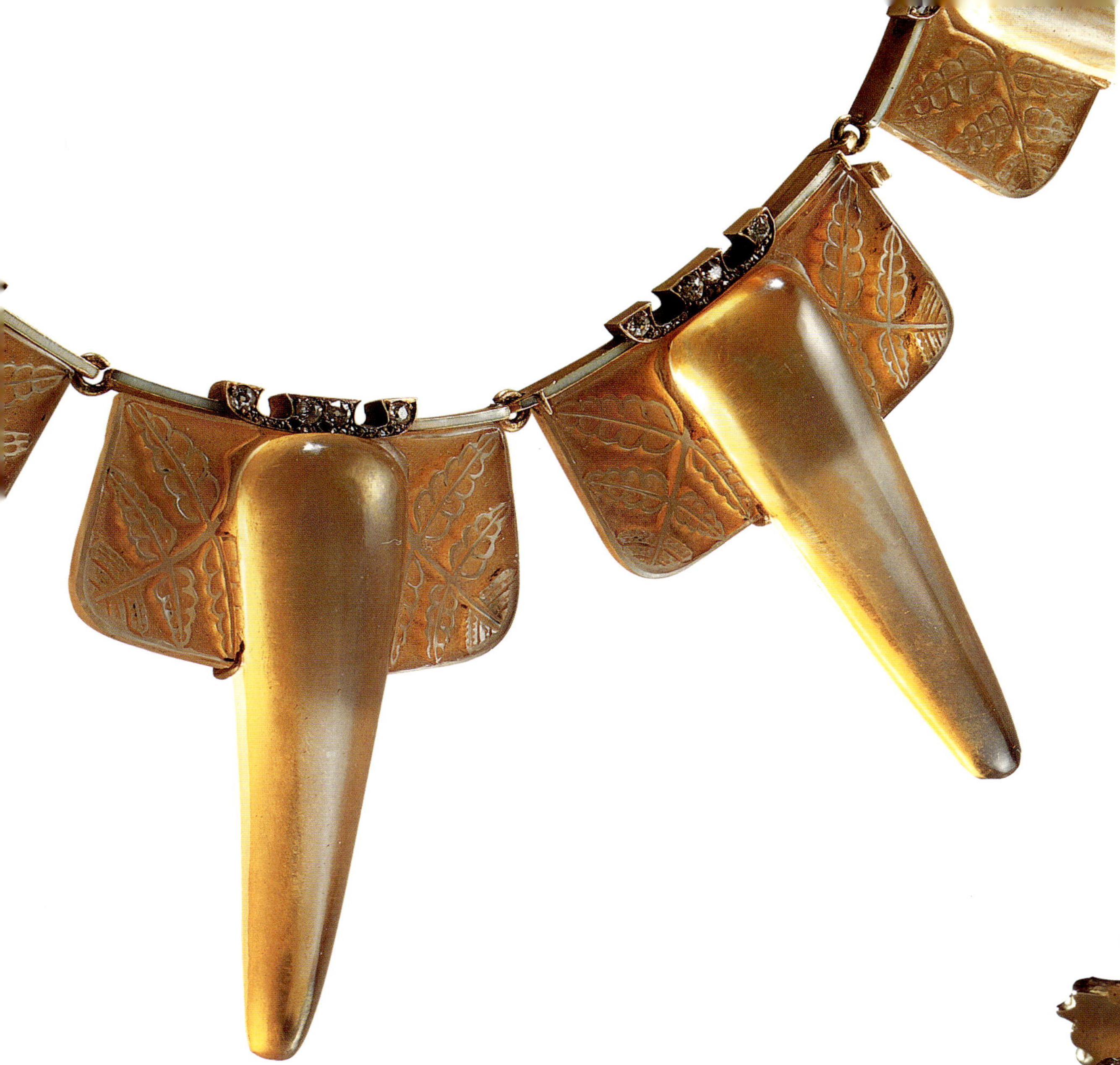

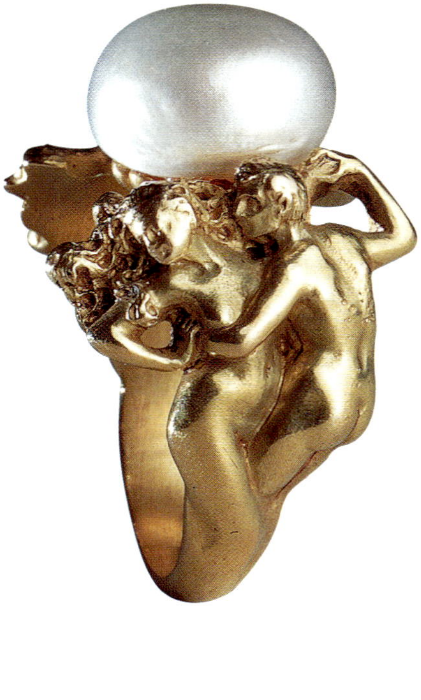

Necklace
Ferns
c. 1902
Cast glass, gold, enamel on gold
(Cat. 87)

Ring
Two Couples
c. 1899–1901
Cast, chased gold, pearl
1 1/8 x 5/8; Diam: 1/2 inches (2.6 x 1.6; Diam: 2.1 cm)
(Cat. 102)

This method was also useful for variants, as when a group of pendants displayed the same relief in the center, but had different mounts. Lalique also occasionally interpreted an idea in varied ways by using the same motif for two or more items of jewelry.

(He separated the rectangular ivory relief on the fish and naiads corsage ornament, Hamburg, Museum für Kunst und Gewerbe, inv. 1900.455, into two medallion-style reliefs in the naiads belt buckle, MCG, inv. 1172. See also cats. 102, 173.)

Pearls and Mother-of-Pearl

Lalique used pearls as a feature in his jewelry compositions in the same way that he did precious and semiprecious stones. From as early as 1893, he showed a preference for the subtle shimmer of white, pink, or gray pearls in their regular, spherical form. But in 1897, irregularly shaped baroque pearls start to appear in his jewelry as well as ordinary pearl drops. Here Lalique was again inspired by Renaissance models. However, whereas in the sixteenth century the large, precious baroque pearls were used to represent the body or trunk of a figure or animal, Lalique gave these exquisite products a separate, independent function as the freely suspended drop of a brooch or pendant. Smaller baroque pearls were used as highlights to provide variation in long chains or as a finishing element for rings. Now and again, several pearls were combined to represent a cluster of flowers, or were positioned as emerging from the mouths of snakes and dragons.

Numerous parallel rows of small pearls were often attached to the center plaques of chokers. Lalique actually preferred this kind of jewelry to flat circular necklaces. Worn on a long, slim neck, the pearl strings of a choker beautifully accentuated the elegant lines of a head with a piled-up hairstyle. They were ideal for the neckband, which could be up to fourteen rows wide and precisely tailored to the conical form of the neck.

Mother-of-pearl, the considerably more affordable product of haliotis (ear shells), found in southern waters, or of different types of oyster, resembles pearl as far as its refractive shimmer is concerned, but can be sawed, engraved, ground, polished, and pierced like horn. Lalique only used mother-of-pearl occasionally, sometimes even in conjunction with horn, for clusters of flowers or the wings of a beetle. In later years, he preferred glass, which was more easily shaped, and coated with enamel, producing a similar effect.

Glass, a Lifelong Passion

Although, in one respect, it was only a small step from enamel to glass, since both materials have a similar chemical composition, one provided color while the other provided form. Lalique recognized, even in the

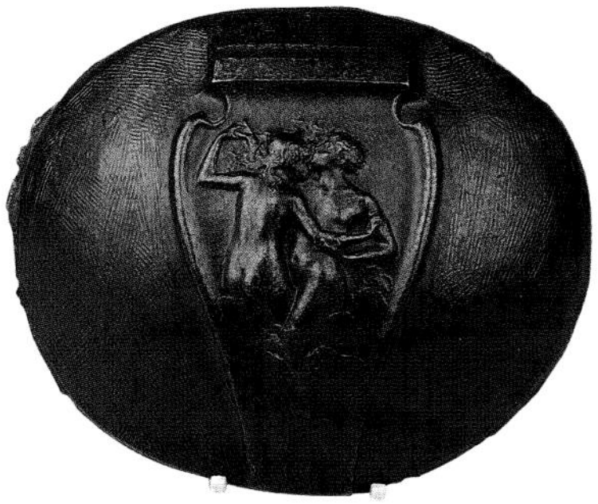

Model for Earring and Finger Ring
Two Couples
1899–1901
Bronze
7 1/2 x 6 1/4 inches
(19 x 16 cm)
(Cat. 173)

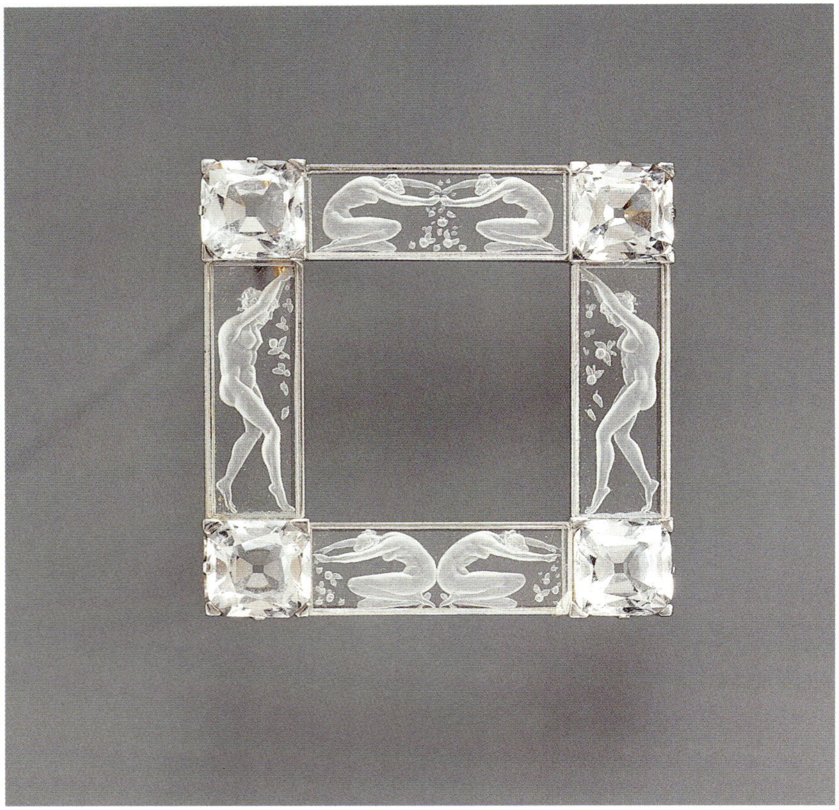

Brooch
Women and Flowers
c. 1904–1905
Gold, glass, diamonds
1 3/4 x 1 3/4 inches
(4.5 x 4.5 cm)
(Cat. 141)

Pendant and Chain
Lilacs
c. 1904–1905
Gold, enamel, engraved glass, diamonds
14 1/4 x 2 1/4 inches
(36.2 x 5.7 cm)
(Cat. 137)

1890s, that he could use glass to embody his concepts of sculptural form and decorative coloring, and indeed, this material absorbed him throughout his life. He experimented extensively with colorless crystal glass, which he fashioned into three-dimensional objects, pressed, cut, and enameled. The intricate shapes of his jewels could be produced in glass with great accuracy. A pale, usually opal-colored coating of enamel then lent the material a mysterious iridescent quality and reduced its transparency. Lalique used the same trick described earlier for glass reliefs, that is, he sometimes placed a brightly colored enameled gold plate behind the glass. However, the effect that was impossible to achieve with ivory here played a dominant role, for the light was reflected. About 1910, Lalique elaborated this effect to produce more than one color in his glass jewelry by setting a colored glass relief on a gold mount enameled in a contrasting color.

With glass, Lalique discovered an outstanding material for interpreting flora and fauna motifs: it was better suited than precious or semiprecious stones for representing, for example, luscious cherries or berries, or the matte, velvety flower of an anemone, rose, or thistle, whose stalks and leaves would stand out in gold and enamel. What could more vividly evoke the freezing cold of a winter landscape than a glass relief with its icy appearance? Lalique coated the surface of the glass with a matte-finish

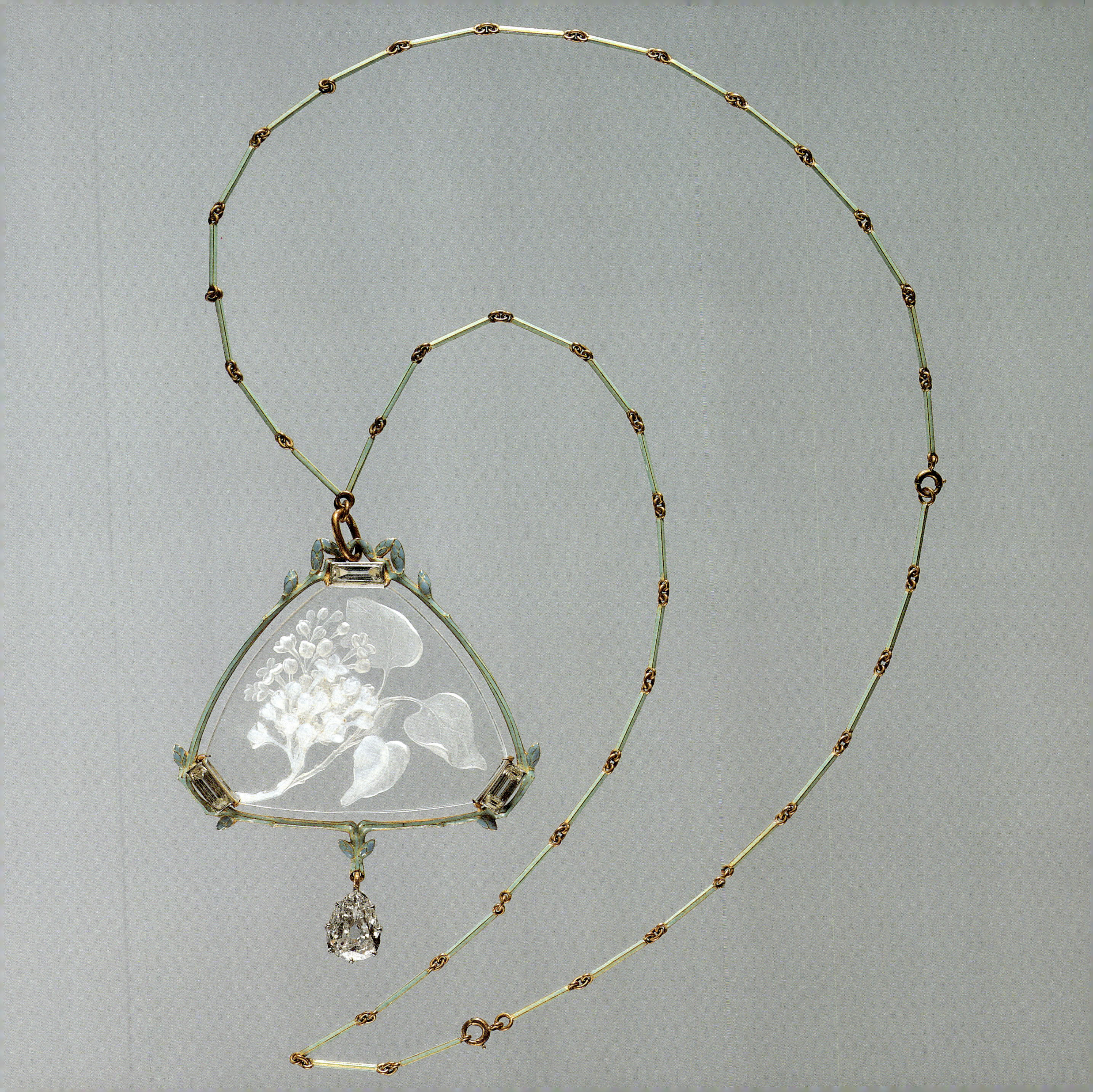

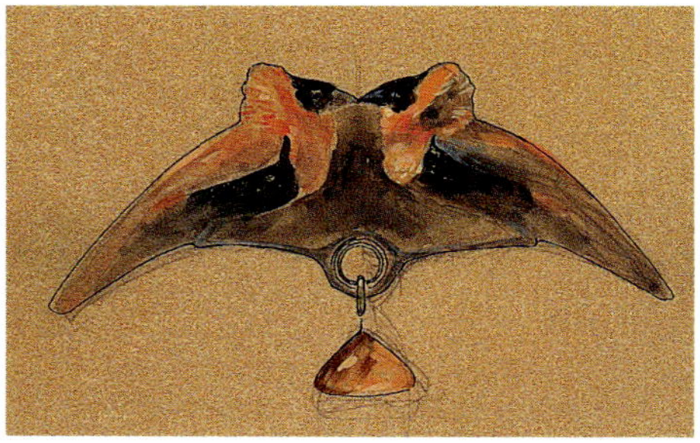

Design
for a Pendant
Two Cocks
c. 1905
Pencil, ink,
watercolor on
paper
10 7/16 x 8 1/2
inches
(27.7 x 21.5 cm)
(Cat. 157)

Pendant
Two Cocks
c. 1905–1906
Cast glass, gold,
copper, *pâte de verre* enamel,
baroque pearl
12 3/8 x 4 7/16
inches
(31.5 x 11.3 cm)
(Cat. 94)

Following double pages
Brooch
Dancing Nymphs in a Frame of Bats
c. 1902–1903
Artificial ivory,
gold, enamel
2 x 3 inches
(5 x 7.5 cm)
(Cat. 112)

Pendant
Dancing Nymphs
c. 1902–1903
Artificial ivory,
enamel, gold,
pearl
2 5/8 x 2 1/4
inches
(6.5 x 6 cm)
(Cat. 113)

Brooch
Dancing Nymphs in a Frame of Butterflies
c. 1901–1902
Gold, enamel,
sapphires, horn
2 1/4 x 1 3/4
inches
(5.5 x 4.5 cm)
(Cat. 111)

Brooch
Dancing Nymphs
c. 1902–1903
Artificial amber,
glass, silver
2 x 2 1/2 inches
(5 x 6.5 cm)
(Cat. 114)

enamel, left the surface dull from cutting, or polished it, depending on the motif. About 1900, ivory was the material predominantly used in the many pendants and brooches featuring representational relief and floral surrounds; by 1905, however, ivory was superseded by glass.

It was around this time that Lalique's jewelry grew increasingly transparent. The artist had clear crystal glass plaques deep-cut from the reverse side by an intaglio method to produce naturalistic representations. These plaques were also often assembled into pendants, into a framework of delicate, enameled branches combined with diamonds. He achieved an amazing three-dimensional effect, for example, in the brooch known as *The Kiss*, with its patinated silver surround, by producing the male head in high relief from the front side, and the female head in bas-relief from the rear (cat. 138).

In the shift to mass glass production about 1908, whole series of pressed-glass brooches, pendants, and hatpins were created—but still in gold mounts—until glass jewelry declined in significance to become merely a sideline in the repertoire of René Lalique, the glass designer, and the elements in a chain were now only held together with silk threads.

The materials Lalique used for his jewelry were often very delicate and liable to crack, particularly the enamels and the glass elements. His jewelry was unusual and exclusive, not only in terms of the materials, but also in dimensions and iconography. Nevertheless, he always ensured that his jewels were wearable by fitting barely visible hinges or joining the individual parts with circular links.

Lalique's use of precious stones and gold in conjunction with so-called non-precious materials such as glass, horn, or ivory revolutionized jewelry design and paved the way for the unusual combinations of materials typical of the Art Deco style. In the process, Lalique confirmed his view that the value of a piece of jewelry lay in its artistry, because only the expertise of the goldsmith, his willingness and ability to try out unconventional techniques, combined with the originality of his ideas, determines the true value of his works.

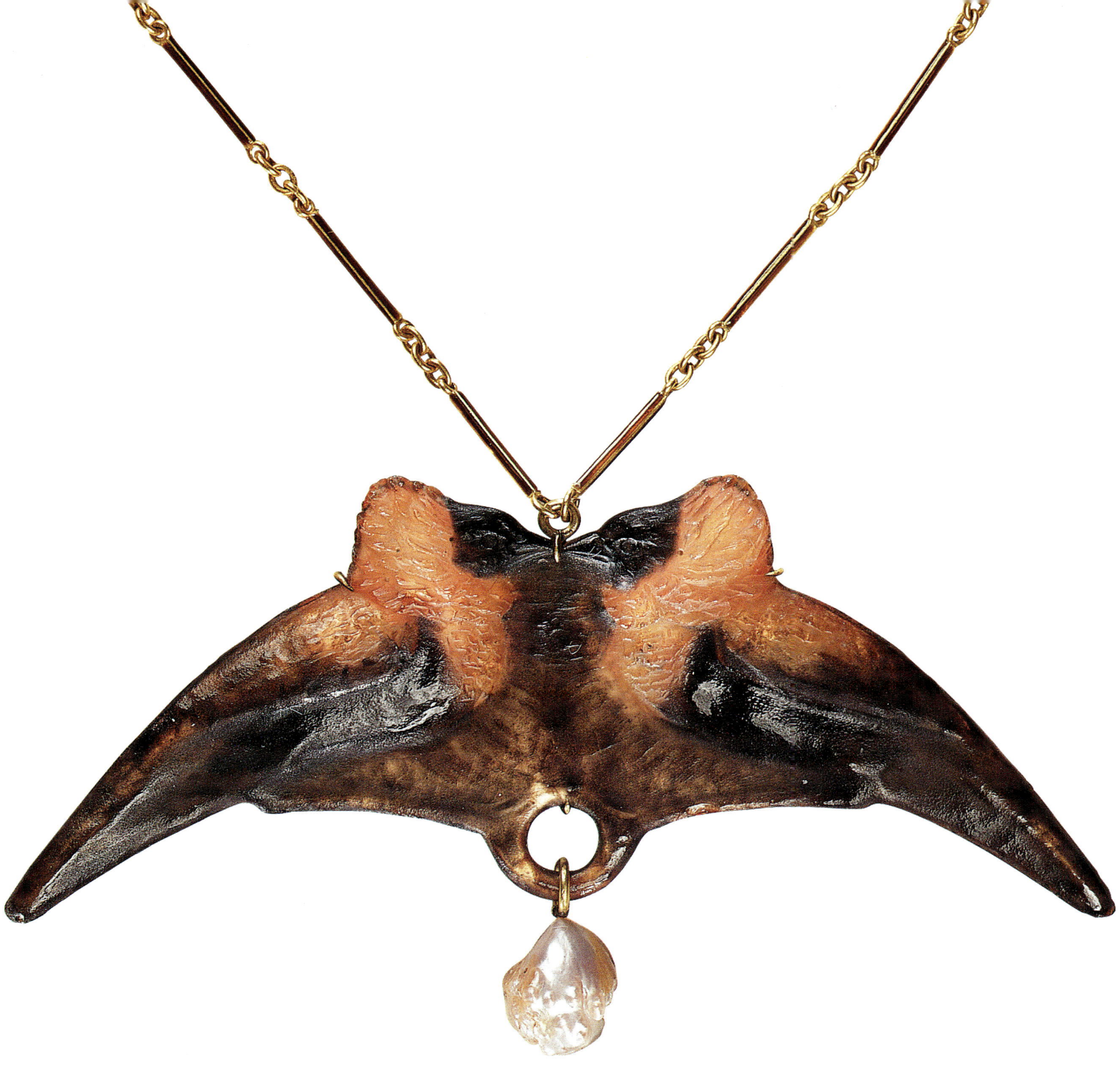

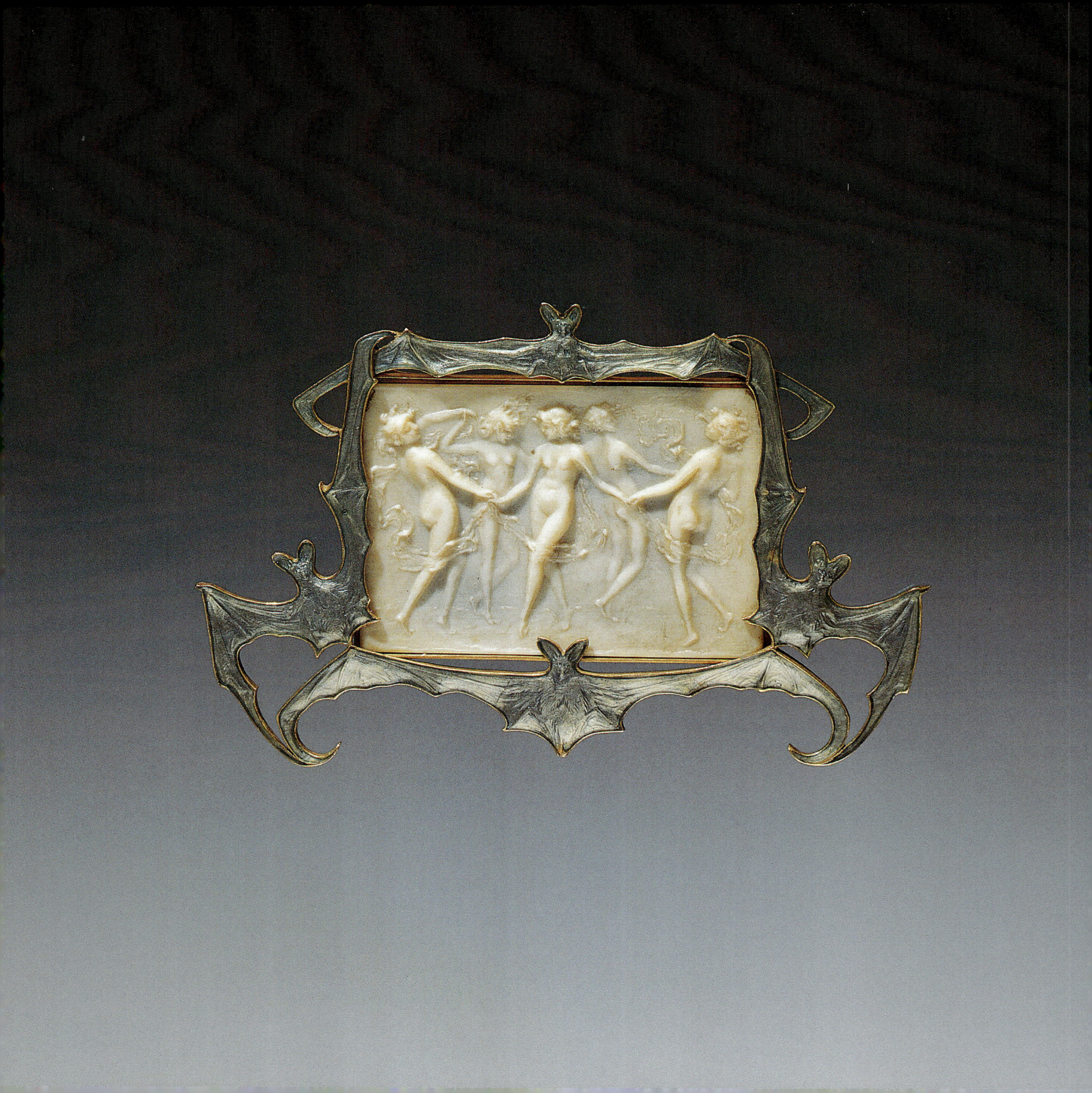

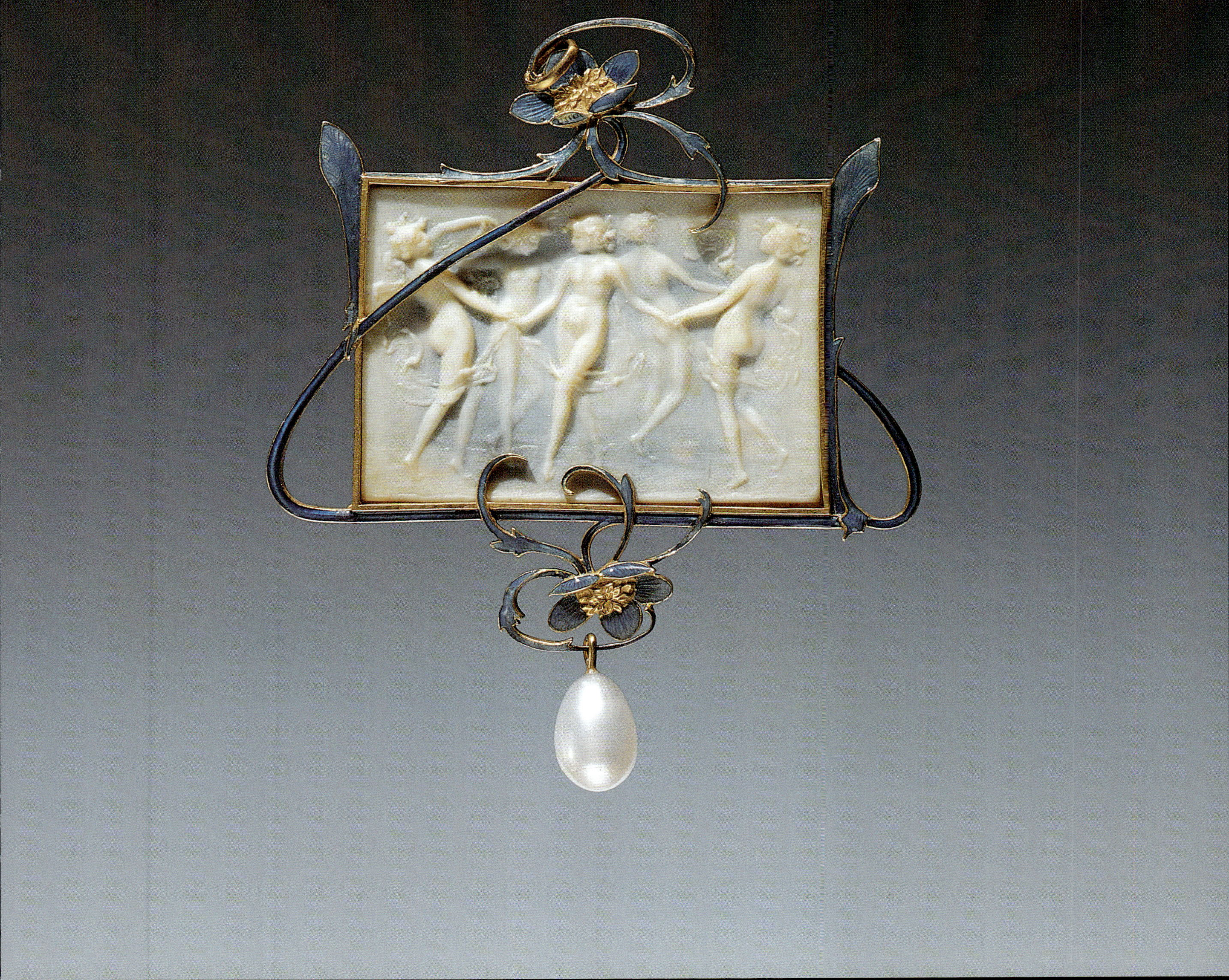

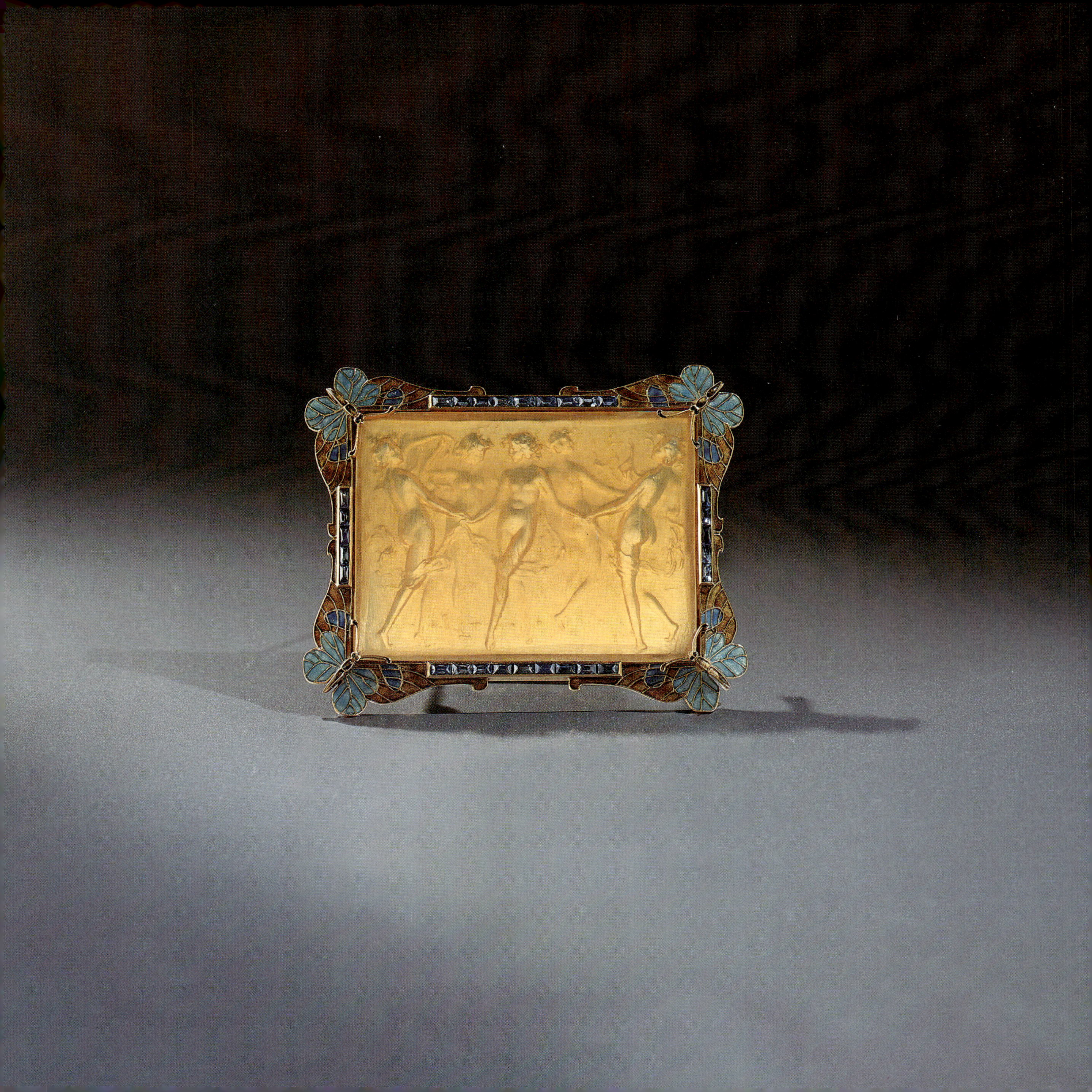

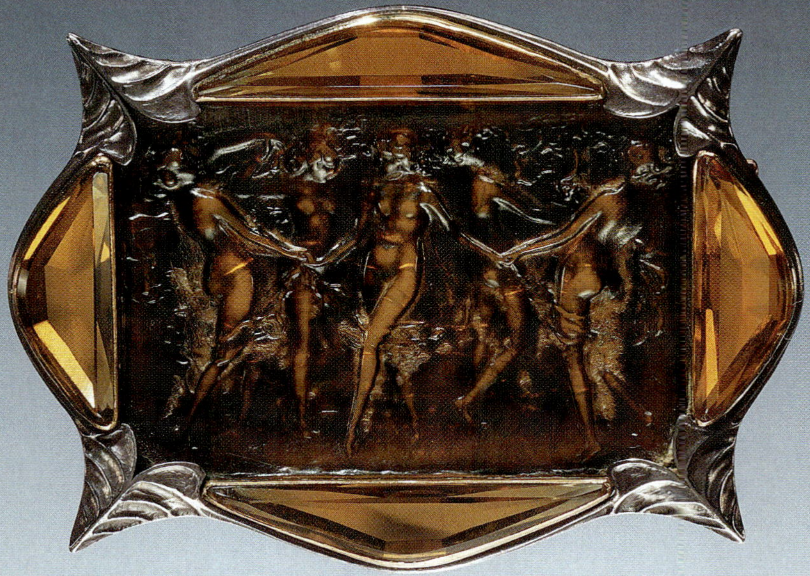

Landscape in the Work of René Lalique

Evelyne Possémé

Pendant
Swans
c. 1898–1900
Chased gold, opaque enamel on gold, *plique-à-jour* enamel
2 1/4 x 1 1/2 inches
(5.7 x 3.8 cm)
(Cat. 31)

The representation of nature in Lalique's jewelry occupies an important if limited place. It manifests itself in a number of motifs: an avenue planted with pines, a landscape with figures, a tree with its reflection, a stretch of water (lake or river) with swans. A study of Lalique's works and their close relationship to photographs taken by the artist himself, however, casts an unexpected light on his working methods. Such works also confirm Lalique's personal affinity with nature. This, in turn, when seen in connection with his correspondence and literary tastes, reveals his fellowship or sense of identity with certain nineteenth-century poets.

René Lalique was no townsman. Born at Ay, in Champagne, he arrived in Paris at the age of twelve to work with the jeweler Vuilleret, a distant cousin. In conversations with his granddaughter Nicole Maritch-Haviland, Lalique would evoke a childhood spent under the wing of a watchful mother, with "long walks in the company of his grandfather, in the early morning on the plains of Champagne, bordered by forests of a somber green harboring a whole little world of birds and insects."[1] Throughout his life, he was to return to the Champagne countryside that had served as the backdrop to his formative artistic experiences. Until his death in 1945, he kept the house that his mother had shared with her sister and that he later inherited jointly with a female cousin, Julia Sevestre.

After Paris, the young Lalique spent the years from 1878 to 1880 continuing his education in London. Although averse to formal studies, he seems to have spent time at the Crystal Palace School of Art and Music at Sydenham, and habituated the South Kensington Museum (later the Victoria and Albert Museum) and the British Museum.[2]

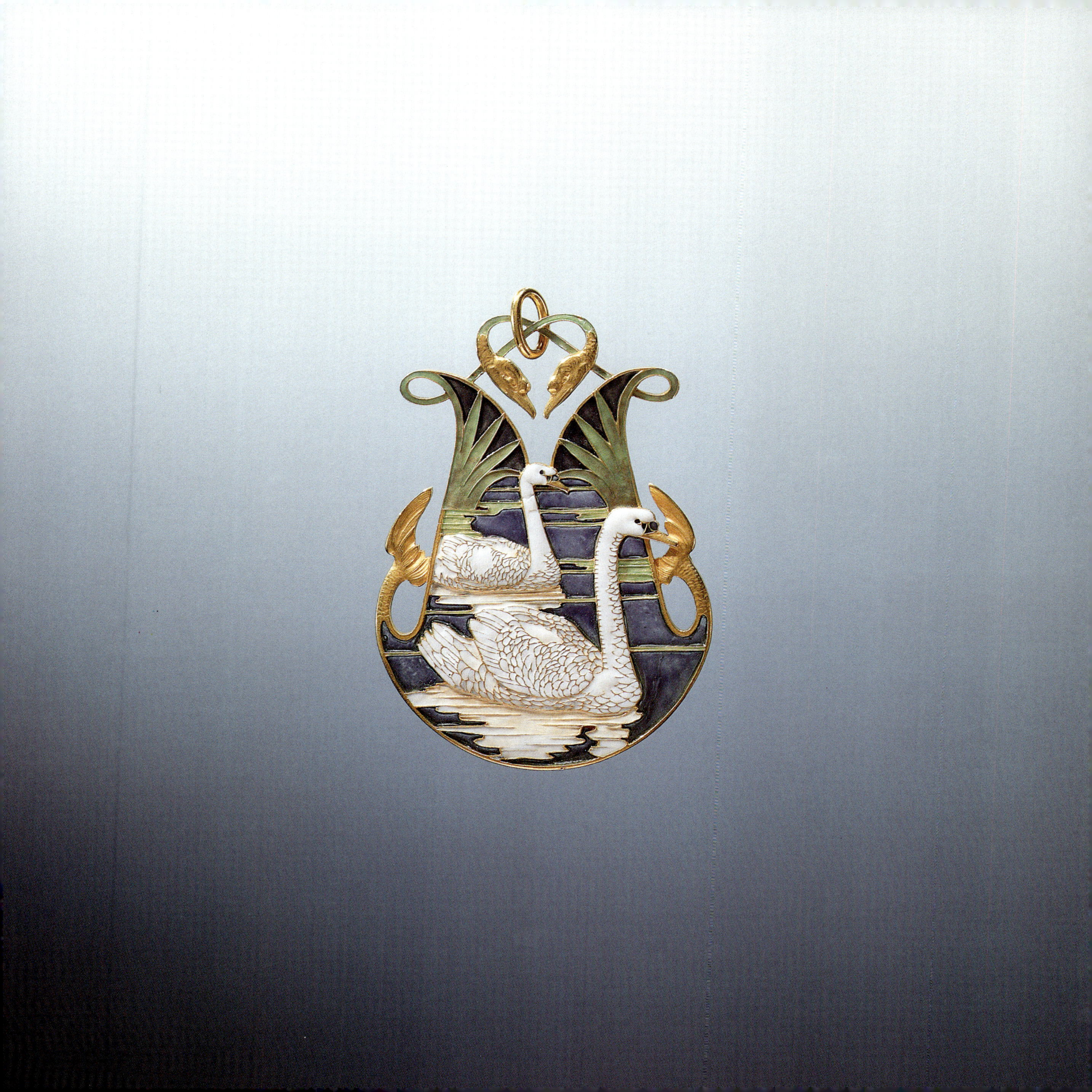

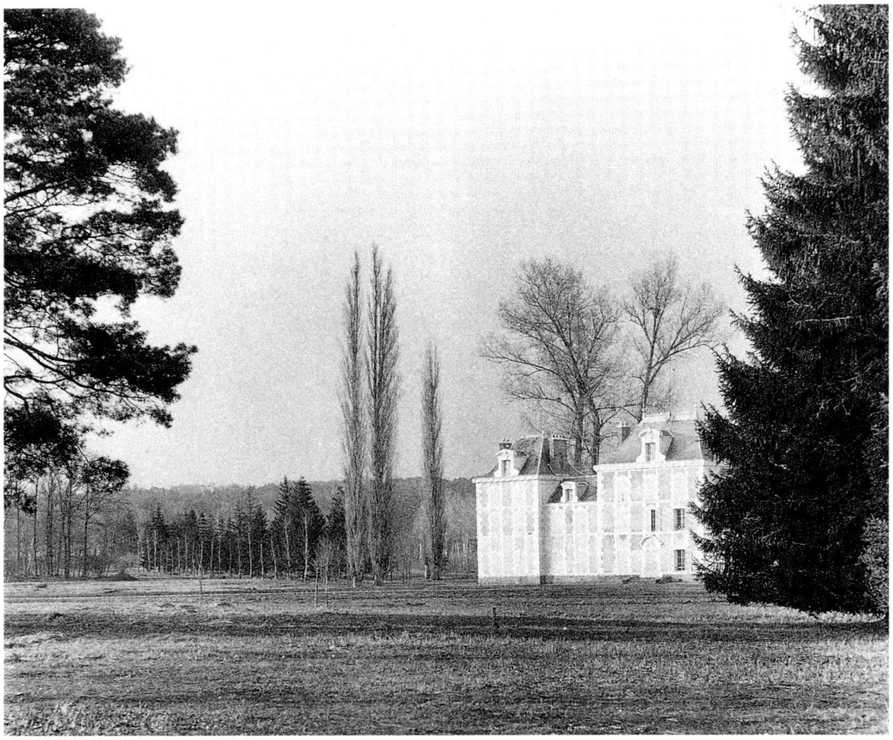

In London, Lalique discovered not only art, but also English literature, particularly Shakespeare, of whom he was to remain a fervent admirer. Moreover, he could scarcely have been unaware of the Arts and Crafts movement in English decorative arts, led at the time by William Morris, but formulated by John Ruskin in the 1860s. In his library, Lalique had a copy of a collection of Ruskin's works in French translation,[3] in which the critic elaborated his ideas concerning nature, trees, and plants. In one text, Ruskin expresses sentiments close to Lalique's: "Although there was no definite religious sentiment mingled with it, there was a continual perception of Sanctity in the whole of nature, from the slightest thing to the vastest;—an instinctive awe mixed with delight, an indefinable thrill, such as we sometimes imagine to indicate the presence of a disembodied spirit."

Throughout his life, Lalique remained empathetic to landscape, to the sensations evoked by beautiful places. As an adult, he often stayed with his family in a manor belonging to his friend, the singer Emma Calvé, situated in the Aveyron, north of Millau, at the end of the deep valley of the Tarn River in southern France. Once, after returning to Paris, he wrote to his wife, who had stayed behind: "My head is still full of fantastic mountain visions, and I dream of fabulous palaces constructed atop those inaccessible summits whence lords would descend....Tell Calvé that I took away with me the very best memories of her and of her fair, cherished land." In the same vein, the letters written during his travels are peppered with rapid-fire notes on the landscapes and towns he went through.

Lalique did more than look upon nature with sensitivity and awe. He saw landscape—and people—with the eyes of a photographer. He was intrigued by the camera and taught photography to his children, Suzanne and Marc, encouraging them to frame shots that would capture fugitive sensations created by a site caught in a certain light. His regular correspondence with Suzanne—conducted when his children were spending summers in friends' houses—often relates to photography.[4] In one letter, dating from before 1914, he sent a photograph with the following note: "I spotted this poor woman sitting on these gray steps; the photo doesn't really capture it, but it was a very beautiful sight." In 1913, after receiving some photographs taken by his children, he offered this advice: "The photographs are fine, but there are more interesting subjects to do at times when the light is good. The courtyard seen obliquely from a window in the kitchen, the trees at the entrance, the bridge, etc." That same year, he asked Suzanne to pass on a message to Marc, who also seemed to have been keen on photography: "Tell him that I am commissioning him to take a photo of the table under the old tree at breakfast time...with the house in the background, and another of the same subject but from the opposite side."

On his own property at Clairefontaine near Rambouillet, Lalique often took photographs himself (fig. 21). Clairefontaine, the site of his earliest endeavors as a master glassmaker, had been given to his wife, Alice, in 1898 (it was sold in 1905). Lalique's granddaughter, Nicole, recalled something her grandfather told her privately: "It was during his walks with Alice in the park at Clairefontaine on the banks of the pond that Lalique would take photographs that gave him a hint of some of nature's more unexpected qualities. These photos were to inspire the landscapes in some of his most audacious jewelry pieces of 1898–1900. He also used the photos he took to breathe new life into a theme which had always been dear to him: the play of light in trees and on water."[5]

The visual relationship between the photographs taken by Lalique at Clairefontaine and certain pieces of jewelry with landscape elements is obvious. But there is other evidence as well that Lalique used photographs as models, as in the annotations recorded on a drawing for a pendant depicting a branch in bloom: "Do another pendant in this/ style directly from nature for the/ leaves, branches and stalks/ the photograph will suffice for/ the flowers."[6]

Such evocations of nature, whether in photographs or jewelry, always return to the same motifs, which express Lalique's

Fig. 21
Lalique's Residence and Grounds at Clairefontaine near Rambouillet
c. 1898–1905

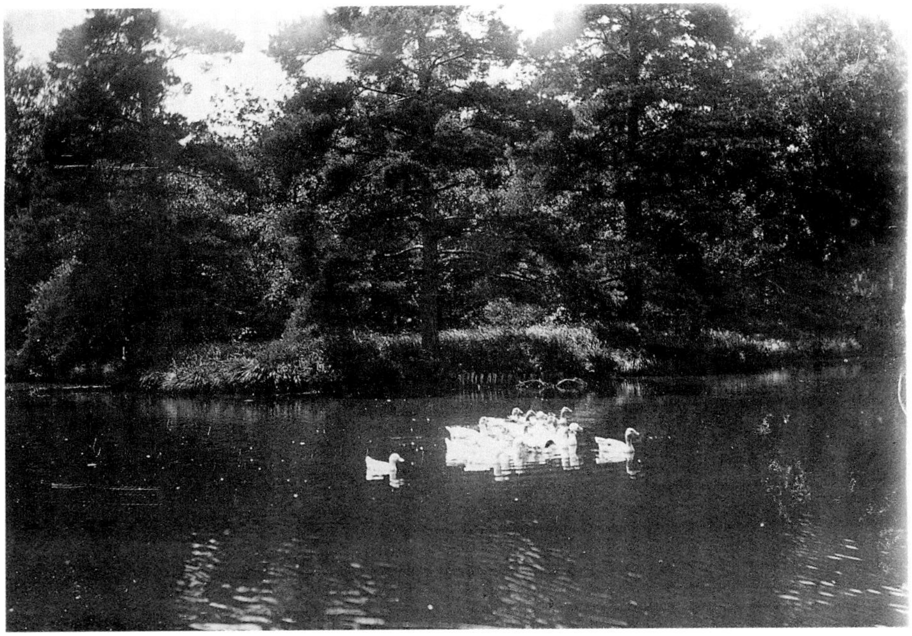

Fig. 22
Lake at
Clairefontaine

Pendant
Two Swans
c. 1897–1899
Chased gold,
enamel on gold,
plique-à-jour
enamel,
diamonds
2 3/8 x 2 1/4
inches
(6 x 5.5 cm)
(Cat. 33)

Following
double page
Fig. 23
Fir Trees in the
Snow at
Clairefontaine

Pendant
Winter
Landscape
c. 1899–1900
Gold, opaque
enamel on gold,
glass, pearl
3 1/4 x 2 1/2
inches
(8.5 x 6.5 cm)
(Cat. 51)

intimate relationship with nature as well as his personal experience: the pine avenue, the firs, the lake or pond, the willows, the swans—all were photographed on his property at Clairefontaine (figs. 22, 23, 25, 26).

All his life, Lalique remained nostalgic for the forests that cloaked the chalk hills around Reims, where as a child he would go for walks. The forest was a place where the soul might find some solace: "Once there, a desire to surrender myself surges forth in my being. Whenever I come here, around midnight, under the spacious trees of this my country, everything, in my now soothed heart, seems to sing of love."

This and other sensibilities about nature Lalique shared with certain nineteenth-century poets. "O! what a beautiful time!" wrote Heinrich Heine, "When the forest trees seemed to entwine their foliage into a triumphal arch, I would move beneath these verdant spans, crowned as if I were the victor!"[7] Paradoxically, this joyful and warm-hearted vision of the forest as the refuge of the poet and of the solitary wanderer never appears in Lalique's works. In the photographs taken on his estate, the avenue of pines strongly evokes the neighboring forest, but his *objets d'art* usually depict a long line of leafless trunks in a winter landscape. In their increasing recession, the trees guide the gaze to a stretch of water bordered by distant leafage. The landscapes reproduced in the drawing in the Lalique Museum Collection (inv. 2.4.346) or on the pendant

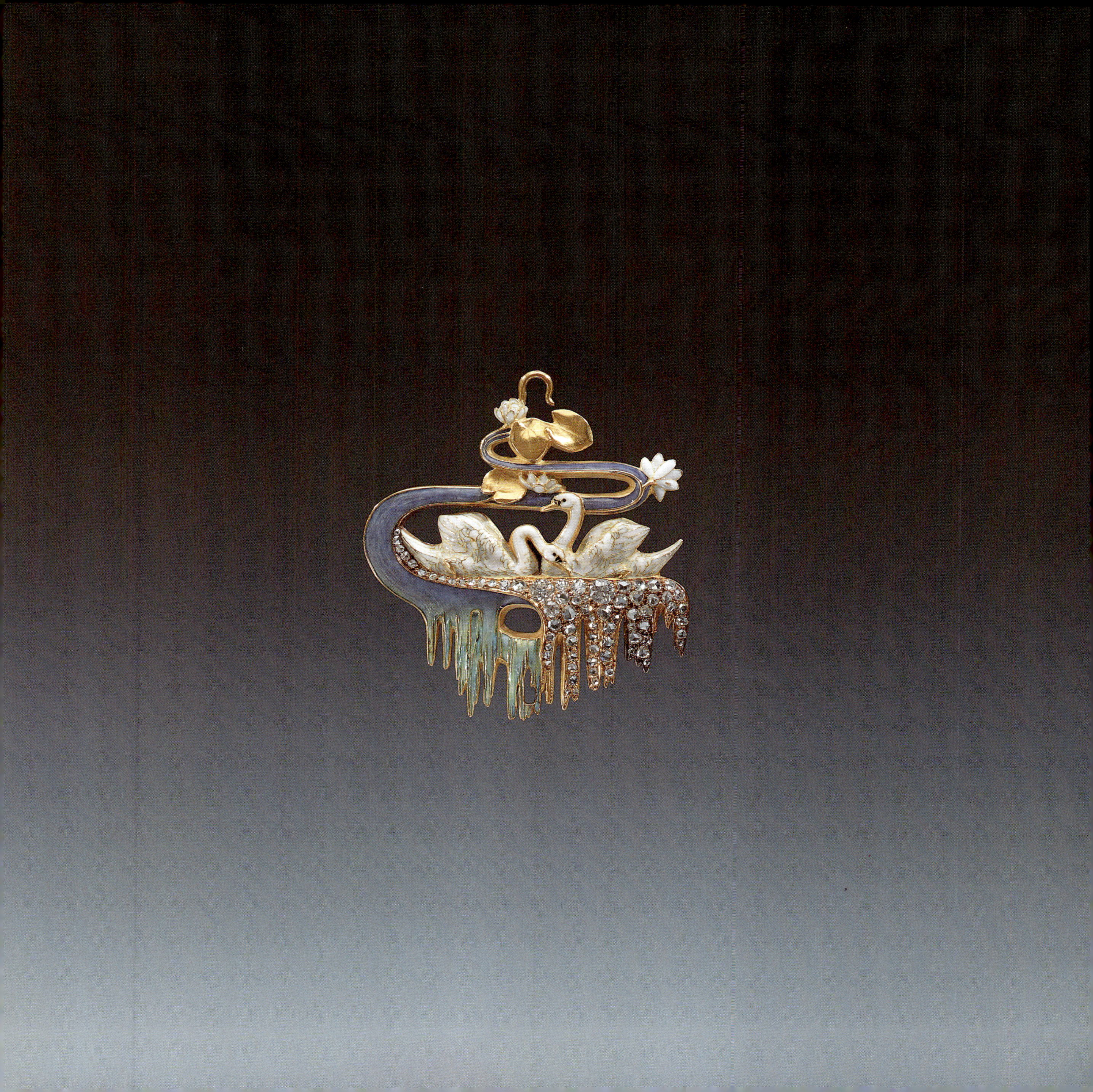

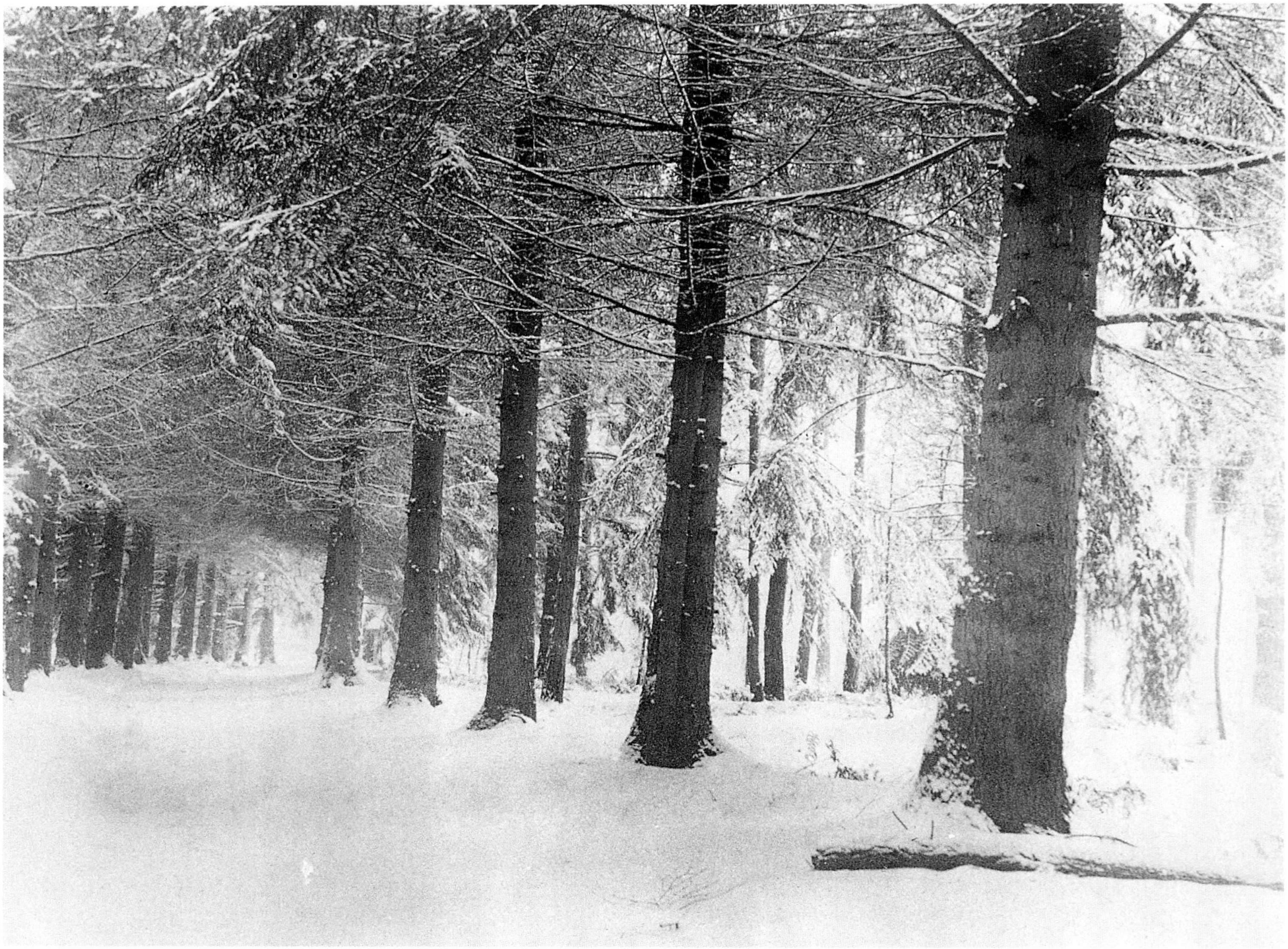

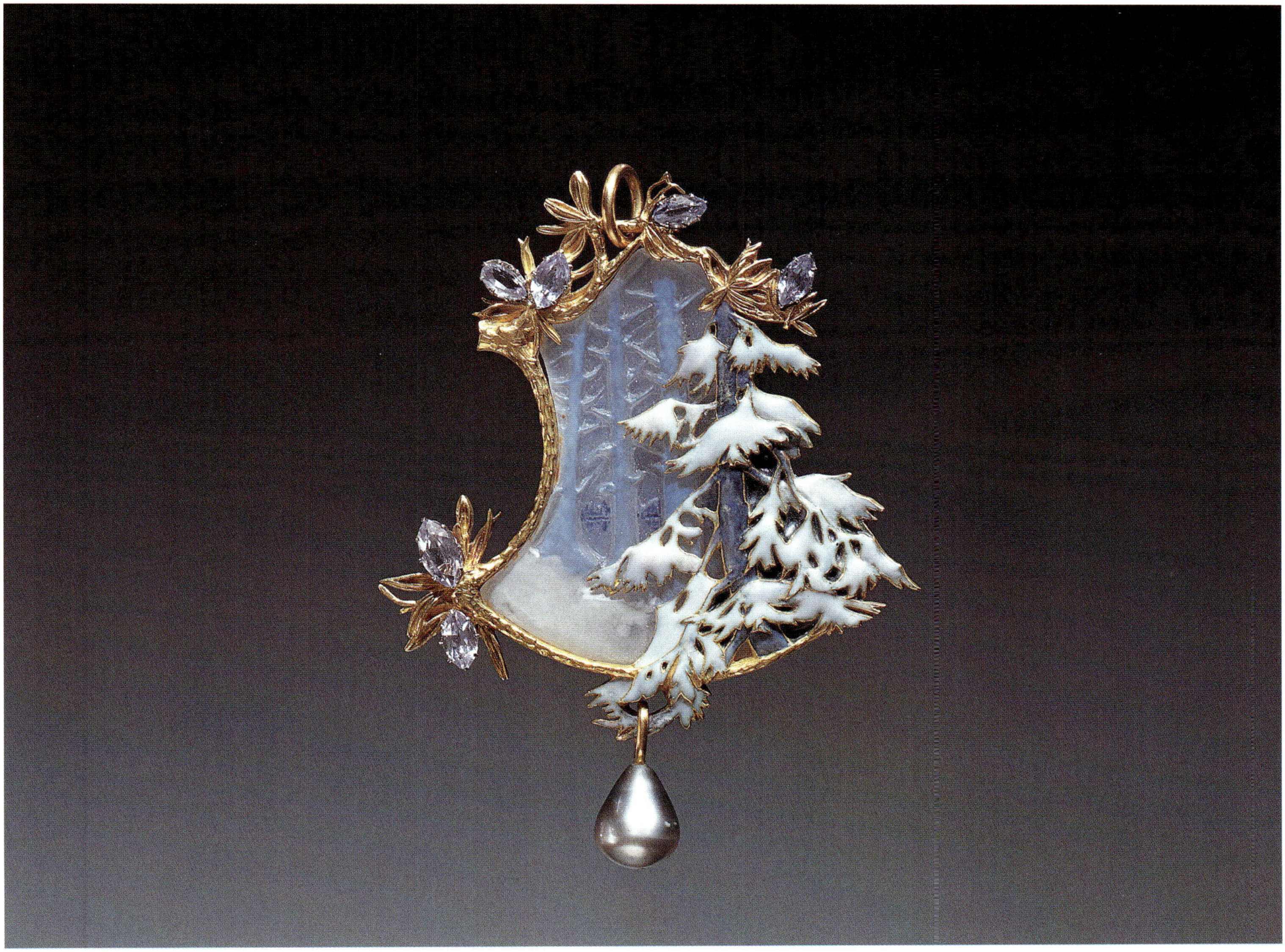

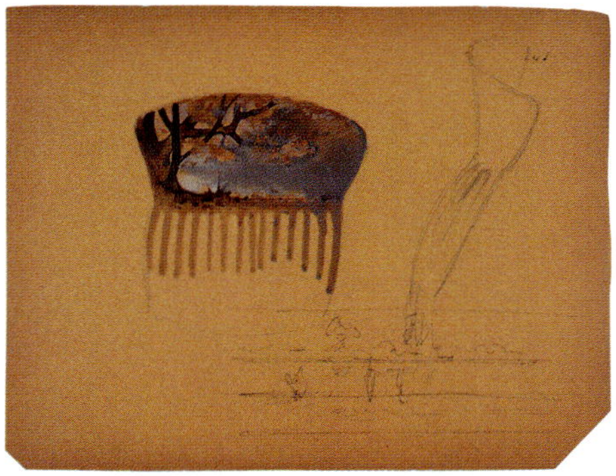

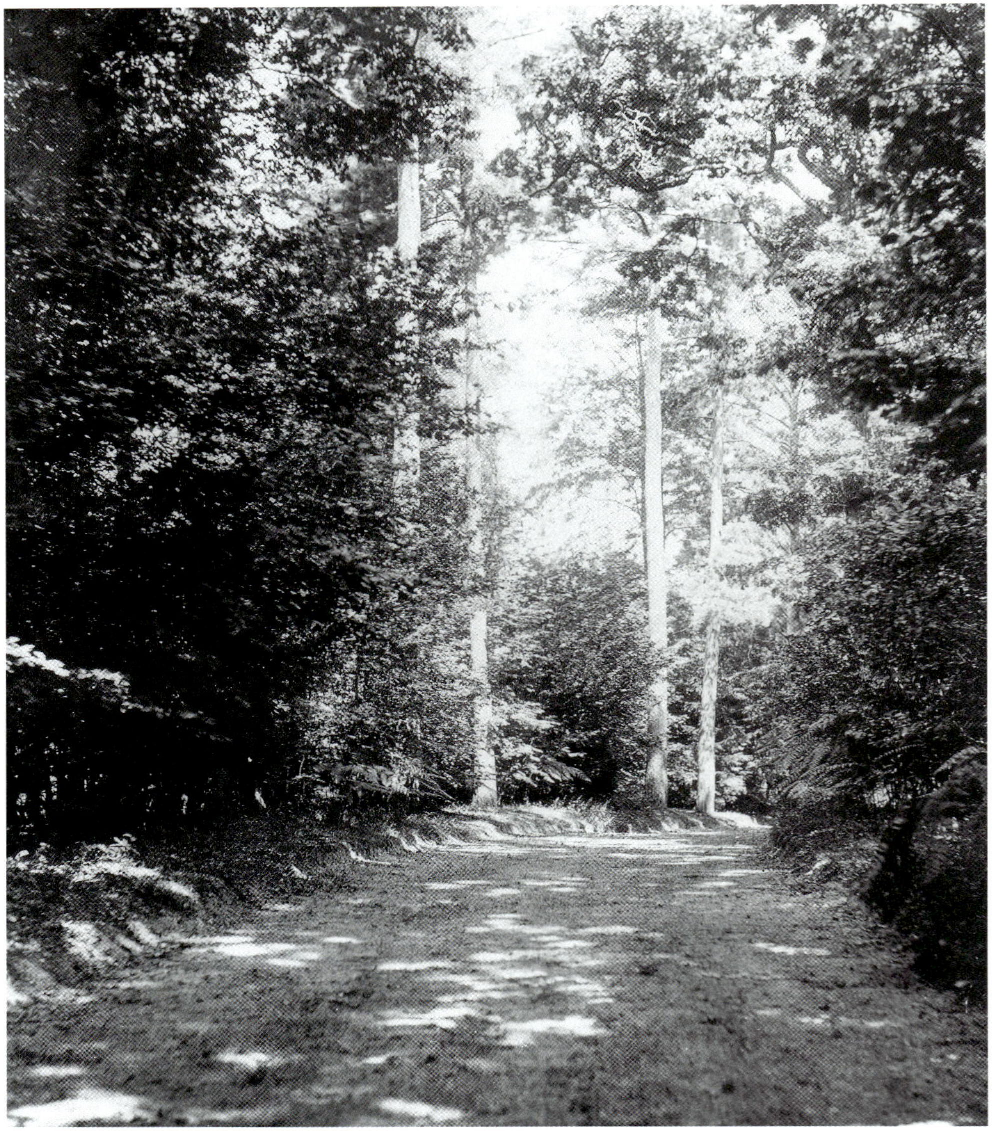

Fig. 24
Design for a
Comb
Paris, Lalique
Museum
Collection,
inv. 1.3.016

Fig. 25
Fir Trees at
Clairefontaine

in the Gulbenkian Museum leave one with an impression of melancholy and loneliness.[8]

Much the same can be said of the vistas of snowcovered firs in Lalique's work, the same trees whose proud solitude Ruskin had already perceived: "But the pine rises in serene resistance, self-contained...they stand on the inaccessible juts and perilous ledges of the enormous wall, in quiet multitudes...upright, fixed, spectral as troops of ghosts standing on the walls of Hades....You cannot reach them, cannot cry out to them:-those trees never heard a human voice, they are far above all sound but of the winds."[9] Lalique reveled in depicting a nature in which the human creature is as nought, where (as with the Japanese) animals, insects, plants, and trees have as much, if not more, importance.

On larger-scale jewelry pieces, for instance, neck plaques or bodice ornaments, Lalique would stretch these woody vistas into long parallel lines of bare trunks, extensions of the pine-bordered avenue, in reference to a type of Japanese print in which trees also fill and modulate the space. Within this arboreal network appear isolated figures taken from the stories of the Round Table or Arthurian legend or else from Shakespeare: Vivien, Morgane, the good fairy who heals wounds, Titania, the queen of the fairies—names full of promise that the artist often scribbled down in his sketchbooks.[10]

To our eyes, a naked female figure seated on a lake's mournful banks on the pendant in Frankfurt looks the incarnation of despair.[11] She cannot fail to evoke Lamartine's lament: "Oh lake! the year has scarcely done its course/And near those waters dear that she should have glimpsed once more/See! I come alone to sit on this stone/On which you saw her once sit!"[12]

The final two lines were cited by Lalique in a letter to his daughter Suzanne in 1937, while he was undergoing treatment at a spa in Aachen. "It is the place where Lamartine's loved one was and it has been chosen for this little monument." Other lines from Heine might apply even more aptly to the description of the scene on the pendant. "Desolate, the stream murmurs like the Styx;/ on the solitary shore a water-nymph is seated,/ wan as death, and silent, like a marble statue;/ she seems deep engulfed in grief."[13]

The woody banks of the lake at Clairefontaine inspired Lalique on more than one occasion. Two drawings particularly, in pencil and chalk, show two naturalistic trees on the banks of a lake.[14] These trees turn up in a study for a comb (fig. 24).[15] On this page, next to a drawing of the piece in profile, appear the teeth of the comb surmounted by a crown decorated by a watery landscape, bordered on the left by the tree trunk. The branches spread over the entire upper section, leaving the bank visible in the foreground; water extends into the background until it reaches some lightly

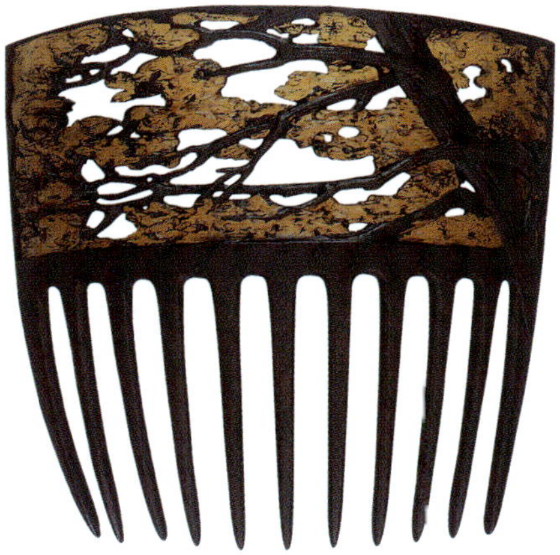

Comb
Tree Branches
c. 1900–1901
Carved horn
with patina
3 7/8 x 4 inches
(9.8 x 10.2 cm)
(Cat. 50)

Following double page
Design for a Watch
Pine Trees
1899–1900
Pencil, ink, watercolor on paper
10 3/4 x 8 3/8 inches
(27.4 x 21.1 cm)
(Cat. 64)

Design for a Watch
Pine Trees
1899–1900
Pencil, ink, watercolor on paper
11 x 8 5/8 inches
(28.1 x 21.9 cm)
(Cat. 65)

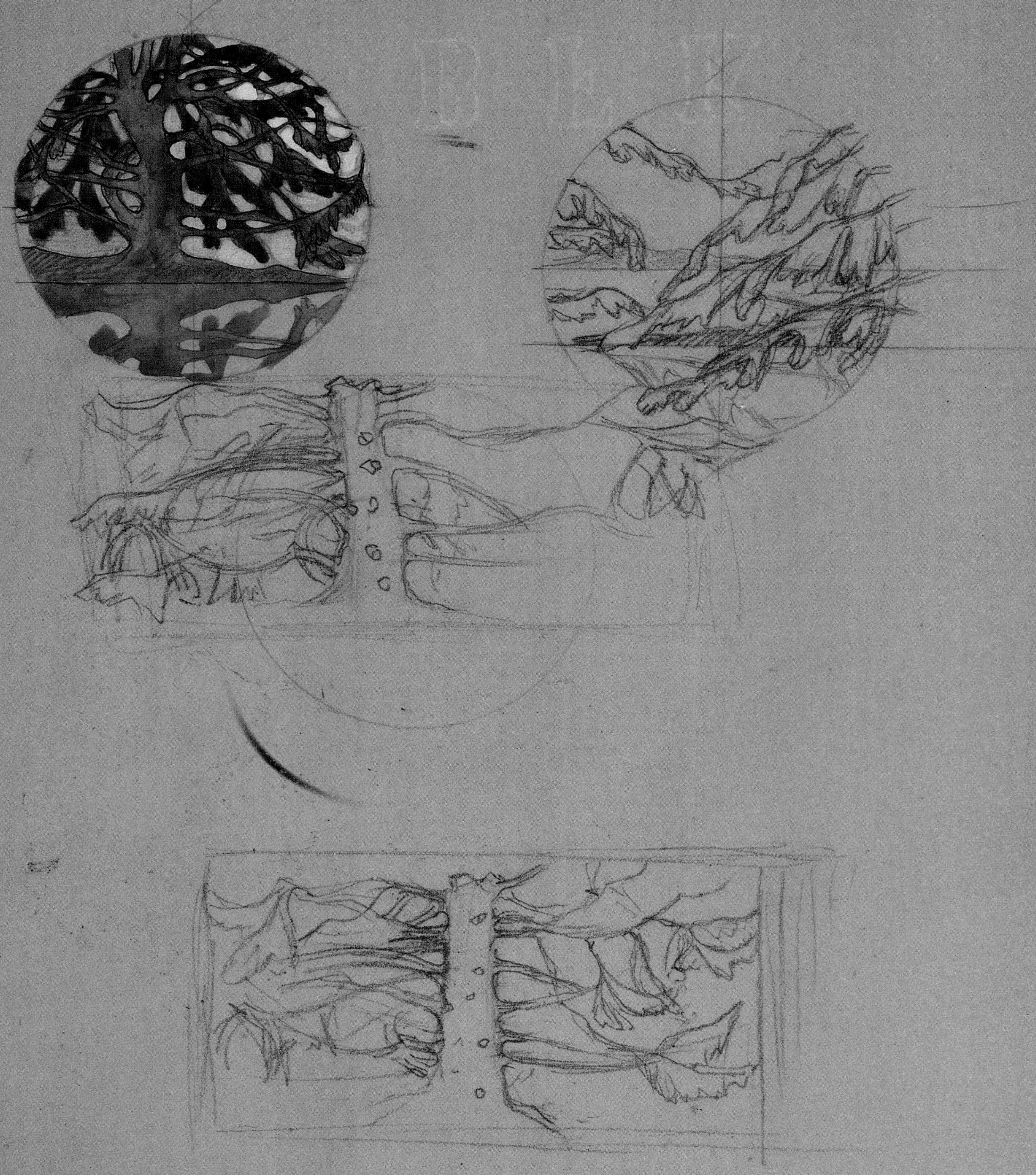

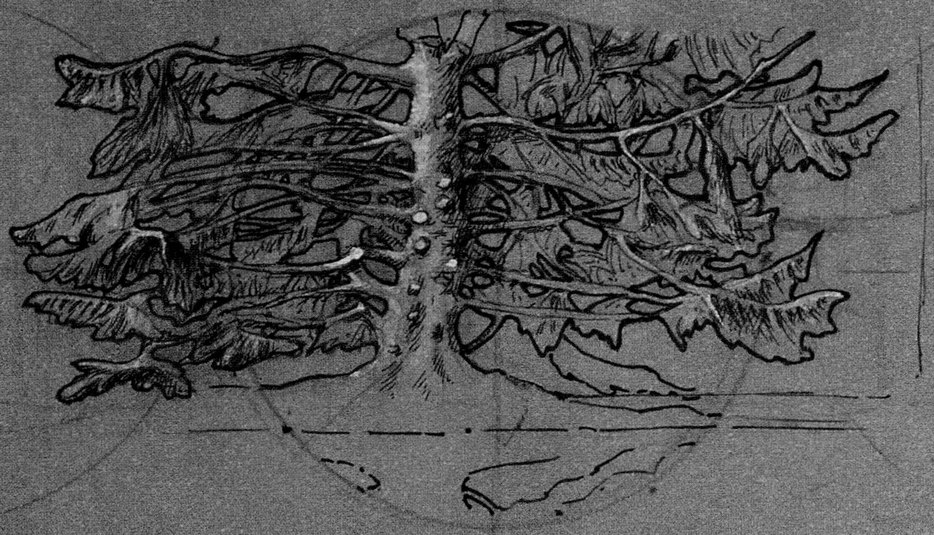

Montre décorée d'un arbre
se reflétant dans l'eau, le terrain
l'arbre et son image dans l'eau
en or — ne pas déformer les cuvettes
les branches se continuent sur la
2e cuvette dessous et sont indiquées
sur la carrure — le fond sera émaillé

pour le 1er Septembre

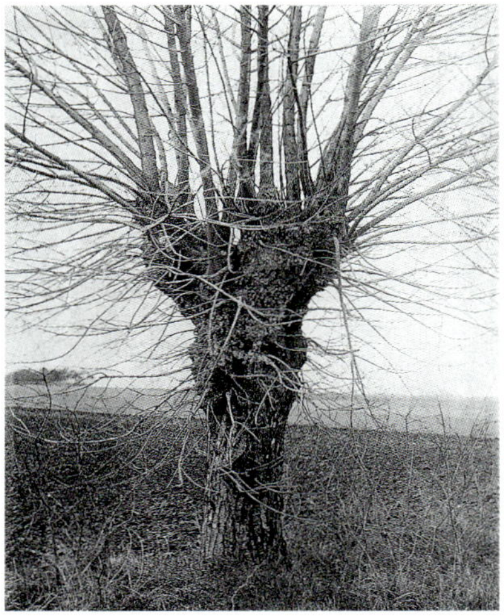

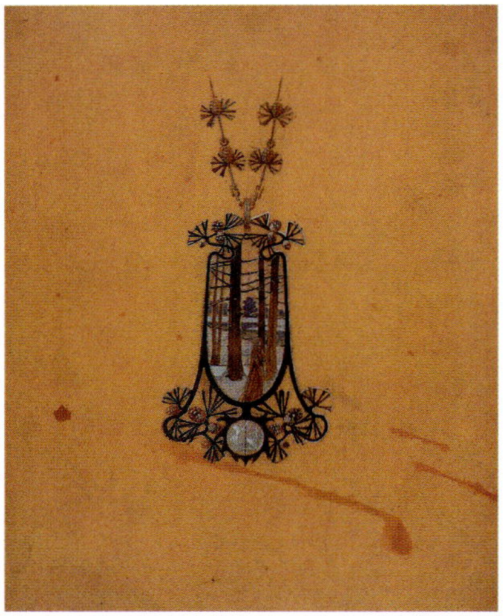

Fig. 26
Willow at
Clairefontaine

Fig. 27
Design for a
Pendant
Paris, Lalique
Museum
Collection,
inv. 2.4.458

Pendant
Dryad and Willows
c. 1900
Chased gold,
enamel on gold,
plique-à-jour
enamel
3 1/8 x 2 1/4
inches
(8 x 5.7 cm)
(Cat. 52)

sketched clumps of shrubbery. At the bottom of the page, the artist has left a thumbnail pencil sketch of various perspectives of the banks, while on the comb itself, the mass of leaves on the tree provides shade for the water below. In this drawing, Lalique's love for his subject is evident in the care he lavishes on the details of the plants, the rendering of the depth of field, the precise positioning of the compositional elements, and the sketching of the reflections of the branches on the water's surface. Lalique has constructed his composition in much the same way as painter would a picture.

The importance of composition is to be found again in two studies for a watch case decorated with a tree (cats. 64, 65).[16] One page contains a number of drawings, two being sketches of a tree trunk, seen from both sides, from which project vertical branches. In the second study, in which Lalique traced a circle to mark the contour of the case, the trunk appears at the center. Two other sketches on the same sheet are oval in form: one shows the reverse side of the watch, where the branches are prolonged so as to meet in the middle; the other, which incorporates touches of color, presents the trunk itself with the leaf-clad branches reflected in the water. This drawing and its companion sheet with an inscription make it possible to see how Lalique developed the decorative design for a watch by stretching the motif out into a long strip, following a technique employed in the design of rings.

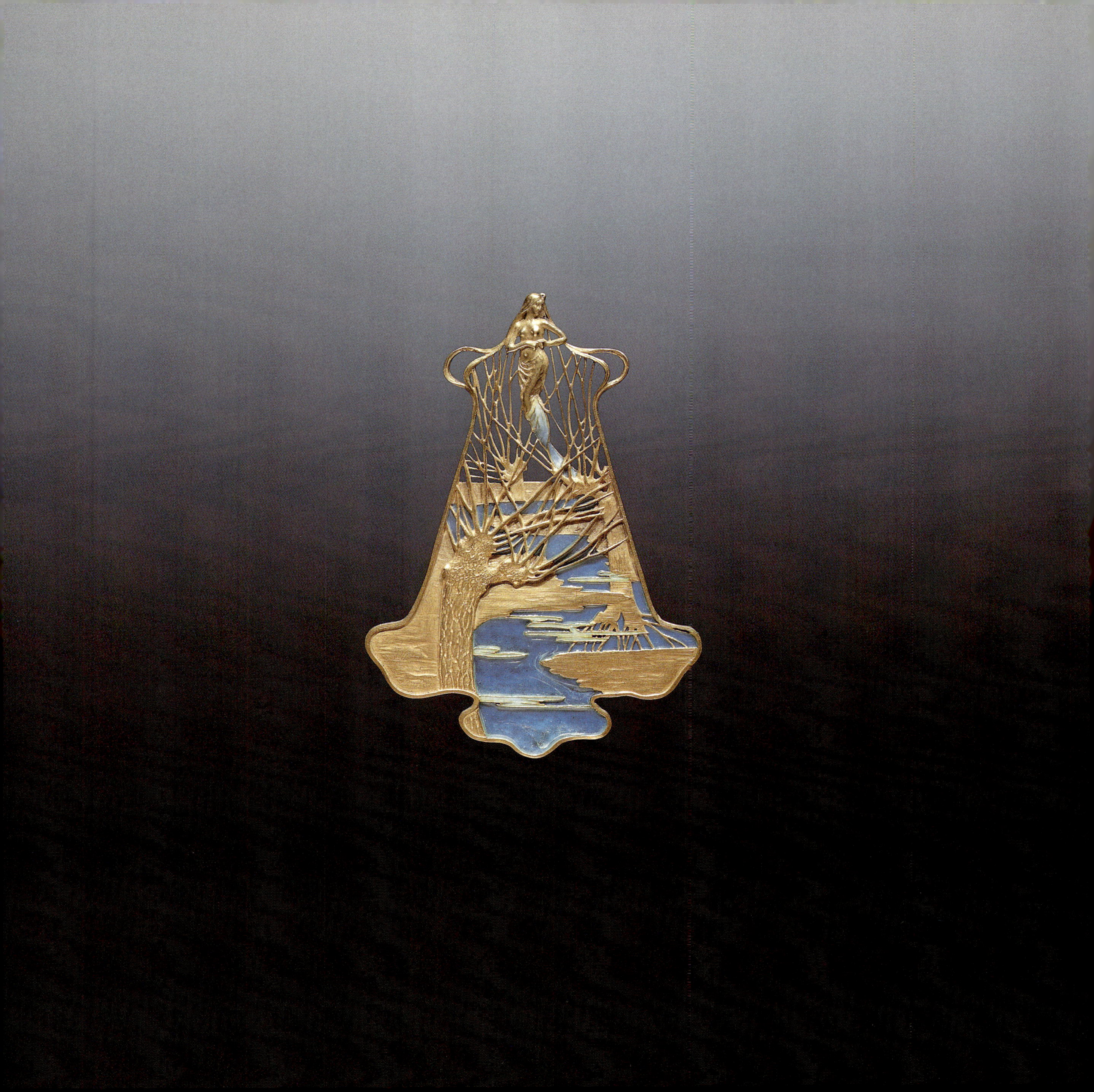

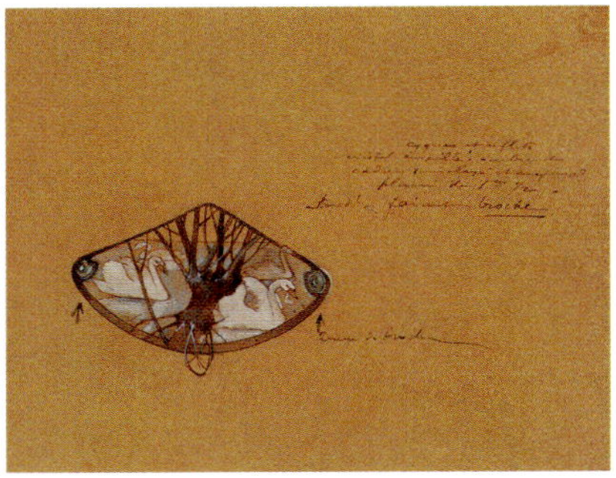

Fig. 28
Design for a Pendant
Paris, Lalique Museum Collection, inv. 2.4.414

Design for a Pendant
Dryad and Willows
c. 1898–1899
Pencil, ink, watercolor, gouache on paper
11 x 8 5/8 inches
(27.8 x 21.8 cm)
(Cat. 66)

These two examples also highlight Lalique's penchant for mirrored surfaces, and especially for reflections of trees in water. The study of reflections becomes the principal subject in a series of willows, a motif that recurs on combs and pendants. On the design for a comb,[17] the crown is decorated by a winding river on whose banks are planted numerous willows that are reflected in the waters. On a drawing for a pendant, the leafless branches of three other willows are reflected in the waters of the river meandering below, while a veiled nymph arises from the topmost branches (cat. 66).[18] A beautiful photograph taken by Lalique shows an enormous willow, its trunk cut lengthwise, stretching out some meager branches toward a desolate expanse from both sides of its quartered bole (fig. 26).

The willow also appears in a drawing for a small triangular pendant; placed in the center, it serves to separate the elegant shapes of swans reflected in the water[19] (fig. 28). Such swans as these, whom Lalique would feed on the banks of his lake at Clairefontaine and enjoy photographing, often recur on his jewelry, their snowy down mirrored and distorted in rippled waters.

In his photographs and drawings, just as in his jewelry, Lalique luxuriates in depicting nature, especially trees, plants, and animals. People are represented by legendary figures: nymphs, fairies, undines, queens, untouchable princesses whose realm borders that of the natural world. His landscapes are composed to express the beauty and grandeur of nature while emphasizing human insignificance and solitude. Lalique redesigns nature, delighting in perspectives that draw the spectator into the landscape. Some of his pieces of jewelry are veritable paintings. In his shoreline landscapes, he betrays an obsession with water's transparency and its reflections, with the mirror surface of the liquid. It is an obsession that pursued him throughout his life and which he later expressed in his work in glass.

Though an admirer of Lamartine, for whom nature provides a solace associated with joys and sorrows, Lalique was no mystic, and nature for him did not imply the existence of a deity. His pantheism is linked to Heine's feeling for nature or, even closer, to that of his contemporary Henri de Régnier, to whose house he had been brought by his friend Edmond Haraucourt, the director of the Musée de Cluny and a poet in his own right. The figures from legend that people Lalique's landscapes and inhabit the trees and plants infuse natural elements with spirituality. Lalique conjures up an unattainable parallel universe which, through dreams, can give heightened force to our sensations and emotions. Through such imagery, he reveals a deep-rooted sensuality, underscored in his work by the importance given to the elements—above all to water, in the guise of calm and undisturbed lakes or rivers winding unhurriedly through banks planted with willows.

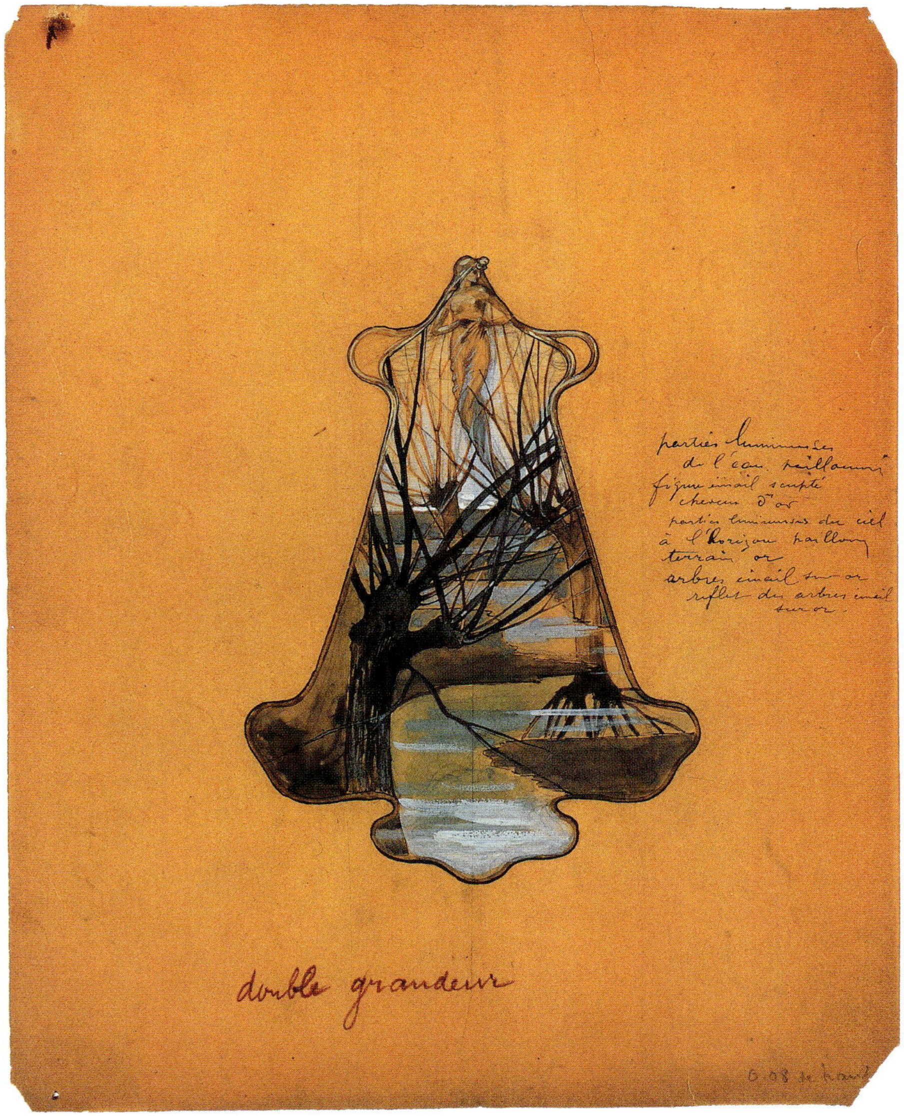
parties lumineuses
de l'eau paillonné
figure émail sculpté
cheveux d'or
parties lumineuses du ciel
à l'horizon paillonné
terrain or
arbres émail sur or
reflet des arbres émail
sur or
double grandeur

Objets d'Art and Glassmaking: René Lalique's Contribution in the Early Twentieth Century

JEAN-LUC OLIVIÉ

Chalice
Figures and Grape Vines
c. 1899–1901
Gold, *plique-à-jour* enamel, carved ivory, glass
4 3/4; Diam: 4 1/8 inches
(12.2; Diam: 10.3 cm)
(Cat. 179)

René Lalique's life can be divided into two successive careers. Just when he was triumphing as a craftsman jeweler around the time of the Exposition Universelle of 1900, he took the first steps in his second calling as a glassmaker. His creations in glass were to become known to a far wider public during the 1925 Exposition Internationale in Paris, and it is these works that constitute the signature style which has endured throughout the twentieth century as one of the truly great names in the French luxury tradition.

Lalique's interest in glass as a material dates from well before he began his career as a glassmaker *per se*. In fact, according to Henri Vever, as early as 1890, the jeweler's partiality to the technique of enameling on gold (a type of glass melting at low temperature onto a metallic base) led him to practical research and experiments in which glass and metal were used in combination.[1] The extraordinary miniature bas-reliefs in glass that he was to incorporate into his jewelry work were the fruit of such sophisticated research.

At the turn of the century, further novel techniques helped Lalique familiarize himself with the potential of glass, knowledge that would later enable him to produce unique glass pieces of exceptional quality. Nevertheless, it was blown-molded and press-molded glass, two techniques closely associated with nineteenth-century industrial culture (although new to Lalique's repertory) that lie at the heart of the artist's aesthetic and commercial triumph, achieved when Lalique became a full-fledged creator of work in glass.

The shift from jeweler to glassmaker can be fixed in the period 1909–12, when Lalique abandoned jewelry altogether. In

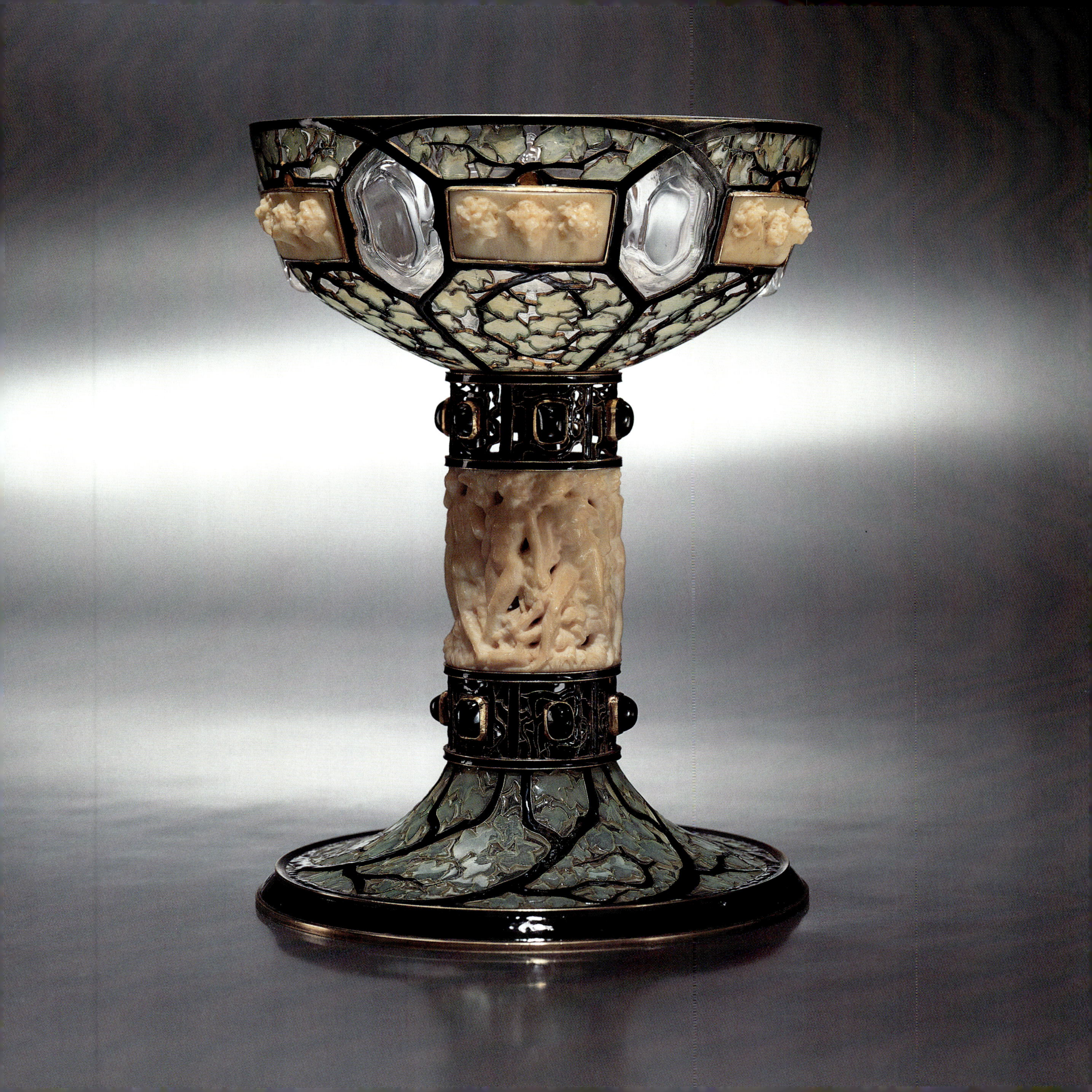

1909, having received his first commissions to produce perfume bottles, he rented and soon after bought a glassworks at Combs-la-Ville near Paris. By 1912, the invitations to visit his shop on the Place Vendôme, sent to amateurs and customers, took the form of a pressed-glass medallion, a proof of his mastery of the new technology.

To better appreciate René Lalique's contribution to glassworking, a few historical remarks on the techniques of mold-blown (*soufflé-moulé*) and pressed (*pressé-moulé*) glass are in order. The principle of blowing glass into containing molds with hollowed-out motifs (which then appeared as reliefs on the glass) is attested in antiquity more or less simultaneously with the invention of blown glass itself. Such practice continued throughout the entire history of glass production, though often only as a subsidiary technique and not always with the purpose of providing figurative ornaments. In the nineteenth century, developments in machine manufacture, metal molds, and finally the use of compressed air opened the way to the mass-produced mold-blown glass which gave new impetus to the glass-packaging industry. All sorts of containers were employed as bearers of commemorative announcements, propaganda, and advertising—witness the celebrated figurative bottles produced by Legras, the large manufactory at Saint-Denis, with which Lalique seems to have occasionally been in contact.

The second technique, which consists in pressing the glass while it remains malleable between a plunger and a mold or die, had also been known since antiquity. But thanks to the progress made during the nineteenth century in the areas of metallic molds and machining, the technique could be employed to produce three-dimensional objects. The press-molded method, generally considered as having been introduced in the United States during the Industrial Revolution, traveled to Europe during the first quarter of the nineteenth century. It gradually transferred creativity to the hands of the inventors of machines and to mold manufacturers. As markets expanded, the technique was put to good use in the low-cost manufacture of designs derived from the repertory of hand-cut glass work. These objects of industrial manufacture continued to employ traditional craft designs.

But the new technology also engendered a whole range of popular, functional, or simply sentimental articles whose shape or decoration was of a ritual, commemorative, or narrative type. Save for a number of objects in the Neo-Gothic manner, the manufacture of pressed-glass goods corresponded only occasionally with the taste of the elite and the decorative styles provided for them by "modern" designers.

Around 1909, Lalique was the first glassmaker to forge a new alliance between nineteenth-century industrial and technical culture and the designs deriving from the

Corsage
Ornament
Bumblebees on
Flowers
c. 1905–1906
Gold, translucent enamel on gold, cast glass, diamonds
2 3/8 x 5 7/8
inches
(6 x 15 cm)
(Cat. 127)

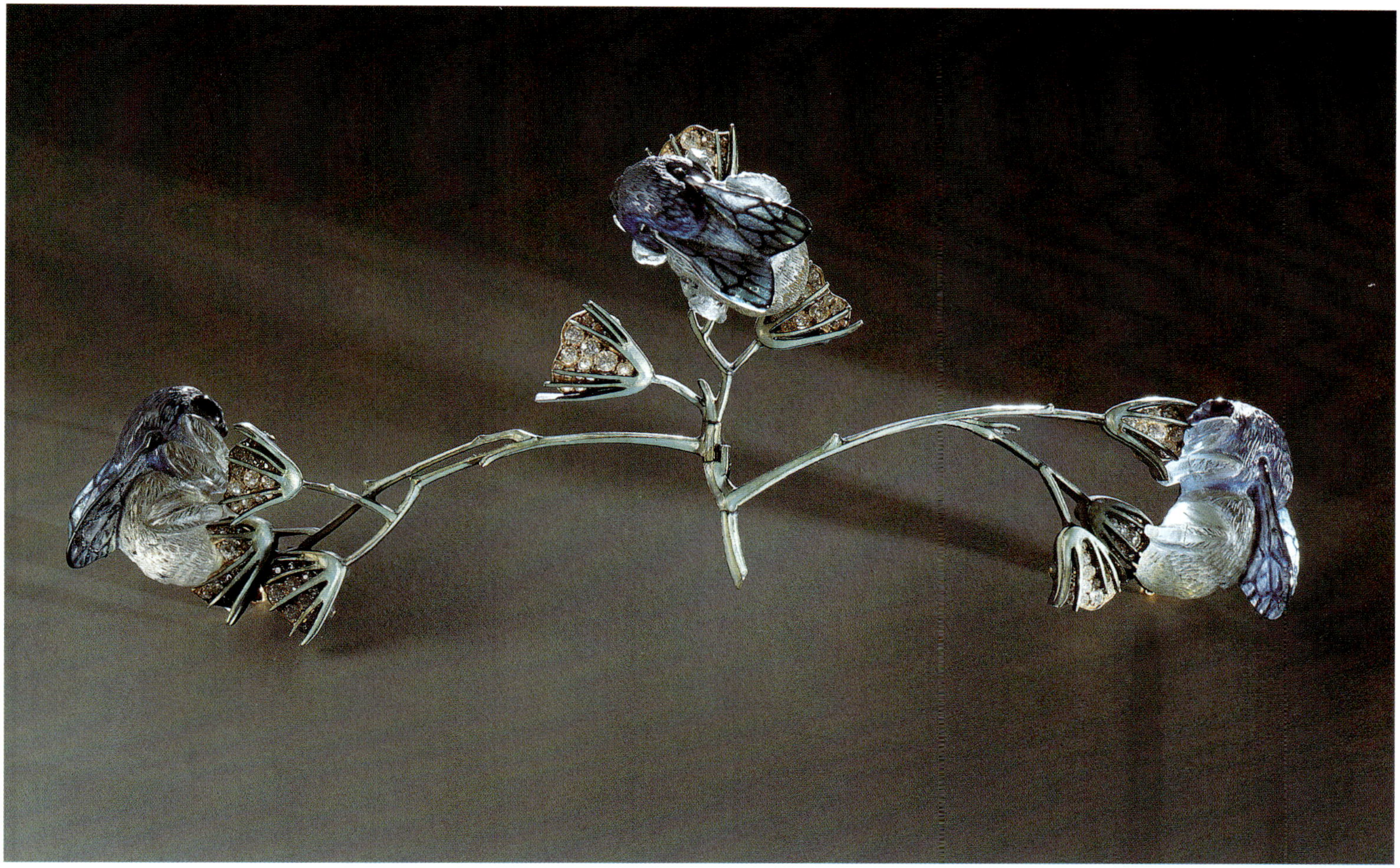

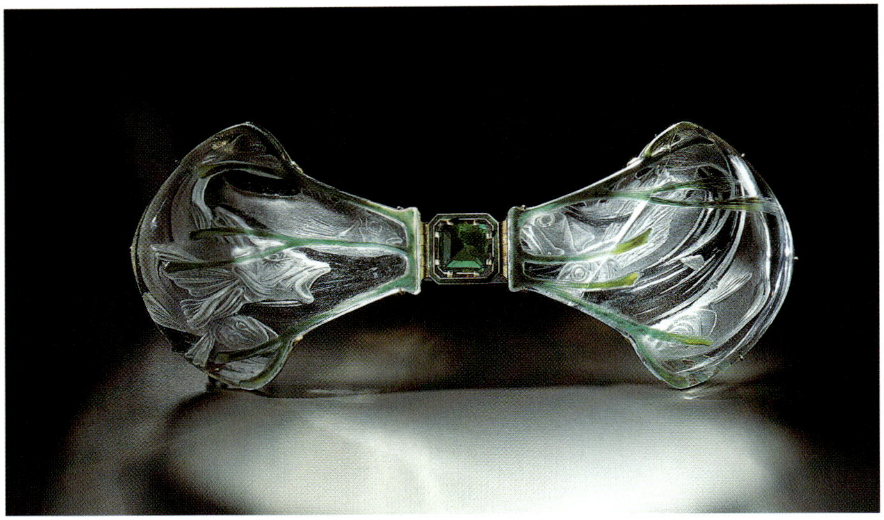

objet d'art, which had been reborn at the end of the century and with which he had been hugely successful as a jeweler. By using these two molding techniques, Lalique was able to integrate into the vocabulary of glassmaking all the human or hybrid, idyllic or phantasmagoric figures that had peopled his jewelry and goldsmith work, without having to resort to the complex processes of traditional master glass craftsmen. The figures in this story-book, dreamy world gradually evolved into more vigorous shapes, where a kind of serene eroticism imbues Neoclassical tendencies, and abstract or stylized ornamentation is animated by powerful rhythms.

The very novelty of Lalique's position seems, in retrospect, one of the most important characteristics of his œuvre, the more so since it turned Lalique into the head of a major manufacturing concern, one that has persevered throughout the twentieth century on the stylistic principles established by its founder.

Lalique's Research in Glass and Glassmaking

In his study on René Lalique published in 1922, Gustave Geffroy states that Lalique "had always been thinking about glass, and had even begun with it some time previously, finding in that ductile yet firm material, as easy to cast as metal, a rich source of quite unexpected potential."[2]

Corsage Ornament *Fish* c. 1903–1905 Gold, enamel, pressed, engraved glass, emerald (now replaced with glass 2 1/2 x 6 1/4 inches (6.5 x 16 cm) (Cat. 131)

Statuette *The Faun's Kiss* Model created c. 1901 Lost-wax castglass 7 7/8 inches (20 cm) (Cat. 192)

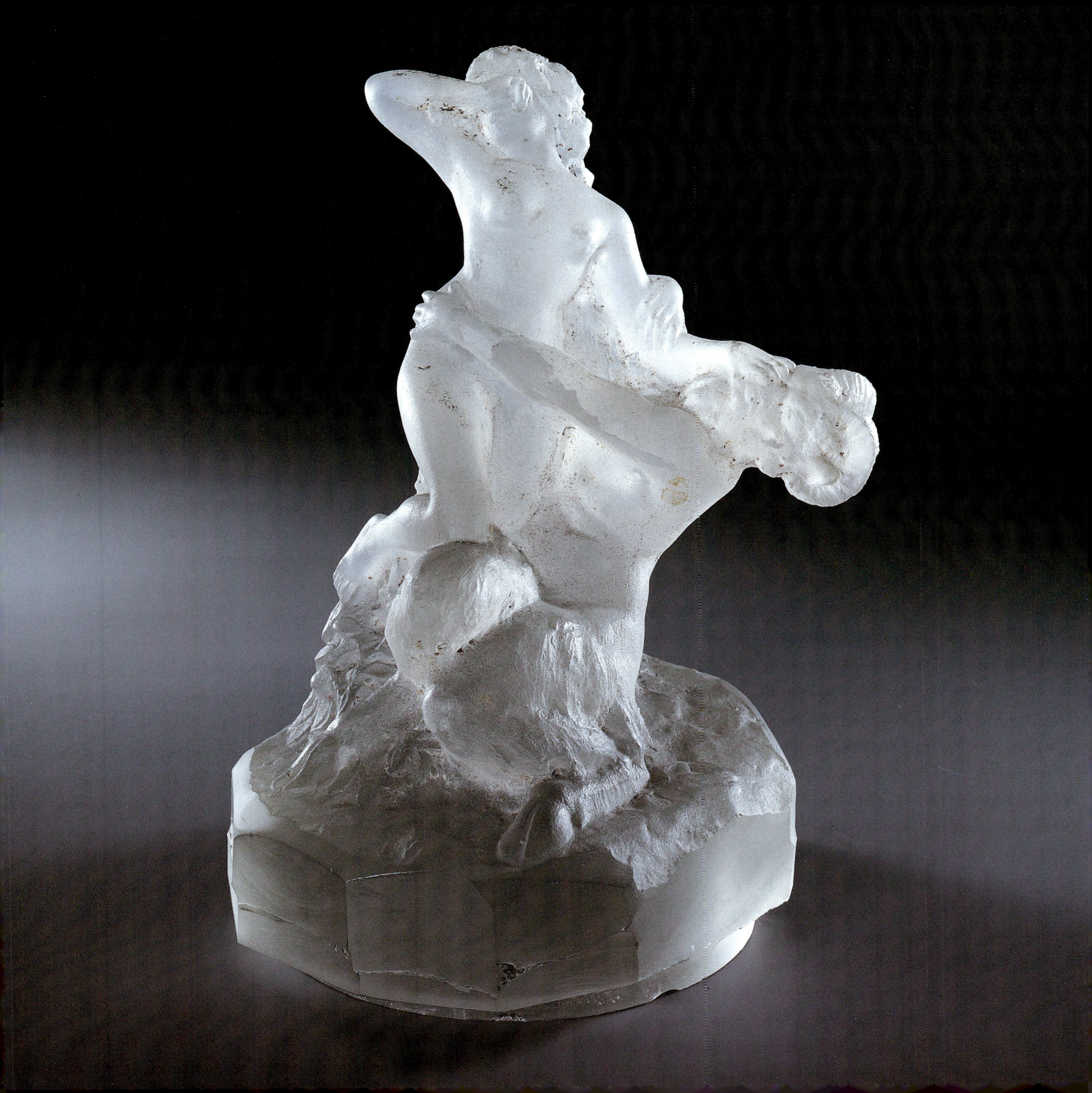

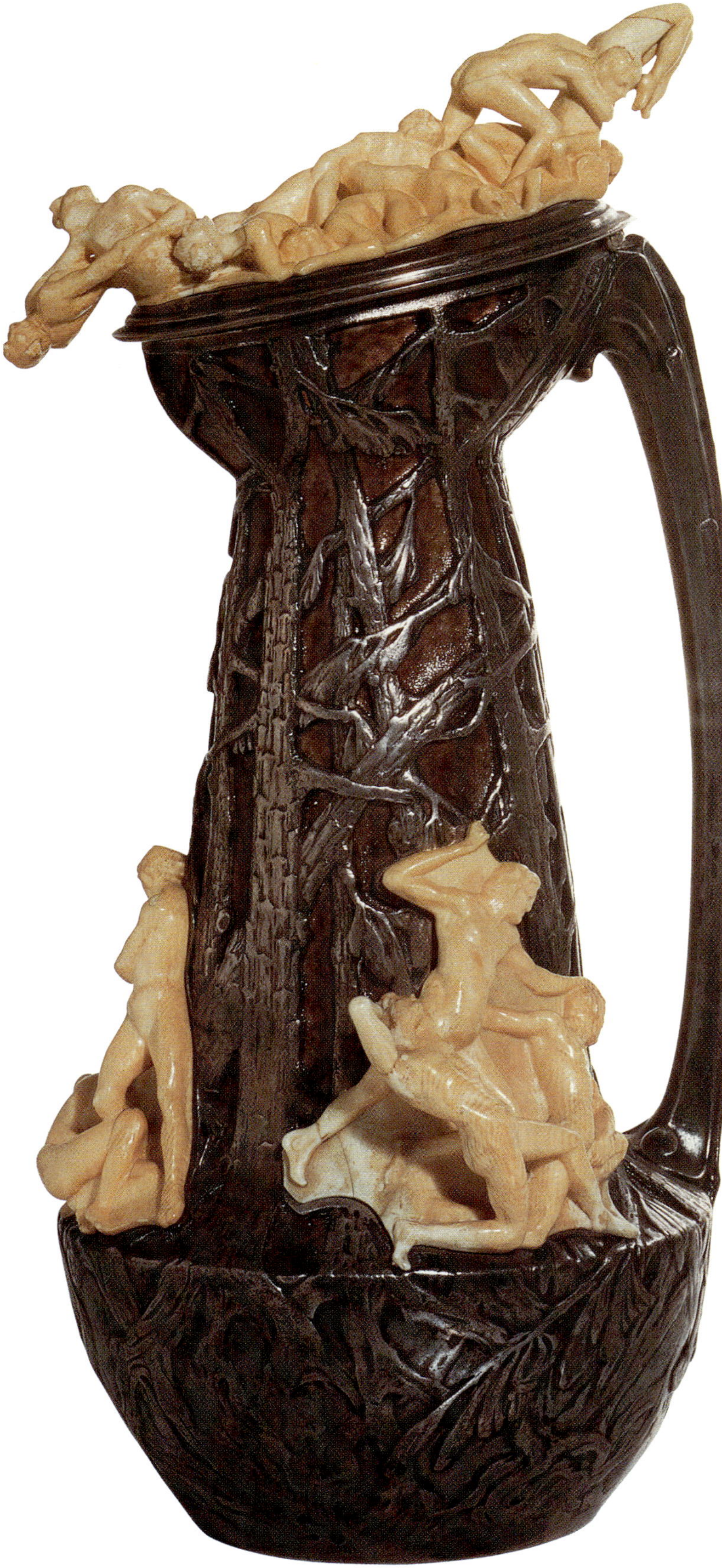

Fig. 29
Ewer
1901–1903
Silver, enamel, ivory
Height: 12 1/2 inches
(Height: 32 cm)
Paris, Private Collection

Goblet
Mulberry Flowers
c. 1899–1900
Blown glass in silver setting
Height: 6 1/4 inches
(Height: 16 cm)
(Cat. 178)

The exact chronology of Lalique's experiments with glass is no longer traceable. But what is important for us is Geffroy's stress on the common ground shared by glass and metal. The new techniques Lalique developed, which derived from the tradition of enameling on metal, were novel and might be compared to the making of glass objects. The metal base effectively became just one stage in the production process, a system that can also be equated to the manufacturing techniques for *plique-à-jour*, that is, translucent, openwork enamel.

The patent for a new manufacturing process for enamels that Lalique was granted in 1891 allowed for the production of relief enamels, since the process enabled metal backing to be turned into a "true hollowed or relief mold." This technique, the result of Lalique's extraordinary skill as an enameler, has points of similarity with a method devised by the sculptor Henry Cros, which he had called *pâte de verre* ("glass paste"). The mineral molds employed by Cros were similar to the metal ones used by Lalique and were destroyed after firing. Lalique specified that his invention allows one "to reproduce sculpture in the round. Appplicable or not to jewelry and ornamental metalwork." These miniature sculptures, molded in a single edition and clinched into the most extravagant pieces of jewelry, represent the earliest glass pieces produced by Lalique.

Subsequently, Lalique manufactured vases and objects, cast or blown into lost-wax refractory molds. By about 1912, such work was on a parallel track with that of a young craftsman in *pâte de verre*, François Décorchemont. Lalique and Décorchemont both stressed the thickness of the translucent glass, with its rough, matte surface, and the forcefulness of a boldly modeled and rhythmically regular motif, rendered with the exceptional precision and vigor that the lost-wax process allows.

This group of single pieces or numbered limited editions sometimes approached monumentality, as a result of the combination of blown work and lost-wax molding, which was unique in the annals of glassmaking. But these works did not provide the foundation for the formal and stylistic evolution of Lalique's art following 1914. After World War I, the decoration of these unique and costly creations remained, for the most part, a repetition of earlier concepts rather than a reflection of the current Art Deco style. This apparent stylistic stagnation, especially noticeable between 1920 and 1925, might be blamed on the taste of Lalique's elite customers. In contrast, the mass-produced models evolved rapidly and independently because their concepts respected both production techniques and the constraints that naturally apply to the production of a series of manufactured items.

Another original series produced by

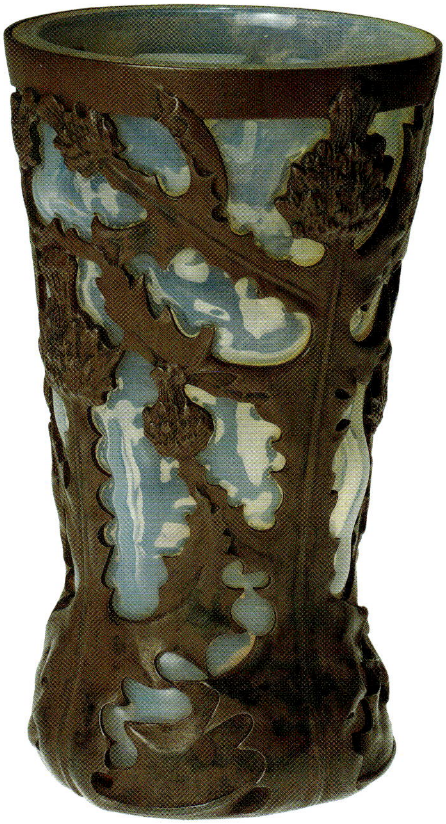

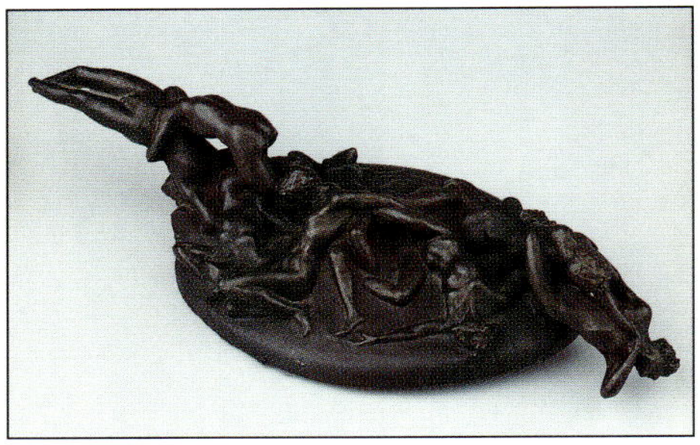

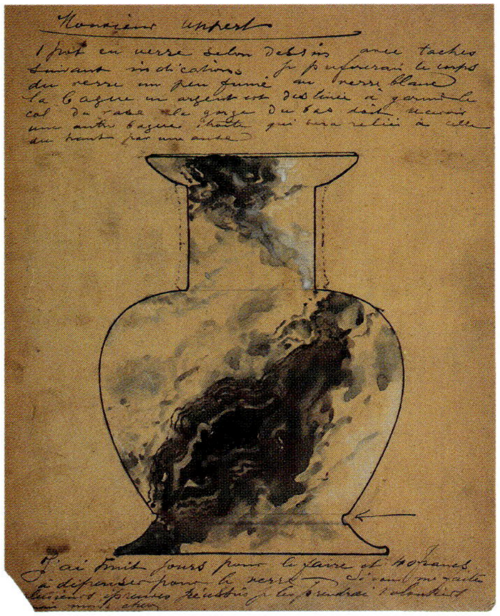

Lalique links glass and metal: a group of objects made since 1898 and deriving from the goldsmith tradition. This "goldsmith work in glass" also has visual similarities to *plique-à-jour*, though it is produced by quite a different technique, the glass being blown into unbacked forms of bronze or silver. The juxtaposition of glass and metal is singularly expressive, while the object's overall design, whose structure is composed of the metal armature, is fixed only when the still workable glass is blown into the gaps provided. The refinement and technical difficulty of joining hot-worked metal and glass means that these objects are extremely scarce, but they remain crucial in Lalique's evolution, since they incorporate the first containing forms decorated in relief and the earliest use of blown glass.

The tinted drawing of a vase decorated with snakes published in *Art et Décoration* in 1898 suggests that at this juncture Lalique used opalescent blown glass—the original coloring of the glass common in the production of French *cristalleries* at the beginning of the nineteenth century. Lalique, who had already employed real opals in a masterly manner in his jewelry, revitalized this tradition. The hue, which ranges from a milky blue to a striking orange, depending on the thickness of the glass and the incidence of light, soon made an appearance in Lalique's glass production. It was above all from the 1920s onward that Lalique, by adapting this coloring of the technique of press-molding which allowed for variable and closely controlled thicknesses of material, created a fashion for shimmering glass which plays as effectively with natural light as with artificial light.

Glass objects blown into metal armatures also form a stage in the evolution of Lalique's attitude to glassmaking techniques. The unique and extremely precious metal components played a role similar to a mount in goldworking, but also served as a mold which permitted great formal liberty without requiring the sophisticated skill of the glassblower. Moreover, among all these figurative ornamental pieces, there are some, such as the ewer in the Museum für Kunsthandwerk in Frankfurt, that resemble a sculpted Dantesque vision. Others, however, take simple forms, such as highly structured chalices and other configurations of a Neoclassical bent. The Bacchic iconography on these chalices (e.g. cat. 181) inspired the friezes of nude figures which are among Lalique's greatest achievements in glass: the Bacchants vase, created in 1927 and still in production.[3]

Three goblets in blown glass and metal, exhibited at the Exposition Universelle in 1900 and reproduced together in one of the catalogues, show Lalique to have been at a particularly fruitful period of stylistic innovation.[4] The goblet in the center, adorned with a mask, presents rhythmically intertwined lines similar to English metalwork such as that by Ashbee. The one on the left,

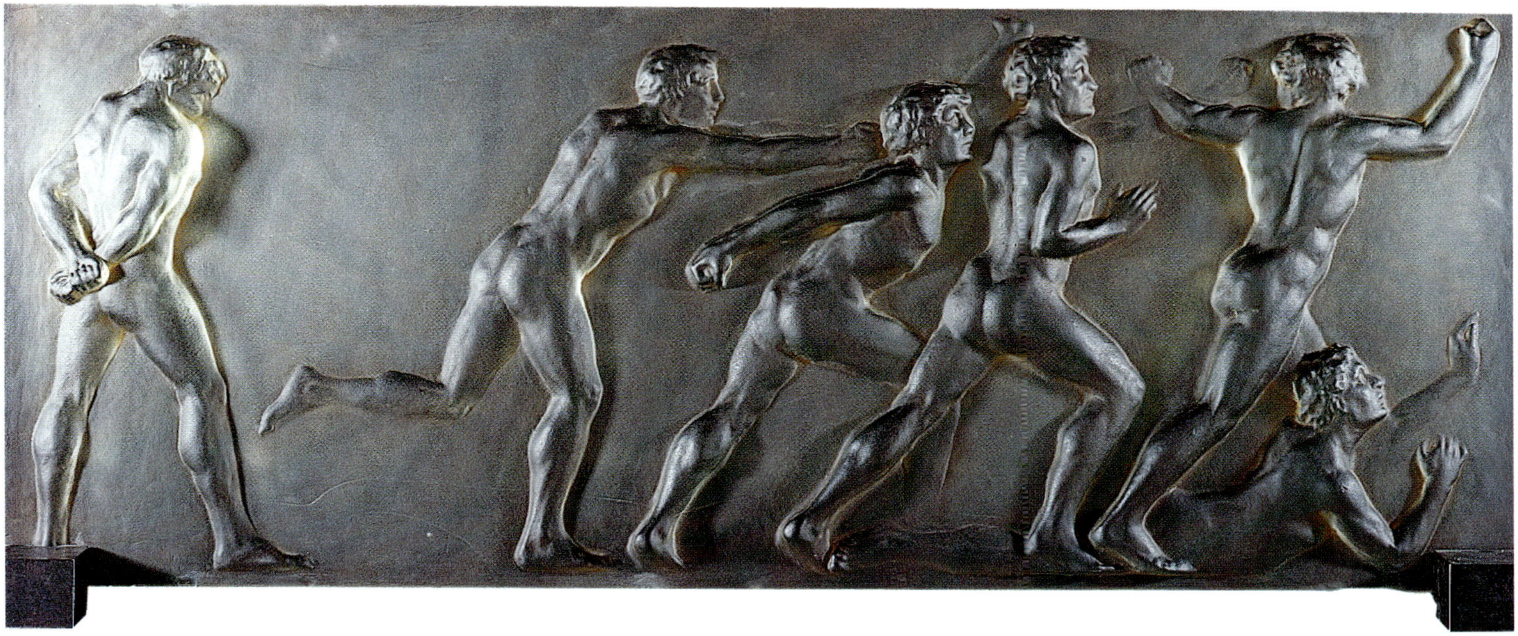

One of Four
Models for
Ewers
Entwined Figures
c. 1901–1903
Bronze
a] 11 x 4 1/2;
b] 7 1/4 x 6;
c] 7 1/4 x 6 3/4;
d] Diam: 6 3/4
inches
(a] 28 x 11.5;
b]18.5 x 15;
c]18.5 17; d]
Diam: 17cm)
(Cat. 176)

Fig. 30
Design for a
Glass Vase
"For M. Appert"
c. 1895–1897
Ink, watercolor
on paper

Panel
Athletes
Model created
c. 1912
Mold-pressed
glass, stained
45 inches
(114 cm)
(Cat. 207)

with a stylized insect motif in a repetitive accelerando rhythm, announces Lalique's work of the 1910s, while that on the right (cat. 178) is an interpretation of his oft-used motif of the thistle, traditionally the symbol of Lorraine. But Lalique combines heraldry and naturalism without the undertones given the thistle by Gallé and the School of Nancy.

Finally, before becoming the head of a true glassmaking workshop, Lalique showed his interest in using decorative glass on an architectural scale in the building of his own sizable home on the Cours-la-Reine in Paris in 1902. His position as a decorator naturally had nothing in common with that of the engineer-architects of the nineteenth century, who were establishing the credo of an architecture in glass and metal. Indeed, Lalique's approach might be understood either as a truly original reading of the tradition of stained-glass windows or else as the glassworking counterpart of the fashion for molded ceramic decors in Art Nouveau architecture.

For two doors of the town house, one giving on to the street and linked with the carved stone decoration on the facade and another inside leading to an exhibition room built onto the mansion, Lalique inserted thick plates of glass molded in bas-relief into a mobile metal structure, thereby devising an entirely novel use for the material.

Glass doors—a common concept today thanks to the progress made in the manufacture and finishing of industrial flat glass—created a shock appropriate to the home of Lalique; Lalique the jeweler (whose name, it had been remarked, rhymed with both *relique* and *magique),* was now preparing his metamorphosis into a glassmaker.[5] The motifs of conifers and athletes, though clearly related to the miniature repertory of Lalique the *fin-de-siècle* jeweler, now served, on a larger scale and with splendid luminosity, as a transition toward the work of the twentieth-century glassmaker. The context in which these masterpieces were manufactured remains obscure, as we do not know whether they were produced in the workshop at Lalique's house at Clairefontaine near Paris or if they were the fruit of collaboration with industry; the latter possibility would have been feasible, given Lalique's personal connections and financial means.

Whatever the case, it should be noted that several years before heading and developing his own glassmaking concern, Lalique had already embarked on the profitable path that would lead to his lofty reputation in the eyes of such exceptional individuals as the couturier and collector Jacques Doucet in 1912 (same model as cat. 207) or Prince Asaka in Tokyo in 1932 as well as for the general public through his exhibitions in Paris, whether temporary (during the International Exhibitions of 1925 and 1937) or else permanent (as for the

Vessel
Two Mermaids
1909
Pressed glass, wheel engraved, stained
4; Diam: 4 7/8 inches
(10; Diam: 12.5 cm)
(Cat. 194)

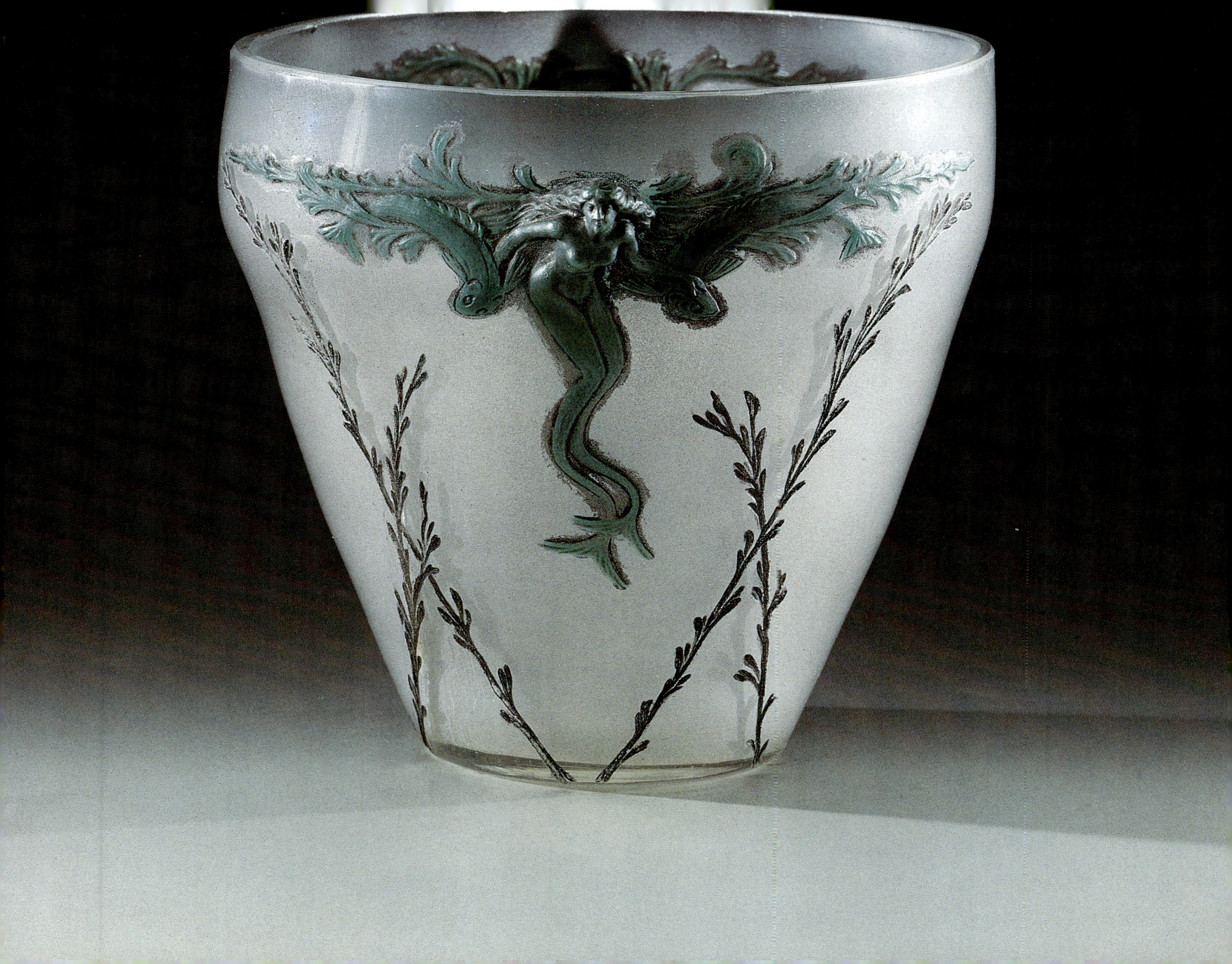

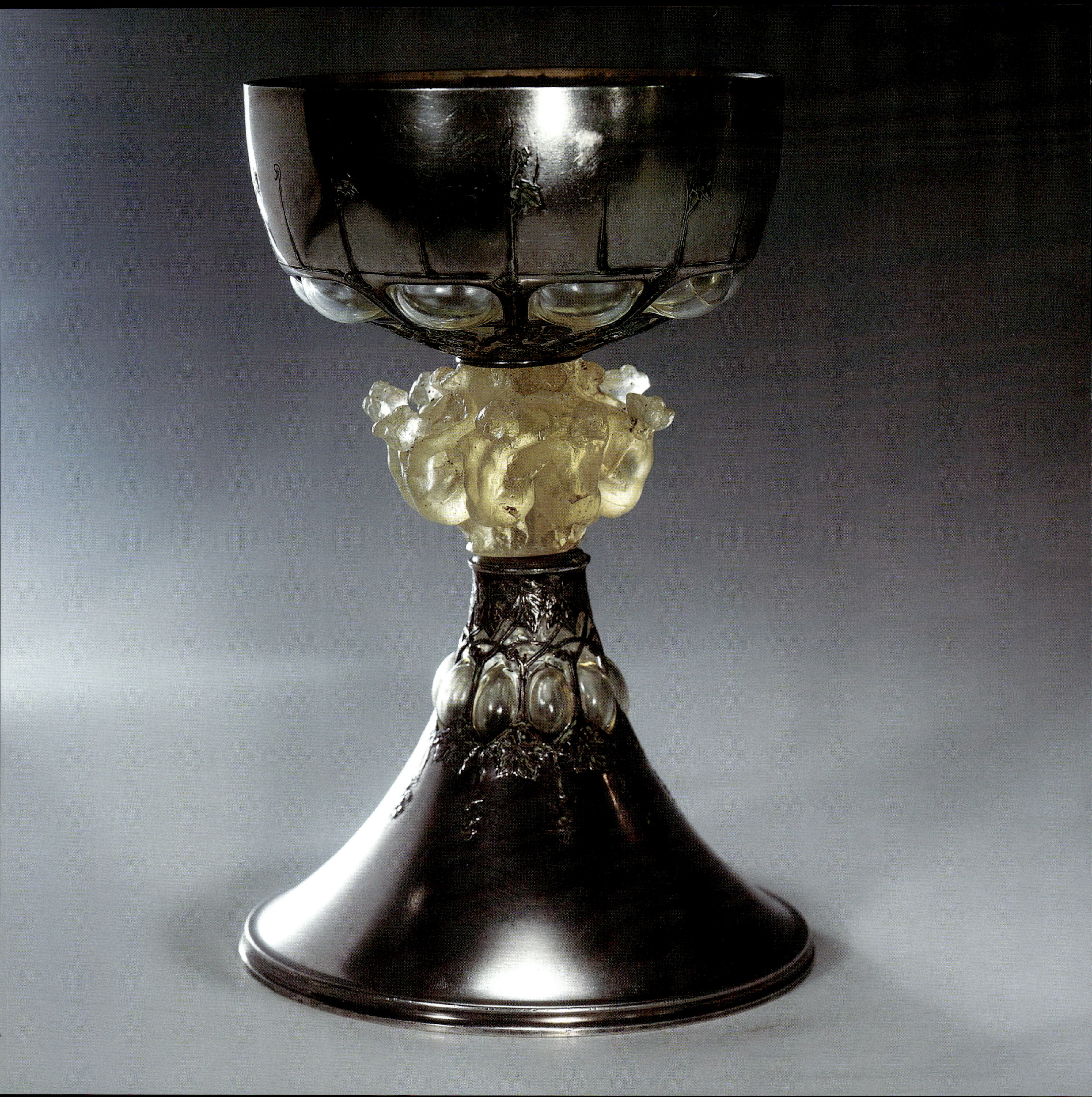

decoration of the Passage du Lido on the Champs-Élysées in 1926).

René Lalique and French Glassmaking at the Turn of the Century

The multicolored effects the glassmaker could obtain by hot-working and the graphic ones created by cold-working with etching acid or the wheel, both derived from principles exploited by Émile Gallé, were the dominant factors in French decorative *verrerie* around 1910, whether for mass-produced or prestige pieces. But the direct or indirect heirs of the School of Nancy, though they had increased the number of their commercial outlets, had reduced their creativity to formulae barely affected by a tardy naturalism: the search for the new had been stifled, but popularization continued apace.

Moreover, the major crystal glassmaking firms, which enjoyed the largest share of the luxury market (including tableware), were preoccupied with the ostentatious aggrandizement of the purity, brilliance, and éclat of lead glass. Their endeavors were limited either to massive size or else to the multiplication of optical effects obtained by cuts that resembled those used on diamonds. Despite sporadic attempts to employ ornamentation based on nature and the sinuous curves inspired by more recent initiatives, the production of these *cristalleries* seemed,

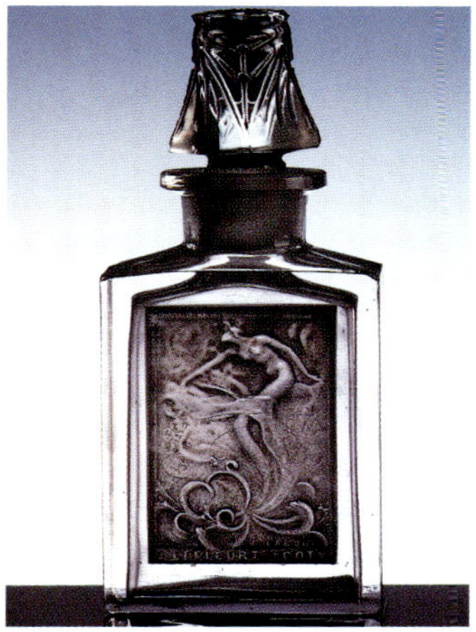

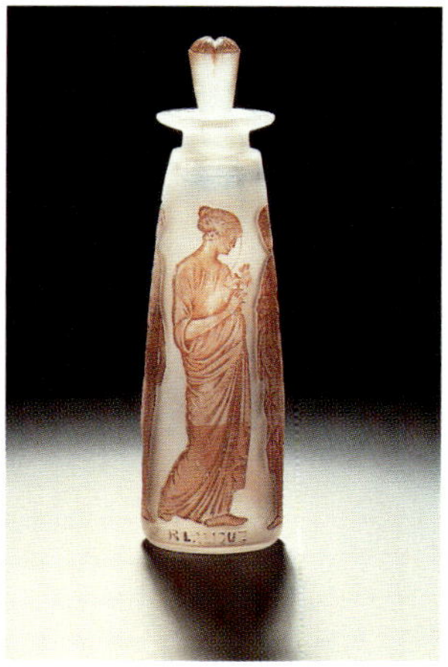

Perfume Bottle
"L'Effleurt"
Label created in 1908; model created in 1912 for Coty
Mold-pressed glass, stopper in mold-pressed glass, stained
4 1/2 x 2 x 1 1/4 inches (11.2 cm x 5 x 3.1 cm)
(Cat. 209)

Chalice
Bacchanal
1902
Silver, enamel, lost-wax cast-glass, blown glass in silver setting
7 1/2 inches (19 cm)
(Cat. 181)

Perfume Bottle
"Ambre antique"
Model created in 1910 for Coty
Mold-blown glass, stopper in mold-pressed glass, stained
6; Diam: 1 1/2 inches (15.5; Diam: 4 cm)
(Cat. 211)

in a revealing reflection of the taste of the period, to be stuck in the opulent rut of Second Empire nostalgia.

At the very beginning of his glassmaking career, Lalique employed monochrome materials, more often translucent than strictly transparent or brilliant. The refinement of his forms comes from their elegant simplicity, while figurative ornaments are assembled in buoyant reliefs that impart rhythm to the energetic lines. Cold-working mechanical or chemical polishing or frosting brings out contrasts between the brilliant and the matte, the smooth and the rough. The reliefs are often underscored by the slight tint of a monochrome patina. Through these techniques, Lalique arrived at his innovative and idiosyncratic technical and stylistic hallmark: acid-worked satin glass. This effect stood in contrast to the fire and brilliance of the traditional crystal-glass product and conferred on Lalique's objects a novel sort of refinement, one no longer based on references to rock crystal or diamond, but created by a specific luminosity, a tactile sensuality which wedded perfectly with the warm intimacy of his decorative glass.

It should also be noted that Lalique's two careers—both based on his talents as a technician, draftsman, sculptor, and coordinator—are built on a rejection of the traditional attributes of wealth. As a creator of jewelry, he had forsaken the use of precious gems, preferring to employ semiprecious stones, enamel, and even unusual materials without intrinsic value, such as horn. As a glassmaker, he discarded both the many-hued splendor of Art Nouveau and the fire of brilliant crystal, preferring a third way which was at once more sober and less costly. Richness was no longer associated exclusively with rarity, nor with countless hours of manual labor, but with the quality of refined and forceful forms and with an extraordinary capacity to play with light.

It was this clean breath of clarity and fresh air that Lalique brought to craft in glass. Molded ornaments allowed for stylistic and iconographical continuity with his work as a jeweler and goldsmith; for example, he often made use of masks or supple, fluid figures such as mermaids and aquatic creatures. This subtle prescription of novel technical developments and stylistic continuity received immediate and vocal plaudits from critics and public alike. To the acclaim from experts and private customers was added a third form of tribute, which proved essential to the growth of the firm—that from other entrepreneurs. The earliest was from the perfumer François Coty. Though the perfume industry, in a market dominated by the notion of the gift, had already put to good use precious packaging and various sales lures, the "look" of any one perfume was generally associated with the color printing used on the paper of the cardboard packaging or on the glued labels applied to undecorated glass bottles. The rare exception was Hector Guimard. At the 1900 Exposition Universelle, in collaboration with the Parfumerie Millot, which was concerned with its global image, Guimard designed an original perfume bottle shape in blown-molded glass; this example, however, seems to have remained unique.

In the association between Coty and Lalique, by contrast, we witness the birth of a new concept in perfume marketing, one that eventually took into account the quality of the glass packaging and, in an entirely novel departure, inseparably linked a particular fragrance, its increasingly evocative and dream-inspiring name, and the molded decoration of its very own container.

The bottle for the perfume "L'Effleurt" embodied the word-play of the name, with its allusions to *effleurer* ("to stroke or brush against"), and to *fleur* ("flower"). The molded decoration of the bottle (cat. 209), the unequivocal sensuality of a naked figure ("une sensualité à fleur de peau," as the French would say) metaphorically evokes the scent given off by a flower in bloom.

This project for Coty also marks a shift in Lalique's approach, as he moved the message—both picture and text—from the label (first in paper, then in glass glued on to the bottle) and had it impressed directly onto the sides of the (mold-blown) glass bottle itself. For another of Coty's fragrances with the classical sounding name "Ambre Antique" ("ancient amber"), Lalique produced a round, columnar vial decorated with modestly draped vestal virgins (cat. 211).

These two examples—among the earliest of Lalique's mass-produced perfume bottles—were to be followed by innumerable commissions from perfumers, who sometimes simply perused and selected from one of the Lalique firm's catalogues a model already being distributed to the public.

The field of experimentation that the emerging perfume market opened up for Lalique is as symptomatic as his most costly creations of his desire to appropriate the tools of industry and mass production without slavishly submitting to their constraints.

The patent he was granted in December 1912, by which new forms could be obtained through "simultaneous, pressing, and blowing," is typical of the sort of hybrid that Lalique thrust upon industrial tradition. Side by side with the development of machine tools, he preserved the variety of his cold-working techniques, which entailed numerous finishing processes for objects that most often received the signature of their creator (no longer underneath or on the back, but visibly on the front)—a signature that soon became the logo of the firm.

It seems appropriate to end this outline of Lalique's contribution to twentieth-century art in glass with the example of perfume bottles, since they are the epitome not only of a new idiom and techniques of decoration but also of Lalique's commercial talent. Without acknowledging his business acumen, it is not possible to explain the originality of his work and his position in the world of modern manufacturing. Draftsman and modeler, a peerless exploiter of the potential of the craft industry during his career as a jeweler, Lalique never forsook the opulent universe of *bijouterie* he created, but managed to graft it onto the experience of industrial glassmaking. His work in glass, although highly varied, achieves a profound unity from an extraordinary confluence: that of a creative craftsman mastering the innumerable vicissitudes of manufacturing in a period of industrial rationalization and growing international markets.

So it was that Lalique invented not only a new style in glasswork but also a novel type of twentieth-century *objet d'art*—a form whose references are no longer aristocratic but well and truly bourgeois.

Hand Mirror
Swallows
Model created
in 1913
Mold-blown
glass, stained
13 3/4 inches
(35 cm)
(Cat. 189)

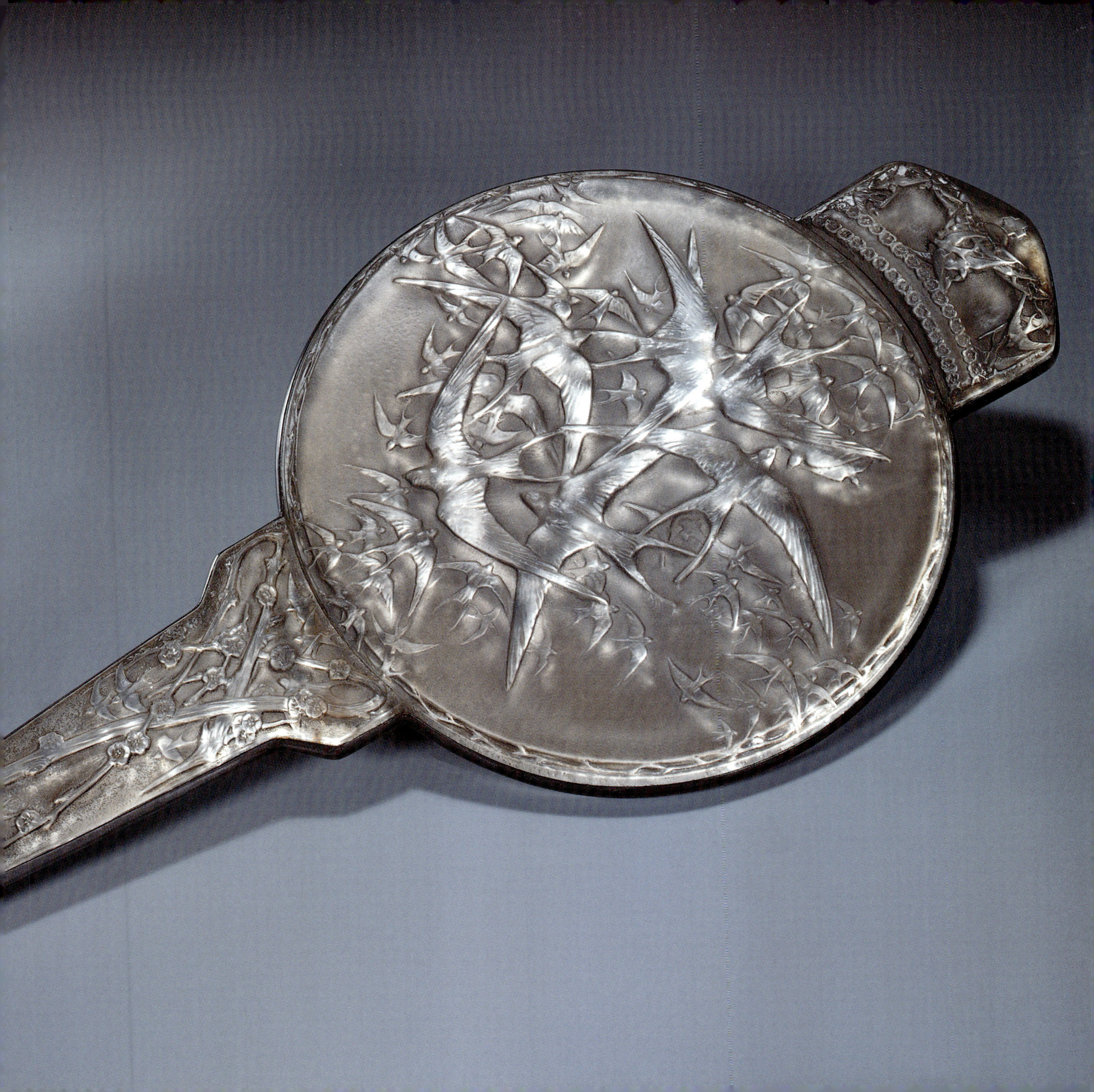

List of Works

Height precedes width precedes depth

I
In Search of the Modern Jewel: 1888–1897

1 **Brooch**
Fish and Bamboo (photo p. 54)
1888
Cast and chased gold
Diameter: 1 1/4 inches (Diameter: 3.1 cm)
Musée des Arts décoratifs, Paris
Gift of Henri Vever 1924, inv. 24520A

2 **Chatelaine-Brooch**
Figure of Time (photo p. 123)
1888–1890
Chased and embossed gold
1 1/2 x 1 1/4 inches (4 x 3.2 cm)
Musée des Arts décoratifs, Paris
Gift of Henri Vever 1924, inv. 24520B

3 **Corsage Ornament**
Song Birds (photo p. 11)
1889 for the House of Vever
Gold, silver, diamonds, rubies
2 x 4 1/4 inches (4.9 x 10.8 cm)
Private collection, New York

4 **Belt** *Coin of Alexander the Great*
c. 1895–1897
Gold, enamel on gold, diamonds, grosgrain ribbon, pearls, antique silver coin
36 1/2 x 1 5/8 inches (93 x 4 cm)
Musée des Arts décoratifs, Paris
Gift of marquise Arconati-Visconti 1916, inv. 20365A

5 **Brooch**
Leaves and Masks
1897–1899
Cast and chased electrum, translucent enamel on gold, pearl
3/4; Diameter: 1 7/8 inches
(2; Diameter: 4.8 cm)
Musée des Arts décoratifs, Paris
Gift of marquise Arconati-Visconti 1916, inv. 20358

6 **Brooch-Pendant**
Butterfly-woman (photo p. 73)
c. 1894–1896
Gold, translucent enamel on gold, diamonds, rubies
2 3/8 x 2 5/8 inches (6 x 6.5 cm)
David Weinstein Collection, New York

7 **Brooch**
Head of a Jester
c. 1896–1898
Gold, enamel, engraved stone
Stamped and etched LALIQUE on back upper right
1 15/16 x 2 inches (4.9 x 5.1 cm)
Virginia Museum of Fine Arts, Richmond
Gift of Sydney and Frances Lewis, inv. 85.251

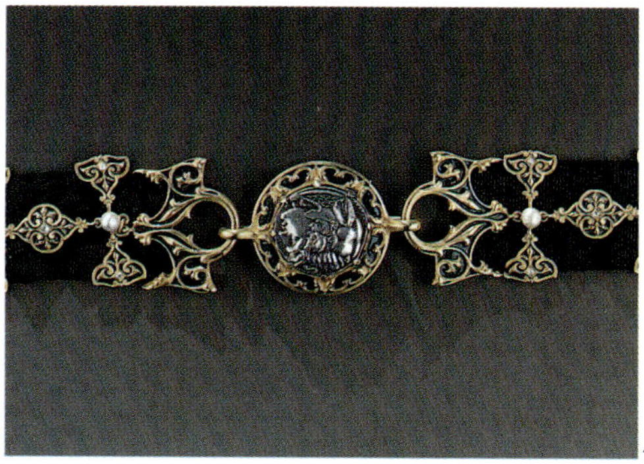
4

8 **Brooch** *Jester*
c. 1897–1898
Cast and chased gold, translucent enamel on gold, pearls
2 x 1 1/2 inches (4.9 x 3.9 cm)
Musée des Arts décoratifs, Paris
Gift of marquise Arconati-Visconti 1916, inv. 20380

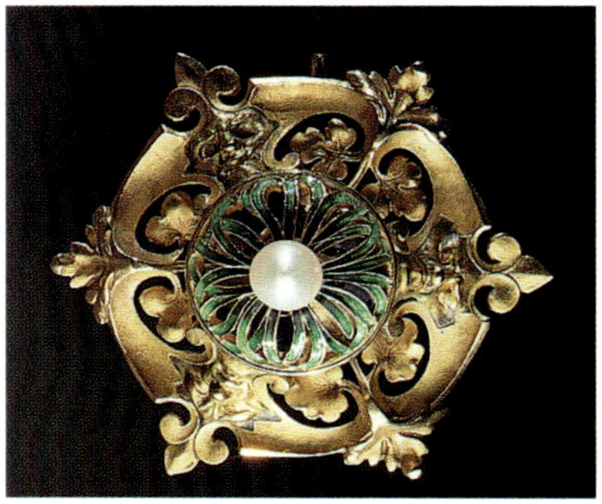
5

9 **Brooch**
Head of Woman with Flower Headdress
c. 1897–1898
Cast, chased and engraved gold, translucent enamel on gold
1 3/8 x 1 1/2 inches (3.5 x 3.8 cm)
Musée des Arts décoratifs, Paris
Gift of marquise Arconati-Visconti 1916, inv. 20370

10 **Brooch**
Woman's Face Surrounded by Pine Boughs (photo p. 50)
c. 1898–1900
Silver, enamel, engraved stone
Signed LALIQUE on back
2 1/4 x 1 5/8 inches (5.7 x 4.1 cm)
Virginia Museum of Fine Arts, Richmond
Gift of Sydney and Frances Lewis, inv. 85.250

11 **Brooch**
Woman in Butterfly Helmet
c. 1897–1899
Engraved agate, silver, gold, enamel
1 7/8 x 2 1/8 inches (7.5 x 5.5 cm)
Private collection, New York

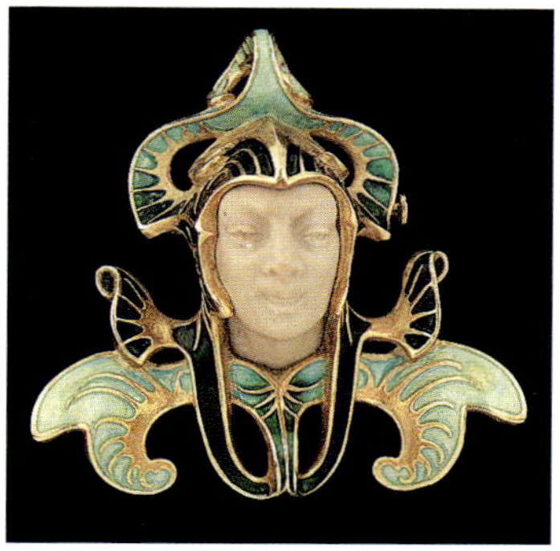

7

12 Necklace *Three Pomegranates* (photo p. 19)
c. 1897
Chased gold, translucent enamel on gold, pearls, opals
Signed LALIQUE on side edge of central pendant
7 5/8 x 7 5/8 x 3/8 inches (19.4 x 19.4 x 0.8 cm)
Virginia Museum of Fine Arts, Richmond
Gift of Sydney and Frances Lewis,
inv. 85.248

13 Necklace
Chrysanthemums (photo p. 117)

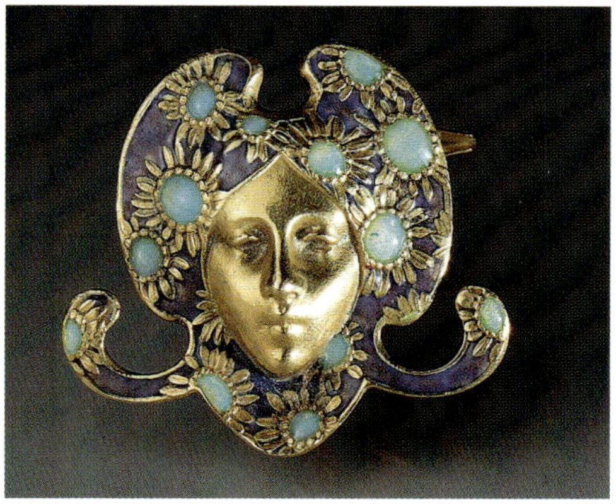

9

c. 1897–1899
Gold, translucent and opaque enamel on gold, pearls
2 1/4 x 13 inches (6 x 33.2 cm)
Musée des Arts décoratifs, Paris
Dechabanne-Binot Bequest 1950,
inv. 36254

14 Brooch
Seaweed
c. 1898–1900
Cast gold, *plique-à-jour* enamel, translucent enamel on gold, sapphire

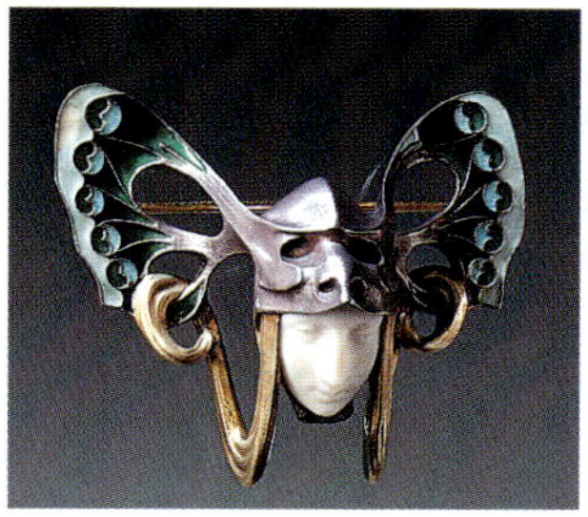

11

Diameter: 1 5/8 inches (Diameter: 4.3 cm)
Musée des Arts décoratifs, Paris
Gift of marquise Arconati-Visconti 1916,
inv. 20367

15 Drawing
A Flight of Swallows
c. 1887
Pencil, ink, watercolor on paper
8 1/2 x 10 1/2 inches (21.6 x 26.4 cm)
Lalique Museum Collection, Paris,
inv. 3.1.075

16 Design for a Corsage Ornament
A Flight of Swallows
(photo p. 10)
1887
Ink on paper
6 1/4 x 9 inches (16 x 22.7 cm)
Lalique Museum Collection, Paris,
inv. 3.1.011

17 Designs for Jewelry
Cherries, Flowers, Birds in a Rocaille Border
c. 1889
Pencil, ink, watercolor, gouache on paper
7 x 9 inches (18 x 22.8 cm)
David Weinstein Collection, New York

18 Design for a Tiara
Dandelions
c. 1885–1890
White gouache on purplish-red-tinted paper
8 7/8 x 11 3/4 inches (22.7 x 29 cm)
Lalique Museum Collection, Paris,
inv. 1.2.030

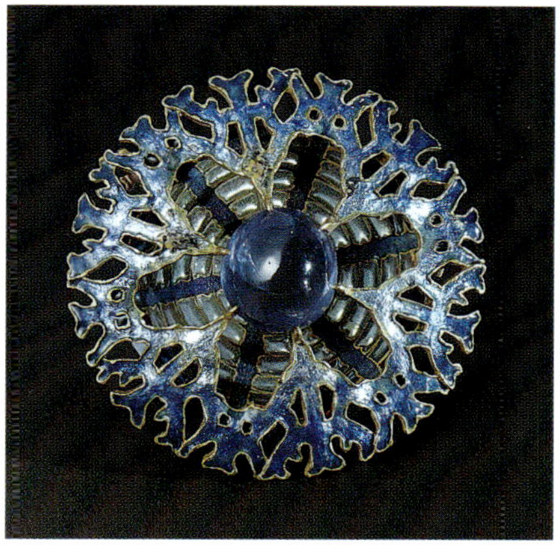

14

19 Design for a Necklace
Five Scrolls (photo p. 18)
c. 1894–1896
Pencil, ink, watercolor on paper
11 x 8 5/8 inches (27.9 x 21.7 cm)
Lalique Museum Collection, Paris,
inv. 2.1.053

20 Design for a Pendant-Brooch (photo p. 116)
c. 1890–1892
Pencil, ink, watercolor on paper
10 7/8 x 8 1/4 inches (27.8 x 22.1 cm)
Lalique Museum Collection, Paris, inv. 3.1.113

21 Design for a Tiara *3 Lotus Blossoms* (photo p. 42)
c. 1893–1895
Pencil, ink on paper
10 3/4 x 8 1/2 inches (27.4 x 21.5 cm)
Lalique Museum Collection, Paris, inv. 1.2.003

22 Design for a Brooch *Renaissance* (photo p. 18)
c. 1893–1894
Pencil, ink, watercolor, gouache on paper
11 x 8 3/4 inches (28 x 22.1 cm)
Lalique Museum Collection, Paris, inv. 3.1.001

23 Design for a Pendant *Head of a Jester*
c. 1896–1898
Pencil, ink, watercolor, gouache on paper
10 3/4 x 8 1/4 inches (27.7 x 21 cm)
Lalique Museum Collection, Paris, inv. 2.4.022

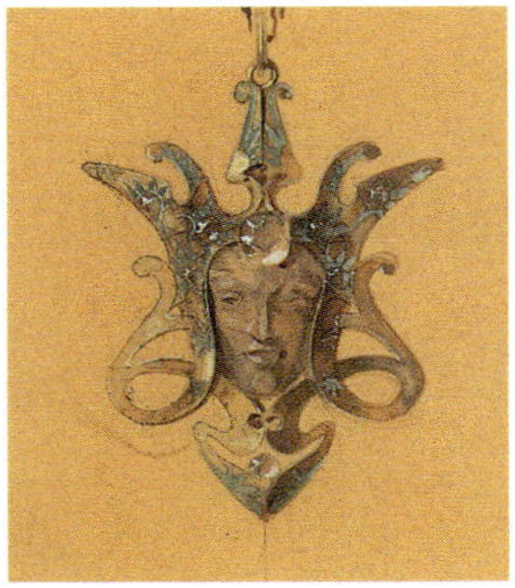
23

24 Drawing *Sarah Bernhardt in Theater Headdress* (photo p. 103)
c. 1894
Pencil, watercolor, gouache on paper
10 1/2 x 8 3/8 inches (26.6 x 21.3 cm)
Lalique Museum Collection, Paris, inv. 1.1.001

25 Drawing *Sarah Bernhardt Wearing Theater Crown for "Theodora"*
1902
Pencil, gouache on paper
10 3/4 x 8 1/2 inches (27.5 x 21.5 cm)
Lalique Museum Collection, Paris, inv. 1.1.008

II
The Modern Jewel: 1897–1900

26 Comb *Two Peacocks in front of Rose Window* (photo p. 20)
c. 1897–1898
Brown horn, patinated in blue and gold, disc of opals
7 1/4 x 3 3/8 inches (18.4 x 8.6 cm)
Musée des Arts décoratifs, Paris
Purchased from the artist 1898, inv. 8755

27 Brooch *Peacock* (photo p. 68)
c. 1897–1898
Chased gold, translucent enamel on gold, moonstones
1; Diameter: 2 1/4 inches
(2.6; Diameter: 6 cm)
Musée des Arts décoratifs, Paris
Purchased from the artist 1899, inv. 9076

28 Pendant *Peacock*
c. 1899–1901
Chased gold, *plique-à-jour* enamel on gold
2 1/4 x 1 1/2 inches (7 x 4 cm)
Private collection, Philadelphia

29 Cravate Pin *Peacock Feather*
c. 1899–1901
Gold, opaque enamel on gold, lapis lazuli
4 1/8; pin head: 3/4 x 1 1/4 inches
(10.4; pin head: 2 x 3.4 cm)
Musée des Arts décoratifs, Paris
Gift of Mrs Carle Dreyfus 1947, inv. 35813

30 Seal Pendant *Scarab*
c. 1899–1901
Gold, translucent enamel on gold, green jasper,
1 1/4 x 1 1/2 inches (3 x 3.8 cm)
Musée des Arts décoratifs, Paris
Gift of Mrs Carle Dreyfus 1947, inv. 35814

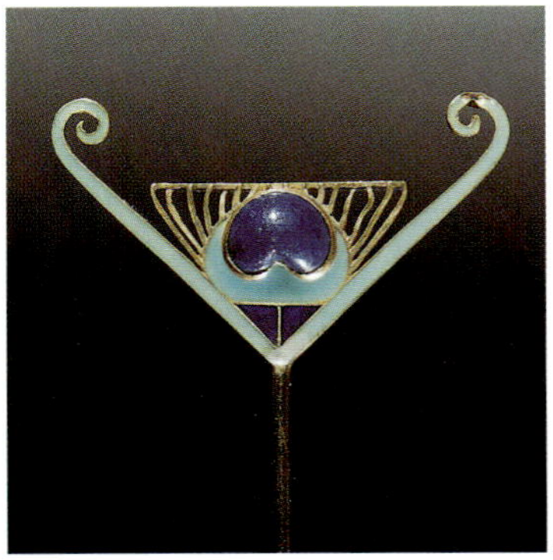
29

31 Pendant *Swans* (photo p. 147)
c. 1899–1900
Chased gold, opaque enamel on gold, *plique-à-jour* enamel
2 1/4 x 1 1/2 inches (5.7 x 3.8 cm)
Private collection, New York

32 Pendant *Swan*
c. 1897–1899
Chased gold, enamel on gold, *plique-à-jour* enamel
3 1/4 x 1 3/4 inches (8.4 x 4.3 cm)
David Weinstein Collection, New York

33 Pendant *2 Swans* (photo p. 151)
c. 1897–1899
Chased gold, enamel on gold, *plique-à-jour* enamel, diamonds
2 3/8 x 2 1/4 inches (6 x 5.5 cm)
Private collection, Philadelphia

34 Ring *Swans* (photo p. 40)
c. 1898–1899
Chased gold, enamel on gold
Diameter: 3/4 inches (Diameter: 2 cm)
Private collection, New York

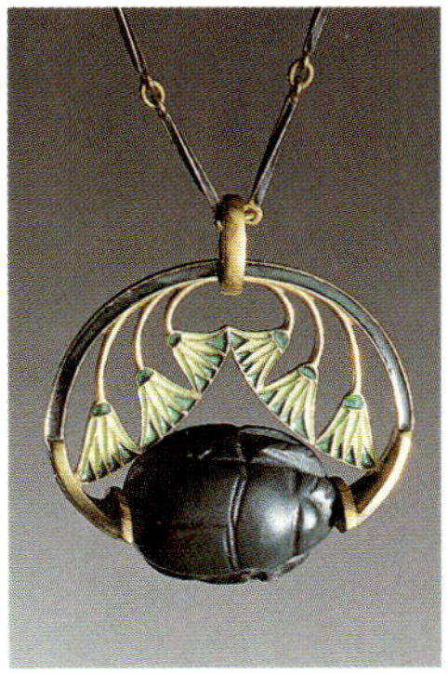
30

35 Pendant
Leda and the Swan
c. 1898–1899
Chased gold, enamel on gold, *plique-à-jour* enamel, sapphire
2 1/8 x 1 7/8 inches (7.5 x 4.8 cm)
Private collection, New York

36 Necklace
Insect Women and

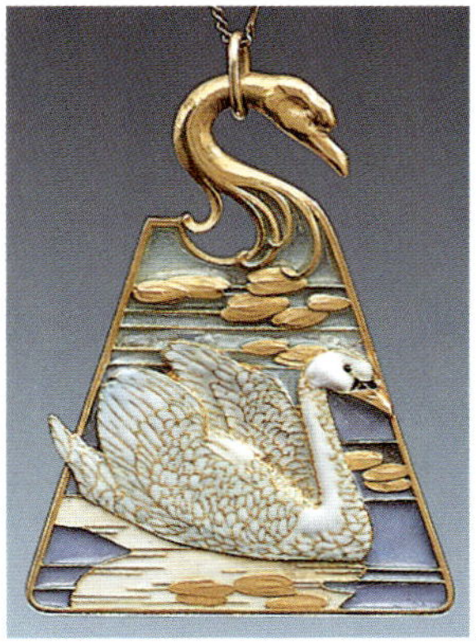
32

Black Swans (photo pp. 36–37)
c. 1898–1899
Chased gold, enamel on gold, *plique-à-jour* enamel, opal, amethyst
Diameter: 9 1/2; large pendants 2 3/4 x 2 1/4; small pendants: 1 3/8 x 1 1/4 inches
(Diameter: 24.1; large pendants: 7 x 5.7; small pendants: 3.5 x 3.2 cm)
The Metropolitan Museum of Art,
Gift of Lillian Nassau, 1985, inv. 1985.114

37 Tiara *Mermaid* (photo pp.22–23)
c. 1897–1898
Bronze with green and brown patina, enamel, carved opals
4 x 5 1/5 x 5 1/4 inches (9.7 x 14 x 13.3 cm)
Musée des Arts décoratifs, Paris
Gift of comte de Ganay in memory of comtesse de Béhague 1939, inv. 34374

38 Brooch
Woman with Dragon Headdress (photo p. 74)
c. 1898–1899
Cast gold, enamel on gold, pearl, carved limestone
2 3/8 x 1 3/4 inches (6.2 x 4.5 cm)
Musée des Arts décoratifs, Paris
Gift of marquise Arconati-Visconti 1916, inv. 20371

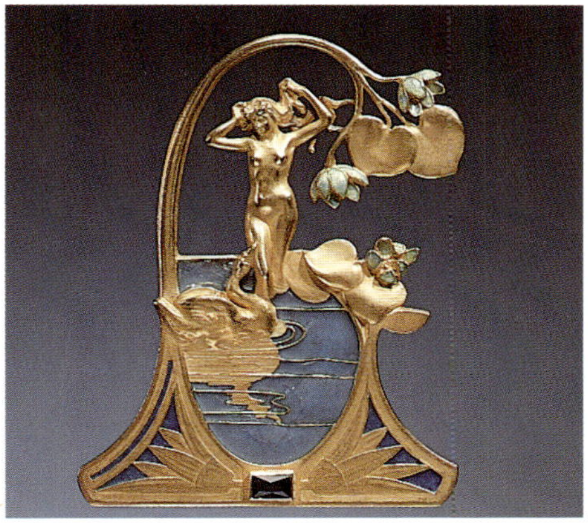
35

39 Dog Collar Plaque
Woman's Profile amid Frogs ("La Princesse au Sabbat") (photo p. 66)
c. 1899
Chased gold, translucent enamel, glass, pearls
Signed LALIQUE on top of frog's eye (top edge)
2 3/16 x 12 x 1/8 inches (5.7 x 30.5 x 4 cm)
Virginia Museum of Fine Arts, Richmond
Gift of Sydney and Frances Lewis, inv. 85.243

40 Brooch
Pansy / Thought (photo p. 69)
c. 1899–1901
Chased gold, engraved enamel on gold, diamonds
1 1/8 x 2 1/4 inches (2.7 x 5.7 cm)
Private collection, New York

41 Pendant and Chain
Woman's Head with Poppies (photo p. 133)
c. 1898–1899
Cast and chased gold, carved white chalcedony, translucent and opaque

enamel on gold, pearl
4 x 2 1/4; chain: 28 1/4 inches
(10.2 x 5.7; chain: 71.6 cm)
Musée des Arts décoratifs, Paris
Gift of baronne Félix Oppenheim 1933, inv. 28867

42 Dog Collar Plaque *"Narcisse"* (photo p. 13)
c. 1899–1900
Chased gold, opaque enamel on gold, glass
2 3/8 x 3 inches (6 x 7.6 cm)
Private collection, New York

43 Dog Collar Plaque *Two Fluteplayers* (photo p. 79)
c. 1898–1900
Chased gold, translucent enamel on gold, opaque enamel, diamonds
2 1/8 x 3 1/8 inches (5.4 x 8 cm)
Private collection, New York

44 Pendant *Woman's Face and Wisteria* (photo pp. 128–129)
c. 1898–1900
Chased gold, opaque enamel on gold
4 x 1 1/4 inches (10 x 3.2 cm)
Private collection, Buenos Aires

45 Ring *Bat* (photo p. 25)
1899
Silver, translucent enamel, moonstone, gold
1/2; Diameter: 3/4 inches
(1.2; Diameter: 1.9 cm)
Musée des Arts décoratifs, Paris
Gift of Mrs Dreyfus-Barney 1966, inv. 40105

46 Watch *Butterflies and Bats* (photo pp. 70–71)
c. 1899–1900
Chased gold, enamel on gold, moonstones
Diameter: 2 inches (Diameter: 5.1 cm)
Private collection, New York

47 Ring *Moth*
c. 1901–1902
Gold, pressed glass, enamel
7/8 x 5/8; Diameter: 3/4 inches
(2.2 x 1.6; Diameter: 2 cm)
Musée des Arts décoratifs, Paris
Gift of Mrs Crépy-Carnot 1981, inv. 49248

48 Comb *Umbel* (photo p. 55)
c. 1897–1898
Blond horn, silver, enamel
5 3/4 x 3 1/4 inches (14.8 x 8 cm)
Musée des Arts décoratifs, Paris
Purchased from the artist 1898, inv. 8755

49 Comb *Landscape with Setting Sun*
c. 1900
Horn, gold, enamel
5 x 4 3/4 inches (12.5 x 12 cm)
Private collection, New York

50 Comb *Tree Branches* (photo p. 155)
c. 1900–1901
Carved horn with patina
3 7/8 x 4 inches (9.8 x 10.2 cm)
Calouste Gulbenkian Museum

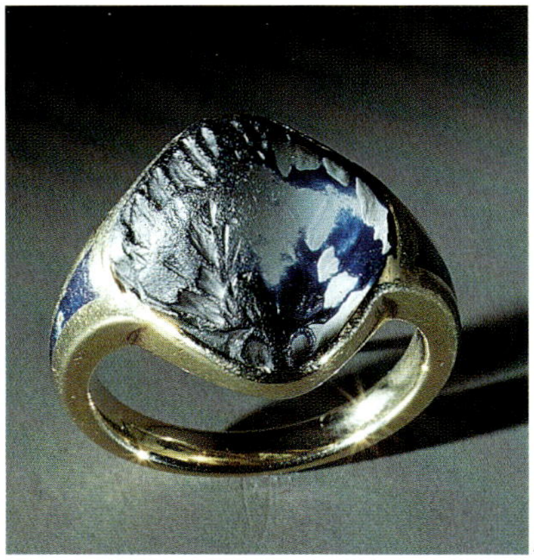
47

51 Pendant *Winter Landscape* (photo p. 153)
c. 1899–1900
Gold, opaque enamel on gold, glass, pearl
3 1/4 x 2 1/2 inches (8.5 x 6.5 cm)
Private collection, New York

52 Pendant *Dryad and Willows* (photo p. 159)
c. 1900
Chased gold, enamel on gold, *plique-à-jour* enamel
3 1/8 x 2 1/4 inches (8 x 5.7 cm)
Private collection, New York

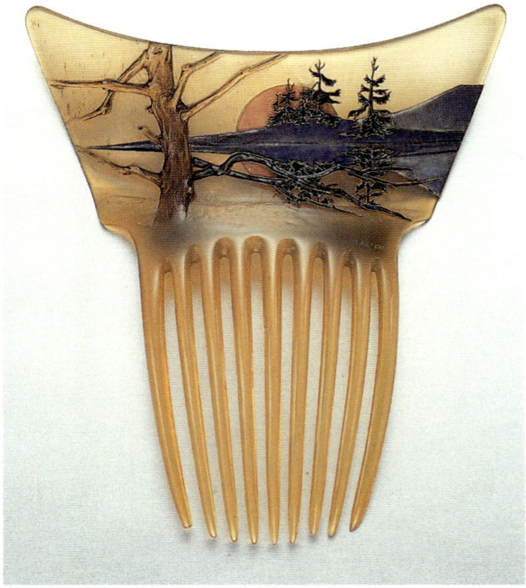
49

53 Bracelet *Iris* (photo p. 16)
c. 1897
Chased gold, enamel on gold, *plique-à-jour* enamel, opals
2 x 7 inches (5 x 17.8 cm)
Private collection, New York

54 Necklace
Hazelnuts (photo p. 41)
c. 1899–1900
Chased gold, translucent enamel on gold, *plique-à-jour* enamel, diamonds, peridots, glass
7 1/2 x 4 3/4; plaque: 2 1/2 x 5 1/4 inches
(19 x 12; plaque: 6.5 x 13.6 cm)
Musée des Arts décoratifs, Paris
Purchased from the artist 1900, inv. 9369

55 Watch
Pine Cones (photo p.126)
c. 1898–1900
Gold, *plique-à-jour* enamel, opaque enamel on glass
2 3/4; Depth: 5/8; Diameter: 2 inches
(7; Depth: 1.5; Diameter: 5 cm)
Musée des Arts décoratifs, Paris
Purchased from the artist 1900, inv. 9370

56 Dog Collar Plaque
Pine Cones (photo p. 106)
c. 1900
Chased gold, translucent enamel on gold, chrysoprases
Central plaque: 2 x 2 1/2;
side plaques: 2 x 1 1/4 inches
(Central plaque: 5 x 6.2;
side plaques: 5 x 3.4 cm)
Musée des Arts décoratifs, Paris
Bequeathed by Mrs Ménard 1968, inv. 41870

57 Necklace *Thorns*
c. 1900
Chased gold, enamel, topaz, pearls
19 x 1 3/4 inches (48.2 x 4.5 cm)
Private collection, Philadelphia

58 Dog Collar Plaque
Ferns (photo p. 52)
c. 1900–1902
Chased gold, translucent enamel on gold, diamonds (now replaced with zircons)
2 x 3 1/4 inches (5.2 x 8.2 cm)
Musée des Arts décoratifs, Paris
Gift of Mrs Maupoil 1968, inv. 41659

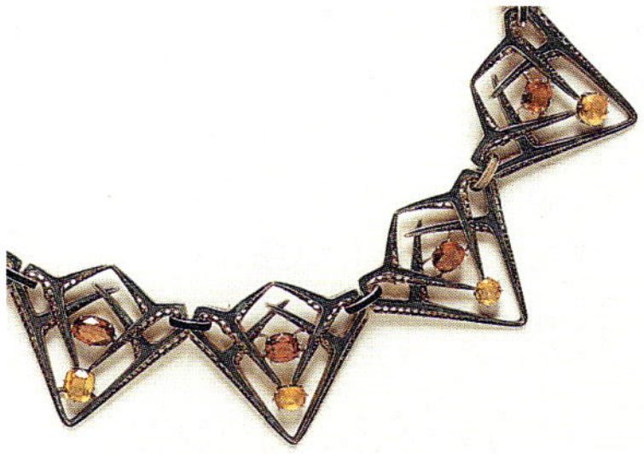

57

59 Design for a Comb
Gothic (photo p. 21)
c. 1897–1898
Watercolor on paper
10 3/4 x 8 3/8 inches (27.2 x 21.3 cm)
Lalique Museum Collection, Paris, inv. 1.3.059

60 Design for a Comb
Peacocks
1897–1898
Pencil, watercolor on paper
10 3/4 x 8 3/8 inches
(27.2 x 21.3 cm)
Lalique Museum Collection, Paris, inv. 1.3.009

61 Design for a Comb
Bats and Moonstones
c. 1898–1900
Pencil, ink, watercolor on paper
10 3/4 x 8 3/4 inches (27.5 x 21.3 cm)
Lalique Museum Collection, Paris, inv. 1.2.002

62 Design for a Dog Collar Plaque
Bats in a Roundel

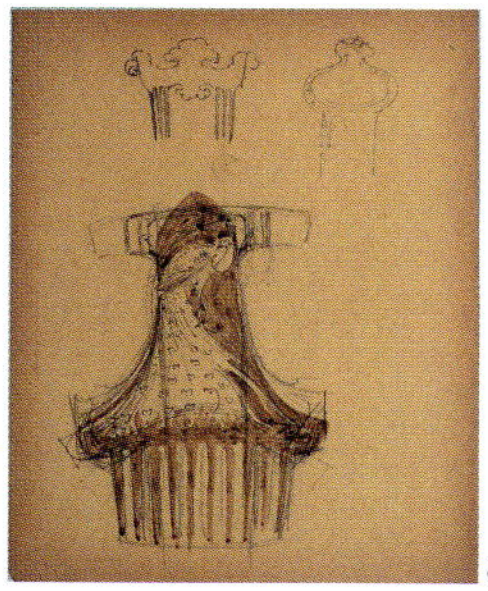

60

c. 1900
Pencil, ink, watercolor on paper
10 3/4 x 8 3/4 inches (27.5 x 21.1 cm)
Lalique Museum Collection, Paris, inv. 2.2.007

63 Design for a Pendant
Two Swans
1898–1900
Pen, watercolor on paper
11 x 8 5/8 inches (28.1 x 21.7 cm)
Lalique Museum Collection, Paris, inv. 2.4.095

64 Design for a Watch
Pine Trees (photo p. 156)
1899–1900

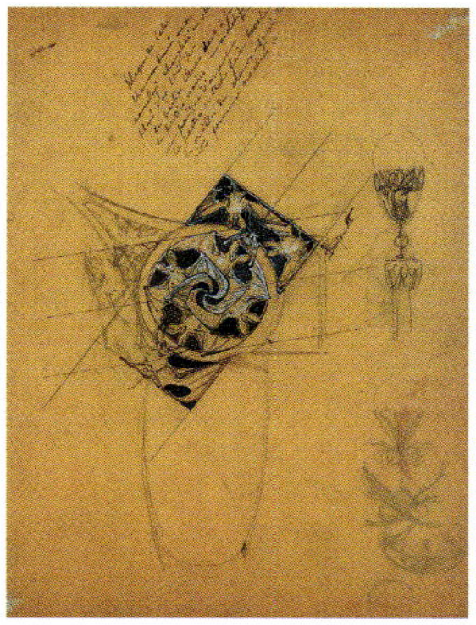

62

Pencil, ink, watercolor on paper
10 3/4 x 8 3/8 inches (27.4 x 21.1 cm)
Lalique Museum Collection, Paris,
inv. 2.2.029

65 **Design for a Watch**
Pine Trees (photo p. 157)
1899–1900
Pencil, ink, watercolor on paper
11 x 8 5/8 inches (28.1 x 21.9 cm)
Lalique Museum Collection, Paris,
inv. 3.6.001

66 **Design for a Pendant**
Dryad and Willows
(photo p. 161)
c. 1898–1899
Pencil, ink, watercolor, gouache on paper
11 x 8 5/8 inches (27.8 x 21.8 cm)
Lalique Museum Collection, Paris,
inv. 2.4.413

67 **Design for a Pendant**
Six Figures in a Forest
c. 1899–1900
Pencil, ink, watercolor on paper
12 x 9 3/4 inches (30.5 x 24.5 cm)
David Weinstein Collection, New York

68 **Design for a Bracelet**
Female Figures in a Thistle Border
1900–1902
Pencil, ink, watercolor, on paper
11 x 8 5/8 inches (28 x 21.8 cm)
Lalique Museum Collection, Paris,
inv. 4.1.081

69 **Design for a Bracelet**
Iris (photo p. 17)
c. 1897
Watercolor on paper
8 5/8 x 10 7/8 inches (21.8 x 27.6 cm)
Lalique Museum Collection, Paris,
inv. 4.1.082

70 **Design for Two Pendants**
Chrysanthemums (photo p. 12)
c. 1898–1899
Pencil, pen, watercolor on paper
11 x 8 5/8 inches (28 x 21.8 cm)
Lalique Museum Collection, Paris,
inv. 2.3.177

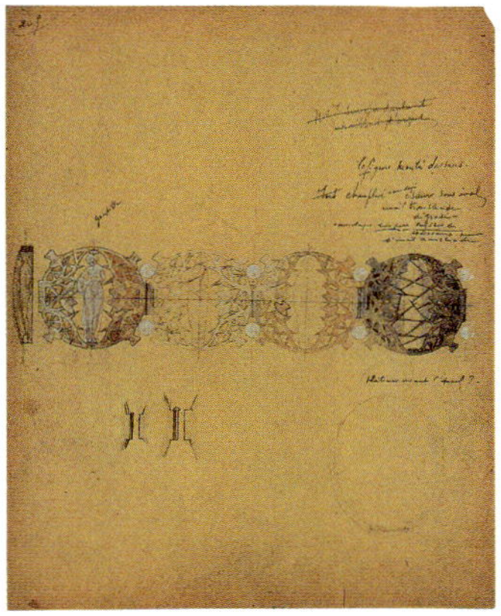

68

II
THE LALIQUE EPOCH
1900–1909

71 **Comb** *Lilies of the Valley* (photo p. 26)
1900
Horn, gold, opaque enamel on gold
6 1/8 x 3 3/4 x 1 3/16 inches
(15.4 x 9.4 x 3 cm)
The Cleveland Museum of Art
Gift of Mrs. A. Dean Perry, inv. 1981.49

72 **Comb** *Ivy*
c. 1900
Horn, gold, translucent and opaque
enamel, sapphires
3 1/2 x 2 1/2 inches (8.9 x 6.3 cm)
Private collection, Philadelphia

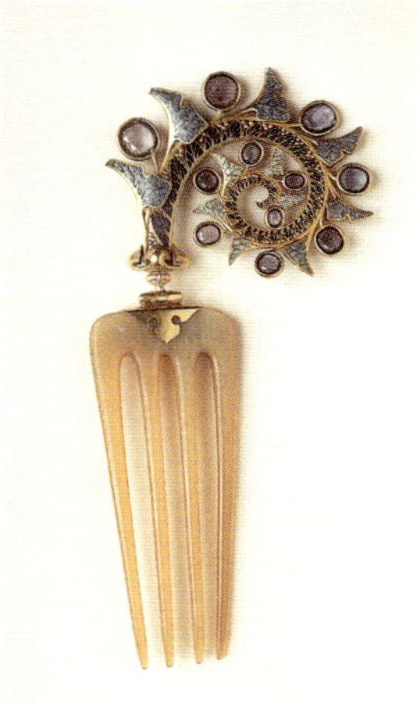

72

73 **Comb** *Cactus* (photo p. 47)
1902–1903
Horn, silver
6 5/8 x 4 3/8 inches (16.5 x 11.6 cm)
Calouste Gulbenkian Museum, Lisbon,
inv. 1159

74 **Hatpin**
Ivy and Clover (photo p. 105)
c. 1900
Chased gold, translucent enamel on gold
7 3/4 x 1 1/4; motif 1 1/4 inches
(19.8 x 3.4; motif 3.3 cm)
Musée des Arts décoratifs, Paris
Gift of marquise Arconati-Visconti 1916,
inv. 20372

75 **Locket Chain**
Birds, Pine Cones, and Flowers
c. 1900–1902
Chased gold, translucent and opaque
enamel on gold, amethysts
66 1/8; motif 3/4 inches (168; motif: 1.8cm)
Musée des Arts décoratifs, Paris
Gift of baronne Oppenheim 1933, inv. 28866

76 Locket Chain
Leaves (photo p. 107)
c. 1898–1900
Electrum, baroque pearls, *plique-à-jour* enamel
6 inches (14.9 cm)
Musée des Arts décoratifs, Paris
Gift of marquise Arconati-Visconti 1916, inv. 20366

77 Tiara *Ivy Leaves* (photo p. 99)
c. 1904–1905
Horn, gold, diamonds, tortoiseshell
Signed LALIQUE on band
$3 \frac{1}{2}$ x $7 \frac{3}{8}$ x 6 inches
(8.9 x 18.7 x 15.2 cm)
Virginia Museum of Fine Arts, Richmond
Gift of Sydney and Frances Lewis, inv. 85.244

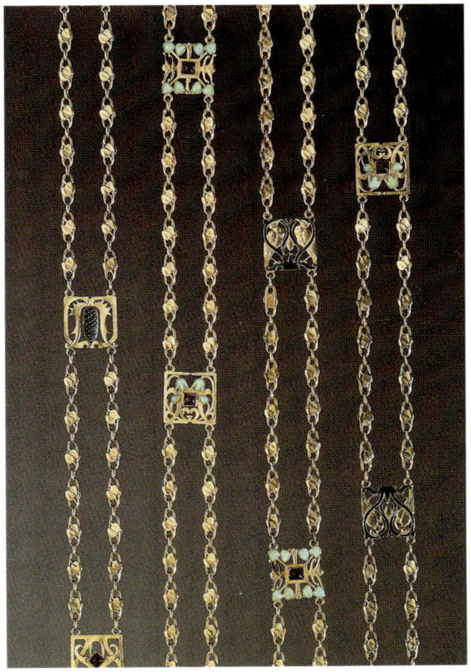

75

78 Tiara
Cattleya Orchid (photo p. 135)
c. 1903–1904
Carved ivory, horn, gold, enamel on gold, diamonds
$4 \frac{5}{8}$ x $8 \frac{1}{8}$ x $6 \frac{1}{4}$ inches
(11.8 x 20.5 x 16 cm)
Private collection, Buenos Aires

79 Watch *Carnation*
c. 1898–1900
Gold, opaque enamel
$2 \frac{3}{16}$ x 3 inches
(7.6 x 5.6 cm)
Private collection, Philadelphia

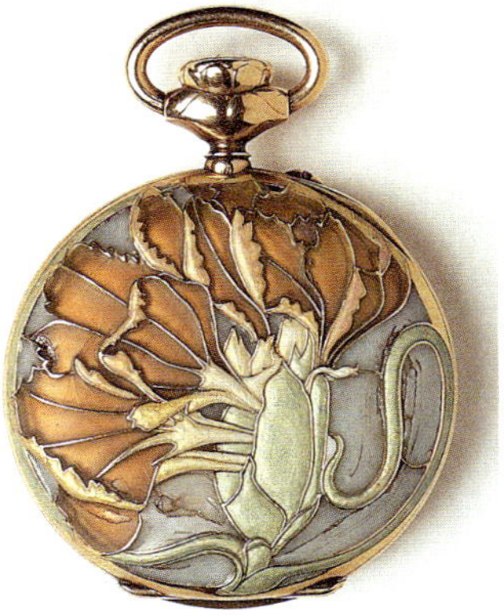

79

80 Ring *Lily*
c. 1899–1900
Gold, opaque enamel on gold
$\frac{1}{2}$; Diameter: $\frac{3}{4}$ inches
(1.1; Diameter 2 cm)
Musée des Arts décoratifs, Paris
Gift of Mrs Dreyfus-Barney 1966, inv. 40104

81 Ring *Flowers* (photo p. 108)
c. 1900
Gold, opaque enamel on gold, *plique-à-jour* enamel, pearls
$2 \frac{1}{4}$; Diameter: $3 \frac{1}{4}$ inches
(3; Diameter: 2.1 cm)
Musée des Arts décoratifs, Paris
Gift of Mrs Dreyfus-Barney 1966, inv. 40106

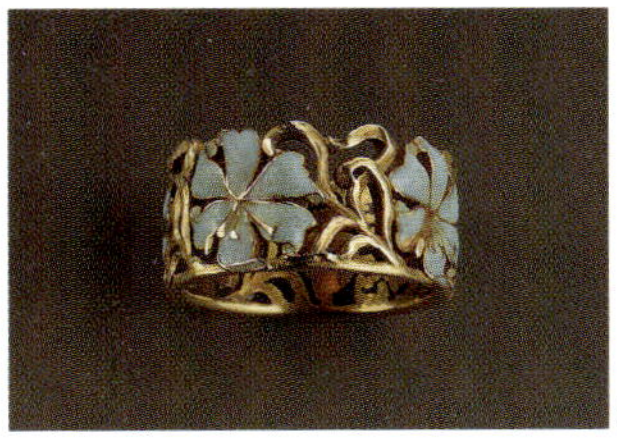

80

82 Ring
Four Lotus Blossoms
c. 1900–1902
Gold, translucent enamel on gold
1 x $\frac{3}{4}$ inches (2.5 x 2 cm)
Private collection, New York

83 Ring
c. 1902
Chased gold, enamel on gold, pearl
$1 \frac{1}{8}$ x 1 x $\frac{7}{8}$ inches
(2.8 x 2.5 x 2 cm)
Private collection, Buenos Aires

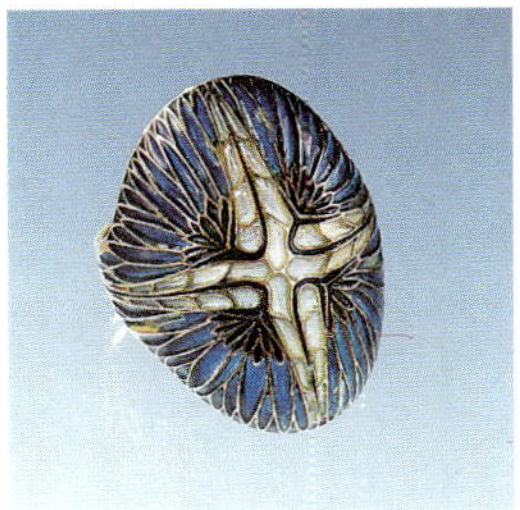

82

84 Hatpin
Flowers and Leaves
c. 1902–1903
Gold, opaque enamel on gold
$6 \frac{1}{2}$ x $1 \frac{1}{4}$ inches (16.5 x 3 cm)
Private collection, New York

85 Bracelet *Thistles*
c. 1901–1903
Chased gold, enamel, opals, pearls
3/4 x 6 3/4 inches (1.8 x 17 cm)
David Weinstein Collection, New York

86 Bracelet
Wheat Stalks (photo p. 115)
c. 1901–1903
Gold, *plique-à-jour* enamel, diamonds
1 1/2 x 7 inches (3.7 x 18 cm)
Musée des Arts décoratifs, Paris
Gift of Mrs Chardin 1978, inv. 46463

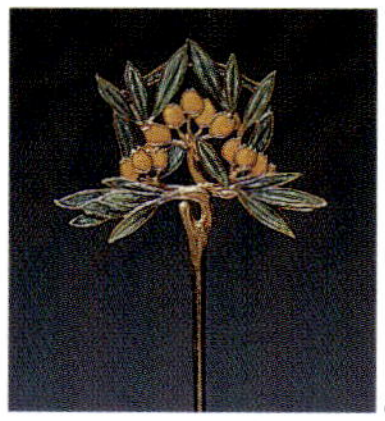
84

87 Necklace
Ferns (photo p. 136)
c. 1902
Cast glass, gold, enamel on gold
Private collection, Buenos Aires

88 Lorgnette and Chain
Wisteria (photo p. 122)
c. 1899–1900
Gold, opaque white enamel on gold,
diamonds, jade, glass
6 1/2 x 40 inches
(16.5 x 101.6 cm)
The Metropolitan Museum of Art
Gift of Mrs. J.G. Phelps Stokes
(née Lettice L. Sands) 1965, inv. 65.154

89 Lorgnette
Lizard (photo p. 110)
c. 1899–1901
Gold, enamel on gold, *plique-à-jour*
enamel, optical glass
6 1/2 x 1 5/8 inches (16.2 x 4 cm)
Musée des Arts décoratifs, Paris
Bequeathed by Mr Reubell 1933,
inv. 30750

90 Necklace *Frogs* (photo p. 67)
c. 1902–1903
Gold, enamel, glass, diamonds
Private collection, Buenos Aires

91 Brooch *Rooster*
c. 1898–1900
Gold, enamel on gold, *plique-à-jour* enamel
3 x 2 1/4 inches (5.5 x 9 cm)
Private collection, Philadelphia

92 Pendant *Two Cocks*
c. 1901–1902
Gold, opaque enamel on gold, diamonds,
sapphire back chased
2 3/4 x 2 inches (6.9 x 5.1 cm)
Musée des Arts décoratifs, Paris
Gift of Mrs Dreyfus-Barney 1966,
inv. 40103

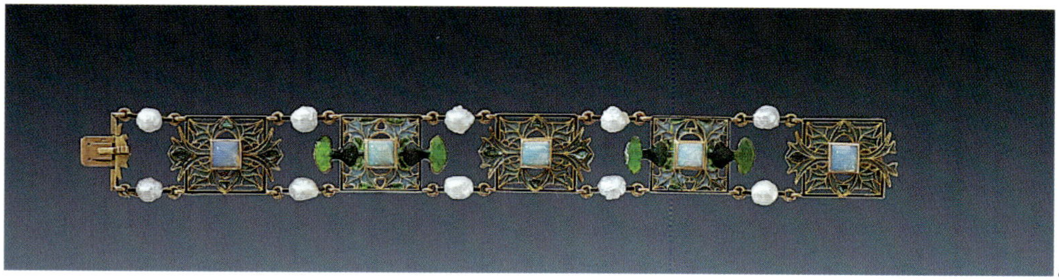
85

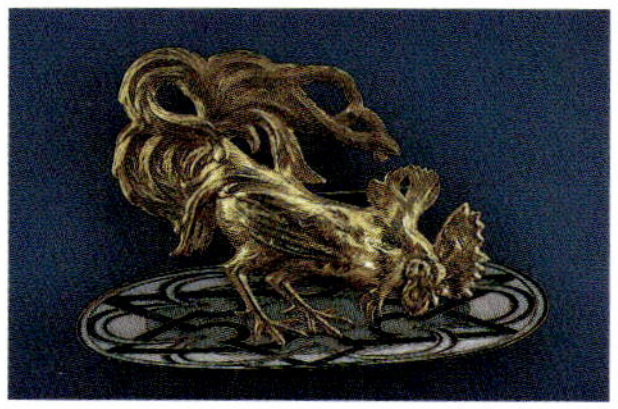
91

93 Buckle
Two Cocks (photo p. 109)
c. 1898–900
Enamel, metal
Stamped LALIQUE
3 3/4 x 5 7/16 x 7/16 inches
(9.5 x 13.8 x 1.1 cm)
Virginia Museum of Fine Arts, Richmond
Gift of Sydney and Frances Lewis,
inv. 85.249 a/b

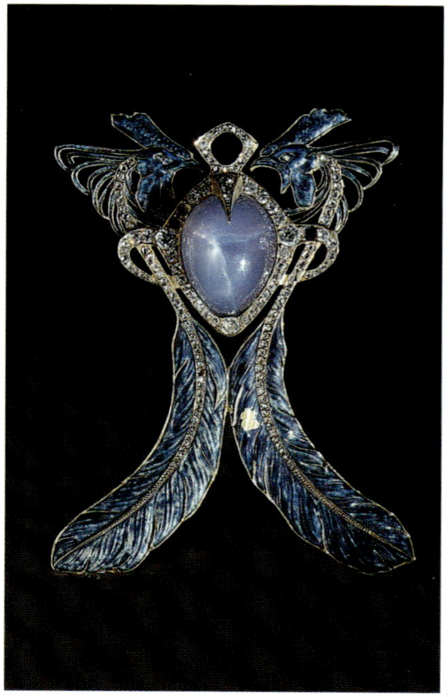
92

94 Pendant
Two Cocks (photo p. 141)
c. 1905–1906
Cast glass, gold, copper, *pâte de verre*, enamel, baroque pearl
12 3/8 x 4 7/16 inches (31.5 x 11.3 cm)
The Corning Museum of Glass, acquired 1990

95 Belt Buckle
Stag Beetles

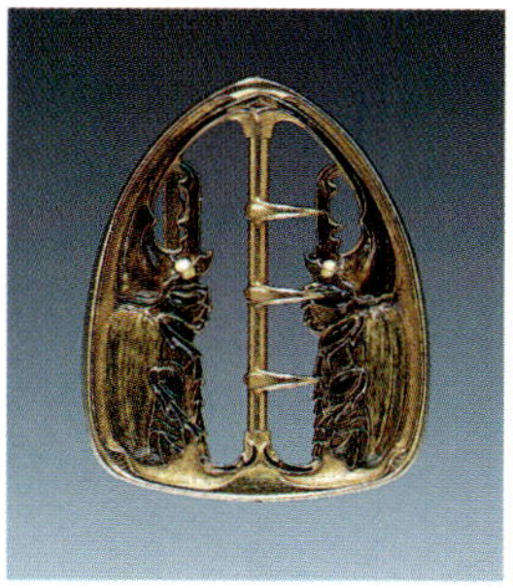

95

c. 1900–1902
Gold, enamel
2 1/2 x 2 inches (6.5 x 5 cm)
David Weinstein Collection, New York

96 Comb
Grasshoppers (photo p. 85)
1902–1904
Carved horn, tourmalines
2 1/2 x 3 1/2 inches (6.4 x 8.9 cm)
The Art Institute of Chicago
Gift of Mrs. Charles J. Morse in memory of Charles J. Morse, inv. 1947.205

97 Pendant *Eagle* (photo p. 28)
c. 1899–1900
Chased gold, enamel on gold, ruby, pearls
2 7/8 x 2 3/8; chain: 24 3/4 inches
(7.5 x 6; chain: 63 cm)
Musée des Arts décoratifs, Paris
Purchased 1995, inv. 996.93

98 Necklace "*Tigers*" (photo p. 81)
c. 1903–1904
Gold, carved horn, tortoiseshell, enamel on gold, agate
Diameter: 4 1/2 inches
(Diameter: 14.4 cm)
The Walters Art Gallery, Baltimore
Purchased from the artist 1904, inv. 57.938

99 Comb
Two Swallows with a Stalk of Oats (photo p. 131)
c. 1906–1908
Gold, carved horn, diamonds
6 1/2 x 8 1/2 inches (16.7 x 21.8 cm)
Private collection, Buenos Aires

100 Brooch
Two Seahorses (photo p. 9)
c. 1902–1905
Chased gold, enamel on gold, *plique-à-jour* enamel, opals, pearls
Stamped LALIQUE upper edge, back
4 x 2 1/2 inches (10.2 x 6.3 cm)
Virginia Museum of Fine Arts, Richmond
The Sydney and Frances Lewis Art Nouveau Fund, inv. 73.46.1

101 Brooch
Three Seahorses

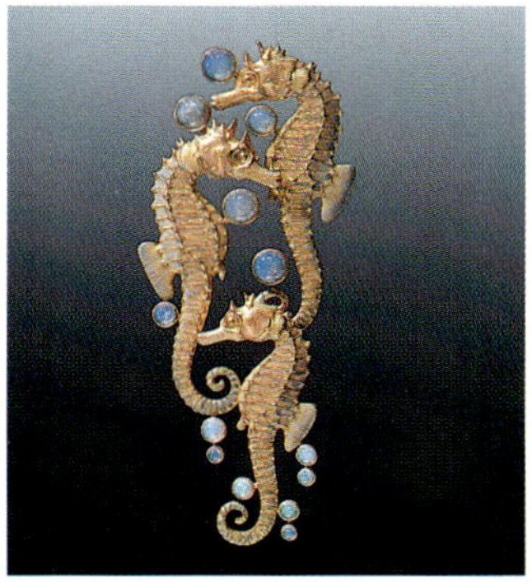

101

c. 1902–1903
Chased gold, *plique-à-jour* enamel, opals
4 1/2 x 2 inches (11.5 x 5 cm)
Private collection, New York

102 Ring
Two Couples (photo p. 136)
c. 1899–1901
Cast, chased gold, pearl
1 1/8 x 5/8; Diameter: 1/2 inches
(2.6 x 1.6; Diameter: 2.1 cm)
Musée des Arts décoratifs, Paris
Gift of baronne Félix Oppenheim 1933, inv. 28864

103 Brooch *Bathers*
c. 1902
Chased gold, carved ivory
Length: 2 1/4 inches (Length: 5.7 cm)
Private collection, New York

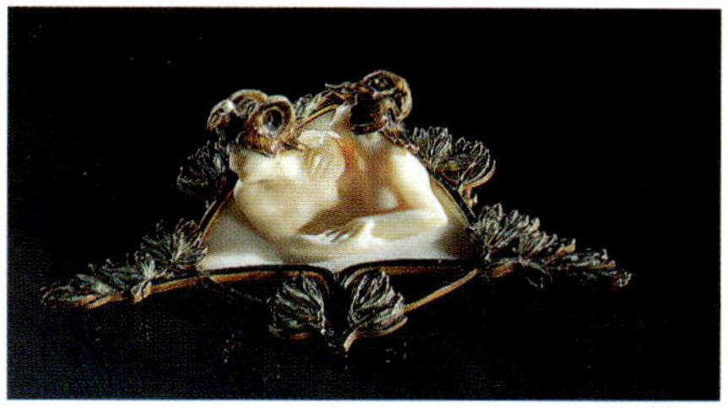

104

104 Brooch
Two Women in Helmets
c. 1901–1902
Chased gold, enamel on gold, carved ivory
2 x 3 3/8 inches (5 cm x 8.5 cm)
David Weinstein Collection, New York

105 Brooch
Women in Helmets
c. 1901–1902
Carved ivory, stone, gilded silver, diamonds
1 x 1 3/4 inches (2.5 x 4.5 cm)
Private collection, New York

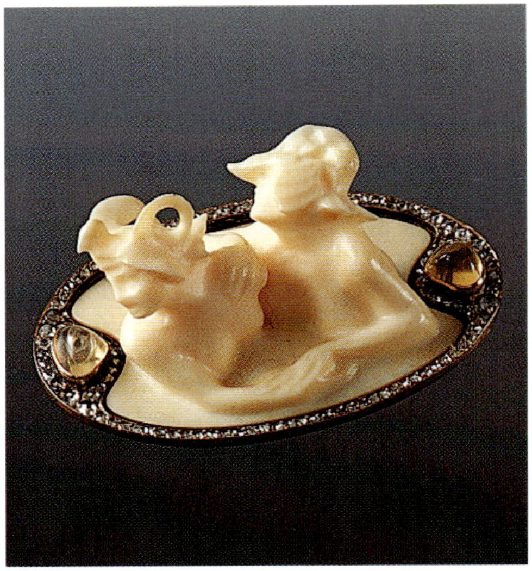
105

106 Corsage Pin Finial or Hatpin *Maenad and Satyrs* (photo p. 95)
c. 1899–1900
Gold, translucent enamel on gold, opal
3 3/8 x 3 7/8 inches (8.7 x 9.7 cm)
Private collection, New York

107 Pendant
Entwining (photo p. 49)
c. 1900–1902
Gold, diamonds, enamel, glass
2 3/4 x 2 3/8; chain: 21 1/4 inches
(7 x 6; chain: 54 cm)
Calouste Gulbenkian Museum, Lisbon
Purchased from the artist 1902, inv. 1164

108 Brooch *Nude Woman*
c. 1900–1902
Gold, enamel on gold, *plique-à-jour* enamel, diamonds, sapphires
1 1/2 x 2 3/4 inches (4 x 7 cm)
Private collection, Philadelphia

109 Hatpin
Bust of an Angel in Profile
c. 1902–3
Gold, enamel, artificial ivory
7 1/2 x 1 1/4 inches (19 x 3.5 cm)
Private collection, New York

110 Pendant
Two Angels (photo p. 48)
c. 1902–1903
Horn, glass, topaz, gold
2 1/4 x 1 1/2; chain: 21 1/4 inches
(5.5 x 4; chain: 54 cm)
Calouste Gulbenkian Museum, Lisbon
Purchased from the artist 1904, inv. 1200

111 Brooch *Dancing Nymphs in a Frame of Butterflies* (photo p. 144)
c. 1901–1902
Gold, enamel, sapphires, horn
2 1/4 x 1 3/4 inches (5.5 x 4.5 cm)
Private collection, Philadelphia

112 Brooch *Dancing Nymphs in a Frame of Bats* (photo p. 142)
c. 1902–1903
Artificial ivory, gold, enamel
2 x 3 inches (5 x 7.5 cm)
Private collection, New York

113 Pendant
Dancing Nymphs (photo p. 143)
c. 1902–1903
Artificial ivory, enamel, gold, pearl
2 5/8 x 2 1/4 inches (6.5 x 6 cm)
Private collection, New York

114 Brooch
Dancing Nymphs (photo p. 145)
c. 1902–1903
Artificial amber, glass, silver
2 x 2 1/2 inches (5 x 6.5 cm)
Private collection, New York

115 Comb
Medallions and Thistles
(photo p. 104)
c. 1901–1903
Horn, enamel, ivory, silver
4 x 4 1/4 inches (10 x 10.7 cm)
Private collection, Philadelphia

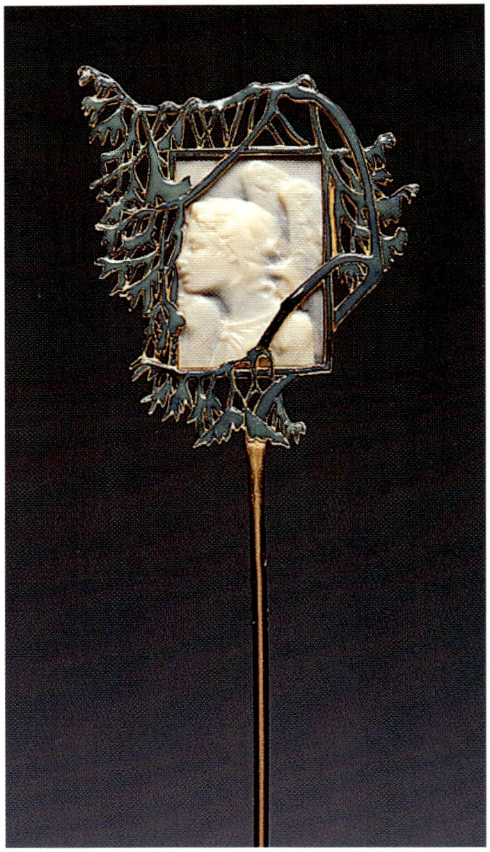
109

116 Pendant
Draped Woman in Budding Branches
c. 1902–1904
Ivory, gold, enamel, stone
3 1/8 x 1 3/4 inches (8 x 4.5 cm)
Private collection, New York

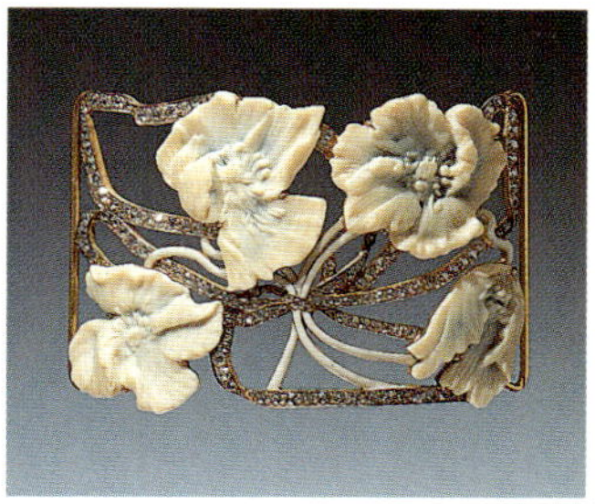
117

117 Dog Collar Plaque
Hawthorn
c. 1902–1903
Artificial ivory, enamel, diamonds
2 x 3 inches (5 x 7.5 cm)
Private collection, New York

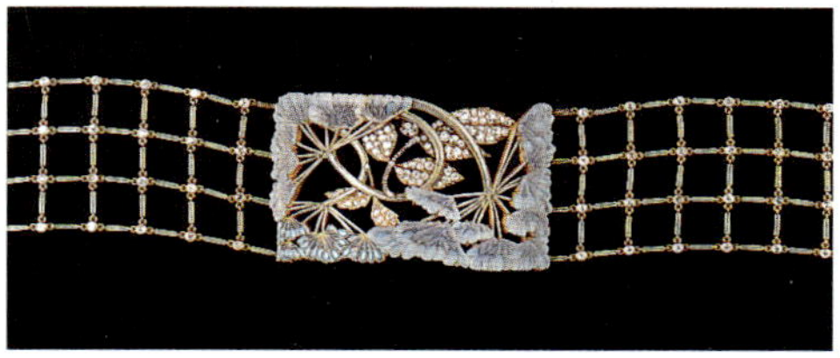
118

118 Dog Collar Necklace
Queen Anne's Lace
c. 1901–1902
Gold, enamel, diamonds, cast glass, pearls
2 1/8 x 13 x 1/4 inches (5.4 x 33 x 0.63 cm)
Virginia Museum of Fine Arts, Richmond
Gift of Sydney and Frances Lewis, inv. 85.245

119 Belt Plate *Thistle*
c. 1901–1903
Gold, *plique-à-jour* enamel, cast glass
2 1/4 x 4 1/8 inches (5.7 x 10.5 cm)
Musée des Arts décoratifs, Paris
Gift of Mrs Dreyfus-Barney 1966, inv. 40101

120 Bracelet *Speedwell*
1900–1902
Gold, enamel, cast glass
3 1/8 x 7 inches (8 x 17.5 cm)
Private collection, New York

121 Brooch
Pine Sprig (photo p. 121)
c. 1900–1902
Gold, enamel, cast glass
2 3/4 x 2 inches (7 x 5 cm)
Private collection, Philadelphia

122 Brooch *Carnation*
c. 1900–1902
Gold, cast glass, enamel, opals
2 9/16 x 2 1/4 inches (6 x 5.5 cm)
Private collection, Philadelphia

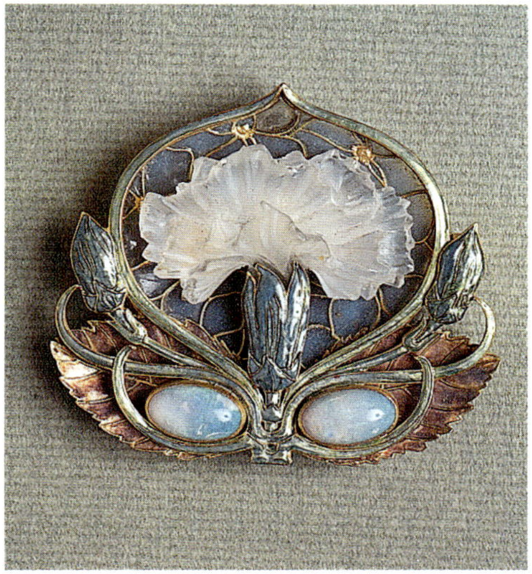
122

123 Brooch-Pendant
Carnations (photo p. 26)
c. 1901–1902
Gold, cast glass, opaque enamel on gold, *plique-à-jour* enamel, pearl
Gold mount stamped LALIQUE on upper right reverse
3 x 2 x 1/2 inches (7.6 x 5 x 1.11 cm)
Virginia Museum of Fine Arts, Richmond
Gift of Sydney and Frances Lewis, inv. 85.246

124 Corsage Ornament
Pansies (photo pp. 88–89)
1903–1904
Gold,enamel on gold, *plique-à-jour* enamel, cast glass, sapphire
3 1/6 x 5 1/2 inches (8.1 x 13.9 cm)
The Walters Art Gallery, Baltimore
Acquired from the artist 1904, inv. 57.943

125 Bandeau *Pansies*
c. 1904–1905
Gold, enamel, diamonds, cast glass
5/8; Diameter: 5 1/4 inches (1.5 ; Diameter: 13.5 cm.)
David Weinstein Collection, New York

126 Pendant *Roses*
c. 1901–1902
Gold, enamel, cast glass, opal, diamonds
2 1/2 x 3 3/4 inches (6.5 x 9.5 cm)
Private collection, New York

127 Corsage Ornament
Bumblebees on Flowers (photo p. 165)
c. 1905–1906
Gold, translucent, cast glass, enamel on gold, diamonds
2 3/8 x 5 7/8 inches (6 x 15 cm)
Musée des Arts décoratifs, Paris
Purchased from the artist 1906, inv. 12745

128 Corsage Ornament
Blackthorn

and Wasps (photo p. 113)
1904
Gold, enamel, pressed glass
1 3/4 x 4 1/2 inches (4.7 x 11.2 cm)
Musée des Arts décoratifs, Paris
Gift of Mrs Desmarais 1983, inv. 54422B

129 Brooch
Female Head with Dragonflies (photo p. 127)
c. 1904–1905
Gold, *plique-à-jour* enamel, mold glass
2 x 6 5/8 inches (5 x 16.8 cm)
Private collection

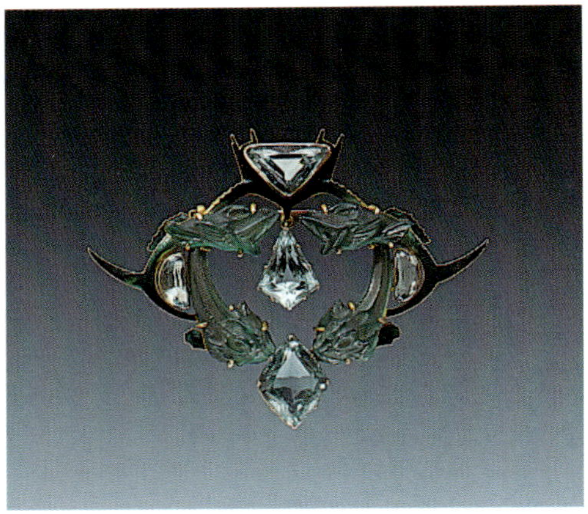

132

130 Handle of a Lorgnette (?)
Sweet Pea with Bust of a Woman (photo p. 27)
c. 1899–1900
Gold, enamel, cast glass
4 1/2 x 2 inches (11.5 x 5 cm)
Private collection, Philadelphia

131 Corsage Ornament
Fish (photo p. 166)
c. 1903–1905

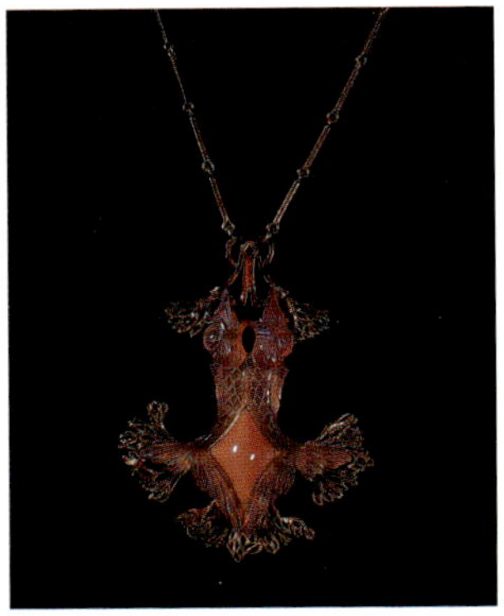

133

Gold, enamel, pressed engraved glass, emerald (now replaced with glass)
2 1/2 x 6 1/4 inches (6.5 x 16 cm)
Musée des Arts décoratifs, Paris
Gift of Mrs Dreyfus-Barney 1966, inv. 40099

132 Brooch *Fish*
1904–1905
Gold, cast glass, enamel, aquamarines
2 1/2 x 3 1/4 inches (6.5 x 8.5 cm)
Private collection, New York

133 Pendant and Chain
Two Fish
c. 1905
Gold, pressed glass, enamel, cornelian
2 3/4 x 2 1/4; chain: 21 1/4 inches
(7 x 5.5; chain: 54 cm)
Lalique Museum Collection, Paris

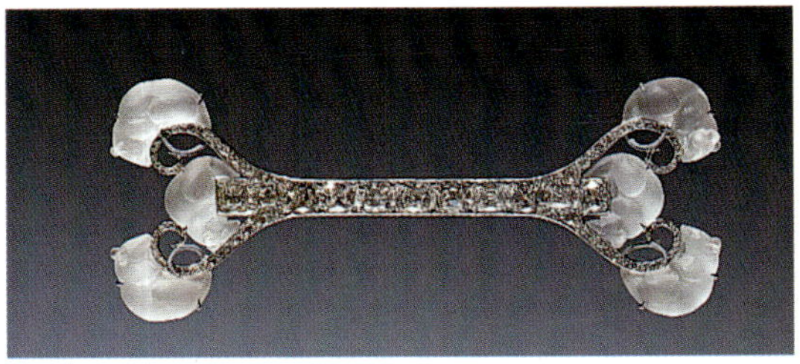

135

134 Brooch-Corsage Ornament
Fish (photo pp. 96–97)
c. 1904–1905
Gold, *plique-à-jour* enamel, diamonds, glass
4 7/8 x 2 3/4 inches (12.4 x 7 cm)
The Metropolitan Museum of Art,
Bequest of Mary Kellogg Hopkins 1941,
inv. 45.28.2

135 Brooch
Mice
c. 1907–1908
Platinum, cast glass, enamel, diamonds
1 1/2 x 3 1/2 inches (4 x 9 cm)
Private collection, New York

136 Pendant and Chain
Honesty Pod (photo p. 84)
c. 1902–1903
Gold, enamel, diamond, pearl (replacing diamond)
Pendant: 2 3/8 x 1 1/2; chain: 21 1/2 inches
(Pendant: 6 x 3.8; chain: 54.6 cm)
The Art Institute of Chicago
Gift of Mrs. Charles J. Morse in memory of Charles J. Morse, inv. 1947.209

137 Pendant and Chain
Lilacs (photo p. 139)
c. 1904–1905
Gold, enamel, engraved glass, diamonds
14 1/4 x 2 1/4 inches (36.2 x 5.7 cm)
The Metropolitan Museum of Art
Gift of Mary F. Failing in memory of her sister, Henrietta Ellison Failing 1944,
inv. 44.123.1

138 Brooch
"The Kiss" (photo p. 76)
1904–1906
Silver, pressed glass
1 7/8 x 2 3/4 inches (4.9 x 7 cm)
Musée des Arts décoratifs, Paris
Gift of R. C. Le Mesnil 1960, inv. 38337

139 Brooch
Doves on Olive Branches (photo p. 93)
c. 1905–1906
Gold, enamel, cast glass, diamonds
6 x 2 1/2 inches (15.5 x 6.5 cm)
Smithsonian Institution, National Museum of American History

140 Pendant-Brooch
"Salammbô" or "Salome" (photo pp. 64–65)
c. 1904–1905
Gold, glass, *plique-à-jour* enamel
3 1/8 x 2 1/2 inches (8 x 6.3 cm)
Private collection, New York

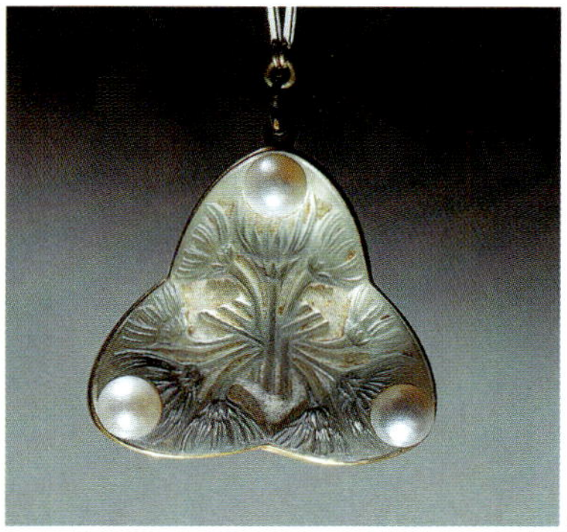
142

141 Brooch *Women and Flowers* (photo p. 138)
c. 1904–1905
Gold, glass, diamonds
1 3/4 x 1 3/4 inches (4.5 x 4.5 cm)
Private collection, New York

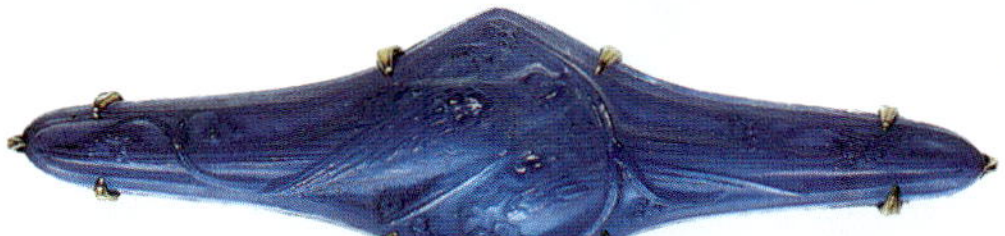
143

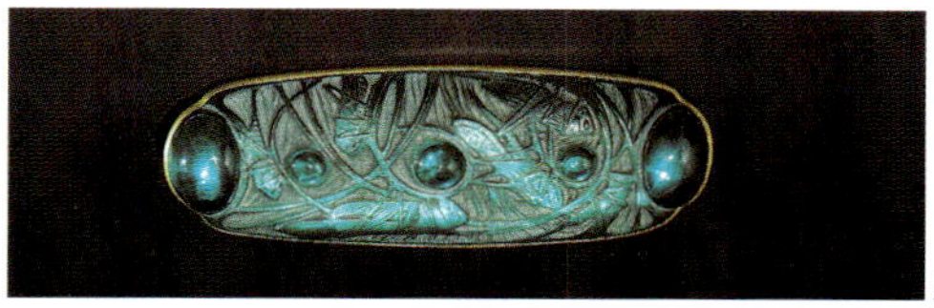
144

142 Pendant and Chain
Aster
c. 1906–1907
Gold, pearls, pressed and stained glass, enamel
1 3/8 x 1 1/2; chain: 20 1/4 inches
(3.5 x 3.8; chain: 51.5 cm)
Musée des Arts décoratifs, Paris
Bequeathed by Mrs Martin-Guelliot 1971, inv. 43643

143 Brooch
Two Pheasants
Model created in 1911, no. 1392
Pressed glass, metal
1 x 3 1/4 inches (2.5 x 8.5 cm)
Lalique Museum Collection, Paris

144 Brooch *Grasshoppers*
Model created in 1913, no. 1400
Gold, pressed glass, enamel
1 1/4 x 3 1/2 inches (3.3 x 9.2 cm)
Musée des Arts décoratifs, Paris
Purchased from the artist 1913, inv. 19292

145 Botanical Study
Wild Turnip
c. 1896–1898
Pencil, ink, watercolor on paper
10 3/4 x 8 1/2 inches (27.5 x 21.5 cm)
David Weinstein Collection, New York

146 Botanical Study
Wild Sweet Pea
c. 1896–1898
Pencil, ink, watercolor on paper
10 3/4 x 8 1/2 inches (27.5 x 21.5 cm)
David Weinstein Collection, New York

147 Drawing *Cock and Sun*
c. 1899–1901
Ink, watercolor on paper
7 3/4 x 5 1/4 inches (19.5 x 13.5 cm)
David Weinstein Collection, New York

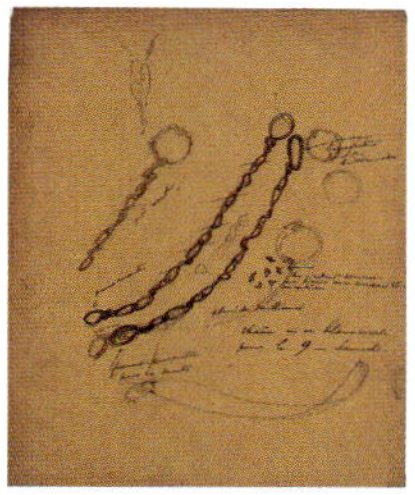
150

148 Design for a Necklace
Butterflies
1902–1904
Ink, watercolor, gouache on paper
10 3/4 x 8 1/2 inches (27.5 x 21.5 cm)
David Weinstein Collection, New York

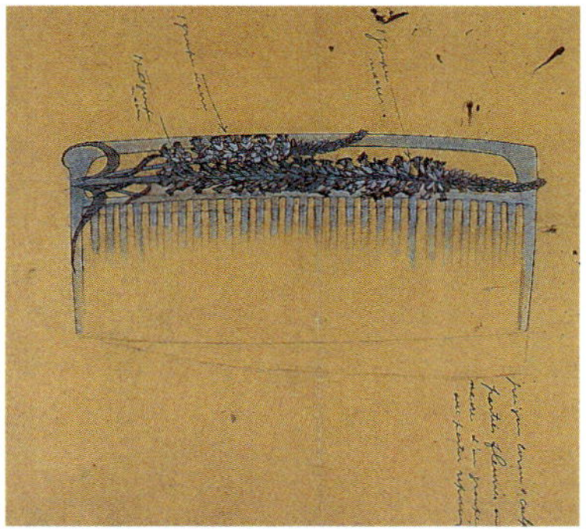
153

149 Design for a Chain
Violets (photo p. 124)
c. 1899–1901
Pencil, ink, watercolor on paper
11 x 8 1/2 inches (27.8 x 21.7 cm)
Lalique Museum Collection, Paris, inv. 2.3.056

150 Design for a Chain
c. 1899–1901
Pencil, ink on paper
10 1/2 x 8 5/8 inches (27.5 x 22 cm)
Lalique Museum Collection, Paris,
inv. 3.6.032

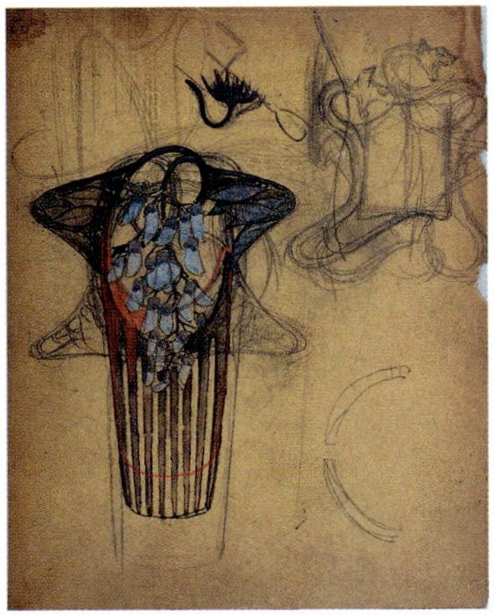

151

151 Design for a Comb
Wisteria
1899–1900
Pencil, watercolor on paper
11 1/4 x 8 3/4 inches (28.4 x 21.9 cm)
Lalique Museum Collection, Paris,
inv. 1.3.019

152 Design for a Corsage Ornament *Pine Boughs and Cones* (photo p. 119)
1905–1906
Pencil, ink, watercolor on paper
11 x 8 5/8 inches (28 x 21.8 cm)
Lalique Museum Collection, Paris,
inv. 3.1.043

153 Design for a Comb
Speedwell
1903–1904

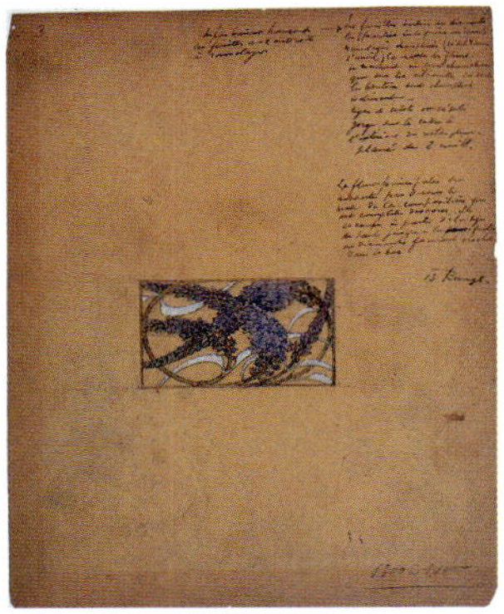

154

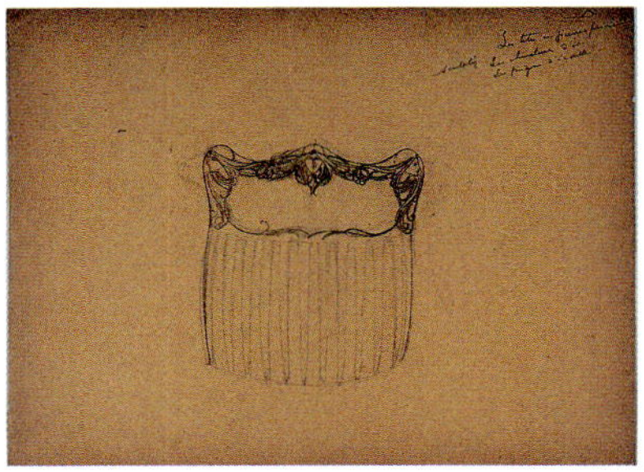

155

Pencil, ink, watercolor, gouache on paper
8 1/2 x 10 3/4 inches (21.5 x 27.5 cm)
Lalique Museum Collection, Paris,
inv. 1.3.113

154 Design for a Dog Collar Plaque
Speedwell
c. 1898–1899
Pencil, ink, watercolor on paper
11 x 8 5/8 inches (27.8 x 22cm)
Lalique Museum Collection, Paris,
inv. 2.2.151

155 Design for a Comb
Three Female Heads
c. 1897–1899
Pencil, ink on paper
8 1/2 x 11 inches (21.5 x 28 cm)
Lalique Museum Collection, Paris
inv. 1.3.002

156 Design for a Pendant
Two Fighting Cocks
(photo p. 112)
c. 1899–1900
Pencil, ink, watercolor, gouache on paper
11 x 8 3/4 inches (28.2 x 21.9 cm)
Lalique Museum Collection, Paris,
inv. 2.4.438

157 Design for a Pendant
Two Cocks (photo p. 140)
c. 1905
Pencil, ink, watercolor on paper
10 7/16 x 8 1/2 inches (27.7 x 21.5 cm)
Collection of the Juliette K. and Leonard S. Rakow Research Library,
The Corning Museum of Glass

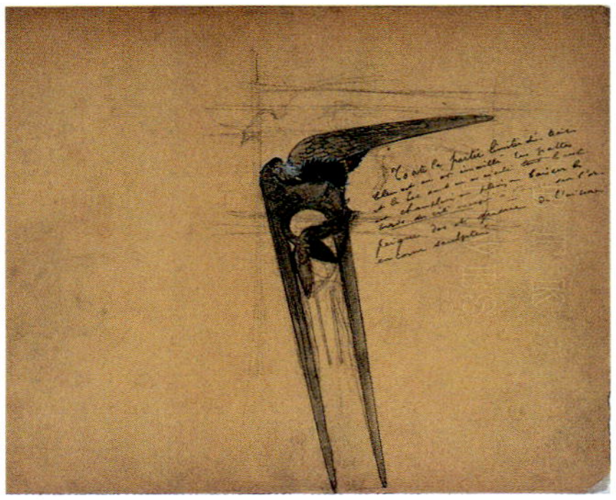

159

158 Design for a Hairpin
Two Swallows with Wheat (photo p. 130)
1906–1908
Pencil, ink, watercolor on paper
8 3/4 x 6 1/2 inches (22.2 x 15.6 cm)
Lalique Museum Collection, Paris,
inv. 1.3.007

159 Design for a Hairpin
Pheasant
1898–1899
Pencil, ink, watercolor on paper
8 1/2 x 4 1/4 inches (21.7 x 11 cm)
Lalique Museum Collection, Paris,
inv. 1.3.142

160 Design for a Hairpin
Grasshopper
1902–1904
Pencil, ink, watercolor on paper
14 3/4 x 8 1/4 inches (27.5 x 21 cm)
Lalique Museum Collection, Paris,
inv. 1.3.144

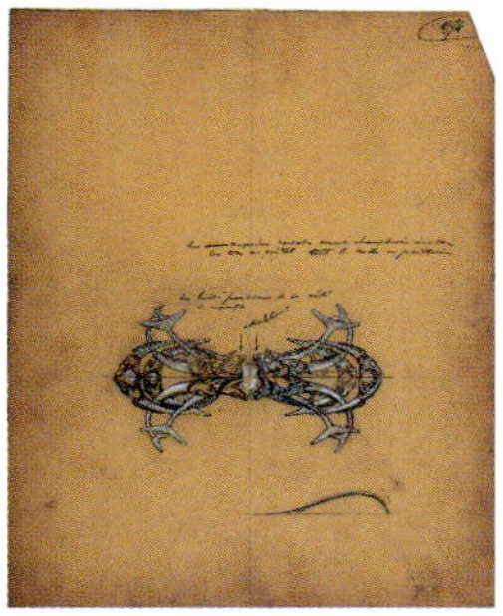

163

161 Design for a Tiara
Bees and Flowers
1905–1906
Pencil, ink, watercolor on paper
10 7/8 x 8 1/2 inches (27.5 x 21.6 cm)
Lalique Museum Collection, Paris,
inv. 1.2.006

162 Design for a Pendant
Entwining
1900–1902
Pencil, ink, watercolor on paper
11 x 8 1/2 inches
(27.9 x 21.7 cm)
Lalique Museum Collection, Paris,
inv. 2.4.060

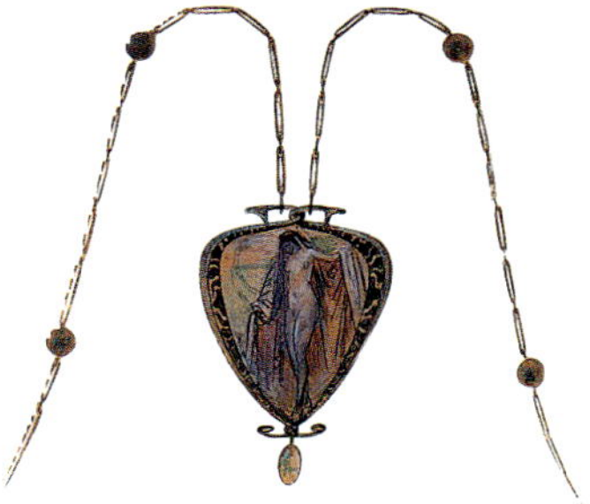

165

163 Design for a Corsage Ornament
Fish
c. 1904–1905
Pencil, ink, watercolor on paper
11 x 8 5/8 inches (28 x 22 cm)
Lalique Museum Collection, Paris,
inv. 3.1.021

164 Design for a Corsage Ornament
Pigeons on Olive Branches (photo p. 92)
c. 1905–1906
Pencil, ink, watercolor on paper
11 x 8 5/8 inches (27.8 x 22.1 cm)
Lalique Museum Collection, Paris,
inv. 3.1.079

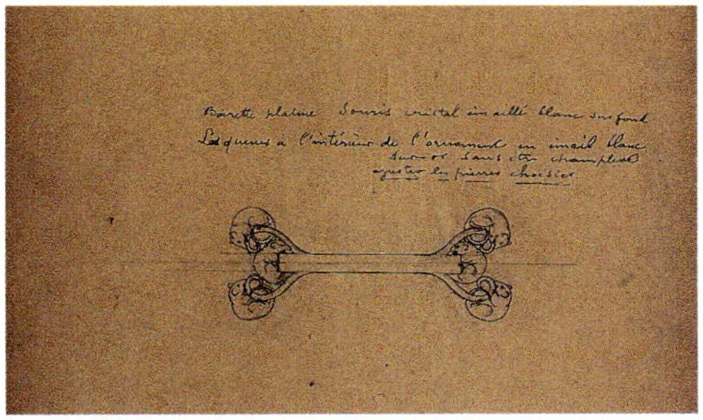

166

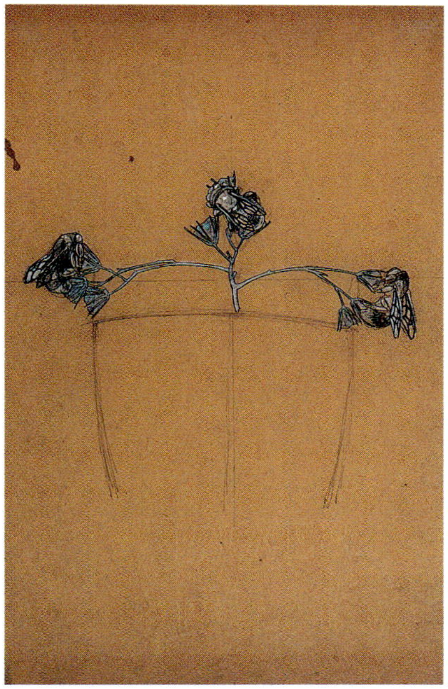

161

165 Design for a Pendant
Woman Enveloped in a Veil in a Border of Snakes ("Salammbô")
c. 1904–1905
Pencil, ink, watercolor on paper
8 5/8 x 11 inches (21.9 x 27.9 cm)
Lalique Museum Collection, Paris,
inv. 2.4.015

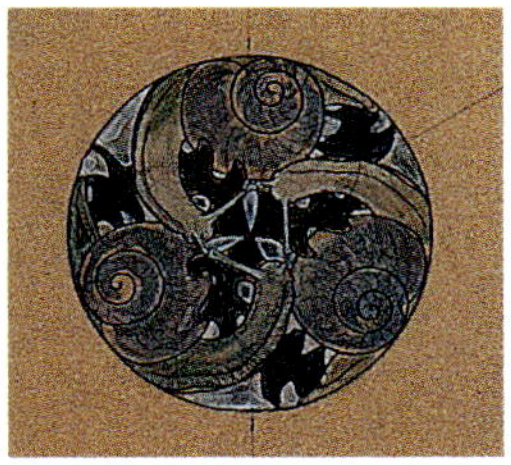

168

166 Design for a Brooch
Mice
1907–1908
Pencil, ink on paper
11 x 8 5/8 inches (27.8 x 21.7 cm)
Lalique Museum Collection, Paris,
inv. 3.2.279

167 Design for a Pendant
Wasps
1906–1907
Pencil, watercolor on paper
11 1/8 x 8 1/2 inches (28.2 x 21.7 cm)
Lalique Museum Collection, Paris,
inv. 2.3.114

168 Design for a Watch
Snails
c. 1899–1901
Pencil, ink, watercolor on paper
11 x 8 5/8 inches (28.1 x 22 cm)
Lalique Museum Collection, Paris,
inv. 3.2.069

IV
FROM CRAFT TO INDUSTRY: OBJECTS, GLASS

169 Mug
Satyr and Vine Shoots
1893
Cast iron model
7 1/4 x 5 7/8; Diameter 4 1/2 inches
(18.5 x 15; Diameter 11.4 cm)
Lalique Museum Collection, Paris

170 Book Cover
"*The Valkyrie*" (photo pp. 56–57)
1893–1894
Leather, silver, ivory
19 3/4 x 15 3/4 inches (50 x 40 cm)
Calouste Gulbenkian Museum, Lisbon
Purchased from the artist 1901, inv. 1142

171 Flacon *Snake*
c. 1898–1899
Silver, jasper
2 3/8 x 1 3/8 inches (6 x 3.5 cm)
Musée des Arts décoratifs, Paris
Gift of Henri Vever 1924, inv. 24508

172 Two Sculptures
Butterfly Woman (photo p. 31)
c. 1899–1900
Bronze
Part of Lalique's display case at the 1900
Exposition Universelle
Each: 39 x 40 x 13 3/4 inches
(99 x 101.5 x 35 cm)
Private collection, New York

173 Model for Earring and Finger Ring
Two Couples (photo p. 137)
1899–1901
Bronze
7 1/2 x 6 1/4 inches (19 x 16 cm)
Lalique Museum Collection, Paris

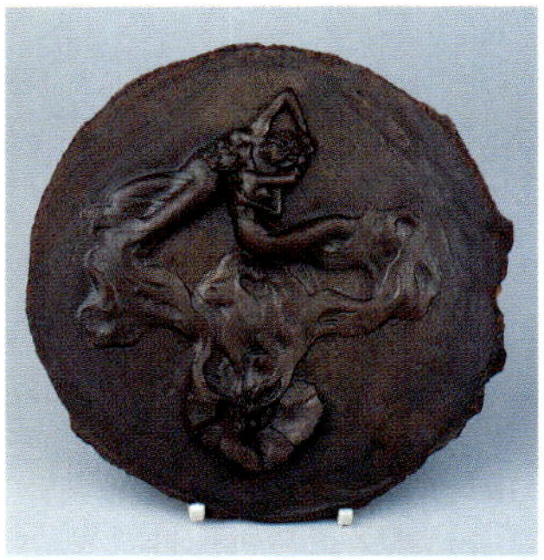
174

174 Model
Two Figures Embracing
c. 1904–1905
Bronze
Diameter: 7 1/8 inches (Diameter: 18 cm)
Lalique Museum Collection, Paris

175 Model for a "Vide-poche"
Face with Wings
c. 1901–1903
Bronze
9 x 2 3/8 inches (23 x 6 cm)
Lalique Museum Collection, Paris

176 Four Models for a Ewer *Entwined Figures* (photo p. 170)
c. 1901–1903
Bronze
a] 11 x 4 1/2; b] 7 1/4 x 6; c] 7 1/4 x 6 3/4; d]
Diameter: 6 1/2 inches (a] 28 x 11.5; b] 18.5 x 15; c] 18.5 17; d] Diameter: 17 cm)
Lalique Museum Collection, Paris

177 Sugar Bowl
Snakes (photo p. 43)
c. 1897–1900
Blown glass in silver setting
8 3/4 x 11 1/2 inches (19 x 28 cm)
Calouste Gulbenkian Museum, Lisbon
Purchased from the artist 1902, inv. 1162

178 Goblet *Mulberry Flowers* (photo p. 169)
c. 1899–1900, no. 820
Blown glass in silver setting
Height: 6 1/4 inches (Height: 16 cm)
Calouste Gulbenkian Museum, Lisbon
Purchased from the artist, inv. 1152

179 Chalice *Figures and Grape Vines* (photo p. 163)
c. 1899–1901
Gold, *plique-à-jour* enamel, carved ivory, glass
4 3/4; Diameter: 4 1/8 inches
(12.2; Diameter: 10.3 cm)
Private collection, New York

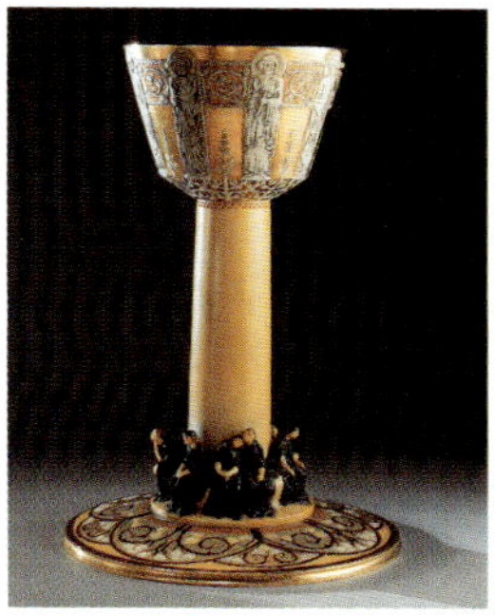

183

180 Chalice
Pine Cones (photo p. 44)
c. 1902
Clear blown glass, lined amber in an engraved silver structure
5; Diameter 3 3/4 inches
(12.2; Diameter 9.5 cm)
Lalique Museum Collection, Paris

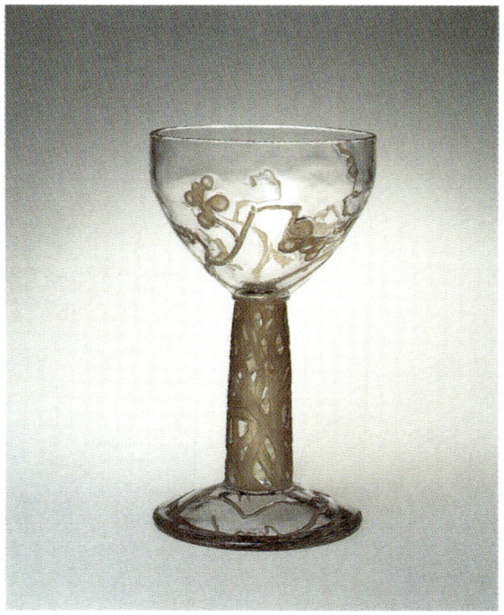

184

181 Chalice
Bacchanal (photo p. 174)
1902
Silver, enamel, lost-wax cast glass, blown glass in silver setting
7 1/2 inches (19 cm)
Private collection, Courtesy of Galerie Moderne, Ltd., London

182 Chalice
Anemones (photo p. 47)
1904
Lost-wax cast glass
Height: 7 1/4; Diameter: 4 1/8 inches
(Height: 18.8; Diameter: 10.5 cm)
Calouste Gulbenkian Museum, Lisbon
Purchased from the artist 1922, inv. 1264

183 Chalice *Apostles*
c. 1903–1905
Gold, translucent and opaque enamel on gold, ivory
12 1/2; Diameter: 5 1/4 inches
(31.5; Diameter: 13.5 cm)
Private collection, New York

184 Chalice *Grapevine*
Model created in 1910
Glass, enamel
7; Diameter 4 inches
(17.8; Diameter 10.2 cm)
The Metropolitan Museum of Art, Purchase Edward C. Moore Jr. Gift, 1923, inv. 23.173.1

185 Parasol Handle Converted to a Seal
Bacchanal
c. 1899–1901
Carved bone, gold
Height: 4 1/4 inches (Height: 10.8 cm)
Private collection, New York

186 Handbag
Two Snakes (photo p. 111)
c. 1901–1903
Silver, silk, leather
9 1/8 x 7 inches (23.1 x 17.9 cm)
Private collection, New York

187 Handbag *Wasps* (photo p. 110)
c. 1901–1903
Silver, moonstones (?)
7 1/8 x 7 1/4 inches (18 x 18.5 cm)
David Weinstein Collection, NewYork

188 Hand Mirror
Stag Beetles and Face (photo p. 61)
c. 1898–1900
Enameled bronze, glass, ivory, mirrored glass
Signed LALIQUE on lower right edge of right plaque
13 3/4 x 7 1/16 x 1 7/8 inches
(34.8 x 18 x 4.5 cm)
Virginia Museum of Fine Arts, Richmond
Gift of Sydney and Frances Lewis, inv. 85.273

189 Hand Mirror
Swallows (photo p. 178–179)
Model created in 1913
Mold-blown glass, stained
13 3/4 inches (35 cm)
Lalique Museum Collection, Paris

190 Stole *Wheat Field*
c. 1906–1907
Silk, metal, gold-lamé, crêpe
124 x 22 7/8 inches (315 x 58 cm)
David Weinstein Collection, New York

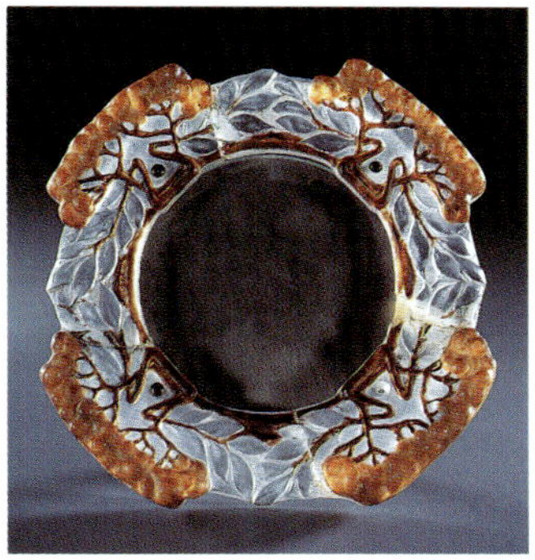

193

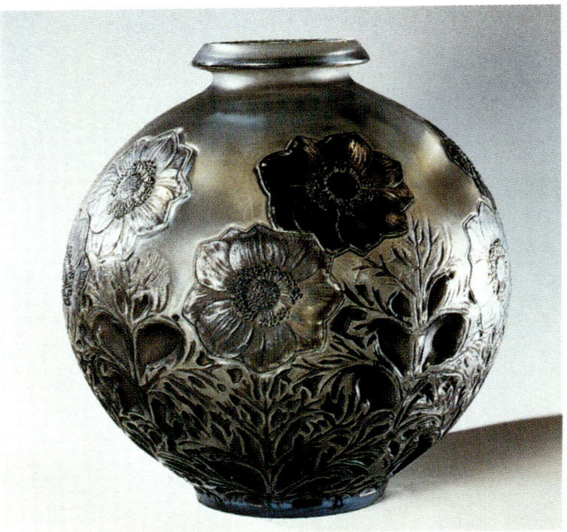
195

191 Stole
Field of Daisies (photo p. 114)
c. 1906–1907
Silk, metal, figured crêpe, gold and brown brocade
124 x 22 7/8 inches (315 x 58 cm)
David Weinstein Collection, New York

192 Statuette
The Faun's Kiss
(photo p. 167)
Model created c. 1901
Lost-wax cast glass
7 7/8 inches (20 cm)
Lalique Museum Collection, Paris

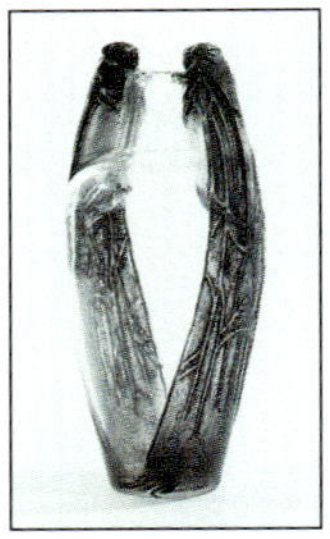
196

193 Frame
Leaves and Fruit
Model created c. 1901
Lost-wax cast glass
Diameter: 4 3/4 inches (Diameter: 12 cm)
Lalique Museum Collection, Paris

194 Vessel
Two Mermaids (photo p. 172)
1909
Pressed glass, wheel engraved, stained
4; Diameter: 4 7/8 inches
(10; Diameter: 12.5 cm)
Musée des Arts décoratifs, Paris
Purchased from the artist 1909, inv. 15954

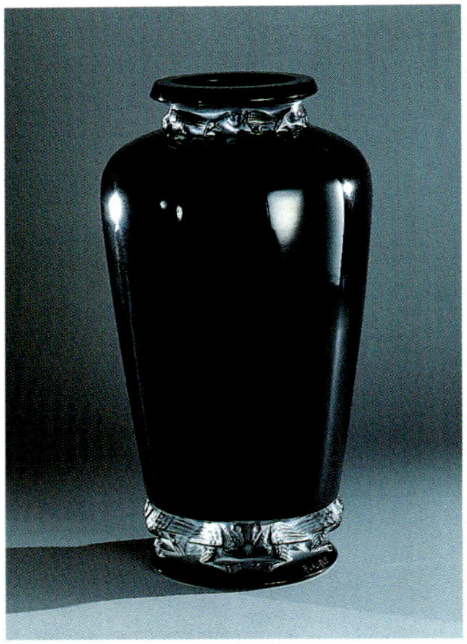
199

195 Vase *Anemones*
c. 1912
Mold-blown glass, cast foil-backed blossoms, enameled
13 3/4 x 12 inches (35 x 32 cm)
The Shapiro Collection, Courtesy of Galerie Moderne, Ltd., London

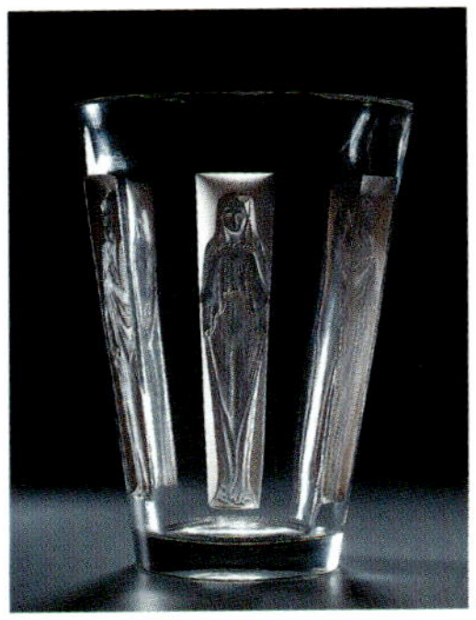
200

196 Vase *Two Cicadas*
Model created in 1912
Mold-blown glass, cicadas applied hot, stained
12 1/2; Diameter: 3 inches
(32: Diameter: 7.5 cm)
Mary Lou and Glenn Utt Collection

197 Vase *Four Scarabs*
1911
Black mold-blown glass, red glass powder applied hot, wheel engraved
9 3/4; Diameter: 10 5/8 inches
(25; Diameter: 27 cm)
Musée des Arts décoratifs, Paris
Purchased from the artist 1911, inv. 18223

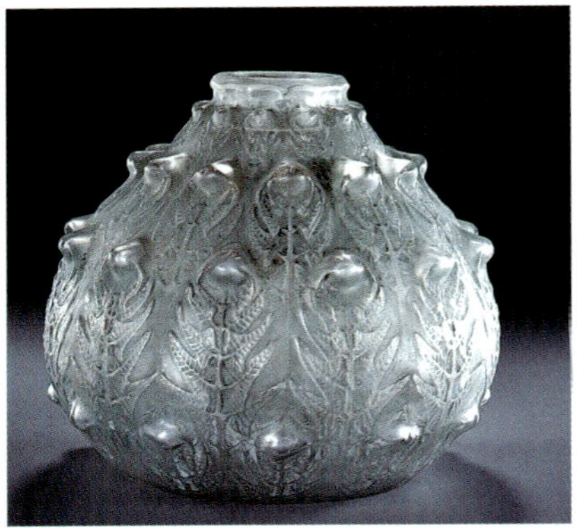
201

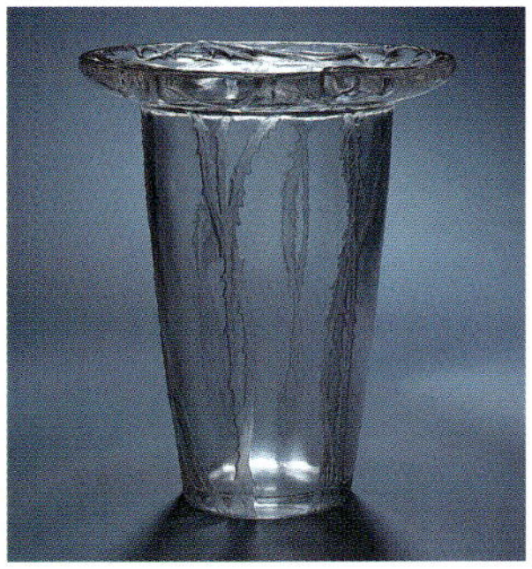

202

198 Vase *Four Masks*
Model created in 1911, no. 878
Mold-blown glass, frosted, stained, engraved
11 1/2; Diameter: 10 1/4 inches
(29; Diameter: 26 cm)
Musée des Arts décoratifs, Paris
Purchased from the artist 1913, inv. 19306

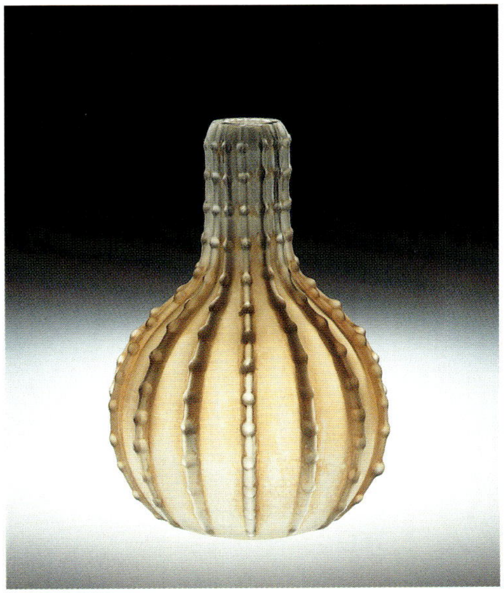

203

199 Vase *Eagle Frieze*
Model created in 1911
Mold-blown glass, polished, frosted
11 3/4; Diameter: 6 3/4 inches
(30; Diameter: 17 cm)
Musée des Arts décoratifs, Paris
Purchased from the artist 1913, inv. 19310

200 Vase-Goblet *Six Figures*
Model created in 1912, no. 903
Mold-pressed glass, stained
7 7/8 inches (20 cm)
Lalique Museum Collection, Paris

201 Vase *Ferns*
Model created in 1912, no. 923
Mold-pressed glass, stained
7 1/2 inches (19 cm)
Lalique Museum Collection, Paris

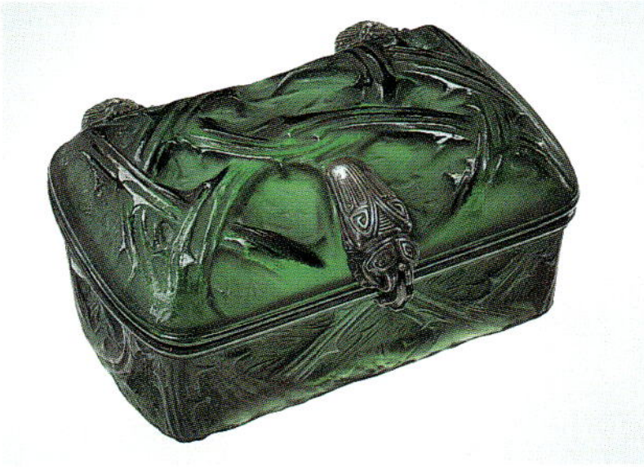

205

202 Vase *Thorn Border*
Model created in 1913
Mold-pressed glass, enamel
6 3/4 inches (17 cm)
Lalique Museum Collection, Paris

203 Vase *"Dentelé"*
Model created in 1912
Mold-blown glass, frosted, stained
7 1/16, Diameter: 5 3/16 inches
(18.9; Diameter: 13.2 cm)
The Corning Museum of Glass
Gift of Dr. and Mrs. Edward F. Lewison

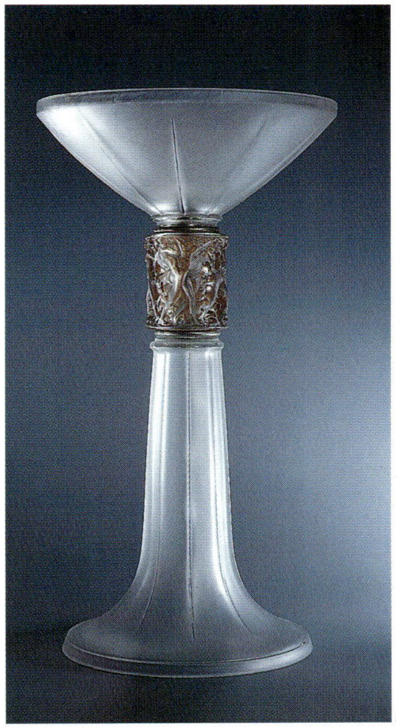

206

204 Box *Lunaria*
Model created in 1914
Mold-pressed glass, stained on silvered ground, maple wood
4 3/4 x 12 1/4 x 7 3/4 inches
(12 x 31 x 19.5 cm)
Lalique Museum Collection, Paris

205 Box *Thorns*
Model created in 1911, no. 352
Mold-pressed glass, stained silvered bronze
3 x 7 x 4 1/8 inches (7.7 x 17.8 x 10.5 cm)
The Corning Museum of Glass

206 Lamp *Ring of Figures*
Model created in 1912, no. 2152
Mold-blown glass, stained, mold-pressed glass, stained
17 1/2 inches (44.5 cm)
Lalique Museum Collection, Paris

207 Panel
Athletes (photo p. 171)
Model created c. 1912, no. 1114
Mold-pressed glass, stained
45 inches (114 cm)
Lalique Museum Collection, Paris

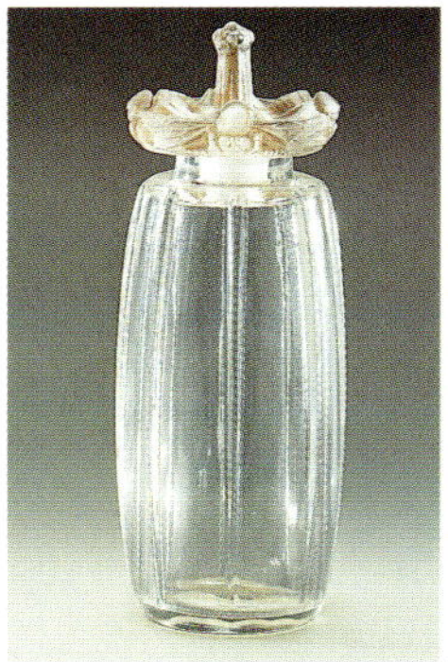
211

208 Perfume Bottle *Fish*
Model created c. 1905
Lost-wax cast glass
Height: 4 inches (10 cm)
David Weinstein Collection, New York

209 Perfume Bottle
"L'Effleurt" (photo p. 175)
Label created in 1908; model created in 1912 for Coty
Mold-pressed glass, stopper in mold-pressed glass, stained
4 1/2 x 2 x 1 1/4 inches
(11.2 cm x 5 x 3.1 cm)
Mary Lou and Glenn Utt Collection

210 Perfume Bottle
"Cyclamen"
Model created in 1909 for Coty
Mold-blown glass, stopper in mold-pressed glass, stained
5 1/2; Diameter: 3 3/4 inches
(14.2; Diameter: 4.6 cm)
Mary Lou and Glenn Utt Collection

211 Perfume Bottle
"Ambre antique" (photo p. 175)
Model created in 1910 for Coty
Mold-blown glass, neck and stopper in pressed glass, stained
6; Diameter: 1 1/2 inches
(15.5; Diameter: 4 cm)
Mary Lou and Glenn Utt Collection

212 Perfume Bottle *"Styx"*
Model created in 1911 for Coty
Mold-blown glass, stopper in mold-pressed glass, stained
4 5/8; 1 1/8 inches (12; Diameter: 3 cm)
Mary Lou and Glenn Utt Collection

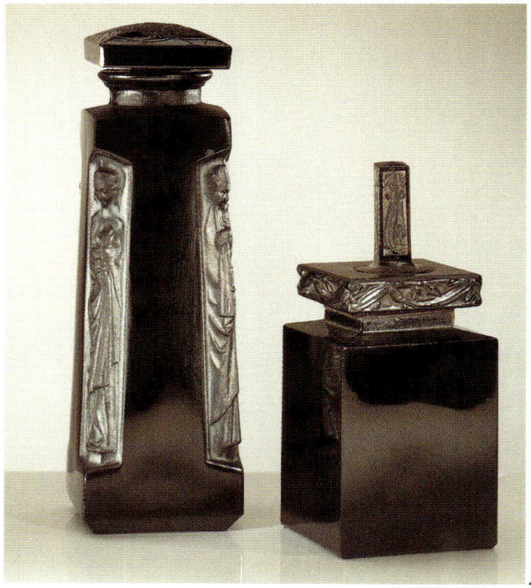
213 214

213 Perfume Bottle
"Au coeur des calices"
Model created in 1913 for Coty
Glass
2 3/4; Diameter: 3 inches
(6 1/2; Diameter: 7 1/2 cm)
Mary Lou and Glenn Utt Collection

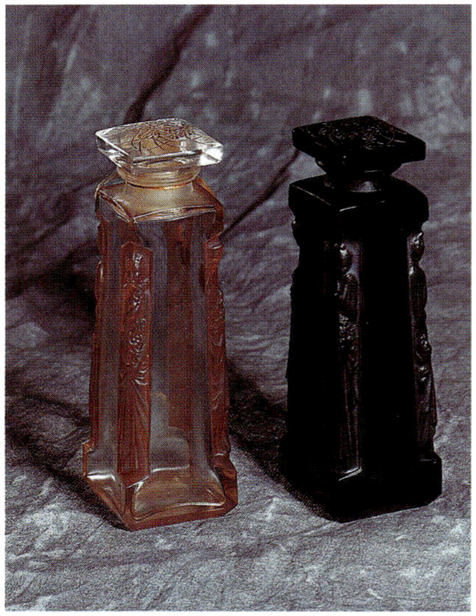
216

214 Perfume Bottle
"Ambre"
Model created in 1911 for d'Orsay
Mold-blown glass, stopper in mold-pressed glass
5 1/4 x 1 1/2 inches (13.2 x 4 cm)
Mary Lou and Glenn Utt Collection

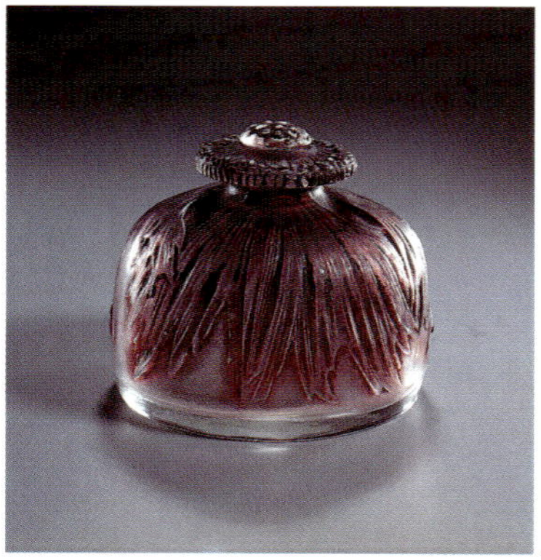
217

215 Perfume Bottle
"Mystère"
Model created in 1912 for d'Orsay
Mold-blown glass, stopper in mold-pressed glass
3 3/4 x 1 1/2 inches (9.5 x 4.2 cm)
Mary Lou and Glenn Utt Collection

216 Perfume Bottle
Quatre Figurines (photo p. 45)
Model created in 1910
Mold-blown glass, neck and stopper in mold-pressed glass, stained
5 1/2 x 1 1/2 inches (13.3 x 4 cm)
Mary Lou and Glenn Utt Collection

217 Perfume Bottle *Poppy*
Model created in 1910, no. 476
Mold-pressed glass, stained
2 3/4 inches (7 cm)
Lalique Museum Collection, Paris

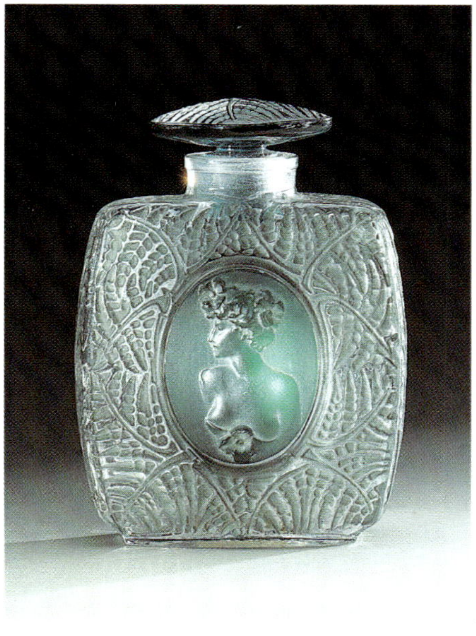

220

218 Perfume Bottle
Lunaria
Model created in 1912
Mold-blown glass, stained, stopper in mold-pressed glass
2 3/4 x 3 inches (7.4; Diameter: 7.6 cm)
Mary Lou and Glenn Utt Collection

219 Perfume Bottle
Capricorn Beetles
Model created in 1912
Mold-blown glass, enamel
3 1/4 x 2 1/4 inches (8.3 x 5.5 cm)
The Metropolitan Museum of Art, Purchase, Edward C. Moore Gift, 1923, inv. 23.173.3

220 Perfume Bottle
Ferns or Busts of Women
Model created in 1912
Mold-blown glass, medallions and stopper in pressed glass
3 3/4 x 2 3/4 x 1 1/4 inches (9.5 x 7 x 3 cm)
Musée des Arts décoratifs, Paris
Purchased from the artist 1913, inv. 19299

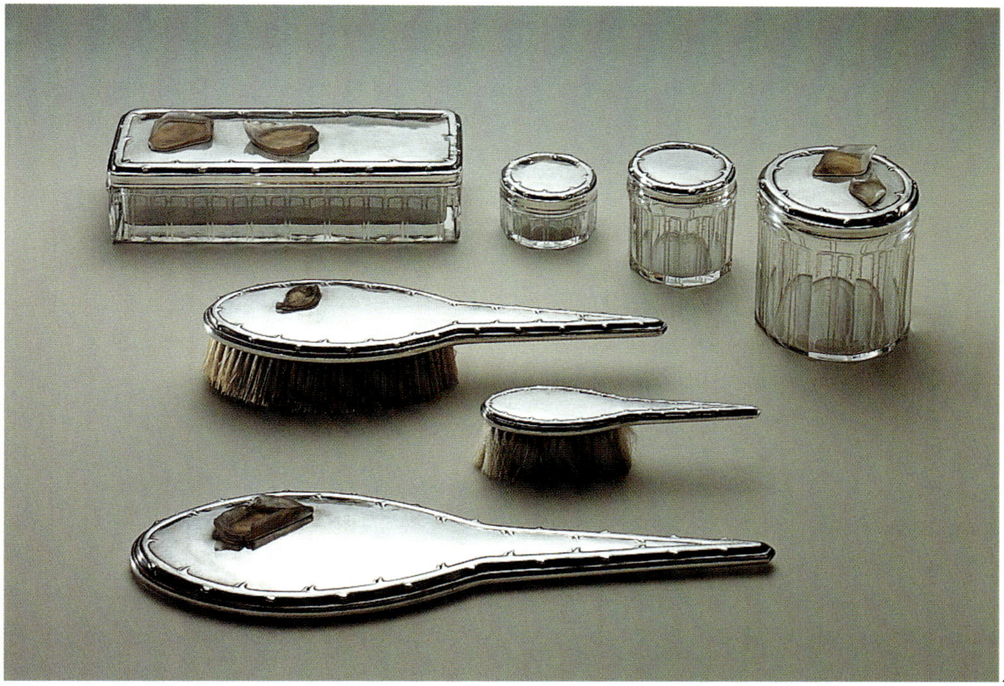

222

221 Perfume Bottle
Two Figures, Stopper with Figures
Model created in 1912, no. 490
Mold-blown glass, stopper in mold-pressed glass, stained

4 3/4 inches (12 cm)
Lalique Museum Collection, Paris

222 Toilet Set *Rose Petals*
Model created in 1909
Silver, mold glass, crystal
a] rectangular box: 2 3/4 x 9 x 3 3/8 inches
(7.1 x 22.8 x 8.9 cm)
b] round box: 4 1/4 x D. 3 3/4 inches
(11 x D. 9.6 cm)
c] round box: 2 7/8 x D. 2 5/8 inches
(7.2 x D. 6.7 cm)
d] round box: 1 1/2 x D. 2 1/2 inches
(4 x D. 6.3 cm)
e] hand mirror: 13 1/4 x 1 1/2 inches
(33.5 x 4 cm)
f] brush: 6 x 1 1/2 inches (15.3 x 4 cm)
g] brush:10 3/4 x 3 inches 27.5 x 7.7 cm)
Private collection, Buenos Aires

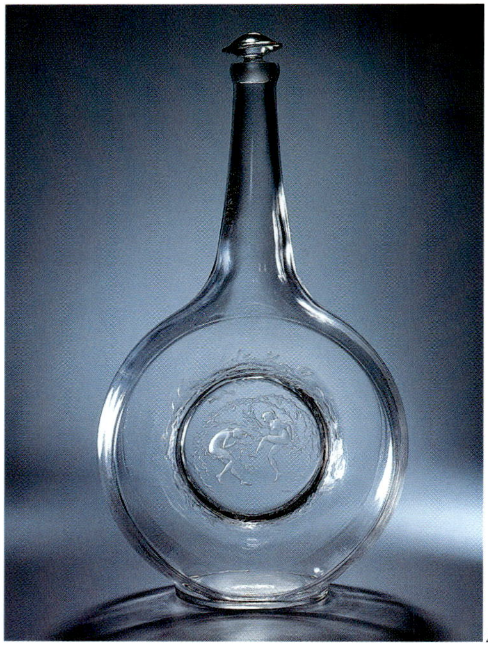
224

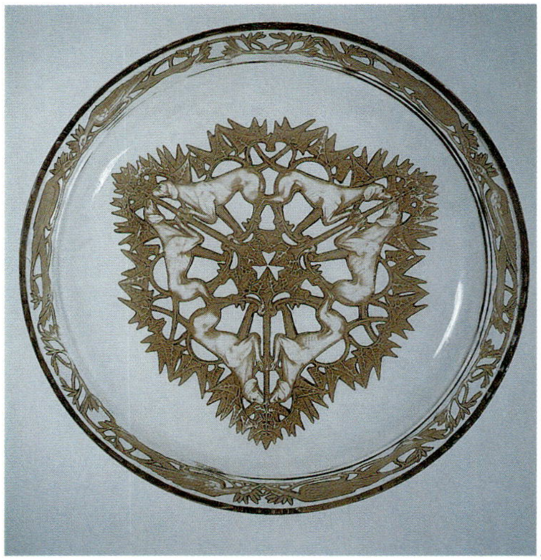
225

223 Carafe
Mermaids and Frogs
Model created in 1911, no. 3150
Mold-blown glass, frosted, stained, stopper in pressed glass
15 1/4; Diameter: 6 3/4 inches
(39; Diameter: 17 cm)
Musée des Arts décoratifs, Paris
Purchased from the artist 1913, inv. 19307

224 Carafe *Two Dancers*
Model created in 1912
Glass
13 1/2 x 7 1/2 inches (35 x 19 cm)
Lalique Museum Collection, Paris

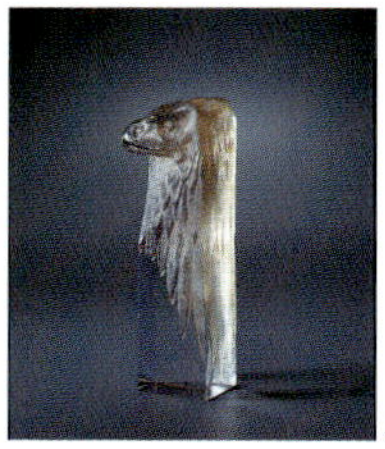
226

225 Plate *Hunting; Dogs*
Model created in 1914, no. 3001
Mold-pressed glass, stained and enameled
Diameter: 8 1/4 inches (Diameter: 21 cm)
Lalique Museum Collection, Paris

226 Seal *Eagle Head*
Model created in 1911, no. 175
Mold-pressed glass, stained
3 1/4 inches (7.8 cm)
Lalique Museum Collection, Paris

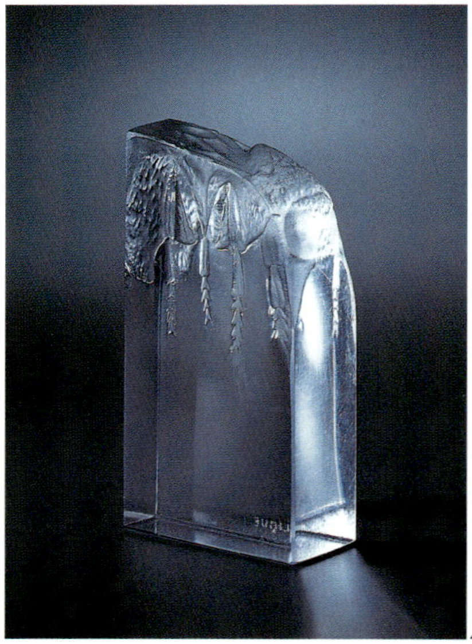
227

227 Seal *Fly*
Model created in 1912, no. 180
Mold-pressed glass
2 5/8 inches (6.5 cm)
Lalique Museum Collection, Paris

228 Seal *Fish*
Model created in 1912, no. 182
Mold-pressed glass
1 7/8 x 2 1/4 inches (4.8 x 5.5 cm)
Musée des Arts décoratifs, Paris

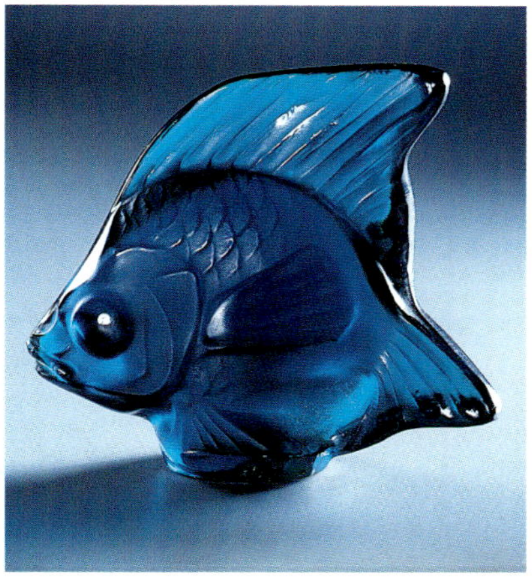

229

Gift of Mrs. Crépy-Carnot 1980, inv. 47740

229 Seal *Fish*
Model created in 1912, no. 182
Mold-pressed glass, green
1 3/4 inches (4.5 cm)
Lalique Museum Collection, Paris

230 Paper Knife *Fish*
c. 1906–1908
Horn
2 1/2 x 19 3/4 inches (6.5 x 50 cm)
Private collection, New York

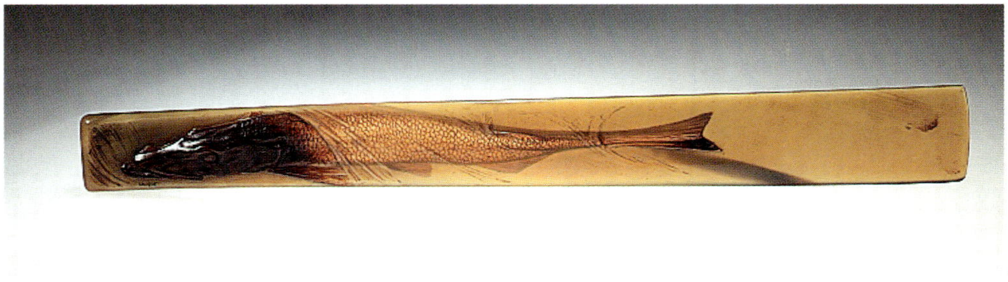

230

231 Medallion
Sarah Bernhardt
c. 1905–1906
Gilded bronze
Diameter: 2 1/2 inches
(Diameter: 6.5 cm)
Private collection, New York

232 Frontispiece
"L'Aiglon" by Edmond Rostand (photo p. 29)
1900
White ink on paper, gold
4 1/2 x 3 inches (11.2 x 7.8 cm)
Private collection, Paris

233 Bookcover
"Chantecler" by Edmond Rostand
1909
Leather
10 x 6 7/8 inches (25.4 x 17.4 cm)
Private collection, Paris

234 Design for a Box
Allegory of War
(photo p. 63)
c. 1898–1900
Collage on paper
10 5/8 x 9 1/2 inches (27 x 24.4 cm)
Lalique Museum Collection, Paris,
inv. 1.1.004

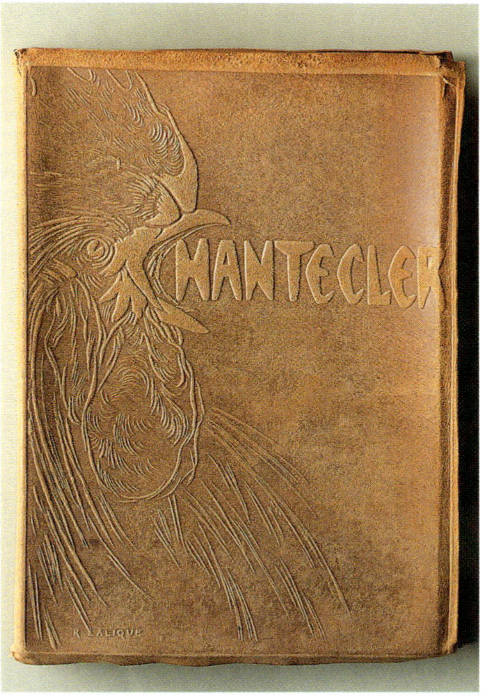

233

235 Design for a Hand Mirror *Stag Beetles and Face* (photo p. 60)
c. 1898–1900
Pencil, ink, watercolor, gouache on paper
15 x 9 7/8 inches (37.8 x 24.9 cm)
Lalique Museum Collection, Paris,
inv. 7.2.035

236 Design for a Fan
Falling Leaves (photo p. 118)
c. 1899–1900
Pencil, ink, watercolor on paper
10 5/8 x 21 inches (27.5 x 53.6 cm)
Lalique Museum Collection, Paris,
inv. 6.1.007

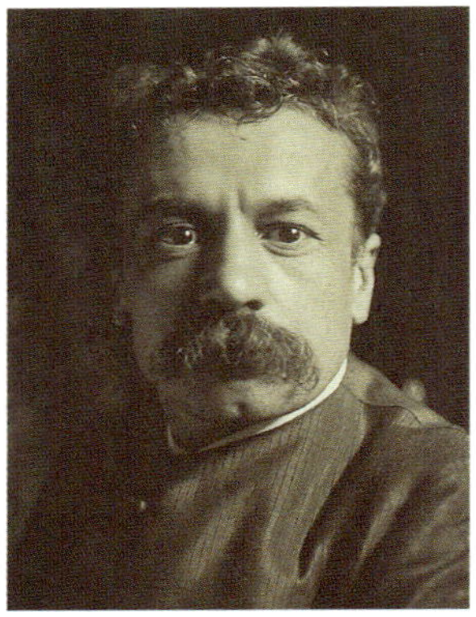

Chronology 1860–1918

Yvonne Brunhammer and Clémentine Vidal

•1860
April 6. Birth of René Jules Lalique at Ay (Marne), the son of a Parisian mercantile agent located on the rue Chapon. Taken back to Paris shortly after his birth, he was to spend his early holidays in his mother's native region of Champagne.

Charles Baudelaire, Les Paradis artificiels.

•1861
June 8. In their Diaries, the Goncourt brothers note the purchase of Japanese drawings on paper at La Porte Chinoise, 36, rue Vivienne, Paris.

August. Adalbert de Beaumont publishes plates from Hokusai's Manga *in his* Recueil de dessins pour l'art et l'industrie.

Charles Baudelaire, second edition of Les Fleurs du mal *(first edition 1857).*

James MacNeill Whistler leaves America and settles in Paris, where he meets Manet.

•1862
E. Desoye's Japanese curio shop opens at 220, rue de Rivoli in Paris.

Gustave Flaubert, Salammbô.

London. Exposition Universelle. A Japanese section comprising 614 objects is organized by Sir Rutherford Alcock, British minister in Japan, and Captain Howard Wyse, British consul at Kabagawa.

London. Foundation of the South Kensington Museum, (later the Victoria and Albert Museum).

•1863
April 20. A Japanese course given by Léon de Rosny starts at the École Impériale et Spéciale des Langues Orientales.

August 13. Death of Eugène Delacroix.

November 15. Eugène Viollet-le-Duc is appointed professor of aesthetics and history of art at the École des Beaux-Arts in Paris and publishes first volume of his two-volume Entretiens sur l'architecture *(1863–72).*

•1864
March 16. A group of industrialists and interior decorators found the Union Centrale des Beaux-Arts Appliqués à l'Industrie.

September 20. A library and a museum are opened at 15, place Royale in the heart of the Marais.

Viollet-le-Duc is named president of the Société du Progrès de l'Art Industriel and publishes Intervention de l'État dans l'enseignement des Beaux-Arts.

The American collector of Japanese books, prints and objets d'art, *John La Farge, takes inspiration from Hokusai for the engraving* Shipwreck *which appears in an edition of Tennyson's poem* Enoch Arden, *published in Boston.*

•1865

June. Following the death of the duc de Morny, the sale in Paris of his art objects, including Japanese bronzes and lacquered objects and furniture.

Gustave Moreau, Leda *(c. 1865–75).*

Whistler exhibits The Princess from the Land of Porcelain *(completed 1863–64) at the Paris Salon. Acquired by Frederick R. Leyland, it was later to be incorporated into The Peacock Room (1876–77).*

London. Completion of the "Japanese Court" at the South Kensington Museum.

•1866

Eugène Rousseau orders a dinner service design in fine faience from Félix Bracquemond with plant and animal motifs borrowed from prints by Hokusai, Hiroshige, Isai, and Hokusen. This service is presented publicly for the first time the following year at the Paris Exposition Universelle.

•1867

April–November. Exposition Universelle on the Champs de Mars in Paris features electric light around the palace perimeter at night. Japan's first official participation with several thousand objects linked to everyday life; a Japanese farm is built in the Trocadéro gardens. The South Kensington Museum acquires 150 objects. The New York firm of Tiffany and Co. exhibits silverware.

August 31. Death of Baudelaire.

Vienna. Museum für angewandte Kunst starts its Japanese collection.

•1868

Posthumous publication of Baudelaire's Les Curiosités esthétiques, *followed by* L'Art romantique *in 1869.*

Lautréamont, Les Chants de Maldoror.

Manet exhibits his portrait of Émile Zola at the Salon (no. 1660) in which is also exhibited a Japanese screen and a print by Utagawa Kuniaki II.

•1869

April 10–November 10. The "Oriental Museum" at the exhibition of the Union Centrale des Beaux-Arts Appliqués à l'Industrie in the Palais de l'Industrie, at which Gustave Moreau makes copies of Japanese prints, albums, and costumes.

Beginning of the publication of L'Ornement polychrome, *under the direction of A. Racinet, printed by Firmin-Didot in color, gold, and silver. Plates xi, xii, xiii, and xiv reproduce Japanese motifs after models on* cloisonné *enamels and textiles.*

Munich. First performance of Wagner's Die Meistersinger von Nürnberg.

•1870

July 19. France declares war on Prussia. September 2. French surrender at Sedan; Second Empire falls on September 4.

Beginning February 15, bi-monthly publication of L'Art pour tous, *founded by Émile Reiber and published by C. Sauvageot. The review regularly reproduces Japanese bronze and ceramic objects.*

Munich. First performance of Wagner's Die Walküre.

New York. John La Farge compiles the chapter "On Japanese Art" for Across Asia and America, *published by Raphaël Pumpelly.*

•1871

January 28. Armistice. Paris falls. May 10. Peace of Frankfurt, France cedes Alsace-Lorraine.

May 21–28. Paris Commune insurrection.

Brussels. Creation of the review L'Art libre *by Camille Lemonnier.*

London. International Exhibition, the section "French Art" organized by Edmond du Sommerand, curator at the Musée de Cluny.

Fire destroys much of Chicago.

•1872

René Lalique is enrolled at the Collège Turgot, where he will remain until the age of fourteen. He begins studying drawing with Lequien, senior, who will instill "excellent principles" into him. He wins first prize for drawing.

Claude Monet, Impression, Sunrise.

Edgar Degas, Foyer de la danse à l'Opéra *(Musée d'Orsay).*

John La Farge meets Dante Gabriel Rossetti, Edward Burne-Jones, and William Morris in London. In New York, he studies glassmaking with Louis Comfort Tiffany at Heidt and Co.

•1873
Paris. Salon des Réfusés.
September 4. Exposition des Beaux-Arts de l'Extrême Orient organized by Henri Cernuschi at the Palais de l'Industrie.
Viollet-le-Duc, Histoire d'une maison.
Rimbaud, Une Saison en enfer.
Vienna. Exposition Universelle takes place in the Prater park and rotunda. An important Japanese delegation returns home with technical information essential for its subsequent industrial development.

•1874
René Lalique leaves Collège Turgot and continues his studies at Fontenay-sous-Bois. In the summer, he makes miniature bouquets of flowers painted with gouache on ivory cards that he sells to small storekeepers in Épernay.
First Impressionist exhibition at Nadar's.
Degas, The Dance Class.
Flaubert, La Tentation de Saint Antoine; *Victor Hugo,* Quatre-vingt-treize.
Camille Saint-Saëns, Danse macabre.
Wagner, Götterdämmerung.
Louis Sullivan attends the École des Beaux-Arts in Vaudremer's studio for a semester.

•1875
May. Lecture by M. Lameire, professor of drawing at the École des Beaux-Arts on the "Decorative arts" in the headquarters of the Union Centrale des Beaux-Arts Appliqués à l'Industrie.
Grand opening of the Paris Opéra, designed by Charles Garnier.
Rimbaud writes Les Illuminations.
Bizet, Carmen.
London. William Morris founds Morris & Co.

•1876
Death of Lalique's father. He enters into an apprenticeship with the jeweler Louis Aucoc for a period of two years. For a few months he takes evening classes at the École des Arts Décoratifs.
Fifth exhibition of the Union Centrale at the Palais de l'Industrie. Alphonse Fouquet presents jewelry for the first time.
Paris. Sale of Oriental artifacts belonging to Siegfried Bing at the Hôtel Drouot auction house.
Stéphane Mallarmé, L'Après-midi d'un faune.
Bayreuth. Opening of the Festspielhaus with Wagner's Der Ring des Nibelungen.
London. At the request of Thomas Jekyll, Whistler undertakes the decoration of the dining room belonging to Frederick Leyland, which was to be fitted out with the painting, The Princess from the Land of Porcelain, *and a collection of porcelain. The room is called Harmony in Blue and Gold, The Peacock Room, and is finished in 1877. It is occupied by Leyland until his death in 1892. It was acquired in 1892 by Charles Lang Freer and installed in the Freer Gallery of Art, Washington D.C. following Freer's death in 1919.*
Philadelphia. First Exposition Universelle in the USA on the occasion of the centennial of American independence.
Far East, September. Departure of Émile Guimet and Félix Regamey. December. Christopher Dresser arrives in Japan.

•1877
Paris. Creation by a group of art lovers of the Musée des Arts décoratifs at the Pavillon de Flore, Palais du Louvre.
Nancy. Émile Gallé takes over as the head of his father's firm, travels in the Swiss and Italian Alps.
Viollet-le-Duc spends time in the Alps as well as at Carcassonne and Toulouse. Completes the chapter on "Architecture" for the Dictionnaire encylopédique et biographique de l'industrie et des arts industriels de la France contemporaine.

•1878
Lalique travels to England, remaining there two years. He attends classes at Sydenham College housed in the rebuilt Crystal Palace. Takes part in decorative arts competitions organized by English reviews and newspapers and spends much time in London museums, in particular the South Kensington Museum.
Paris. Exposition Universelle on the Champ de Mars and on the Colline de Chaillot where Davioud erects the Palais du Trocadéro, a center

for festivities, concerts, congresses, and lectures. Peace is honored with Bartholdi's head of the Statue of Liberty: "Peace is only possible with Liberty." Contributions recorded include those from Émile Gallé, with glasswork and ceramics which reflect the eclecticism of the times, and Alphonse Fouquet, presenting gold and enamel jewelry inspired by the Renaissance.

The Japanese section at the Trocadéro includes pieces recently brought back by Guimet and intended to be exhibited in the museum he is organizing in Lyon.

The vogue for things Japanese invades the decorative arts in France and throughout Europe, but also in New York, witness the goldwork pieces that Tiffany and Co., at the urging of Edward Chandler Moore, sends over to the Paris Exposition.

Bing opens a shop selling Far Eastern art at 19, rue Chauchat.

London. Rutherford Alcock publishes Art and Industries in Japan.

•1879

Viollet-le-Duc, Histoire d'un dessinateur: Comment on apprend à dessiner.

September 17. Death of Viollet-le-Duc at Lausanne.

Ferdinand Cheval begins building his "Ideal Palace" at Hauterives (Drôme).

Lyon, September. Guimet sets up a museum, a library, and a school following the models of the South Kensington Museum and the Union Centrale.

Pierre Loti, Aziyadé; *Émile Zola,* Nana.

London. Sale at Chelsea of Whistler's house, "The White House", and of his collections, furnishings, screens, and Japanese books. Christopher Dresser creates his earliest objects in glass and silver.

New York. Louis Comfort Tiffany founds the interior decorating firm Louis C. Tiffany and Associated Artists, together with Coman and Wheeler (1879 or 1880).

•1880

Back in Paris, Lalique starts working in the rue de Saintonge as a designer for one of his relatives, a M. Vuilleret, who is discouraging: "You want to do designs for jewelry, but that'll lead nowhere!"

Exhibition of works by Viollet-le-Duc at the Musée de Cluny. An article dedicated to Lalique in the first number of La Revue des arts décoratifs, *published jointly by the Union Centrale and the Société du Musée des Arts Décoratifs.*

Rodin, maquette for the Gates of Hell *(1880–1917) intended for the Musée des Arts Décoratifs, which was to set it up on the site of the Cour des Comptes, quai d'Orsay.*

Gustave Eiffel, Garabit Viaduct (1880–84).

Eugène Grasset designs furniture for the residence of the printer Charles Gillot.

Bing's first voyage to Japan.

First William Blake exhibition in Boston.

•1881

René Lalique spends one year at Auguste Petit *fils*, rue de Chabanais.

French Minister of Education, Jules Ferry sponsors a law on free primary education.

Edmond de Goncourt, La Maison de l'artiste, *in which he describes the Far Eastern art cabinet in his house at Auteuil.*

Louis Sullivan enters as project designer at Adler's, Chicago.

•1882

René Lalique sets up on his own and supplies a large number of manufacturers and jewelry outlets, such as Jacta, Aucoc, Renn, Gariod, Hamelin, and Destape, etc. He takes classes in sculpture modeling with Lequien junior in a school in Paris, now the École Bernard Palissy. He takes up etching.

Creation of the Union Centrale des Arts Décoratifs from the merger of the Union Centrale des Beaux-Arts Appliqués à l'Industrie and the Société du Musée des Arts décoratifs.

March 28. Law on mandatory school education and the secular nature of teaching.

First performance of Wagner's Parsifal.

•1883

Despite encouragement from the jeweler Charles Arfvidson, Lalique fails to publish a planned journal on industrial art which, was to have employed engraving techniques to spread ideas for new models. He agrees instead to contribute to the trade journal *Le Bijou*, founded in 1874, which is above all directed at jewelry-makers from abroad.

Paris. Bing renovates and enlarges his shop on the corner of rue de Provence and rue Chauchat.

A retrospective exhibition of Japanese art is organized at the Galerie Georges Petit, from the collections of Parisian dealers such as Bing himself and other amateurs and artistes, for example, Sarah Bernhardt. At the Palais de l'Industrie, the first annual Salon of Japanese painters organized under the auspices of the Union Centrale des Arts Décoratifs.

Huysmans, L'Art moderne.

Nietzsche, Also Sprach Zarathustra *(1883–91).*

Barcelona. Gaudí begins building the Sagrada Familia.

Venice. Death of Richard Wagner.

•1884

Lalique forms a two-year partnership with Varenne, who sells on his designs executed in bright yellow gouache on a black ground and marked "Lalique et Varenne, rue de Vaugirard, 84" to various makers. Lalique's drawings are presented at the Exposition Nationale des Arts Industriels, held in the Louvre, on the occasion of the display of the Crown Jewels in the Salle des États. They attract the attention of Alphonse Fouquet: "I was not aware of the existence of any contemporary jewelry designers, and at last, here is one!"

Paris. Eighth exhibition of the Union Centrale des Arts Décoratifs: "Stone, Construction Wood, Earth and Glass." Émile Gallé exhibits enameled glasswork with Eastern and naturalist motifs as well as multilayered glass pieces inspired by Chinese examples in the same material. First Salon des Indépendents.

Puvis de Chavannes, Le Bois sacré aux Muses et aux Arts. *Rodin,* The Burghers of Calais.

Huysmans, À Rebours.

Brussels. Octave Maus founds the XX (Knopff, Ensor, Finch, etc.). First Salon at the Palais des Beaux-Arts.

•1885

Lalique accepts Jules Destapes' proposal to take over his jewelry workshop on place Gaillon: "I made up my mind and my conversion was complete." He then devotes himself for a number of years to pure *joaillerie,* assisted by craftsmen overseen by Paul Briançon, who will remain Lalique's collaborator for twenty years.

Paris. Death of Victor Hugo.

Émile Zola, Germinal.

Van Gogh, The Potato Eaters.

Naval officer Julien Viaud (Pierre Loti) in Japan.

•1886

Lalique's first marriage, to Marie-Louise Lambert, with whom he has a daughter, Georgette (dies December 12, 1910).

Paris. Jean Moréas publishes "Un Manifeste littéraire: le Symbolisme" in Le Figaro. *Édouard Drumont,* La France juive.

Paul Gauguin at Pont-Aven produces his first ceramics at Chaplet's workshop, winter 1886–87.

Brussels. Renoir, Monet, Redon at the Salon des XX.

Chicago. Sullivan and Adler, Auditorium *(1886–89); stained-glass windows by Healy and Millet.*

•1887

Lalique moves into larger premises at 24, rue du Quatre-Septembre. The *Flight of Swallows* parure acquired by Boucheron. Starts working in enamel and gold.

Paris. First exhibition of Les XX, Galerie Georges Petit.

Pierre Loti, Madame Chrysanthème.

Dayton, Ohio. Edward Colonna brings out his Essay on Broom-Corn *and sends a copy to Louis Comfort Tiffany.*

•1888

Lalique produces his earliest pieces of *plique-à-jour* jewelry, with decoration inspired by Antiquity and Japan (as dated by Henri Vever).

Paris, May. Bing brings out the first issue of the monthly Le Japon artistique, *publication continues until April 1891. Alphonse Mucha begins his Paris career as an illustrator and poster artist.*

London. Charles Robert Ashbee, Arthur Heygate Mackmurdo, and Walter Crane found the Guild and School of Handicraft and the National Association for the Advancement of Art and Its Application to Industry.

•1889

"In 1889, I moved one rung up the ladder, and, once I'd obtained what I was looking for, work came more easily to me." Lalique participates in the Exposition Universelle as an anonymous collaborator with Vever and Boucheron. *Song Birds* brooch, signed VEVER on the edge, Lalique's hallmark on the pin and perhaps the tulle or matt brooch bordered with jewelwork, (as reproduced in Vever's *La Bijouterie française au XIXe siècle* (1908, p. 697) and dated by him 1889).

Vever and Boucheron both obtain grands prix, Alphonse Fouquet a gold medal for his final public presentation with pieces of jewelry that have hardly changed since 1878: chimerae are a theme much in vogue.

Paris. Exposition Universelle commemorating the centennial of the French Revolution. Gustave Eiffel builds his 300-meter high Tower on the Champ de Mars. Émile Gallé—"Homo Triplex" as Roger Marx dubs him—presents works in glass and ceramic as well as furniture. The Wallace Fountains in Paris.

Inauguration of the Musée Guimet, Place d'Iéna.

Henri Bergson, Essai sur les données immédiates de la conscience.

Budapest, November 20. Gustav Mahler gives the first performance of his First Symphony.

Chicago. First house by Frank Lloyd Wright at Oak Park.

•1890

Lalique moves his workshop which now employs around thirty craftsmen to 20, rue Thérèse, on the corner of the avenue de l'Opéra.

He designs its furniture and, with the aid of the two sculptors, Alphonse Ledru, father and son, decorates the walls and ceilings with female riders.

Meets Alphonse Ledru's daughter, Augustine-Alice Ledru.

Clément Ader, first flight in an airplane.

Van Gogh commits suicide.

Odilon Redon, Les Yeux clos.

Austria. Otto Wagner is appointed to redesign Vienna's architecture.

St Louis. Sullivan and Adler build the Wainwright Building.

•1891

Lalique undertakes research on glass, showing his earliest experiments to Jules Henrivaux and Léon Appert.

Paris. First Nabis exhibition.

First of Gauguin's voyages to Tahiti.

Claude Monet, Les Nymphéas.

•1892

Paris, May 4: birth of Suzanne, daughter of René Lalique and Augustine-Alice Ledru. Lalique starts out on the road that will culminate in the total reconception of the *bijou*: "In 1892, I had to make a truly exceptional effort to shake myself loose of all I had done hitherto. I worked ceaselessly, making drawings, models, studies, and technical trials of all types without a moment's rest, striving to achieve new results, to create something that has never been seen before."

Paris. Palais de l'Industrie, "Les Arts de la Femme," organized by Union Centrale des Arts Décoratifs. At the Galerie Durand-Ruel, exhibition of the Rose+Croix (Toroop, Hodler, Knopff, etc.). Loïe Fuller at the Folies Bergère.

Maurice Maeterlinck, Pelléas et Mélisande. *Jules Massenet,* Werther.

Chicago. Louis Sullivan publishes Ornament in Architecture.

•1893

Lalique takes part in the goldsmiths' competition organized by Union Centrale des Arts Décoratifs, the subject being "a drinking vessel in metal." He obtains a second prize (500 francs) for the *Thistles* goblet and is awarded a medal with honorable mention for the *Pampas and Satyrs* vase. According to Henri Vever, Lalique produces a large oval cameo "in glass in various hues, simply molded without retouching," representing a standing female nude doing her hair (Vever, 1908, p. 713).

Oscar Wilde publishes Salome, *illustrated by Aubrey Beardsley.*

Edvard Munch, The Scream. *Massagier and Loti,* Madame Chrysanthème *at the Théâtre Lyrique, Paris.*

Chicago. World Columbian Exposition commemorating the fourth centenary of the discovery of America. Sullivan builds the Transportation Building.

•1894

Lalique exhibits for the first time at the Salon de la Société des Artistes Français in the sculpture section: a cover for a music case, *The Valkyrie,* in homage to Richard Wagner. Lalique meets Sarah Bernhardt, makes jewelry for Victorien Sardou's Gismonda, produced on October 31 at the Théâtre de la Renaissance. The poster is designed by Alphonse Mucha.

Hector Guimard works in England and Scotland. Bing organizes exhibitions of Oriental art in cities on the East Coast of the United States. He is entrusted with a research mission on art in America, discovers Tiffany's and the stained-glass windows by John La Farge and Louis Comfort Tiffany.

Brussels. Henry Van de Velde publishes Déblaiement d'Art. *Foundation of* Libre Esthétique.

•1895

For the first time, Lalique exhibits glass pieces at the Salon, among which the 1893 cameo. That year, the Société des Artistes Français opens a decorative arts section to which he sends a group of newly designed jewelry pieces, for instance a "dragonfly with wings spangled with amethysts and yellow sapphires" and a large Renaissance-style fastener decorated with a *plique-à-jour* female nude (Vever, 1908, pp. 723–24). Participates at Bing's first Salon de l'Art Nouveau.

Paris, December 26. Inauguration of Louis Bonnier's newly fitted-out "Galeries de l'Art Nouveau" on the site of Bing's Eastern art store. Some of the foremost European and North American artists from every discipline take part: Louis Comfort Tiffany, with glass pieces and stained-glass windows after works by Toulouse-Lautrec, Bonnard, Ranson, and Maurice Denis.

Bing brings out his report on his journey to the USA, La Culture artistique en Amérique.

•1896

Lalique wins a medal for his Salon offerings: they include a number of pieces of goldwork, "among which a round vase with a handle for the Grand Duke Alexis, a drinking vessel for M. Germain Bapst, and a large chest that was much criticized. As far as we are able to recall, this last represented the chariot of Fortune or the Triumph of Wealth: the handles were made in human shape, both men and women, and executed in high-relief bronze." (Vever, 1908, p. 726). For the first time, Lalique exhibits a *bijou* in ivory and a silver appliqué bracelet.

Munich. Founding of the review, Jugend.

Athens. First modern Olympic Games.

•1897

Lalique exhibits at the Salon a vitrine of horn and ivory combs, some of which are acquired by Parisian museums; the Musée de Luxembourg purchases a large poppy in gold, brilliants, and *plique-à-jour* enamel that today belongs to the Musée d'Orsay.

In the Gazette des Beaux-Arts there appears an article by Émile Gallé, who considers Lalique the inventor of the "modern *bijou*." Lalique takes part in the Exposition Internationale in Brussels and win a grand prix. He is made a Chevalier of the Légion d'Honneur.

Robert de Montesquiou, Roseaux pensants. *Eugène Grasset,* La Plante et ses applications ornementales.

The first appearance of several decorative arts journals: Art et Décoration, *in Paris; in Vienna,* Ver Sacrum, *the publication of the Secession;* Dekorative Kunst—*under the aegis of Julius Maier-Graefe—which was soon to become* L'Art Décoratif.

•1898

Lalique's contribution to the Salon represents a formal and thematic repertoire of his work: combs and tiaras, corsage ornaments, pendants and brooches, rings and bracelets, all realized in gold and enamel, enriched with colored gemstones, with a penchant for opal, (the whole linked to the cults of

Nature, of Woman, allusive to Symbolist culture, and reminiscent of Oriental and Renaissance art). Henri Vever writes about Lalique in *Art et Décoration*. Lalique acquires a property at Clairefontaine where he sets up a glassmaking workshop.

Philippe Wolfers, Medusa *pendant.*

Peter Behrens, The Kiss.

Deaths of Gustave Moreau, Stéphane Mallarmé, Puvis de Chavannes, Charles Garnier, and Edward Burne-Jones.

•1899

Lalique creates the Bérénice costume tiara for Julia Bartet.

Roger Marx devotes an important article to Lalique's work in Art et Décoration.

Henry Van der Velde designs the furniture for Julius Maier-Graefe's "Maison Moderne".

•1900

September 1. Birth of a son, Marc, to Lalique and Augustine-Alice Ledru. Lalique's contribution to the Exposition Universelle in Paris is much remarked upon: "Lalique triumphed in unparalleled fashion; a dense and fervent crowd gathered round to see works that were on everyone's lips." (Vever, 1908, p. 738). Lalique is at the summit of his creative power. His customers belong to the international aristocracy, to the worlds of business, politics, theater, and the arts, and include great collectors such as Martine de Béhague, the marquise Arconati-Visconti, Calouste Gulbenkian, and Henry Walters.

Numerous articles appear in specialized journals, one by the writer Pol Neveux in *Art et décoration*, another by Léonce Bénédite for *La Revue des Arts Décoratifs*. Lalique is raised to an Officer of the Légion d'Honneur. Lalique's vitrine at the Exposition Universelle is contrasted with Georges Fouquet's, with its jewelry after designs by Alphonse Mucha and Henri Vever, which drew on work by Eugène Grasset.

Lalique is the great success at the Exposition Universelle, together with Émile Gallé who shows marquetry glass with themes inspired by nature and its flora and fauna.

Paris. Hector Guimard designs the Metro entrances. The Vincennes-Maillot metro line comes into service.

USA. Theodore Roosevelt is president.

•1901

At the Salon, Lalique exhibits light-colored and white *bijoux* in which glass occupies a crucial place. They are presented in a vitrine flanked on all four corners by what critic Gustave Geffroy described as "glass snakes which have the bright, grayish transparency of flowing ice."

Paris. Foundation of the Société des Artistes Décorateurs.

Victor Prouvé, Émile Gallé, Louis Majorelle, and the Daums found the École de Nancy.

Paris. Opening of Georges Fouquet's store, rue Royale, interior decoration by Mucha.

Émile Gallé, crystal vase, blown in several layers, with appliqué seahorses, dated and with a dedication to Joseph Reinach, Captain Dreyfus's defense attorney.

USA. Gustav Stickley founds the magazine The Craftsman.

•1902

On July 8, Lalique marries Augustine-Alice Ledru and settles in a town-house at 40, Cours-La-Reine where his private residence, workshops, and outlets are combined (architect M. Feine). Lalique himself designs the decoration of the balconies and the stonework entrance door surround; it is inspired by "every species of pine." This is also the theme of the molded-glass door leaves, whereas the hall is decorated with panels representing athletes in the antique style.

Lalique takes part in the International Exhibition of the Decorative Arts in Turin. Among the jewelry he exhibits at the Salon are blown-glass dishes set in a metal armature.

Paris. Sale of the Japanese art collection belonging to Charles Gillot.

Claude Debussy, Pelléas et Mélisande.

Weimar. Henry Van der Velde is director of the Kunstgewerbeschule.

New York. Louis Comfort Tiffany becomes

vice president and artistic director of Tiffany & Co. on the death of his father.

•1903
Lalique takes part at the first Salon d'Automne founded by Frantz Jourdain. Exhibits alms purses, one being embroidered with two interlocked silver snakes.

Paris. Exhibition of Islamic art at the Musée des Arts décoratifs.

Vienna. Josef Hoffmann founds the Wiener Werkstätte with Koloman Moser.

•1904
Lalique takes part in the Louisiana Purchase Exposition in St. Louis. Travels to the USA with his wife, Alice, staying over briefly in New York then going to St. Louis and thereafter to Buffalo.

The collector Henry Walters acquires the ensemble of Lalique's jewelry today housed at the Walters Art Gallery, Baltimore.

Closure of both Bing's and Maier-Graefe's galleries.

Nancy, September 23. Death of Émile Gallé. L'Exposition d'Art Décoratif organized by the Société Lorraine des Amis de l'Art.

Paris. First performance of Tristan and Isolde *at the Opéra.*

•1905
Paris. Lalique opens a shop on the Place Vendôme. Takes part in the Exposition d'Art Décoratif at Liège; Pol Neveux is the head of the committee.

Lalique composes a frieze, *La Flore de France*, embroidered by Madame Ory-Robin.

Paris, May 29. Grand opening of the Musée des Arts décoratifs, at the Pavillon de Marsan, in the Louvre.

Brussels. Josef Hoffmann begins building the Palais Stoclet (1905–11).

Austria. Sigmund Freud, Three Contributions to the Theory of Sex.

Richard Strauss, Salome.

•1906
Lalique takes part in the "Dentelles et Broderies" exhibition at the Pavillon de Marsan with a showcase of collars decorated with facing cockerels, and peacocks, embroidered in silver and gold and inlayed with glass flowers (dating from 1904), and with appliqué gold-lamé embroidery and strings which had already appeared in Liège in 1905.

Death of Cézanne.

•1907
At the Salon, Lalique exhibits scarves in gold lamé silk produced by the firm Bianchini-Férier et Cie. Three of these are acquired by the Musée des Arts décoratifs.

Picasso, Les Demoiselles d'Avignon.

New York. Gustav Mahler conducts at the Metropolitan Opera.

Cologne. Hermann Muthesius founds the Deutscher Werkbund.

•1908
In the Exhibition "Parure de la Femme" at the Musée Galliera Lalique displays fabulous combs: one, an ivory, gold and brilliant-set orchid is close to the example in the Walters Collection. He begins to work with François Coty.

Cubist paintings by Braque and Picasso. Brancusi, The Kiss.

Adolf Loos publishes "Ornament und Verbrechen."

New York. Matisse and Rodin at Alfred Stieglitz's 291 Gallery.

•1909
Lalique rents a glassmaking concern at Combs-la-Ville to the east of Paris; produces his first perfume bottles for Coty: "L'Effleurt." Earliest patent for a glass-molding process "applicable to the manufacture of bottles, decanters, and all types of vessels whose aperture is narrower than their inner dimensions" (application February 16, 1909; patent issued February 17, 1910).

At the Salon, he shows engraved-glass and diamond *bijoux*, as well as a "showcase with toiletry *objets d'art*," one of which was probably the perfume bottle, "Cyclamen," for Coty. Also exhibits the vessel with two sirens acquired by the Musée des Arts décoratifs.

Death of Augustine-Alice Ledru.

January: Le Figaro *publishes Marinetti's* Futurist Manifesto.

Paris. First performances by the Ballets Russes at the Théâtre du Châtelet.

Maeterlinck, L'Oiseau Bleu.

Richard Strauss, Elektra.

•1910

Lalique takes part in the exhibition "Glassmaking and Crystalware" at the Musée Galliera, with dishes and chalices including the dish with vine stems and figures, acquired by Gulbenkian in 1902 (inv. 1177).

Paris. Exhibition of the Deutscher Werkbund at the Salon d'Automne.

The Ballets Russes perform Stravinsky's Firebird.

Vienna. Strauss, Der Rosenkavalier.

•1911

Lalique takes part in the Exposition Universelle of Decorative Art in Turin. French participation is organized by UCAD. He also exhibits at the Salon of the Société des Beaux-Arts. First show devoted solely to glasswork in the gallery on the Place Vendôme.

Claude Debussy, The Martyrdom of St. Sebastian. *The Ballets Russes perform Stravinsky's* Petrushka *at the Théâtre du Châtelet.*

Vienna. Death of Gustav Mahler.

Odilon Redon decorates the library of the Abbey of Fonfroide for Gustave Fayet.

•1912

Last jewelry exhibition on the Place Vendôme. Lalique makes the glass slab doors for Jacques Doucet's residence on avenue du Bois. Designs the interior fittings of the Coty building, in New York, and a large glass bay decorated with branches and poppy flowers covering the entire facade.

Bernard Shaw, Pygmalion.

Thomas Mann, Death in Venice.

USA. Woodrow Wilson becomes president.

•1913

September 30, Lalique purchases the glass making concern at Combs-la-Ville. Applies for a patent for "the decoration of glass or other transparent substances with motifs illuminated by means of concealed of unconcealed sources of light" (application August 1, 1913; patent issued August 4, 1914) He is now a full-fledged glassware industrialist; he perfects glass making processes that will allow him to produce both unique pieces in lost-wax as well as series through blown-molded and press-molded techniques with a felt-wheel finish or patination.

Marcel Proust, À la Recherche du temps perdu. *Apollinaire,* Alcools. *Maurice Barrès,* La Colline inspirée. *Freud,* Totem and Taboo.

New York. Armory Show.

•1914–18

World War I.

In 1918 or 1919, Lalique travels to Lorraine and Alsace searching for premises better suited for glass production than Combs-la-Ville, and above all to look for qualified craftsmen. He first goes to Saint-Louis and then on to Meisenthal, but without success. His means of production are contrary to those then employed at the Cristalleries Saint-Louis glassworks, for example. It appears that the plant he acquired at Wingen-sur-Moder was proposed to him by Alexandre Millerand (an admirer of his work in glass) who also aided him in the project.

Official gifts to Mrs. Wilson on the US presidential trip in France December 1918 include a corsage ornament by René Lalique. It is an earlier work, but the Paris town council finds the subject in keeping with the circumstances: eight glass doves on olive branches set with diamonds (in fact these were pigeons; see drawing cat. 164).

• 1945

May 5. Death of René Lalique.

Notes

The Lalique Epoch

1. Henri Clouzot, "L'époque Lalique ou les origines de l'art moderne," excerpted from *La Revue Mondiale*, in *La presse et l'exposition des oeuvres de René Lalique, organisé par le Musée des Arts Décoratifs au Pavillon de Marsan, Palais du Louvre, février et mars 1933* (Paris: Impressions Modernes Pierre Guyot, 1933), n.p.
2. Doubtless this is the brooch referred to by Henri Vever: "Around 1896, [Lalique] made a corsage ornament in glass; a large brooch representing Winter, with groups of crystals on the finely colored snowy trees; it was a truly original invention. The piece was ordered from Russia"; Vever, *La Bijouterie française au XIXe siècle*, III (Paris: H. Floury, 1908; reprint, Florence: S.P.E.S., 1975), p. 714. Lalique executed several brooches and pendants on the theme of a winter's landscape, either in enamel or glass; an enamel piece was purchased by the Hamburg Museum für Kunst und Gewerbe at the 1900 Exposition; see *René Lalique: Jewelry, Glass*, exh. cat. (Paris: Musée des Arts décoratifs, 1991), no. 210. We are aware of a number of versions of this type in glass, one acquired by Calouste Gulbenkian in 1900 (qv. cat. Gulbenkian, 1989, no. 154 and *René Lalique: Jewelry, Glass*, no. 148), and another now in a private collection in New York (cat. 51).
3. Clouzot, "L'Époque Lalique," n.p.
4. Vever, *La Bijouterie française*, p. 702.
5. Ibid., pp. 706–708.
6. Roger Marx, "René Lalique," *Art et Décoration*, 6 (1899), p. 15.
7. Vever, *La Bijouterie française*, pp. 709–10.
8. See Sigrid Barten, *René Lalique: Schmuck und Objets d'Art, 1890–1910* (Munich: Prestel-Verlag, 1977), p. 569 and fig. 1796. The portrait of Émile Gallé now belongs to the Musée de l'École de Nancy.
9. When he sold a piece, Lalique would also supply the gouache that had served as its blueprint. The first drafts, on the other hand, he would keep for himself. More than three thousand sheets, often annotated in his own hand, have been preserved by his granddaughter, Marie-Claude Lalique, daughter of his son Marc. For the most part they now belong to the Musée de la Société Lalique in Paris; see Marie-Noël de Gary, "The Book of Truth: Lalique's Jewelry Drawings," in *René Lalique: Jewelry, Glass*, pp. 116–29.
10. See Evelyne Possémé, "Landscape in the Work of René Lalique," pp. 146–161 below.
11. Vever, *La Bijouterie française*, pp. 703–04.
12. Ibid., p. 702, ill.; Barten, *René Lalique*, no. 332, ill.
13. Pol Neveux, "René Lalique," *Art et Décoration*, 8 (1900), pp. 129–30.
14. Philippe Burty, *Les Émaux cloisonnés anciens et modernes* (Paris: J. Claye, 1868).
15. The poppy pin was acquired by the Musée du Luxembourg in 1897 and entered its collections the following year; it was transferred to the Musée National d'Art Moderne, and, in 1987, to the Musée d'Orsay (inv. OAO 46). The dragonfly-woman corsage ornament is one of the strangest and most symbolically charged of the works Lalique produced around 1897–98; acquired by Calouste Gulbenkian in 1903, it is at present at the Museu Calouste Gulbenkian in Lisbon (inv. 1197).
16. On February 12, 1891, Lalique applied for a patent for a new enamel-producing process, issued on May 15 of that year, no. 211.367: "An enamel-making process enabling enamel to be produced in any desired thickness, and whereby it is also possible to reproduce sculpture in the round. Applicable or not to jewelry and ornamental metalwork"; see *René Lalique: Jewelry, Glass*, p. 247.
17. Vever, *La Bijouterie française*, p. 710.
18. Henri Vever and Léonce Bénédite give the date of this meeting as 1891, but it is 1894, if one refers to the correspondence between Lévy-Dhurmer and the jeweler; see Evelyne Possémé and Anne Vanlatum, "Scenic Mirages," in *René Lalique: Jewlery, Glass*, pp. 70–71.
19. Bing's outlet on rue Chauchat in Paris was a meeting place for the Orientalists and for all devotees of Japanese art. Between May 1888 and April 1891, he published a deluxe review, *Le Japon Artistique*, comprising a repertory of "Documents concerning art and industry" selected from examples of Japanese art and destined to inspire contemporary artists and artisans. It

constitutes today an invaluable text for understanding how artists and collectors at the end of the nineteenth century viewed Japanese art.

20. Émile Gallé, "Les Salons de 1897: Objets d'art," *Gazette des Beaux-Arts*, 18 (September 1897), pp. 247–48.

21. Ibid., p. 230.

22. The senior Ledru had been a marble-cutter in the studio of Rodin, who was the major inspiration behind his work; see Arthur Maillet, "Le Salon des Champs-Élysées," *L'Art Décoratif Moderne* (June 1895), pp. 174-75 (Ledru exhibited some pewter vases with handles in the shape of nude female figures). According to Vever (*La Bijouterie française*, p. 709), the two Ledrus often collaborated with Lalique, "executing his compositions in relief." Is it possible to conclude that they transmitted the Rodin influence one can discern in some of Lalique's jewelry pieces as well as in several other objects? Lalique and Rodin knew each other and one of the sculptor's letters refers to the two artists collaborating (Evelyne Possémé, "Lalique: Artist and Magician," in *René Lalique: Jewelry, Glass*, Paris, 1991, p. 132 and n. 7).

Reminiscences of Rodin are clear in the Lalique works that introduce the nude male or female figure before 1900. For example, there is an ivory brooch (cat. 103) where the posture of one of the female bathers recalls Rodin's *Kneeling Fauness* of 1886, which was also to appear in the *Gates of Hell* tympanum, on which Rodin was working by 1880 and whose tumbling bodies made such an impression on the jeweler. Lalique recalled both this theme and its sculptural treatment in the nudes modeled on a ewer in glass and bronze or ivory produced around 1901–02 (cat. 176).

23. Raitif de la Bretonne [pseudonym of Jean Lorrain], "Pall-Mall Semaine. Samedi 14 mai. Au Champs-de-Mars, Galerie des Machines, section objets d'art," *Le Journal*, May 22, 1898.

24. Frederick Leyland kept this controversial interior decoration until his death in 1892. The whole décor was acquired in 1904 by Charles Lang Freer (1854–1919) to house the ceramics collection in his Detroit residence. After his death in 1919, it was installed permanently in the Freer Gallery of Art, Washington, D.C., where it is known as The Peacock Room.

25. Henri Vever, "Les Bijoux aux Salons de 1898," *Art et Décoration*, 3 (1898), pp. 169–78.

26. Quoted by Roger Marx, "Les Maîtres décorateurs français: René Lalique," *Art et Décoration*, 6 (1899), p. 20.

27. "Je sais un bijoutier amoureux des opales/ En vain le tenterait le plus pur diamant/ Il ne ciselera que la gemme aux feux péles,/ Dont l'irisation l'a choisi pour l'amant..."; Robert de Montesquiou, *Les Paons* (Paris: E. Fasquelle, Éditeur, 1901), p. 348.

28. Robert de Montesquiou, *Roseaux pensants*, 1897, p. 169; see Philippe Thiébault, "Two Literary Friendships," in *René Lalique: Jewelry, Glass*, pp. 39–40.

29. Pieces of a religious character seem to make their appearance after 1900, for example, the two angels pendant (cat. 110), and the Apostles chalice (cat. 183).

30. Museu Calouste Gulbenkian, inv. 1134, Gulbenkian cat., 1989, no. 744; *René Lalique: Jewelry, Glass*, no. 164, ill. pp. 42–43.

31. In tribute to her blonde hair, Liane de Pougy had given Natalie Barney the nickname "Moonbeam"; see Jean Chalon, *Chère Natalie Barney: Portrait d'une séductrice* (1976; ed. Paris: Flammarion, 1992).

32. Roger Marx, "Les Maîtres décorateurs français," p. 17 n. 6.

33. Neveux, "René Lalique," p. 130 n. 13.

34. Ibid., p. 130.

35. Ibid., p. 129.

36. Vever, *La Bijouterie française*, pp. 738–39.

37. Ibid., p. 740.

38. Neveux, "René Lalique," p. 129.

39. Henri Clouzot, "L'Époque Lalique," n.p.

40. These virtuoso pieces are itemized in Lalique's reference and account book for the 1900 Exposition Universelle as belonging to a private collection.

41. Museu Calouste Gulbenkian, inv. 1208, cat. Gulbenkian, 1989, no. 798; *René Lalique: Jewelry, Glass*, no. 127, ill. p. 36. The original yellow diamond has been replaced by an amethyst. Described in the account book as a "cockerel head [tiara] enameled in brilliant yellow," 37,000 francs.

42. In the Gulbenkian version (Museu Calouste Gulbenkian, inv. 1216, cat., 1989, no. 804; *René Lalique: Jewelry, Glass*, no. 163, ill. p. 19.), the serpents' jaws are not equipped with the lugs which, in the original piece, fixed the pearls.

43. Museu Calouste Gulbenkian, inv. 1197, cat. 1989, no. 790; *René Lalique: Jewelery, Glass*, no. 162, ill. p. 25. Inscribed in the account book (see note 40 above) for the sum of 10,000 francs.

44. Léonce Bénédite, "La Bijouterie et la joaillerie à l'Exposition Universelle de 1900: René Lalique (premier article)," *Revue des Arts Décoratifs*, 20 (1900), p. 201, ill. Cited in Lalique's account book as no. 8: "Corsage ornament chrysophrase beetles, decoration in gold joaillerie," 12,000 francs. Acquired by Madame Goupy.

45. Cited in Lalique's account book as no. 22. "1 Bee corsage pin," 2,000 francs, acquired by M. Pietro Herohn (?).

Kunstindustrimuseum, Copenhagen; *René Lalique: Jewelry, Glass*, no. 206, ill. p. 130.
46. Madame Waldeck-Rousseau was the wife of Pierre Waldeck-Rousseau (1846–1904), lawyer and politician, président du Conseil from June 1899 to June 1902. He had earlier defended Gustave Eiffel in the Panama corruption trial (January 1893). Mme. Salles-Eiffel was the engineer's daughter.
47. Bénédite, "La Bijouterie et la joaillerie," p. 208 n. 44, ill.
48. See *Art et Décoration*, (1901), and Barten, *René Lalique*, no. 599.
49. Tristan Destève, "La Maison de René Lalique", *Art et Décoration* 12 (1902), p. 161.
50. In 1912, Lalique once more took up the theme of the athletes in a two-part glass door for the living room in the private residence of the couturier Jacques Doucet on the avenue du Bois in Paris; it was transported in 1928 to Doucet's converted studio in Neuilly. The panel at the Musée Lalique in Paris is a variant (cat. 207).
51. Émile Molinier, "Les Objets d'art aux Salons," *Art et Décoration*, 9 (1901), p. 191.
52. Gustave Geffroy, "Les Salons de 1901: René Lalique", *L'Art Décoratif*, 13 (1901), pp. 89-91.
53. Lalique took out patents concerning glass between 1909 and 1914 (*René Lalique: Jewelry, Glass*, p. 247). No. 409.412, applied for on February 16, 1909 and issued on February 17, 1910: "A glass-molding process applicable to the manufacture of bottles, decanters, and all types of vases whose aperture is narrower than their inner dimensions." No. 449.192, applied for on December 16, 1911 and issued December 17, 1912: "A process for the manufacture of glass receptacles and other objects by simultaneous molding, pressing and blowing." No. 472.382, applied for August 1, 1913 and issued August 4, 1914: "A process for the decoration of glass or other transparent substances with motifs illuminated by the means of concealed or unconcealed sources of light." No. 475.348, applied for on February 10, 1914 and issueed on February 16, 1915: "A manufacturing process for objects in decorated glass or crystal, permitting in particular, the ornamentation of such pieces by means of undercut motifs, and further enabling the most minute details of the mold to be reproduced on the decorated object."
54. Félix Marcilhac, *Catalogue raisonné de l'œuvre en verre de René Lalique* (Paris: Éditions de l'Amateur, 1989), p. 55.
55. See note 46 above.
56. Raymond Poincaré (1860–1930), président du Conseil from January 1912 to January 1913 and President of the Republic from 1913 to 1920. Louis Barthou (1862–1934), a collector of glass, including pieces by Maurice Marinot. Barthou was killed during the assassination of Alexander II of Yugoslavia at Marseilles on October 9, 1934.
57. See *René Lalique: Jewelry, Glass*, "A Critical Sampler," p. 245.
58. Quoted in Maria Teresa Gomes Ferreira, "Lalique and Calouste Gulbenkian," in *René Lalique: Jewelry, Glass*, p. 59.
59. Calouste S. Gulbenkian, *La Transcaucasie et la Péninsule d'Apchéron: Souvenirs de voyage* (1891: 2nd ed. Lisbon: Fundação Calouste Gulbenkian, 1989).
60. José de Azeredo Perdigão, *Calouste Gulbenkian, Collector*, trans. Ana Lowndes Marques (Lisbon: Fundação Calouste Gulbenkian, 1969).
61. Ibid., p. 86.
62. Robert de Montesquiou, *Les Paons*, p. 348 n. 27

The Physics and the Metaphysics of Jewelry: "Something That Has Never Been Seen Before"

1. Benvenuto Cellini (1500–1571), sculptor and goldsmith, was born and died in Florence. He worked at the French court between 1540 and 1545. The excellence of his art and his adventurous life inspired Berlioz to write his opera Benvenuto Cellini (1838). In 1855, the jeweler Mollard, having found in Cellini's *Autobiography* an account of a translucent enamel process given by the goldsmith to François I, experimented with the process and was granted a patent in 1855; see Henri Vever, *La Bijouterie française au XIXe siècle*, III (Paris: H. Floury, 1908; reprint, Florence: S.P.E.S, 1975), p. 418.
In 1881, Vever and his brother inherited the business of two generations of Lorraine jewelers who had settled in Paris in 1871. Artist-jeweler and a major collector of Japanese prints, Vever was to trace the history of French jewelry from the Empire to the Third Republic in three volumes whose style and intelligence equal the quality of the information given.
2. Ibid., p. 710.
3. Gustave Kahn, "L'art de René Lalique" in *L'Art et Les Artistes*, 1 (April–September 1905), pp. 147–48.
4. Paul Robert, *Dictionnaire alphabétique et analogique de la langue française* (Paris: Société du Nouveau Littré, 1960).
5. Jean Chevalier and Alain Gheerbrant, *Dictionnaire des symboles* (1969; ed. Paris: Robert Laffont et Éditions Jupiter, 1982). I have used this work throughout the present article for the interpretation of symbols.
6. Edgar Munhall, *Whistler and Montesquiou: The Butterfly and the Bat* (New York: The Frick Collection; Paris and New York: Flammarion, 1995), p. 38.

7. Théophile Gautier, *Émaux et camées* (1852; ed. Paris: Claudine Gauthot-Mersch, Gallimard, 1981), p. 10.
8. Jules Michelet, *La Sorcière* (Paris: Hetzel, 1862).
9. In the laboratory that Lalique had installed on the rue Thérèse, Vever saw "very curious" pieces in glass, made between 1890 and 1892, among which "a little head of St. John the Baptist, full of expression"; Vever, *La Bijouterie française*, pp. 712–13.
10. See Yvonne Brunhammer, *Le Beau dans l'utile: Un musée pour les arts décoratifs* (Paris: Découvertes Gallimard, 1992), no. 145.
11. Viollet-le-Duc, *Entretiens sur l'architecture* (Paris: A. Morel, 1872), XV, p. 205.
12. The opposition between *natura naturans*—the vital energy of the Baroque—and *natura naturata*—encoded by classicism—is rehearsed by Eugenio d'Ors, *Du baroque*, trans. A. Rouardt Valéry (Paris: Gallimard, 1935).
13. Evelyne Possémé, "Japonisme et bijoux Art Nouveau," in *Mode et japonisme*, exh. cat. (Paris: Musée de la Mode et du Costume, 1996).
14. Wagner, quoted by Baudelaire, "Richard Wagner and Tannhäuser in Paris" (1861), in *The Painter of Modern Life and Other Essays*, trans. Jonathan Mayne (Oxford: Phaidon Press, 1964); French ed. in *Oeuvres complètes* (Paris: Éditions de la Pléiade, Gallimard, 1976), II, p. 792.
15. Édouard Dujardin, the inventor of "stream of consciousness" in the novel, founded *La Revue Wagnérienne* in 1886 before going on to create, in 1888, *La Revue Indépendante*, edited by Gustave Kahn. With Jean Moréas and Paul Adam, Kahn had already founded the journal *Le Symboliste* in 1886. It was on that occasion that the Decadents took on the name of Symbolists.
16. "Richard Wagner and Tannhäuser in Paris," in *The Painter of Modern Life*, p. 116; *Oeuvres complètes*, p. 784.
17. "Modernity," in *The Painter of Modern Life*, p. 12; *Oeuvres complètes*, p. 694.
18. Eugène Grasset, "L'Art Nouveau," lecture given at the Union Centrale des Arts Décoratifs, published in the *Revue des Arts Décoratifs*, 18 (1897), p. 144. Calouste Gulbenkian, passionate collector of Lalique's work, played a decisive role in placing the oeuvre in a museum context.
19. Sérusier's nearly abstract painting, made on a cigar box cover, now in the Musée d'Orsay, represents a landscape reflected in water. For Sérusier's friends, it was the revelation of what art had to be; thus they called it *Le Talisman*.
20. Frazer first published *The Golden Bough: A Study in Comparative Religion* in 1890.
21. For the portrait of La Berma in the role of Racine's *Phèdre*: Marcel Proust, *Within a Budding Grove*, II, in *Remembrance of Things Past*, trans. C.K. Scott-Moncrieff (London: Chatto and Windus, 1981), III, pp. 22–30; *À la recherche du temps perdu* (Paris: Éditions de la Pléiade, Gallimard, 1954), I, pp. 448–51.
22. Baudelaire, "Correspondances": "La Nature est un temple où de vivants piliers laissent parfois sortir de confuses paroles."
23. The capital letters are borrowed from Baudelaire's "Woman," chapter X of *The Painter of Modern Life*, pp. 2931; *Oeuvres complètes*, p. 713.
24. Ibid.
25. "Je suis belle, ô mortels, comme un rêve de pierre"; Baudelaire, "La Beauté," in *Les Fleurs du mal*.
26. The Peacock Room is now at the Freer Gallery of Art, Washington, D.C.
27. Munhall, Whistler and Montesquiou, p. 62 and fig. 56. The piece is in the Hunterian Art Gallery, Glasgow.
28. Charles Cros, *Le Collier de griffes*, collection of poems posthumously published in 1908.
29. Munhall, *Whistler and Montesquiou*, p. 36.
30. Annie Sidro, *Le Carnaval de Nice et ses fous* (Nice: Serre, 1979), p. 82.
31. Joris-Karl Huysmans, *À Rebours*, 1884 (*Against the Grain*, trans. Robert Baldick (London: Dover, 1971). This cult book for the Decadents marked the author's break with Zola, to whom Huysmans had once appeared as the great hope of the Realist school.
32. Charlus is an omnipresent character in *À la recherche du temps perdu*; see the "temptation scene" (*Le Côté de Guermantes*, 1921; ed. cit., II, pp. 284–96, and V, pp. 390–406.
33. "I will be esteemed for having loved without concealment,/ that which, for others, inspires only fear"; Robert de Montesquiou, in *Les Hortensias bleus, suivi de pages choisies* (1896; ed. Paris: Éditions des Autres, 1979), p. 171.
34. As described by Pierre Loti, quoted by Arthur Gold and Robert Fizdale, *The Divine Sarah: A Life of Sarah Bernhardt* (New York: Alfred A. Knopf, 1991), p. 217. 35. The name she used in referring to her entourage.
36. Ibid., p. 260.
37. "Celle qui ne meurt pas tant qu'elle fut aimée"; Montesquiou, "La couche de la morte," in *Poètes d'aujourd'hui*, Ad van Reyer and Paul Léautaud, eds. (Paris: Mercure de France, 1922), p. 44.
38. See Giovanni Lista, *Loïe Fuller: Danseuse de la Belle Époque* (Paris: Stock-Somogy, 1994), p. 271.
39. "The Exhibition of Jewellery by René Lalique," *The Studio*, 35 (July 1905). This

argument derives from the Arts and Crafts movement. Ruskin's preference was for raw, uncut stones. Elsewhere, criticism was aimed at Lalique's elitism and at his bending to Parisian fashion.

William Morris suggested that the artist should not make choices just because fashion wills it but only when he believes in its beauty. See Norah C. Gillow, *William Morris: Ornements et Motifs* (Paris: Bookking International-Bracken Books, 1988), p. 14.
40. "All too many Herodiades, Cleopatras, Theodoras, too many *Flowers of Evil* and *Hortensias Bleus*," wrote Albert Thomas, "Les Bijoutiers modernes à l'Exposition Universelle," *L'Art Décoratif*, no. 25 (1900). The references are to Mallarmé's Hérodiade; to two of Sarah Bernardt's roles when "Shakespeare's lips" touched "the rings on her fingers" (Edmond Rostand) and Victorien Sardou was writing for her; and to Baudelaire and Montesquiou.
41. Lista, *Loïe Fuller*, p. 271.
42. Baudelaire, *The Painter of Modern Life*, chap. XI; *Oeuvres complètes*, p. 714.
43. "Les parfums, les couleurs et les sons se répondent," in "Correspondances."
44. Émile Gallé, "Les Salons de 1897: Objets d'art," *Gazette des Beaux-Arts*, 18 (September 1897), p. 247.

The Reception of René Lalique in America: 1901–1920

1. On the reception of jewelry at the Exposition Universelle of 1900 see Léonce Bénédite, "Le Bijou à l'Exposition Universelle," *Art et Décoration* 8 (1900), pp. 65–82; and Pol Neveux, "René Lalique," *Art et Décoration* 8 (1900), pp. 130–36, which is elaborately illustrated with Lalique pieces. The availability of Neveux's review in the United States was instrumental in helping to spread interest in Lalique.
2. Irene Sargent, "René Lalique: His Rank among Contemporary Artists," *The Craftsman* 3 (1902–1903), p. 68.
3. For Lalique's work in the Musée du Luxembourg see Roger Marx, "René Lalique," *Art et Décoration* 6 (1899), pp. 20–21. On the early pieces collected by the Musée des Arts Décoratifs in Paris see Yvonne Brunhammer, "History of a Collection: The Musée des Arts décoratifs," in *René Lalique: Jewelry, Glass*, exh. cat. (Paris: Musée des Arts décoratifs, 1991), pp. 188–201. Marx considered Lalique to be a strong supporter of modernism, which reinforced the critic's own position as a member of the aesthetic elite that was running the art in Paris at the turn of the century.
4. On Stickley, see Mary Ann Smith, *Gustav Stickley, The Craftsman* (Syracue: Syracuse University Press, 1983); John Crosby Freeman, *The Forgotten Rebel: Gustav Stickley and His Craftsmen Mission Furniture* (Watkins Glen, NY: Century House, 1996).
5. Smith, *Gustav Stickley*, p. 34. Sargent actively wrote for *The Craftsman* between 1901 and 1905. For further reference see Cleota Reed Gabriel, "Irene Sargent: Rediscovering a Lost Legend," *Courier* 14, no. 2 (Summer 1979), pp. 4–9.
6. Sargent, "René Lalique," p. 72.
7. Ibid., pp. 65–66.
8. Tristan Destève, "The Workshops and Residence of M. René Lalique," trans. Irene Sargent, *The Craftsman* 4 (1903), pp. 1–8.
9. Interest in Lalique's workshops coincided with the general appraisal of other artisan shops organized at the time. It would also have paralleled the ways Stickley organized or used his workmen.
10. Irene Sargent, "A Minor French Salon," *The Craftsman* 4 (1903), pp. 450–59. The Salon in question was the Société des Artistes Français. Tiffany may have been castigated for not being French rather than for the true quality of his pieces.
11. Ibid., p. 456. Sargent valued the criticism of Verneuil, who had composed the original review for *Art et Décoration*.
12. Ibid., pp. 458–59. Sargent opposed the invasion of pure commercialism and protested its effect on the decorative arts.
13. P. Verneuil, "The Insect in Decoration," trans. Irene Sargent, *The Craftsman* 5 (1903–04), pp. 573–74. The fact that Sargent translated this article indicates the value Americans placed on "nature" worship in the decorative arts.
14. See "René Lalique from the German of Dr. H. Pudor in 'Dokumente des Modernen Kunst-Gewerbes,'" *The Craftsman* 5 (1903–04), pp. 619–20.
15. Beverly K. Brandt, "'Worthy of carefully selected' American Arts and Crafts at the Louisiana Purchase Exposition, 1904," *Archives of American Art Journal*, 28, no. 1 (1988), p. 3. This author is indebted to Jill Miller of the University of Minnesota for calling his attention to the range of pieces exhibited in St. Louis in 1904.
16. Ibid., p. 13. Brandt commented: "The display might have had a long-term impact on the evolution of American arts and crafts in the early twentieth century had the display received better exposure in the press."
17. Ibid.
18. See *Official Catalogue of Exhibits—Department of Art* (St. Louis: Official Catalogue Company, 1904), p. 167, under the rubric "Group 14, Original Objects of Art Workmanship," no. 109.
19. Will H. Low, "The Field of Art, St. Louis," *Scribner's Magazine* 37 (June 1905), p. 766. Low noted that tradition was

abandoned in "the self-styled art nouveau, where the work of Lalique and his followers found an expression which to the writer's mind amply justified itself, however much in works of larger scope this nascent style may be questioned."

20. *Official Catalogue of Exhibits*, p. 167.

21. "Tiffany and Company, at the Saint Louis Exposition," *The Craftsman* 6 (1904), p. 181.

22. Ibid., p. 182. The article carefully noted that Tiffany also created a collection that was shown outside the competition in St. Louis, that is, the Paris Salon, where his work received the designation Hors Concours. Once again the American press underscored this parallel with France.

23. Brandt, "'Worthy of carefully selected' American Arts and Crafts," p. 11.

24. For reference to Alice Roosevelt's visit see "Women Throng Station to see Miss Roosevelt," *St. Louis Post Dispatch* (May 26, 1904), with a photograph on the front page of Miss Roosevelt dressed in the height of contemporary fashion. She provoked ongoing discussion in the St. Louis press, including "President's daughter Becomes Guest of Honor on Appearance at Illinois Building Dedication," *St. Louis Post Dispatch* (May 27, 1904), and "Miss Roosevelt's Visit Causes a Reduction of the St. Louis 400 to 100," *St Louis Post Dispatch* (May 31, 1904). Interest in all of President Roosevelt's children, especially Alice, appeared in other newspapers, including a major piece (with extensive photo coverage of the children) entitled "President Roosevelt's Interesting Children," *Chicago Sunday Tribune* (June 19, 1904).

25. "A Rare Collection, Of Jewels Exhibited in the Art Palace," *World's Fair Bulletin* (October 1904). Following the earlier visit by Alice Roosevelt, this article called attention to the fact that the socially prominent, among hundreds of others, had frequently visited the installation. The present author is indebted to the assistance of the Missouri Historical Society in locating this reference.

26. See "Group at the Maryland Building, St. Louis, June 8," (Baltimore) *Sun* (June 12, 1904); a second article, "Homeward from Fair," *Sun* (June 13, 1904). Significantly, the *Sun* also reported on President's Roosevelt's interest in approaching financial magnates, including George G. Gould of New York. This might explain why Miss Gould accompanied Miss Roosevelt to St. Louis and the Lalique installation. For reference see "Gould at White House," *Sun* (June 15, 1904).

27. Walters is not mentioned in any newspaper article from Baltimore as going to the World's Fair with the official group. For reference to the Walters family as collectors see "The History of the Collection," in *William R. Johnston, The Nineteenth Century Paintings in the Walters Art Gallery* (Baltimore: Walters Art Gallery, 1982): pp. 13–28. Additional information on Henry Walters is found in *Richard H. Randall, Jr., Jewelry Ancient to Modern* (New York: Viking Press, 1979): especially the foreword.

28. Johnston, *The Nineteenth Century Paintings in the Walters Art Gallery*, which does not, however, provide specific information on the dates Walters visited the St. Louis Fair. In discussions with the present author, Johnston verified Walters's attendance at the St. Louis Fair. A receipt in the Walters Art Gallery archives confirms this purchase of Lalique works.

29. Ibid., p. 247. Johnston that pieces by Lalique were not among those listed in the French section of the *Catalogue général . . . de St. Louis* (1904) and were shown, therefore, in Lalique's own exhibitions of *Objets et bijoux d'art* in Department D, Manufactures, Palais des Manufactures. This documentation, however, does not discuss the pieces shown by Lalique in Department B—Art and Listed under "original Objects of Art Workmanship," no. 109, as "Collection of Objects of Art" and found in the Official Catalogue of Exhibits . Were Lalique's pieces shown in more than one location? Clearly, the press covered the Palace of Arts, where social elites viewed Lalique's installation. For further reference see William R. Johnston, "Henry Walters' First Purchases of Jewelry," *Antiques* 119 (July 1981): pp. 1356–57.

30. For the pieces Walters owned, see Randall, *Jewelry Ancient to Modern*, pp. 248–53. Walter's interest in Lalique can be compared with that of the wealthy businessman Calouste Gulbenkian. See Maria Teresa Gomes Ferreira, "Lalique and Calouste Gulbenkian," in *René Lalique: Jewelry, Glass*, pp. 54–69.

31. On different aspects of Lalique's career see Yvonne Brunhammer, "Lalique: A Story in Two Parts," in *René Lalique, Jewelry, Glass*, pp. 16–35.

32. Information supplied by Yvonne Brunhammer in a letter to the present author, November 12, 1997. Mme. Brunhammer's information is drawn from personal letters addressed by Alice Lalique to her daughter Suzanne from April 16, 1904 to May 19, 1904.

33. See "List or Manifest of Alien Passengers for the U.S. Immigration Officer at Port of Arrival," SS *La Savoie* sailing from Le Havre, April 16, 1904 and arriving at the Port of New York, April 24, 1904, no. 1696, National Archives, Washington, D.C. Among those traveling with the Laliques on the *Savoie* were Léon Leroy, a jeweler, who

gave his destination as the St. Louis World's Fair, French Department, and Auguste St. André de Lignereux, who was going to St. Louis as the French Consulate to the city. This author is indebted to Karla Cosgriff for her help in the location of these documents.
34. Alice Lalique to Suzanne Lalique, letter of May 7, 1904 from the Hotel Lorraine, Lindell Boulevard and Boyle Avenue, St. Louis.
35. "Society at Home and Abroad, Personal and Otherwise," *New York Times*, June 11, 1905. The present author is indebted to Alastair Wright for his assistance in locating this article.
36. Ibid. Most critics made a similar distinction between Lalique's achievements and more traditional ways in jewelry.
37. Ibid.
38. See J. Nilsen Laurvik, *Rene Lalique*, (New York: Haviland and Company, 1912). The Lalique and Haviland families were connected through marriage. This information has been provided to the author by Mme. Nicole Marich-Haviland, Lalique's granddaughter. J. Nilsen Laurvik was the director of the San Francisco Art Association and chief organizer of the art section of the 1915 Panama Pacific International Exposition in San Francisco. It was his intention to establish a museum in San Francisco.
39. Ibid., p. 4.
40. Ibid., p. 12.
41. See "A New and Great Craftsman in France," *The Craftsman* 23 (1912–13), p. 75.
42. Ibid., p. 76.
43. Information provided by the National Museum of American History, Smithsonian Institution, inv. 55862 and 55863.

Lalique and Fashion

1. José de Azeredo Perdigão, *Calouste Gulbenkian, Collector*, trans. Ana Lowndes Marques (Lisbon: Fundação Calouste Gulbenkian, 1969), p. 80.
2. *L'Art et la Mode*, no. 2 (1890), p. 14.
3. Jean Cocteau, *Reines de France* (Paris: Grasset, 1952), p. 141.
4. *L'Art et la Mode*, no. 27 (1897), p. 342.
5. *L'Art et la Mode*, no. 2 (1890), p. 14.
6. Comtesse de Pange, *Comment j'ai vu 1900* (Paris: Grasset, 1962), p. 116.
7. In 1910 rows of pearls seemed to fall out of favor, in part due to the number of imitations being produced; see *L'Art et la Mode*, no. 2 (1910), p. 32.
8. *L'Art et la Mode*, no. 37 (1902), p. 729.
9. Sigrid Barten, *René Lalique: Schmuck und Objets d'Art, 1890–1910* (Munich: Prestel-Verlag, 1977), from an article by Fritz Minkerslinz on the 1900 Exposition Universelle.
10. Ibid.
11. Paul Poiret, *En habillant l'époque* (Paris: Grasset, 1930), p. 28.
12. François Mathey points out that the overall structure of jewelry corresponded to that of dress; see his preface to *Le Bijou 1900/Modern-Style Jewelen*, exh. cat. (Brussels: Hôtel Solvay, 1965).
13. Nadine Gasc notes quite rightly that it is a pity that Lalique never designed "dresses to serve as caskets for his jewelry" like William Morris; see "Lalique: A Major Influence on Fashion," in *René Lalique: Jewelry, Glass*, exh. cat. (Paris: Musée des Arts Décoratifs, 1991), p. 92.

Materials and Techniques in the Jewelry of René Lalique

1. About 1910 Lalique succeeded, for example, in mass producing elaborate reliefs for perfume bottles, by waiting until the end of the production process to attach the base of the container; see Félix Marcilhac, *Catalogue raisonné de l'œuvre en verre de René Lalique*, 2nd ed. (Paris: Éditions de l'Amateur, 1994), pp. 59–69.
2. Lalique drew particularly on Renaissance models in a corsage ornament produced between 1893 and 1894 bearing a female torso and volutes, which served as a cloak clasp; see Sigrid Barten, *René Lalique: Schmuck und Objets d'Art, 1890–1910* (Munich: Prestel-Verlag, 1977), no. 903. Lalique's comments on the design (cat. 22) contain an etching based on the finished object and a self-portrait, which demonstrates his artistic pride vis-à-vis this work and his personal affinity with the Renaissance.
3. Henri Vever, La *Bijouterie française au XIXe siècle*, III (Paris: H. Floury, 1908; reprint Florence: S.P.E.S., 1975).
4. Roger Marx, "René Lalique," in *Art et Décoration*, 6 (1899), p. 15. The majority of the drawings are now in the Musée Lalique, Paris.
5. Only a few of these colleagues are mentioned by name, among them Paul Briançon, Georges-Pierre Deraisme, Hofmann, Chardon, and Eugène Feuillâtre; see Barten, *René Lalique*, p. 79.
6. The Belgian designer Philippe Wolfers, for example, used a completely different approach, choosing gemstones in colors which sharply contrasted with the enamel.
7. As Lalique was known for his fondness for the opal, in 1901 Alphonse Fouquet even dedicated a poem to him entitled "L'Opale."
8. The availability of ivory depended on Belgium. In 1893–94, King Leopold II had taken measures to ensure that ivory from

the Belgian-controlled independent kingdom of Belgian Congo was made available to artists of his country. These included the sculptor and goldsmith Philippe Wolfers, who from 1897 to 1905 devoted himself to producing Art Nouveau jewelry in the Lalique genre.
9. Vever, *La Bijouterie française*, p. 719: "Having modeled the jewel, I was certain of achieving the most faithful reproduction of the effects which I had sought to create, without the intermediary of engravers or other craftsmen."

Landscape in the Work of René Lalique

1. The author would particularly like to thank Madame Nicole Maritch-Haviland, daughter of Suzanne Lalique and granddaughter of René Lalique, for her invaluable help and generosity. With exemplary patience, Mme. Maritch-Haviland replied to my numerous questions, allowed me to consult her archives, and share her memories. Her memoirs concerning her family, and especially René Lalique himself, will be published shortly. All the letters and Lalique's remarks quoted in this article have their source in the Maritch archives or her memoirs. The majority of these letters are now housed at the Musée d'Orsay and the Musée des Arts décoratifs.
2. Lalique enthusiastically returned to London and its museums in 1894, when he traveled there with Sarah Bernhardt and her entourage. (He was making designs of stage jewelry for her.) The visit is documented in his correspondence with Alice Ledru, then his companion and mother of his daughter Suzanne, born two years earlier. It was during this visit that Lalique formed a friendship with the set designer Marcel Jambon.
3. Ruskin, *Pages choisies*, introd. Robert de la Sizeranne, 2nd ed. (Paris: Hachette, 1909). The volume was given to Lalique's daughter Suzanne (now collection Maritch-Haviland). The passage quoted is from Ruskin, "The Moral of Landscape," in *Modern Painters*, part IV.
4. The correspondence between Lalique and Suzanne began in 1907–1908, when the artist's wife, Alice, became ill with the disease that would ultimately lead to her death in July 1909.
5. The photographs are today in the Musée d'Orsay.
6. "Refaire un pendant dans ce/ genre d'après nature pour les/ feuilles, les bois et les tiges/ la photographie suffira pour/ les fleurs." Most of Lalique's drawings for jewelry today remain the property of the Musée Lalique, Paris. The annotated drawing quoted here is inv. 2.4.479. I am glad to have the opportunity to express my thanks to Mme. Catherine Vincent-Dolor, Director of Public Relations at the Maison Lalique, who gave me permission to consult the drawing.
7. Heinrich Heine, "Waldeinsamkeit," lines 121–24, from *Lamentationen*, published in *Romanzero*, 1852.
8. See the pendant with landscape, c. 1899–1900, and its related drawing, in the Museu Calouste Gulbenkian, in Sigrid Barten, *René Lalique: Schmuck und Objets d'Art, 1890–1910* (Munich: Prestel-Verlag, 1977), nos. 621, 621a.
9. Ruskin, "The Leaf Shadows," in *Modern Painters*, part VI, chapter IX.
10. These sketchbooks are conserved in the Musée d'Orsay. The first page of the sketchbook inscribed with these names bears the number 588–47.
11. Barten, *René Lalique*, no. 648.
12. Alphonse de Lamartine, "Le Lac," in *Méditations poétiques*, 1820: "O lac! l'année à peine a fini sa carrière,/ Et près des flots chéris qu'elle devait revoir,/ Regarde! Je viens seul m'asseoir sur cette pierre/ Où tu la vis asseoir!"
13. Heine, "Waldeinsamkeit," lines 141–44.
14. Barten, *René Lalique*, nos. 1783, 1784.
15. Musée Lalique, inv. 1.3.016.
16. Musée Lalique, inv. 2.2.029 and 3.6.001; Barten, *René Lalique*, nos. 1509, 1509a.
17. Barten, *René Lalique*, no. 86, a drawing given to the Bibliothèque Nationale by Mme. Pol Neveux. The Neveux were friends of Lalique.
18. Musée Lalique, inv. 2.4.413; Barten, René Lalique, no. 616.
19. Musée Lalique, inv. 2.4.414 and 5.1.001.

Objets d'Art and Glassmaking: René Lalique's Contribution in the Early Twentieth Century

1. Henri Vever, *La Bijouterie française au XIXe siècle*, III (Paris: H. Floury, 1908; reprint, Florence: S.P.E.S., 1975), pp. 711–14.
2. Gustave Geffroy, *René Lalique* (Paris: L'Art Décoratif Moderne, 1922), p. 8.
3. Félix Marcilhac, *Catalogue raisonné de l'œuvre en verre de René Lalique* (Paris: Éditions de l'Amateur, 1989), no. 997.
4. *René Lalique: Jewelry, Glass*, exh. cat. (Paris: Musée des Arts décoratifs, 1991), p. 157, there reproduced from Gustave Geffroy, *Les Industries artistiques françaises et etrangères à l'Exposition de 1900*.
5. The rhymes on Lalique's name appeared in Robert de Montesquiou's *Roseaux pensants*, 1897; see Yvonne Brunhammer, "The Lalique Epoch," p. 24 above.

Selected Bibliography

Barten, Sigrid. *René Lalique, Schmuck und Objets d'Art 1890–1910*. Munich: Prestel-Verlag, 1977.

Bayer, Patricia, Mary Lou, and Glen Utt. *Lalique, Perfume Bottles*. New York, 1990.

Bayer, Patricia, and Marc Waller. *René Lalique*. London, 1988.

Bury, Shirley. *Jewellery Gallery. Summary Catalogue*. London, 1982.

Calouste Gulbenkian Museum. *Catalogue*. Lisbon, 1989.

Dawes, Nicholas M., Thomas Moving, and Jérôme Lawton. *Lalique, a Century of Glass for a Modern World*. New York, 1989.

Geffroy, Gustave. *René Lalique*. Paris, 1922.

Lalique, Marc, and Marie-Claude Lalique. *Lalique par Lalique*. Lausanne, 1977.

Lalique, Marie-Claude. *Lalique*. Geneva, 1988.

Laurvik, J. Nilsen. *René Lalique*. New York: Haviland and Company, 1912.

Lorel, Camille, Henry Menetrier, and Roger Farjon. *Catalogue Guide Illustré de la Collection Charles Lebeau*. Boulogne-sur-Mer, 1926.

Marcilhac, Félix. *R. Lalique, Catalogue raisonné de l'œuvre en verre de René Lalique*. Paris: Éditions de l'Amateur, 1989.

Mortimer, Tony L. *Lalique, Jewellery and Glassware*. London, 1989.

Musée des Arts décoratifs. *René Lalique: Jewelry, Glass*. Paris: Musée des Arts décoratifs, Réunion des musées nationaux, 1991.

Musée d'Orsay. *Catalogue Sommaire Illustré des Arts Décoratifs*. Paris, 1988.

Percy, Christopher Vane. *Lalique Verrier. Guide du Collectionneur*. Lausanne, 1977.

Sturm, Fabienne Xavière, and Anne Winter-Jansen. *Bijoux Art Nouveau*. Geneva, 1982.

Vever, Henri. *La Bijouterie française au XIXe siècle*. 3 vols. Paris: H. Floury, 1908; reprint Florence: SPES, 1975. 1906–1908, 3 vols.

Wolfgang Scheffer. *Werke um 1900. Kataloge des Gewerbemuseums Berlin I*. Berlin, 1966.

Selected List of Exhibitions

•1900 Paris Universal Exhibition.

•1902 Turin International Exhibition of Modern Decorative Arts. May–October.

•1904 St. Louis Universal Exhibition.

•1905 London Works of René Lalique. Agnew & Sons Gallery.

•1910 Buenos Aires International Exhibition.

•1911 Turin International Exhibition of Industry and Labor

•1925 Paris International Exhibition of Modern Decorative and Industrial Arts.

•1933 Paris Le Decor de la Vie sous la IIIe République de 1870 à 1900. Pavillon de Marsan, Louvre. April–July.

•1937 Paris International Exhibition International Exhibition of Modern Day Arts and Techniques.

•1937 Paris Le Décor de la Vie de 1900 à 1925. Pavillon de Marsan, Louvre.

•1952 Zurich Um 1900 Art Nouveau und Jugendstil aus Europa und Amerika zur Zeit der Stilwende. Kunstgewerbemuseum.

•1960 New York Art Nouveau. Art and Design at the Turn of the Century. The Museum of Modern Art. June 6–September 6; Pittsburgh Carnegie Institute. October 13–December 12; Los Angeles County Museum, January 17–March 5, 1961; Baltimore The Baltimore Museum of Art, April 1–May 15, 1961.

•1960 Paris Les Sources du XXe Siècle, Musée National d'Art Moderne. 1960–1961.

•1961 London International Exhibition of Modern Jewelry 1890–1961, Goldsmiths' Hall. October 25–December 2.

•1961 Turin Mode, Fashion, Dress.

•1962 Düsseldorf Juwelen, Kunstmuseum.

•1963 Pforzheim Goldschmiede Kunst des Jugendstils Schmuck und Gerät um 1900. Schmuckmuseum.

•1963 Brussels L'Art et la Cité. Palais des Beaux-Arts.

•1964 Munich Sécession, Munich. Haus der Kunst, March–May.

•1964 Frankfurt Kleinodien. Museum für Kunsthandwerk.

•1965 Brussels Le Bijou 1900. Hotel Solvay. May.

•1966 Paris Les Années 25. Musée des Arts décoratifs. March–May.

•1967 Ostend Europa 1900.

•1971 Nuremberg Gold und Silber. Schmuck und Gerät, von Albrecht Dürer bis zur Gegenwart. Norishalle.

•1971 Durham From Slave to Siren. The Victorian Woman and her Jewelry from Neoclassic to Art Nouveau. The Duke University Museum of Art.

•1972 Munich Weltkulturen und Moderne Kunst. Haus der Kunst. June 16–September 30.

•1972 Amersfoot Sieraad 1900–1972. Zonnehof. August 2–October 1.

•1975 Brussels Art Déco 1925. Société Générale de Banque. September 30–October 30.

•1975 Tokyo 1900–1925. Picture of Carefree Years. Isetan department store. October 2–13.

•1976 Houston Art Nouveau Belgium France. Rice Museum March 26– June 27; Chicago The Art Institute. August 28–October 31.

•1976 Paris Cinquantenaire de l'Exposition de 1925. Musée des Arts Décoratifs. October 15, 1976–February 2, 1977.

•1978 Zurich René Lalique. Museum Bellerive. May 25–August 13.

•1979 Paris Paris–Moscou 1900–1930. Centre Georges Pompidou. May 31–November 5.

•1980 Copenhagen Paris 1925. Magasin du Nord. April 14–30.

•1980 Grasse 3000 Ans de Parfumerie. Musée d'Art et d'Histoire. July 22–October 22.

•1980 Paris Les Réalismes 1919–1939. Centre Georges Pompidou. 17 December 17, 1980–April 20, 1981.

•1981 Moscow Paris 1900–1930. Pushkin Museum. May 27–1 November 1.

•1981 Tokyo 1900 in France. Art Gallery Mitsukoshi. August 11–30; Osaka Art Gallery Mitsukoshi. September 8–20; Sapporo Museum of Modern Art. September 26–October 24; Kurashiki November 10–22.

•1982 Paris New Glass—Verriers Français Contemporains—Art et Industrie. Musée des Arts Décoratifs. April 12–July 5.

•1983 Paris L'Exposition des Expositions Universelles. Musée des Arts décoratifs. June–December.

•1983 Osaka International Design Festival. Paris 1925: Between Tradition and Design. October 22–November 9.

•1985 Baltimore Art Nouveau Jewelry by René Lalique. Baltimore. The Walters Art Gallery; Richmond Virginia Museum of Fine Arts; Fort Worth Kimbell Art Museum; Los Angeles Los Angeles County Museum of Art.

•1986 Seoul 100 Years of Glass Art in France. Ho-Am Gallery. September–October.

•1987 London The Jewellery of René Lalique. Goldsmiths' Hall. May 28–November 22.

•1987 Pforzheim René Lalique, Schmuckkunst um 1900. Schmuckmuseum. September 26–November 22.

•1987 Munich Die Nibelungen. Bilder von Liebe, Verrat und Untergang. Haus der Kunst. December 5, 1987–February 14, 1988.

•1987/1988 Munich René Lalique. Schmuckunst um 1900. Bayerisches National-museum; Hamburg Museum für Kunst und Gewerbe.

•1988 Tokyo René Lalique, Master-Glassmaker. Metropolitan Teien Art Museum.

•1988 Paris Le Japonisme. Galeries Nationales du Grand Palais. May 17–August 15; Tokyo National Museum of Western Art. September 23–December 11.

•1989 Munich Pariser Schmuck: vom 2. Kaiserreich zur Belle Epoque. Bayerisches Nationalmuseum. December 1, 1989–March 4, 1990.

•1990 Paris Hymne au Parfum, Deux Siècles d'Histoire dans les Arts Décoratifs et la Mode. Musée des Arts de la Mode. October 17, 1990–February 3, 1991.

•1990 Paris De Manet à Matisse. Sept Ans d'Enrichissements au Musée d'Orsay. Musée d'Orsay. November 12, 1990–March 10, 1991.

•1991 Tokyo Masterpieces of French Glass and Crystal at the Musée des Arts Décoratifs, 1800–1990. Suntory Museum of Art. July 30–September 16.

•1991 Paris René Lalique, Jewelry Glass. Musée des Arts Décoratifs. October 22, 1991–March 1992.

•1992 Tokyo René Lalique. The National Museum of Modern Art. May 23–July 12.

•1995 Montreal Paradis Perdu: L'Europe Symboliste. Musée des Beaux Arts. June 8–Oct. 15.

Picture Credits

Original photography © David Behl: cats. 11, 31, 32, 33, 34, 35, 40, 42, 46, 49, 51, 52, 82, 84, 85, 101, 105, 106, 111, 112, 113, 114, 115, 117, 121, 130, 132, 135, 140, 172, 179, 183, 186; fig. 20, p. 132.
© 1996, The Art Institute of Chicago. All rights reserved: cat. 136.
© 1997, The Art Institute of Chicago. All rights reserved. Photo Bob Hashimoto: cat. 96.
© 1996 The Cleveland Museum of Art: cat. 71.
The Corning Museum of Glass: cats. 94, 157, 203, 205.
Det Danske Kunstindustriemuseum, Copenhagen: fig. 6, p. 39.
Calouste Gulbenkian Museum, Lisbon: cats. 50, 73, 107, 110, 170, 177, 178, 182; fig. 8, p. 59; fig. 9, p. 75.
Lalique Museum Collection. Photos André Brumaire: 16, 19, 20, 21, 22, 59, 60, 65, 69, 70, 133, 143, 150, 151, 153, 154, 155, 159, 161, 163, 164, 165, 166, 168, 174, 176, 189, 192, 193, 200, 201, 202, 206, 207, 217, 224, 225, 226, 227, 229, 234, 235, 236; fig. 24, p. 154; fig. 27, p. 158; fig. 30, p. 170.
Lalique Museum Collection. Photos Laurent Sully Jaulmes, Musée des Arts décoratifs: 23, 24, 64, 66, 68, 149, 152, 156, 158.
Lalique Museum Collection, Paris: frontispiece p. 2, cats. 173, 180; fig. 3, p. 30; fig. 7, p. 46; fig. 13, p. 90; fig. 28, p. 160.
Copyright © The Metropolitan Museum of Art, New York: cats. 36 (© 1995), 88, 134 (© 1996), 137 (© 1996), 184 (© 1996).
Musée des Arts décoratifs, Paris. Photos Laurent Sully Jaulmes: cats. 1, 2, 4, 5, 9, 13, 14, 26, 27, 29, 30, 37, 38, 41, 45, 47, 48, 54, 55, 56, 58, 62, 74, 75, 76, 80, 81, 86, 89, 92, 97, 102, 127, 128, 131, 138, 142, 144, 194, 199, 220; fig. 1, p. 12; p. 204 *(original photo Paul Haviland)*.
Musée des Arts décoratifs, Paris, Vever archives: fig. 4, pp. 32–33.
Musée de la Mode et du Textile, Paris. Collections UCAD-UFAC. All rights reserved. Photo Joël Leiter: fig. 17, p. 102.
Musée de la Mode et du Textile, Paris. Collections UFAC. All rights reserved: fig. 18, p. 102.
Musée de la Mode et du Textile, Paris. All rights reserved. Photo Laurent Sully Jaulmes: fig. 19, p. 102.
Musée d'Orsay ADAGP © Photos RMN- J.G. Berizzi (original photos René Lalique): fig. 21, p. 148; fig. 22, p. 150; fig. 23, p. 152; fig. 25, p. 154; fig. 26, p. 158.
Private collection, Buenos Aires: cats. 44, 78 *(photo Laurent Sully Jaulmes)*, 83, 87, 90, 99, 222.
Private collection, Courtesy of Galerie Moderne, Ltd., London: cat. 181.
Private collection, New York: cats. 3, 11, 31, 34, 35, 40, 42, 43, 46, 49, 51, 52, 53, 82, 84, 101, 105, 106, 109, 112, 113, 114, 117, 132, 135, 140, 141, 172, 179, 183, 186, 230.
Private collection, Paris: cats. 232, 233; fig. 16, p. 101 *(photo Lafayette)*; fig. 29, p. 168.
Private collection, Philadelphia: cats. 33, 57, 72, 79, 91, 111, 115, 121, 122, 130; fig. 20, p. 132.
Private collection: cat. 129.
The Shapiro Collection, Courtesy of Galerie Moderne, Ltd., London: cat. 195.
Smithsonian Institution, National Museum of American History: cat. 139.
Mary Lou and Glenn Utt Collection: cats. 196, 209, 211, 213, 214, 216.
© 1985 Virginia Museum of Fine Arts, Richmond, VA. Photo Katherine Wetzel: cat. 123.
© 1990 Virginia Museum of Fine Arts, Richmond, VA. Photo Linda Loughran: cat. 7.
© 1996 Virginia Museum of Fine Arts, Richmond, VA. Photos Katherine Wetzel: cats. 10, 12, 39, 77, 93, 100, 118, 188.
© Roger Viollet, Paris: fig. 15, p. 100.
The Walters Art Gallery, Baltimore: cats: 98, 124.
David Weinstein Collection: cats. 6, 32, 85, 95, 104, 187, 190, 191.
Photos © Yvonne Weisberg: fig. 10, p. 83; fig. 11, p. 85; fig. 12, p. 87.
Collection of the Woodrow Wilson House Museum, Washington D.C. Photo William K. Geiger: fig. 14, p. 92.

Jacket front: Dog Collar Plaque, "*Narcisse*," c. 1899–1900. Gold, enamel, glass. 2 3/8 x 3 inches (6 x 7.6 cm). Private collection, New York. *Photo David Behl.*

Jacket back: Tiara, *Cattleya Orchid*, c. 1903–1904. Carved ivory, horn, gold, enamel on gold, diamonds. 4 5/8 x 8 1/8 x 6 1/4 inches (11.8 x 20.5 x 16 cm). Private collection, Buenos Aires. *Photo Laurent Sully Jaulmes.*

Photoengraving by Colourscan, Singapore
Color separations, printing, and binding by Pollina S.A., Luçon, France
Printed on Maine Club glossy 150 g/m² - Numéro d'impression: 74342